Holy Intoxication
to Drunken Dissipation

Holy Intoxication to Drunken Dissipation

Alcohol Among Quichua Speakers in Otavalo, Ecuador

BARBARA Y. BUTLER

UNIVERSITY OF NEW MEXICO PRESS   ALBUQUERQUE

Printed in the United States of America

10 09 08 07 06   1 2 3 4 5

Library of Congress Cataloging-in-Publication Data

Butler, Barbara Y., 1949–
    Holy intoxication to drunken dissipation : alcohol among
Quichua speakers in Otavalo, Ecuador / Barbara Y. Butler.
        p. cm.
    Includes bibliographical references and index.
    ISBN-13: 978-0-8263-3814-3 (pbk. : alk. paper)
    ISBN-10: 0-8263-3814-3 (pbk. : alk. paper)
    1. Quechua Indians—Alcohol use—Ecuador—Otavalo.
2. Quechua Indians—Ecuador—Otavalo—Rites and ceremonies.
3. Quechua Indians—Ecuador—Otavalo—Religion. 4. Drinking
customs—Ecuador—Otavalo. 5. Earthquakes—Ecuador—
Otavalo. 6. Social change—Ecuador—Otavalo. 7. Otavalo
(Ecuador)—Social conditions. 8. Otavalo (Ecuador)—Religious
life and customs. 9. Otavalo (Ecuador)—Social life and customs.
I. Title.
    F2230.2.K4B88 2006
    305.898'323086612—dc22

                                                    2005029795

Design and composition: Melissa Tandysh

Contents

Preface

How I Came to Tell This Story

IT WAS EARLY DECEMBER 1977 and chilly in the shade of the roofed veranda, *curridur*, where a clean reed mat had been dragged out for us to sit on, and I wrapped my long skirt as best I could over my legs to keep them warm. Copying the other women, I sat with my legs tucked to the side, but they soon went to sleep since, as I was told months later, my technique was wrong—I put too much weight on my thigh. On my first visit to Huaycopungo, where I was hoping to do research, I was carefully watching, trying to comply with what others were doing and straining, only partially successfully, to follow the conversation around me. Yolanda Hidalgo, a *mestiza*[1] schoolteacher from San Rafael, was asking Isabel Criollo Perugachi, a *runa huarmi* (indigenous woman) who spoke fluent Spanish, if she would be willing to help me with the research for my Ph.D. dissertation in her community. Isabel was four years younger than I but, like me, married and a mother. Unlike me, she was already expecting her second child and lived in her parents' one-roomed house with her husband, daughter, and her six siblings. The Instituto Otavaleño de Antropología had sent me to Yolanda because she and Isabel had served as assistants to a Spanish anthropologist, Berta Ares Quejía, several years earlier. Both local women helped Berta research the large religious festivals that were sponsored by indigenous individuals from the surrounding communities, although they took place in San Rafael, the parish seat (see Ares Quejía 1988). The mestizos who inhabited the town of San Rafael directed the sponsors of the festivals, or at least thought they did, since they considered themselves the overlords of the indigenous peasants and representatives of civilization in one of the more backward outposts of Otavalo cantón.[2] While Yolanda's family was notorious for its exploitation of the indigenous people in the parish, many *runacuna*, the Quichua plural for indigenous people, considered her a friend. She had started the first elementary classroom for indigenous children in Huaycopungo. Yolanda and Isabel's conversation was hard for me to follow because they often used Quichua words and phrases or local idioms in Spanish with which I was not yet familiar.

Isabel's mother, Dolores Perugachi, hovered in the background looking distinctly uncomfortable with the proceedings, although when we arrived, she had made what I came to learn were the appropriate welcoming gestures. Grabbing a broom and stepping from the shade of the veranda into the brilliant sun of midday at high altitude on the equator as we talked, Dolores began dramatically sweeping the yard, the twelve-inch long strands of coral beads hanging from her ears swinging back and forth as much from her emotion as the physical motion of her work. All the while, she muttered under her breath in Quichua—loud enough to be heard but not directed at anyone in particular. This, I later learned, is the traditional way for indigenous women to make their opinions known in public, in contrast to men, who are expected to address a group directly and openly. Despite their indirect delivery, women's opinions are not taken lightly. In fact, these muttered public asides often contain far more emotional information, positive or negative, than those of influential men, who must persuade with a soft and humble voice of authority. Dolores was constrained in speaking directly by the presence of a San Rafael mestiza and schoolteacher, even one she knew and trusted more than most, and a prestigious white foreigner from the United States. But it was her daughter she was trying to influence. Although Isabel's family members were proud of her extraordinary level of education (eighth grade) and activities in support of the indigenous community, they were frequently exasperated at how her work challenged their expectations for a daughter and made demands on them as well. When Yolanda and I were walking back to San Rafael after Isabel agreed to work with me and we had said our good-byes, I asked Yolanda what Quishpe Dulu Mama, as she was called, had been saying.[3] She was warning Isabel, Yolanda said, that now that I had come, I would become close to the family, become part of their hearts and their lives, and then go away, never to return, as she claimed Berta Ares Quejía had done before.[4] The threads of interdependence so painstakingly woven between us could be broken in an instant. Airplanes high in the sky and heading north, Dolores later told me, made her want to cry, imagining Berta or even me up there disappearing forever into the clouds.

Perhaps Mama Dulu's words are responsible for the fact that her family, in successively more distant concentric circles of relationship, and others in Huaycopungo have been woven into the permanent fabric of my life even now, almost thirty years later. She threw

Fig. 1. Dolores Perugachi Quishpe
sorting *totora* reeds, 1978
(PHOTO BY AUTHOR)

down a challenge that I, young, idealistic, and determined, could not help but try to meet. I never got that scene out of my head. But I had help in making that implied plea unforgettable. Community leaders still work tirelessly to catch me in the webs of connection and reciprocity they so eagerly spin, in part because I contribute financially to their community development projects as a way to repay the community for its collaboration in my doctoral degree. For my demonstrated commitment to them, they wish to claim me as a transnational community member.[5] It would be a mistake to draw the conclusion that a financial motive is the sole activating force in this vital relationship, since from their point of view strong affection is expressed and deepened through material reciprocity. They claim with some passion that it is my *moral* support that has been most valuable to them. Many individuals envy those others who have made me their *comadre*, the all-important relationship between the parent and the godparent of a child, since I have continued to honor those relationships over time. In May of 1978 I became the baptismal godmother of Isabel's second child and first son, born on the first of March. Isabel had been seized with back labor pains as I drove us home from a trip to the shrine of the Virgin of Las Lajas, just over the Colombian border. Luckily Ricardo waited to be born until we had returned to Huaycopungo, although we still tease him that he was almost a Colombian. He is now married and has a young son. In July of 2004, I accepted my seventh and eighth godchildren, Isabel's brother's daughter and her second son Alberto's baby boy, and attended the high school graduation of another godchild, Isabel's third son out of five.[6]

Isabel and her husband, José Manuel Tituaña Amaguaña, and I are growing old together. Their oldest child and only daughter, Susana, married hurriedly in 1994 after her son was born. She had been lonely while finishing a two-year post–high school degree in Quito, the capital city, and José, from the neighboring community of Cachiviro, had been a persistent suitor. As each relative arrived for the celebration, we would take a walk and together vent our feelings of frustration in both words and tears that Susana was throwing her hard-won education and other assets away on a young man who was not her equal. Even I had known her since she was three. Since Susana hadn't been able to bring herself to tell me in advance and showed up shamefaced to meet me in Quito with a baby in her arms, my deep shock and disappointment were all too real. Still, despite the honesty of my emotion, I couldn't help laughing inside as we enacted what countless other families had done over the millennia. Furthermore, no one seemed to question for a moment the naturalness of a *gringa* in the backstage scene of relatives grieving at a wedding. I had a familiar pang of guilt over my continuing the schizophrenic dance of outsider/insider perspective that is essential to participant observation.

We are all accustomed to José now and he's part of the family, and it's the other adult children's choices we agonize over, one by one. None of us believed what everyone older told us, that our children can bring us more heartache as young adults than they do even as teenagers. I have had only one opportunity to return the favor and host a compadre in my home in Wisconsin. In 1995 a relatively new compadre, the husband of José Manuel's sister Elena, Alfonso Farinango, came to Chicago to sell the Ecuadorian handicrafts he had previously sold at a shop in the Canary Islands.

What Kind of Story This Will Be

There are three points I would like to draw from the introductory vignette and its aftermath. One is that I'm telling a story in what follows, a true story up to a point, but one that has a beginning, middle, and end. Real life doesn't stand still for those markers of drama and resolution to endure for long, but human beings constantly frame lives at many levels of generalization—from their own to that of their community or nation—in those terms. This will be one of the themes I will explore in what follows, namely the power of the stories that we think and hear and tell each other to guide our lives, both on the individual level and, in this case especially, as social groups. Our cultural myths serve us as dynamic guides to negotiate the material world in which we are embedded.

However, this is a story written mainly for a North American audience about a part of the world that is both similar and very different from our own. In order to make sense of it, the reader must learn a great deal of cultural information—like what it means in indigenous Otavalo for women to whisper loudly enough to be heard, or where visitors are expected to sit, or how local ethnic and class divisions are acted out. This is an ethnography in a relatively traditional sense—a book detailing the culture and society of a particular place at a particular time. That means that cultural information is recorded here so that in years to come other researchers, both professional and avocational, may be able to answer questions about the relationship of the past way of life in Huaycopungo to the present. I will try to keep the boring detail to a minimum or to segregate it into endnotes or appendices when appropriate.

I believe that foreign observers deserve to hear what Catherine Allen, quoting Malinowski, called "the hold life has" (Allen 1988, quoting *The Argonauts of the Western Pacific* [1922] 1961, 25) or what I sometimes think of as the Disney version of a way of life. All of us grow up in a world where many people tell us why our way of life is good, what a truly admirable person is like, how the different individuals and institutions in our world can work together to create a worthy whole, how we can all be heroes of our cultural stories. Contrarily, we have customary expectations about how things can go badly wrong, what makes for a truly bad person, and what we must guard against as a group. This set of cultural myths is always an idealized and imperfect model of what really happens; sometimes it's even oppressively wrong. Nonetheless, it is an important part of the reality in which we live—to use Clifford Geertz's expression—the webs of significance we ourselves spin and in which we are suspended. In order to understand the lives of the people in the story to follow, readers must be conversant with these cultural myths before they can begin to deconstruct them. Social and cultural change over time is dependent upon the interpretations held by those undergoing the transformation, operating on and molding the hard facts of the situation at hand. In the story I will tell, what once was the ideal came to be seen as the feared misdirection that led to everything falling apart. Readers must be prepared to see what is going on in two different ways at once, because both are in some ways true.

Lastly, this vignette from the very start of this story, almost three decades ago, should introduce you to what kind of research, what kind of relationships to "data," to people, and to anthropology as a social science inform this account. If closeness to the people and culture can be placed on a continuum, I am far removed from the up-close perspective of a native, whether mestizo or indian,[7] or even of someone who has lived a long time in the area. First, I am a foreigner, however long and deep has been my involvement with Ecuador over the years. Second, anthropology has been a deliberately chosen lens through which I have interpreted what I see, hear, and feel from my first acquaintance with Huaycopungo, and nearly my first acquaintance with Otavalo. Sometimes, as an outsider, I have the advantage of seeing particular local social norms that natives take so for granted that they think they are natural, rather than cultural. But my own deeply ingrained social norms sometimes keep me from seeing others at all, and my analysis of social life is therefore skewed and oversimplified.

Nor does this study fall on the end of the continuum characterized by anonymous and controlled data collection. My research has involved forging a social place for myself in Huaycopungo, including intimate relationships that have persisted over years and the more recent role of a regular community benefactor. Furthermore, systematic, numerically significant data collection has been relatively rare since my dissertation. This has resulted from a number of factors, most important because the length of most of my visits has not been great enough for me to balance to my satisfaction my social obligations to people with relatively intrusive and coercive research. The reader and I are therefore probably both acutely aware of my role in creating the following truth/fiction. This is my interpretation, with the richness and bias of intimacy. My compadres, especially the dozen or so with whom I am particularly close, have had a competitive advantage in shaping this account, although they certainly do not all agree with each other, over other people in and around the community. In recent years I have chosen more often to simply listen to hours of their disputes and discussions with relatives, neighbors, and friends rather than to administer surveys or employ other sophisticated means of data collection, even to the informal asking of questions. In the ideal study these two methodological poles should be given equal weight.

I am a white, Anglo-Saxon, middle-class American woman, now middle-aged. My personal and scholarly history is inextricably tied to my experiencing and imagining Ecuador in its three geographic regions. In 1970 I married a foreign student from the coast of Ecuador and the following year went to live with him in Guayaquil, the largest city in the country and the main port to the Pacific Ocean. During my original two years in Ecuador, I made a visit to the Oriente, the Amazonian jungle region, which convinced me, then and there, to go back to graduate school in the United States in anthropology. My experience of the jungle had confirmed for me the Western literary tradition that gives the jungle great creative power, if not in some mystical sense then because the jungle, or its symbolic representations, so effectively mobilized my own human power and creativity. That these traditions were interwoven with native South Americans' own beliefs that the tropical forests are a primordial source of spiritual knowledge and power was something I would learn only later.

However, since 1977, the Quichua-speaking people in the Andean cantón of Otavalo have been one of my main preoccupations.[8] Although I began our association for my dissertation research in 1977, *research* now seems a misleading, distancing word to use for the shared experiences of the past twenty-eight years. The "friendship" (American gloss) or ritual kinship (*compadrazgo*; Otavalo gloss)[9] I have shared with Isabel Criollo Perugachi, who began as my research assistant, has mediated all my professional and personal associations. No term actually does justice to the rewarding complexities of this relationship. While I try to explain the relationship to Americans by saying she is one of my best friends, she tells people there that I am like a mother to her, which embarrasses the American me, but in which I recognize the same claim of shared pleasure and unconditional support between women. While she is nonplussed to proclaim the symmetrical aspects of our relationship while delighting in the hierarchical ones, I struggle to eliminate the paternalistic parts associated with my greater wealth and social prestige in the wider society, following my middle-class, and 1960s-nurtured, ethic of egalitarianism. To be honest, this inequality of economic and symbolic capital is a treasured resource from her point of view, and the richly rewarding maternalism that results serves to satisfy what is usually only an impossible desire, imaginatively enacted in traditional ritual or now viewed passively on television soap operas. For these people, who are both poor and low on the local social hierarchy, enticing wealth and power into a commitment to share the bounty is a highly valued but generally elusive goal.

As a result of Otavalo norms of ritual kinship, many of my family and friends have shared in this relationship with the large extended kindreds of my comadre Isabel and her husband, José Manuel. We are all comadres and compadres to each other, regardless of age or generation. My close ties also include many individuals in their extended families, and she is not the only person I would call a personal friend. This relationship has served personal, family, and community aims for them as well—emotional, social, economic, and political. It continues by phone, mail, fax and now, since June of 1999, e-mail when we are not together, as do many other relationships there.

I first visited Otavalo in 1972, but came to Ecuador for dissertation research in September of 1977. I left the field that first time in April of 1979, anxious to be with my daughter whom I had left with her father on a visit home the previous September. In the summer of 1982, I returned to Huaycopungo for a three-month postdoctoral study of beliefs and practices related to anger sickness, *colera*.[10] In 1987 I made a one-week trip to Ecuador, during which I visited Huaycopungo and saw firsthand the recent and devastating earthquake damage. As part of three weeks in Ecuador in 1988, I spent one week interviewing community members about the recent changes in community life. In 1989 I stayed in Ecuador two weeks; I spent considerable time with my compadres but did no explicit interviewing. In 1990 I spent three weeks in Huaycopungo pursuing issues of changes in drinking. In 1991 I spent two months in Ecuador, trying to learn more about the role of religious and political movements in the changes in Huaycopungo. In the years since I have continued to make a number of four-day to two-week visits, at least once a year, and, as stated above, we frequently are in touch when I am not there. E-mail has become more common in recent years, although faxes and telephone calls are not unusual.

Increasingly my visits are defined and guided by my ritual kinship relationship and my relationship as minor financial patron to the community, not by my desire to *study* the lives of Otavaleños. Nonetheless, if I time my visit to coincide with San Juan, the summer solstice celebration that lasts for a week in late June and occupies a position of significance similar to that of Christmas for North Americans, I join the other returning family members. Since small groups of family and friends sit for hours during this period exchanging

news and analyzing the advances and losses of the past year for themselves, their extended families, their community, the region, and even
the country as a whole, I need only listen carefully to acquire a price-
less summary of current events and trends while playing the socially
acceptable role of visitor. Quite naturally, the conversation sometimes
steers into areas of particular interest to me.

Huaycopungo is overall a very poor community, though not as
poor as some in Otavalo cantón. As I got to know more people better
in the first decade or so of my visits, our relationships increasingly
included symmetry and complementarity along with the hierarchy
that frequently gave me a superordinate position. As a white, rich[11]
North American, I was more often treated as a superior than an equal,
and only very rarely as a subordinate to local indigenous authorities.
Perhaps it is more accurate to say that this theme of complementarity/
hierarchy has been the incessant background or foreground of our relationships, continually being highlighted, denied, negotiated, suffered,
or enjoyed by each of us, as it is in their other relationships.

The people of Huaycopungo are not totally without advantages in
the relationship with me. While they have most often displayed respect
and humility in the presence of outsiders like myself, there have been
social activists among them for many decades who have challenged
these restrictive norms of interaction and a very few who have been
downright hostile. Furthermore, although I have the power to come
and go, when I am there I am on their turf. For all the mutual adjusting and readjusting to real and imagined expectations of the other, it
seems that I have the advantage as a student of culture, because I am
immersed in theirs. They have a relative advantage as teachers who
have greater knowledge of the norms and therefore can exercise greater
control over the shape of the relationship. In fact, I sense that some of
them would prefer that I remain slightly retarded regarding their culture, because they can remain my protectors and have more control
over what I know, do, and say. Whereas, as an anthropologist I prefer
to come alone rather than bring friends and family from the United
States, because our talk and our activities are then more likely to stay
focused on community life, they prefer it when they can talk to and
interact with a number of gringos and learn as much as possible about
gringo etiquette, values, and fashions. And they are moved to tears of

joy when they convince my friends or family to don their clothing and join in dancing. Because of their financial disadvantage and need of my material generosity, I often grudgingly accept exchanges of assistance in menial labor and verbal performances of gratitude that replay feudal scenes of peasant obeisance to their lord and master. If I don't let my friends carry my suitcase, then they cannot repay me in any way and therefore remain anxiously in my debt. Nor can they ask me again when the need inevitably returns. Sometimes I petulantly grab my suitcase back and carry it myself, resenting my placement in the category of helpless nobility. Nor are they entirely unaware of the feminist and personal struggles for autonomy to which my generation in the United States has made me heir and which sometimes has me snatching back suitcases from my male friends and my father as well.

In the last several years, a number of community leaders—led by the inimitable José Manuel Aguilar, who has been a founder and director of the evangelical church Jesus de Nazareth, president of the Asociación Agrícola Huaycopungo, which was founded to continue a suit for land stolen in the colonial period, and president of the community council, to name just a few of his official positions—have made a request. These leaders hope that when my book is published, I will make it available to them. After all, say some, as a student of their history I have talked to the elders in the time before the recent convulsive changes in their cultural life. They need that account and will need it even more in the future to help their children negotiate the interchange between the two cultures. It is with a heavy feeling of responsibility that I proceed in this endeavor, which began with my desire to understand and articulate that understanding for people in my own country. Furthermore, over the years I became increasingly aware that these leaders wanted to be named in the account and I would have to directly address the conflict between the professional norms of anthropology, which prescribes pseudonyms to protect community members, and their desire for recognition. In the summer of 1999, I convoked a meeting of the community council, asking them to invite any other leaders they wished, to discuss the pros and cons of using pseudonyms in the manuscript. Although I tried to explain the rationale for pseudonyms and highlighted the possible negative consequences to them of using their official names, they unanimously agreed that full names be used.

They again expressed their confidence that I would be able, from my conversations and observations of the culture over the years, to record their cultural history in a work that could serve as a resource for their descendants in years to come. Another source of their confidence, they said, came from the words of the elders who talked to me twenty years ago. Since they infrequently spoke openly to outsiders, if they talked to me, they must have told the truth. I tried to suggest that perhaps they shouldn't trust me so much, and gave them several possible scenarios in which my motives or judgments might violate their best interests, even inadvertently, but they thought my self-deprecation was funny. As shown in studies by Rappaport (2004) and Wogan (2004), my converting their recent history into written form immeasurably increases their value and influence in the world. Wogan writes the following of his examination of indigenous Salasacans in the central Ecuadorian Andes: "What emerges is a picture of writing as a fundamental symbol of power, so fundamental that it can stand beside more well-studied symbolic forms as a window into indigenous relations with the outside world" (108). After the English version, they want versions in both Spanish and Quichua to be produced, which will arguably have a greater local effect on the meaning of their existence, and I agreed to make that happen in some form.

Their confidence in me strikes me as naïve, not because of any particular ineptitude or insincerity on my part, but because there is always a significant and unpredictable potential for interpretive disagreement with such an account, disagreements that could lead to serious and negative political consequences. Furthermore, one account written by a North American professional anthropologist could come to have greater authority than warranted, overriding other interpretations that local people, whether indigenous and not, might want to make. Or contrarily, an account written by a foreign anthropologist could attract especially negative scrutiny by national researchers, who understandably resent the generally greater exposure given to works by North rather than South American professionals.

More than anything else, working for a small Native American tribe in Wisconsin whose people *are* able both to understand the norms and institutions in which I take part, as well as to criticize them in depth, taught me how my actions as an anthropologist were not as implicitly free of political taint nor as morally unambiguous as I had previously believed. Scholarship is not simply pursuing the enhancement of human knowledge. The norms of face-to-face, nonstranger interactions and community loyalty were as strong local determinants of the exercise of my work role in Wisconsin as of my researcher role in Ecuador. However, whatever "love" I demonstrated for individuals or the community as a whole, as some on the reservation described it, did not free me from responsibility for the intended or unintended political consequences of my actions, any more than it did for the reservation community members themselves. There, excited by the concept of cooperative research, I wanted to offer my services to help design and carry out any research project the tribe itself was interested in, but "research" was a politically loaded term, carrying more disadvantages than advantages. It was often less risky to proclaim my identity as social worker than as anthropologist. Many leaders urged me to carry out research clandestinely, because they trusted my motives, but they would not support me before the tribal council and help obtain official approval for any research project. I learned a lot, but I did not carry out systematic research of any kind.

I am not trying to express a policy here, simply to address the day-to-day working out of specific relationships, which have never been and will never be fully fixed. To be perfectly honest, I used to have nightmares of facing rigged tribunals where torture and death are the only possible outcomes of my gringo presumption. My understanding of the ethical, practical, and moral (that is, how to be a good friend/comadre) dimensions of these questions has been enhanced by realizing to what extent my compadres and I share this fervent desire to understand each other's cultures. This book is, in part, about the attempts of individuals as part of families and an ethnic community to re-create their social identity in the changing context that is contemporary Ecuador and in spheres of transnational culture in a global village. Negotiating intimate relationships, despite the symbolic and real gulf between our positions in world politicoeconomic systems, has been part of that struggle, at least for some individuals in Huaycopungo. The United States, whether seen as a role model or a world oppressor, is a powerful image in the creation of Ecuadorian national identity. It is also key for Otavalans in their renewed representations of themselves, whether they see the Americans as more sympathetic to them as exotic indigenous people than are Ecuador's prejudiced mestizos, or whether they share the national view of resisting the third-rate, third world image with which Americans saddle Ecuador and Ecuadorians. If they and I, and our friends and families, can recognize that our different cultures both contain knowledge and power and that these powers are of a complementary nature, we will be better served. The alternative has most often been, at least officially, granting knowledge and power only to the societies of South America that have European roots, and sometimes even more to those of North America. With a mutual recognition of the value of indigenous culture, it will be possible for those who still identify themselves and are identified as Andean "Indians" to regain the stature of people of value in the nation, in the world, and in their own hearts that they lost over and over and over again following the Spanish conquest. They can stop defining and forging their culture specifically in opposition to the national one as a way to salvage a sense of cultural dignity in a society that exploits them, a method that inevitably leads to their battling the insidious argument that their domination is due to those differences, which demonstrate their obvious inferiority. Since North America is currently more powerful in the world as a whole than Ecuador or South America, if individual North Americans ratify a different but complementary view of indigenous worth, it is a symbolic, if ephemeral, defeat for the standard local hierarchical arrangement of peoples and a victory for indigenous Otavalans struggling to maintain their dignity in their native land.[12]

Finally, this preface began with the story of how Isabel's mother Dolores's mumbled complaint that I would get in their hearts and then disappear marked a change in the course of events, turning my collaboration with some influential people in Huaycopungo from temporary dissertation research into a lifelong commitment. In the process who we are has been redefined, as has what kind of community Huaycopungo is. This does not imply my power as an actor but instead my significance as a symbol for those local leaders determined to exercise agency on behalf of their community in an era of expanding civil rights. The only remarkable thing I did was continue to show up. Nor is it the absence of a firm dividing line between "truth" and "fiction" that I wish to call attention to, except to make clear my storytelling role in this narrative about other peoples' lives and stories; rather, I want to point to the power of our continually created and re-created stories, from the level of the individual to the "world system," to channel and change our emotional, social, and physical behavior in reciprocal ways. This examination of drinking alcohol as a practice and as a problem underlines the power of everyone's relatively fleeting or more durable interpretations to motivate behavior and normative change. Stories told with compelling symbolic images about reverberative places, like the Amazon forests or the slopes of Mount Imbabura, or moments, like a major earthquake in the story to come, are the most powerful of all.

A Note on Verb Tense

Deciding how to use the past and present tenses in this manuscript has not been easy or straightforward. Part II was relatively simple, since it addresses issues that were current when I wrote them, although they will all be past once the book is published. Part I presented a much greater challenge. Anthropologists have long used what they call the "ethnographic present" tense to call attention to the enduring nature of culture. Using the past tense carries the risk of implying that cultural continuities are less important than what has changed and that everything is on the chopping block at all times. On the other hand, the ethnographic present can give a false impression of timelessness. Adhering strictly to either the past or the present tense for consistency in part I would have been highly unsatisfying, since my goal was to follow tiny threads of change and continuity through the thicket of complexities to clarify their relationships.

Part I not only describes the events and situations occurring in a stretch of time that is past; it also presents a baseline set of cultural assumptions and an idealized depiction of a way of life, as much as possible from the local point of view—at least when the locals are in a self-justifying mood. Of these cultural assumptions a few have disappeared absolutely, some have altered only in appearance, some affect the older people more than their descendants, and some continue unchanged. After all, the norm cascade that is the subject of this book allowed locals to see themselves as faithfully replicating the past even as they made an about-turn. In order to communicate this sense of a world and a people as they should be through time, the present tense is very helpful, but not sufficient. In what follows, I try to favor the present tense and confine my use of the past tense to statements that would be seriously misleading in the present tense. I suspect, however, that I am more freewheeling in my use of tense than that implies, throwing in a pinch of this and a dollop of that, just as I cook, rather than carefully measuring to replicate a recipe each time. I heartily apologize to those who find this use of tense disconcerting. For those who are only slightly thrown off balance, I am unrepentant; if you are jarred into awareness of the many voices and constant dialogue in any culture about what is old-fashioned, forgotten, or tried and true, my choices were justified.

Acknowledgments

SINCE I FIRST WENT TO ECUADOR IN 1971, I started my research in 1977, and this book began to sprout in 1991, I am tempted to thank everyone who supported me or the research or the writing in any way for the last thirty-four years. But that's an autobiography, with which I won't burden the reader.

The top of my list for recognition for their part in crafting this book are the hundreds of people in Huaycopungo and the rest of Otavalo cantón who have shared parts of their life with me. Not only would I love to put the names of everyone close to me here, but I also know they would welcome this tiny simulacrum of fame. However, I found the task very difficult because of my fears both that the list would be too long and that I would inevitably forget someone important. When I enlisted my assistant and comadre Isabel Criollo to help, she began to list all the people we had ever interviewed. Here I will only single out a few community leaders: Antonio Criollo (Anga Andu)[1], Rafael Otavalo (Ila Rafi), José Otavalo (Ila Jusi), Rigurio Andrango (Curaga Rigurio), Luis Andrango (Curaga Lucho), José Manuel Aguilar (Damiano Jusi Mali), Pedro Aguilar (Damiano Pidru), José Maria Criollo (Chirichi Jusi Maria), Francisco Otavalo (Ila Francisco), Segundo Aguilar (Huayco Segundo), Francisco Mendes (Lurico Pachu), José Manuel Otavalo

(Ravil Jusi Mali), José Mendes (Pachi Muyu), José Manuel Tocagon (Chico Jusi Mali), Isabel Criollo (Anga Sabila), and Asciencia Criollo (Anga Asciencia). While the list consists almost entirely of men's names, as is culturally appropriate in this context, their wives are all recognized as essential parts of a male/female partnership, as is the one husband who is also not named here.

Many individuals from Huaycopungo and the surrounding area have become characters in the text and I beg their forgiveness for insufficiently understanding them or oversimplifying their lives to make a point. All have generously expressed their trust in me and agreed to let me use their lives in this way. All expressed their wish to have their correct names used, despite my attempts to justify the use of pseudonyms. For those who aren't mentioned but who know they have played an important part in my understanding of Otavalo, please know that I'm eternally grateful. Some of them are no longer with us and I offer a prayer for their peaceful rest. Many of them want me to publicize their history for the benefit of the next generation, and I humbly beg their understanding for my writing the book I wanted to write. And I promise that this book and more accessible versions will appear in Spanish and Quichua before long.

My parents, Thomas Y. and Clara W. Butler, have clearly helped me in too many ways to count, including a recent return visit to Huaycopungo in July 2004, which meant so much to me, community leaders, my godchildren and compadres, and community members in general. The Butler Charitable Foundation's contributions have aided the community in perfecting grant-writing and reporting skills and in pursuing community development projects that have fostered community pride and solidarity. My sister Marjorie; my daughter, Marisa; my ex-husbands, Ricardo Rivero and P. Sudevan; and my one-time childcare assistants, Zoila Quezada and Jackie Purcell Callister, the latter also a photographer, were part of some stages of my involvement with Huaycopungo, contributing in a positive way to the nature of my experience and my resulting interpretations and understanding. Marjorie, Ricardo, and my parents, who returned this past summer (2004) after many years, made more visible to me how much healthier people are now compared to twenty-five years ago and how much their standard of living has improved. My sister Bonnie and her husband,

Paul Bunning; my nieces Jessie and Caitlin; my friends John Morser, Tracy Honn, and Cynthia Sanford have joined me in Huaycopungo in more recent years and have been very important to my understanding of my continuing relationships with people there. Most important to me has been their sharing of experiences with me, and thus points of reference, so I no longer felt so alone and unable to talk to anyone who would understand. Their fresh eyes gave me renewed interest in things that I had taken for granted, and their enormous pleasure in their experiences there justified to me my own commitment and many returns.

In the list of scholarly influences and support, I begin with Norman Whitten who, following in the footsteps of Joseph Casagrande,[2] has devoted many years of research, writing, teaching, and mentoring to the benefit of all who are interested in Ecuador, especially in the United States. When I was visiting Puyo in 1972 it was his American students I met, including the prospective Ecuadorian student Marcelo Naranjo, who inspired me to apply to graduate school in anthropology. Although my application to the University of Illinois got lost in the mail from Ecuador, his example was an important goad to my future career. Next, I must give thanks to Enrique Mayer who, with his legendary generosity, used his position as head of the Center for Latin America and the Caribbean at the University of Illinois to reconnect me to academic anthropology and Latin American studies after a hiatus and thus inspire me to think about writing this book. I had finally arrived to spend a year at the University of Illinois almost thirty years after my application to grad school entered the Ecuadorian postal system in 1972, and twenty years after I had received my Ph.D from the University of Rochester.

Suzanne Wilson, a graduate student in sociology and part-time employee of the Center for Latin America and the Caribbean at the University of Illinois–Urbana-Champaign when I was there and now an associate professor at Gustavus Adolphus College, continued reading, commenting, cheerleading, and other invaluable tasks for years after I returned to Wisconsin from the University of Illinois and deserves significant credit for this book getting written. My first Quichua teacher, Remigio Caceres in Ilumán, Imbabura and my next, Carmen Chuquin at the University of Wisconsin–Madison deserve my grateful recognition for their patience and for sharing so many insights into the language and culture. American anthropologists Leo Chavez, Lawrence Carpenter, Jeffrey Ehrenreich, and Judith Kemp were all in the field with me during my original dissertation research—the first two investigating in Otavalo and the second two visiting from their site among the Coiaquer in far northwest Ecuador. Our interactions between 1977 and 1979 were key for my original analyses of the culture.

Academic advisors during my years as a student and postdoctoral fellow included Alfred Harris and Fitz-John Porter Poole at the University of Rochester, and later Arthur Rubel at Michigan State University. The support of anthropologists Ann Millard and Barbara Rylko-Bauer from Michigan State University and Kenyon Stebbins, whom I met at Michigan State University but who is now retired from the University of West Virginia, also made my persistence in getting this story to print possible.

For their wonderful books, *The Hold Life Has* and *Food, Gender, and Poverty in the Ecuadorian Andes*, I express my gratitude to Catherine Allen, whom I have never met, and Mary Weismantel, with whom I spent one lovely day in Huaycopungo, because they inspired me to believe that I could write an ethnography of Huaycopungo.

The Department of Philosophy, Anthropology, and Religious Studies at the University of Wisconsin–Stevens Point and my many colleagues there, particularly Dona Warren and Corinne Dempsey, have supported my work in significant ways. My year at the Institute for the Humanities at the University of Wisconsin–Madison in 1996 was a taste of academic heaven that got this manuscript's first draft done.

Ada Deer, one of the heroes of Menominee Restoration and a recent head of the Bureau of Indian Affairs, was a mentor from the University of Wisconsin–Madison for my three years of social work at the Stockbridge-Munsee Reservation in Shawano County, Wisconsin. Many people there, particularly at the health center between 1987 and 1990, further refined my understanding of alcohol use and abuse and the particular challenges faced by indigenous minorities. Dave Besaw, Nancy Miller-Korth, Lynn Miller, Lorraine Miller, and Larry Ziereis must be singled out for special mention, although I remember so many others who challenged my naïve assumptions and deepened my thinking.

I must also thank the alcoholics in my personal life who led me to Al-Anon, and my special Saturday morning group in Stevens Point whose collective wisdom is also responsible for my embracing the challenge of writing this book.

My dissertation research in Ecuador, done while a graduate student in the University of Rochester's Department of Anthropology, was financially supported by the University of Rochester travel grants, the Organization of American States, and the Wenner-Gren Foundation for Anthropological Research. Assistance in later years came from the National Institute of Mental Health grant to Michigan State University's program in Medical Anthropology and the University of Wisconsin–Stevens Point's University Professional Development Committee.

The Ecuadorian Instituto Nacional de Antropología e Historia and Instituto Nacional del Patrimonio Cultural approved the proposals for formal research on a number of occasions, and I greatly appreciate their support. The Instituto Otavaleño de Antropología and Department of Anthropology at the Pontificia Universidad Católica del Ecuador also provided assistance and encouragement during the early years of the research.

Although I started with a predisposition to distrust publishers, from the many horror stories with which I had been regaled over the years and a frustrating experience with a different university press, I was overwhelmed with gratitude for the universally professional, helpful, and comradely way this project progressed at the University of New Mexico Press. The Spanish expression *mil gracias* (one thousand thank yous) better expresses my gratitude to editor and "Princess o' Power" Evelyn A. Schlatter, with whom I began the process, and to her successor Maya Allen-Gallegos, than any readily available expression in English. My copyeditor Robin DuBlanc's patient artistry inspired in me a limitless sense of awe and appreciation that I can never repay.

To conclude, I want to dedicate this book to two of Huaycopungo's most inspiring leaders, my friend and longtime comadre, Isabel Criollo Perugachi and my friend and soon-to-be compadre, José Manuel Aguilar Mendez. In consonance with local practice and consistent with my own feelings, I need to recognize their spouses at the same time—the man who has grown in my estimation every year since I met him, Sabila *cumari's* husband, José Manuel Tituaña Amaguaña, and Taita Damiano's wife, Dolores Villagran Hinojosa. Our era will end soon, my friends, and we will leave the interweaving of the past with the present for a better future to our children and grandchildren. You will leave a formidable legacy and I can only hope I came close to doing it justice in this account.

January 2005

Fig. 2. Isabel Criollo Perugachi, with her
sons Luis Antonio and José Alberto,
and José Manuel Aguilar, 2000
(PHOTO BY AUTHOR)

Machapashun:
Let's You and I Get Drunk

The Culture of Drinking as a
Window into a Changing World

THE LAST SEVERAL decades of the twentieth century have brought profound transformations in the lives of the indigenous people of Otavalo cantón in highland Ecuador. One highly symbolic behavior—the ritualized sharing of alcoholic beverages—also changed dramatically, from being valued as a means to achieve a holy intoxication that fostered communion with people and spiritual forces to being judged by the participants as a route to drunken dissipation and community disintegration. By attending to the changing beliefs and behaviors regarding ritual drinking, we can illuminate larger questions about Otavalan society and culture in a period of transformation, particularly how people in an extremely challenging social and economic environment create a sense of agency for themselves in the pursuit of a satisfying present and a better future. One of the greatest challenges facing Otavalans is their being a generally despised and oppressed ethnic minority in their own land. Because drinking was part of religious ritual, the story to follow is also one about worldview and religious practice. And since religious beliefs and rituals are central to the creation and re-creation of ethnic identity, as a means to ensure cultural continuity in both implicit and explicit counterpoint to the dominant culture, then this is a study of more general cultural transformation as well. By following the cups of corn beer or sugarcane brandy from hand to hand and around the paths linking the homes of one community, we will be treated to a panorama of the fondest dreams and goals, as well as the inevitable failures and contradictions, experienced by the individuals and families who want their actions to enrich that community, just as it nourishes them.

Such changes are occurring in the lives of all indigenous people in Ecuador, not only those in the highly populated highland region, and throughout Latin America (for example, Cancian 1992; Eber 1995; Colloredo-Mansfeld 1999; Meisch 2002). In Otavalo, people considered indian have been gradually emancipated from a position marginal to the national economy, where they constituted a pool of actively or potentially coerced labor for all non-indians. At the same time, the subsistence adequacy of the peasant agricultural adaptation that in some ways shielded them from the economic and cultural pressures of the dominant society and the world system has decreased significantly. As their economic and political life changes, a variety of religious missionaries compete for attention with the previously monopolistic Catholic Church. A national indian political movement, popularly called El Movimiento Indigena in Spanish, has also posed a successful challenge to the government, its land-use policies, its defense of human rights, and its provision of basic services for indigenous Ecuadorians. Home life, work, and festive or ceremonial activity are all being transformed, as are the rules for how the symbolically potent food and drink exchanged in these spheres of activity are produced, distributed, and consumed. Today, when celebrants offer a glass with the word *Machapashunchic* (Let's get drunk together), they are as likely to be pouring from a bottle of Coca-Cola as ladling homemade corn beer from a tall pottery jar.

The following account will examine the indigenous side of the evolving conjuncture of two Ecuadorian social groups, one that defines itself and is defined by the dominant society as indigenous to the land, and the other, their mestizo neighbors, who see their ancestry as taking greatest significance from a European immigration to a new world of progress.[1] It is dogma for most mestizos that their approach to living is superior and it is virtually unthinkable that there could be two equally valuable alternatives, even for those who might cherish childhood memories of eating and playing with indigenous servants or the servants' children in the *campo*, or countryside. It is not a question of two cultures in contact, but of the less evolved resisting, and perhaps not deserving, the civilizing properties of the modern, however lacking it may be in the simple joys of a more primitive life.

The juxtaposition and intermixture of these social categories continue to produce novel forms of culture and relationship that cannot be understood without reference to both at the same time. Nor can contemporary expectations and norms be understood without reference to the history of these cultural conflicts and compromises. The fact that, in Ecuador, indigenous social identity and physical existence is dependent upon a wider society that judges its own high value in reference to the stigmatized status it accords its indigenous neighbors means that indigenous people must create models of themselves, their world, and their effectiveness in the world at this interface. They seek help both from the secular and spiritual powers that originate outside their indigenous world as well as from those they can consider autochthonous. To ritually link their cultural adaptations to metaphysical and sacred principles, whether Christian or native, helps legitimate them absolutely, despite the pressures from the outside world to control, change, or denigrate anything indigenous. While one can find indigenous beliefs, behaviors, and symbols today that are echoed in chronicles of the precolonial period, one can find others that are of European or more recent origin, but that nevertheless serve as potent symbols of indigenous identity today. Attention to the complex interweaving of these traditions will be a goal in what follows, although a precise unraveling of all the threads is impossible.

As stated above, this generalized account is presented from the indigenous point of view. For that reason, the reader can find only a shallow view of mestizo Ecuadorians. The indigenous movement, which I like to call a civil rights movement in recognition of the similarities between this movement and that of African Americans in the United States, has changed relations between indigenous people and mestizos in Otavalo to an astonishing degree, and throughout the nation in a lesser but still highly significant way. At any particular time, relationships between mestizo and indigenous Ecuadorians were highly varied. While indisputable and proactive racists have likely always existed as they do today, most mestizos were racists only passively. Despite the social system in which they lived, they were often capable of great tolerance and kindness as neighbors. Some discriminated only on the basis of class and some seemed immune to the power of social hierarchies in their lives. Those at the margins could slide back and forth between making common cause and close personal relationships with indigenous people, and some of those had indigenous parents or grandparents. A book about ethnic relations in Ecuador would be far more complex and nuanced than this one and for that I apologize to my Ecuadorian friends, acquaintances, and relatives by marriage and godparenthood, not just to mestizo but to indigenous readers as well. Relations of power can twist real human relations into unrecognizable and often grotesque shapes, and perceived ethnic or racial differences become grist for this nightmarish mill. Individuals have only a limited ability to resist this milieu, so this account should in no way be seen as an indictment of people.[2]

Despite the fact that we may see complex and shifting combinations of color, pattern, and texture in the fabric being woven from five hundred years of cultural conjunctures, Otavaleños still see themselves in a powerful opposition to the outside world of *mishu jinticuna*, literally "mestizo people" or nonindian Ecuadorians.[3] This may be a cultural myth, but it has considerable social reality. Their social origins and their contemporary reality must take into account this polarized world, even as it shifts its shape and content. Recent indigenist political movements on the regional, national, and international scenes have only reinforced this dichotomy between indigenous and nonindigenous peoples, while economic and social changes have simultaneously reduced it.

A Historic Introduction to the Clashing Cultures of Alcohol Use

On the eve of the Spanish conquest of the Inca Empire, peoples throughout the Andes brewed beer from corn and other grains. They believed that this alcoholic beverage, called *asua* in the Ecuadorian dialect (Quichua) of the Quechua language, to be a gift from the gods, one that had special powers to metaphysically transform persons and relationships and to mediate between men and gods. There were other valuable wild or domesticated plants and animals with similar transformative powers, among which were *coca* leaves, guinea pigs, and hallucinogenic drugs such as *ayahuasca*.[4] When they drank beer during the most powerful ceremonies, pre-Columbian andeans consumed as much as they could and tried to attain and demonstrate publicly a state of inebriation so total that they left consciousness behind. The spirits of the universe enjoyed the animating properties of alcohol as much as did humans and were attracted to the scene of ritual drinking by offerings people made to them for their shared pleasure. While this pattern bore some similarities to tolerated folk Catholicism on the Iberian Peninsula as well, even in Europe it was always subject to suspicion by the Catholic hierarchy, ever mindful of the threats to its hegemony posed by European paganism, Moorish religion, and Judaism.

The conquering Spaniards came to the New World with a very different view of drinking alcohol. For them only wine had a comparable role, capable of symbolizing sacred tenets of their culture. Wine represented Western civilization and as such it transformed human animals into civilized beings when taken daily as a part of meals. During the Catholic mass, it was ritually converted into the blood of the sacrificed Jesus Christ, binding potential sinners into a redemptive communion with God. Civilized people drank wine daily, but in moderation. It was a divinely sanctioned staple food, a means to spiritual communion, and a source of healing.

Most other forms of drinking and types of alcohol, however, symbolized quite the opposite—the power of evil to undo civilization and endanger God's dominion over the world. Drunkenness existed, but righteous men, obeying the commandments of God, could never look upon it with favor. Since human nature was always flawed, alcohol intoxication could be tolerated, and even enjoyed as a personal release from social and religious strictures, but never considered a path to God. Among the urban bourgeois, it was always amoral and sometimes even immoral. Drinking to intoxication threatened the civic order, which served as a public sign of the correct functioning of the hierarchical order and political institutions, with their linked sacred and secular justifications.

During the earliest years of the Spanish colonization of the New World, when wine was in disastrously short supply, there was discussion among Spaniards about whether asua, the andean form of alcohol, could be substituted during the mass, but that proposal was resoundingly defeated (Crosby 1972, 5). The colonists who proposed the substitution were unlikely to have noticed the parallels in cultural practice with regard to wine and asua; the argument was made on the grounds of practicality and was defeated on the grounds that Spanish tradition was sacred and andean practice uncivilized. Once Peru's first wine vintage was successfully produced in 1551, barely nineteen years after the conquest had begun, the official Spanish response hardened into a condemnation of indian drinking of corn beer as a behavior representing the primitive, and possibly idolatrous, nature of the Andean people they were subduing.⁵ One cleric went so far as to say that God had not deigned to provide wine to these New World heathens because he did not consider them worthy of becoming Christians (72).

Some colonial Spanish missionaries, such as Acosta, recognized "the dangers to Christian doctrine and morality" (MacCormack 1991, 264) of indian ritual drinking. However, as time went on, many others found uncontrolled drinking by the poor, whether indigenous or not, to be understandable by virtue of their degraded position in society and incapacity for living the fully moral life of the bourgeois Christian. As Dean explains, arguments over whether such native practices as festive dancing menaced hispanic-Catholic civic and cultural domination often focused on drinking. "Interestingly, placing the blame on the consumption of alcohol seems to have been a way of glossing over the menace and minimizing the threat of dancing Indians. Early on, Hispanics chose to understand (and consequently dismiss) the discontent of the colonized as the irrational misbehavior of drunken Indians" (1999, 58).

Other missionaries and colonial authorities allowed suspected andean sorcerers/shaman to deny their idolatrous activities by claiming to have been incapacitated due to simple drunkenness (Griffiths 1996, 88). While the practicing shaman became drunk in order to gain access to spiritual power, this truly different Spanish justification of drinking allowed them to escape punishment for idolatrous behavior. They could privately practice traditional spirituality for the indigenous community as long as they publicly denied the religious meaning of their use of alcohol and other drugs to the hispanic authorities and accepted the hispanic designation of themselves as simple drunks. Allen claims that the importance of ritual devotion to the animated landscape and coca-leaf chewing intensified after the forced imposition of Christianity (1988, 35). Thus began an intercultural dialogue with far-reaching consequences for native andean people.

Over time, indian drunkenness became a sign more of indigenous moral weakness to the colonial and republican authorities than of religious resistance, although it remained a potential source for secular rebellion. Catholic saints' days were marked by enthusiastic drinking on the part of native celebrants under the accepting eye of the local priest and mestizo neighbors, who often gratefully sold alcohol to further indian revels and line their own pockets. "Es evidente que en el indigenado la tendencia al alcoholismo existía desde la prehistoria; luego se la oficializó con propaganda del Estado y después de los particulares: *'Tome el trago tal o cual'* con lo cual las cosas no han mejorado" [It's evident that the tendency to alcoholism has existed since prehistory; later it became official with the state and, later, private interests advertising, "Take this or that brand of trago," which has not improved the situation (Bonifaz 1975, 90; my translation)].

By encouraging drinking in connection with Catholic worship, authorities hoped to channel indian enthusiasm into approved realms of belief and behavior and away from both native religion and indigenous rebellion. One might say, however, that the Catholic priests played right into the hands of native cultural resistance. Perhaps they had no choice, since whatever constraining policy they made would eventually be subverted wherever possible. Because the colonial authorities and the subjugated natives continually jockeyed for relative advantage in their unequal relations with one another, it is hard to confidently assign any set of indigenous actions to a category representing simply acceptance of domination or resistance to it, or the policies of the controlling elite to simply subjugation or tolerance for native agency.

From the early colonial period to the present, tension between the native andean and the hispanic approaches to indian drinking has continued unabated within many indigenous communities in the Andean region. Indian alcohol use can be characterized either as the uncontrolled moral weakness of a conquered and uncivilized people (following the Euro-American model) or (in the Native American tradition) as devotion to God and other forms of divinity through the joint consumption of alcohol by men and spirits to the point of reaching a mind-altering state of inebriation. Both discursive traditions have offered advantages and disadvantages to the indigenous population over time. Each of these contrasting views of heavy drinking has served indigenous people as a source of both symbolic and real resistance to the dominant society at one time or another.

Although most andean natives became Catholic in the centuries following the Spanish conquest, much of the two religious and cultural traditions remained largely juxtaposed rather than completely synthesized (Wachtel 1977; Taussig 1980), with differing combinations and contrasts in different geographic areas. Indigenous andeans followed religious beliefs and practices that had roots in both worlds, contrasts that they continued to recognize and dramatize rather than combine into a new synthesis. Like the accused sorcerers during colonial times, andean natives until the present were frequently forced to encourage the stereotyping of themselves as hopeless drunks in order to continue forms of worship that had remained meaningful, while the dominant Catholic society either ignored or encouraged their drinking. This paradoxical acceptance of the outsider's view of indian drinking for certain purposes and the adherence to heavy ritual drinking as religious tradition constituted both solutions to a set of problems and, especially as time went on, a devastating curse.

When I first visited Huaycopungo in Otavalo in 1977, the people there were experiencing serious problems due to heavy drinking but still defending it as sacred tradition. However, in 1987 a devastating earthquake galvanized the people of Huaycopungo to make a public commitment to change their lives, especially their drinking, since all natural disasters are God's way of punishing people for having gone astray. They interpreted this message from God to be directed at the forms of their religious life, specifically getting drunk. While the changes that would increase alcohol-related problems and the people's attention to them had already been developing, the earthquake provided the justification needed for an abrupt change of direction, a *pachacuti*, or world reversal, in andean tradition. At its most comprehensive, a pachacuti inspires fear, since it mirrors the original pachacuti that created the world as we know it. In andean popular characterizations of the origin times, nonpeople lived below ground, ate children, grew rotted plants in the dark, and so on. A total pachacuti might result in returning to that inverse existence. Still, the occurrence, even the orchestration, of a smaller pachacuti can stave off a reversal of such disastrous proportions.

The story of this comprehensive change in drinking norms, religious life, and the content of indigenous ethnic identity will be explored in the chapters to come. What did the consumption of alcohol mean to the people of Huaycopungo before the reforms? How and why did they come to be ready for a message from God about their religious drinking? How it occurred, specifically the abrupt community acceptance of an altered social charter, will be explained as a "norm cascade" from applications of game theory to rapid shifts in publicly held preferences. The book will conclude with an examination of the meaning of those changes for their future as indigenous people.

My Introduction to Drinking in Otavalo

The first time my attention was drawn to indigenous drinking was between 1971 and 1973, when, after finishing my undergraduate degree in Latin American studies, I went with my Ecuadorian husband to live in his country. During those years, I frequently saw drunken indians stumbling onto the bus and then passing out in their seats, lying unconscious on the sides of roads, or reeling around the markets muttering curses in Spanish, and I heard many Ecuadorians "explain" this phenomenon to me. As I began to read the anthropology literature on the Andes more closely, I found it emphasized heavy drinking among the indigenous people. A major theme in Ecuadorian representations of the highland natives stresses their pattern of drinking to unconsciousness in public places as exemplary of their intrinsic inferiority or animal nature. In another, more sympathetic, twist on the same theme, heavy indian drinking resulted from the indians' brutal postconquest experience, which degraded their culture from the civilized forms of the Inca era and returned it to a more primitive, subhuman state. Quotes from three authors writing at different times in the twentieth century (all quoted in Bonifaz 1975) illustrate this point. The first attempts to partially excuse the indians by laying the blame on the harsh work conditions imposed by their masters for exacerbating a well-developed alcoholism, while the last two simply highlight that supposed propensity for alcohol abuse in the nature and culture of the indigenous andeans themselves.

No es que el indio buscara en la "Chicha" o cerveza de maíz y más tarde en el alcohol de caña, el lenitivo, el olvido de sus dolores y sufrimientos sino que el vicio arraigado ya en ellos, tomó mayor desarrollo cuando el aumentodel trabajo aumentó el consumo de sus fuerzas y disminuyó su energía vital.

[It's not that the indian would search for the palliative, for the forgetting of his pains and sufferings in "chicha," or corn beer, and later in cane liquor, but that the vice now deeply rooted within them develops more quickly when an increase in work further sapped their strength and diminished their vital energy. (Alfredo Espinoso Tamayo in 1918, quoted in Bonifaz 1975, 90; my translation)]

El alcoholismo es el vicio más nefasta que la {la raza} degrada.

[Alcoholism is the most ghastly vice that degrades it [the race]. (Professor Aquiles Pérez in 1947, quoted in Bonifaz 1975, 79; my translation)]

Cualquier pretexto es bueno para una borrachera.

[Any reason at all justifies a good drunk. (Bonifaz 1975, 89; my translation)]

When I returned to Ecuador to do field research for my doctoral dissertation in 1977, advice from individuals and written sources led me to expect that I would be pressured to join in the drinking. Furthermore, they said, a refusal to drink would brand me an evangelist and, therefore, an enemy of the traditional community. They were right. Getting publicly drunk for the first time in Huaycopungo was indeed a milestone in my becoming acceptable as a person in the community. I was no longer a complete outsider—someone to be treated with suspicion and hostility in an effort to make me so uncomfortable I would leave. By drinking with them, I had behaved in a *runa* (human/ indian) way and had agreed to share in the most potent symbolic act of sharing and group relatedness—drinking to intoxication. Furthermore, I had done so in the potential presence of powerful spirits, who had been invited to join the festivities, and who could therefore spiritually sanction the commitment I had made to a long-term relationship with the people of the community. By thus demonstrating my willingness to participate in group values and behavior I became acceptable, as more than a casual visitor, but certainly as less than a full member.

That day I had been drinking in many homes, since it was summer, the season of life-cycle ceremonies, and had been encouraged to consume a particularly large quantity of alcohol at a house-building celebration where my assistant's maternal uncle, whom we will meet again in the first chapter, was supervising the roof raising. This pressure, as we will come to understand in the first chapter, combined teasing, with its mix of humor and aggression, and high seriousness. When I could drink no more, my assistant escorted me back to her home, where I passed out in the corner. The fact that I vomited repeatedly, barely waking from my stupor to crawl on all fours like a dog to the same mysteriously chosen spot in the dirt-floored house, was not a response to drinking that is valued in Huaycopungo, nor one I would ever care to repeat. Nevertheless, it was expectable and reassuring that, as a young woman, albeit with the full complement of adult statuses—*cusayuc*, *huahuayuc*, and *huasiyuc* (married, a mother, and homeowner)—and a gringa, I show this weakness with respect to getting drunk. Indeed, such communal drinking to intoxication represents not only one of the pleasures of social life but one of its burdens. I had been willing to make this sacrifice for social relatedness by letting go of my rational control and allowing myself to be sick. But I had not done so ignorantly. Like all runa, I had a personal protector from within the community who escorted me home and watched out for me while I slept it off.

However, the offer of drinks to outsiders did not always result in such a socially integrative experience; young American tourists without personal protectors within the community were sometimes encouraged to drink with abandon, and when they were completely plastered, dragged to the edge of the Pan-American highway without shoes, jacket, camera, watch, and other gringo desirables. Stories of such exploits were the source of much local amusement.

To become thus immersed in a completely different culture of drinking, one that turned on its head the quotidian Ecuadorian theories of indian drinking, demanded my attention more effectively than any observation alone. The indigenous practice that most renders plausible the negative characterizations of nonindian observers is that individual control over the amount drunk or over the effects publicly shown is not a value, nor does one try to hide one's drunkenness from certain people. In fact, a lack of motor control and even "passing out" is the expressed, official aim of communal drinking. What frequently goes unrecognized by outsiders to indigenous culture is that, with total intoxication the normative goal, self-control is exercised by exaggerating the intoxication displayed while moderating the amount actually consumed. Both men and women do it, women most of the time and men when they are not centrally involved in the ceremonial action and have no time for a hangover. When I first got drunk, I had neither noticed nor mastered that technique. I naïvely thought that I had to keep downing those gourd bowls of *chicha* (corn beer) until I was really and truly three sheets to the wind, all the while probably unconsciously trying to show off how well I could "hold" my liquor. Few things could so clearly violate European ideas of civilized behavior as this normative surrender to and exaggeration of total, public intoxication.

What makes the contrast in expectations appear even more appalling to those who judge indigenous behavior on the basis of their own culture is the fact that young men do not give up their heavy drinking as they age into responsibilities and dignity, as we North Americans and mestizo Ecuadorians expect. Old men, and even old women, are among the *most* likely to be reeling around drunk or sleeping it off on the side of the footpaths, since age confers greater prestige and drinks are shared preferentially with those of the highest status. Intoxication is sacred because it facilitates exchanges among people, between people and the spirits, and between people and the Christian God—

exchanges that can change essential states of being. The elaborate rules of drinking etiquette and their deep spiritual significance are often ignored by majority Ecuadorians and other Euro-American observers, or dismissed as instinctual, childish, devil-inspired, deluded, or perverted habits of thought and behavior.

By drinking so much on that first occasion I staked a claim on a physical constitution, social prowess, and innate spiritual strength that were highly valued but known to be extremely rare. Only the most obviously gifted and ambitious men, and surpassingly unusual women, would obey the letter of the law, so to speak, and actually consume alcohol in such great quantities. Either I had been innocently duped into becoming plastered, as they had previously experienced with naïve and friendly young North Americans, or I was claiming some thrilling and unexpected powers. People were immediately reassured that it was the former. I eventually learned how to publicly accept the principle of social and spiritual surrender to commitment through shared drinking without actually putting my own self in harm's way. It was relatively easy for me, because my local friends were, and are, always anxious to protect me and conscious of the special ignorance that makes my need for protection especially acute.

Later chapters will give a fuller explication of the rich symbolic significance of the frequent offerings of alcoholic beverages, either as a single drink for personal consumption or as a larger container from which one can serve many others, and the almost unanimous acceptance of those offerings until recent years. However, despite this use of drinking to bind community members together and to reproduce all that is good in the cosmos, in the late seventies it seemed to me that the negative consequences of alcohol use, such as wife beating, accidents, fights, and alcohol dependence, were far more common and disruptive than the ideal would have it. Such misfortunes were said to be part of the world as it is, never wholly good or not-good, and thus part of the experience of drinking as well. Indian life was hard and there was no getting away from that. The level of personal risk that is acceptable among economically and politically dominated people is always greater than that deemed tolerable by those capable, through the combination of wealth and power, of exercising greater control over the comfort and safety of their own lives. Still, ritualized drinking was supposed to increase the good and minimize the suffering, not cause greater suffering as it increasingly seemed to be doing.

At the time, minority voices in Huaycopungo, primarily those few new converts to evangelical Protestantism, argued strongly against drinking at all, but their point of view could be seen only as a challenge to all normative behavior. A number of factors—including an increase in money, a decrease in agricultural production relative to population, an increase in the availability of sugarcane brandy (*aguardiente*, known locally most often as *trago*), and a decrease in the availability of asua (the Quechua word for corn beer, called *chicha* in Ecuadorian Spanish), coupled with community beliefs that food was grown, not purchased, and that surplus, including money, was to be used for ceremonial activity—all seemed to have led to increased consumption of alcoholic beverages. How to characterize drinking, then, as a problem or as sacred behavior, or even as both, and what to expect from the future, were issues that occupied my attention, despite the fact that my dissertation topic bore little relationship to drinking. The recognition that this issue was highly political, since indian drinking was a powerful symbol of racial or cultural inferiority in a national system then bent on ethnocide, or the deliberate destruction of a culture (Stutzman 1981; Whitten 1981), was an important goad to making these issues into a problem that I could neither easily solve nor easily forget.

My return visit in 1987, after five years away, put an end to the mystery of what would happen to the drinking beliefs and behaviors that, in 1979 and 1982, had seemed to me to pose a double bind for the people of Huaycopungo. It had become acceptable, even mandatory, to criticize traditional drinking publicly. There and then my attention was finally hooked and I decided to pursue these issues in more depth. In the meantime, I had increased my expertise in alcohol and other drug issues by following my postdoctoral training in medical anthropology with a master's degree in social work and work in mental health outreach at an Indian Health Service clinic on a small reservation in Wisconsin.[6] Despite my best intentions to distance myself from AODA (alcohol and other drug abuse) problems in social work when I was in school—I even skipped the courses—our mental health programs on the reservation, like those everywhere, were tailored to the sources of funds, and the most-funded problem area of the late 1980s was AODA. As I become more knowledgeable, I found that the conventional wisdom about alcohol use and abuse, while hardly monolithic, shed little light on either the spiritual and integrative role of heavy alcohol use in Huaycopungo before 1987 or the rapid shift in both ideology and behavior in the late 1980s. The case seemed to demand documentation and further investigation.

The intense interest in the role of alcohol abuse among Native American communities in North America further committed me to unravel the complexities of the situation in Otavalo for comparative purposes. The year 1985 saw the publication of *A Poison Stronger Than Love*, an anthropologist's shocking account of Anishinabe people in Grassy Narrows, Ontario, who succumbed nearly unanimously to the gamut of social pathology fueled by continual drinking (Shkilnyk 1985). In 1986 filmmakers in Canada produced an inspiring documentary, *The Honor of All*, about the remarkable recovery of another Canadian band of Anishinabe from similarly widespread alcohol abuse and dependence (Lucas and Tanaka 1986). The following year, the Indian Health Service declared that alcohol abuse was the number one public health problem for native people in the United States. All of these sources profoundly affected the thinking about social service programs on the reservation where I worked.

There are both striking similarities and striking differences in the culture of alcohol use in native America north and south of the current border between the United States and Mexico. Making and drinking fermented beverages was an extremely rare pre-Columbian practice north of the border. The manufacture and consumption of alcohol was introduced to northern native America by European explorers, conquerors, and settlers. However, south of the Rio Grande River, alcohol preparation and consumption was highly institutionalized, especially in the regions of elaborate civilization, Mesoamerica and the Andes. Nonetheless, the European conquest and colonization created a monolithic racial/ethnic category of "Indians" from the myriad language groups extant in the New World in 1492. And despite their very different drinking history, the new Euro-Americans of North, Central, and South America all reported a supposed predisposition to alcohol abuse among the American natives. This startling fact alone justifies the examination of South American patterns in an attempt to shed light on North American problems. Understanding the creation of the "problem" of alcohol "abuse," in both its material and symbolic senses, can further our understanding of how to prevent or reduce the human suffering involved. The suffering is real and alcohol is deeply implicated, but the contrary perspective of seeing alcohol as a gift from the gods with myriad positive benefits also deserves a second look. For the Otavalan Ecuadorians among whom I studied, all things of great power can as easily help as harm human beings. Keeping that in mind may help us avoid polarizing the issue and condemning indian drunkenness unequivocally.

The Book's Organization

CONTRAST AND COMPLEMENTARITY

This book is organized by contrasts—the most obvious being the before and after of part I and part II, with 1987 the fulcrum point for the seesaw's swing of change. Another contrast is that between the dominant society of mestizos and whites in Ecuador and the world of indigenous Ecuadorians in Huaycopungo, which has such a profound effect on who the runacuna are and who they want to be. Furthermore, anthropological studies of the Andes have frequently called attention to the salience of dualisms and their interrelationships in native thinking. Not only has this way of thinking about the world invaded my consciousness in trying to understand the lives of my friends in Huaycopungo, but it has characterized the way they have approached the cultural dilemmas that have faced them for centuries and that continue to face them in the new global village. It deserves a short introduction here.

The longer I lived among the people of Huaycopungo, sharing conversations and interpreting their words, the more I began to see and accept paradoxes—A is true and so is its opposite, B—as a generally satisfying position, especially when expressing the core truths of existence. Contrarily, mutually exclusive opposites—A is true, so B must be false—which had previously seemed simple common sense to me, came to seem inherently unstable and troubling. As my friends and acquaintances in Huaycopungo put it, men were dominant as heads of households overall, but so were women; the spiritual powers of the heavens were superior to those of the earth, but the opposite proposition seemed equally true. The Catholic God trumped native deities, except when he didn't. The hierarchically superior were, paradoxically, inferior, and the weak were likely to triumph. These positions would vacillate, and any seeming resolution would be an illusion, likely to create an abrupt and destabilizing reversal of the previous position. Only after struggling with my own blurry perceptions of this kind of thinking for some time did I begin to study the scholarly treatment of dual forms, including paradoxes, among andeans by North American anthropologists. As early as 1978, in an ethnographic study of a Peruvian andean society, Billie Jean Isbell coined what has become a standard metaphor in andean studies when she called contemporary andean culture "a kaleidoscope of mirrored images" (1978, 11).

Of special note in the scholarship on dualism in the ancient and contemporary Andes is the extraordinary dynamism of the system, with opposed pairs engaging in continual exchanges, periodically changing places, devolving into constituent twins at telescoping levels, battling for primacy, and exchanging essence to create hybrid forms, while never losing their position as opposites. One image from European culture that visually illustrates this intermingling of motion and position is the contra dance, where the original placement of opposed pairs in a line is scrambled in a number of predetermined forms throughout the dance, while being restored at its end. If the opposing lines of couples remained static, without the exchanges and interweaving of both lines and individual couples, it would not be a dance. Frozen snapshots of those beginning, intermediate, and ending positions all have social reality in andean thought, but the ideal model for a living universe is the continuing and human-fostered dynamic, whose symbolism frequently begins with the opposition of pairs.

All wholes of any significance—like the cosmos or the earth or the community or even God, to name a few—are often thought to consist of two complementary parts. As an example, an important organizational schema for local and regional space is to divide the land into two opposed but interactive sides: Upper Side, or *Janan Shaya,* and Lower Side, or *Urai Shaya.* This division has consequences for both social and spiritual life.

At the same time that the pairing of opposites invokes cooperation in making a whole, it consistently provokes conflict, such as the struggle over boundaries between the shayas, incompatible sexual strategies of men and women, the nature of the sun to both nourish and scorch or the rain to irrigate and flood, or the competition between siblings for privilege in the distribution of parental resources. This conflict is believed to create a dynamic force that can also be harnessed for the benefit of people and the world around them. It is not simply destructive but can be a source of creative power, like the sexual struggle between men and women that leads, through sexual intercourse, to the production of the new generation.[7] Of course, the discordant forces can escalate to the point of destruction, but humans have responsibilities, such as ritually reversing their relationship with others or with natural forces, designed to restore balance. Nor is the balance ever expected to be static; it is in constant oscillating movement. Similarly, the endless struggle between the runa people and the dominating mestizo society can, with care and God's goodwill, be turned to the people's advantage.

Metaphors invoking the relationships of the genders are particularly common for describing the alternately conflicting and complementary roles of other mirrored entities in the universe. According to Isbell, "sexual complementarity is perhaps the most pervasive concept used to classify cosmological and natural phenomena" (1978, 11), to which we could add social phenomena as well. Men and women are fundamentally different but highly interdependent, and this type of contrast and complementarity can be found throughout social, geographic, and spiritual worlds. A complex society includes those who command and those who obey, the land includes warm lowlands and cold highlands, and spiritual power lies complementarily in the earth and the sky. Andeans often treat the married pair as a single social person.

Furthermore, each polarized side contains the original polarity within it—when male is contrasted with female, the male side continues to be divisible into male and female, as is the female (Allen 1988). These opposing pairs can be related hierarchically or in a balanced equality. The relationship of the genders is more often used to express an equal relationship, while the relations of gods and humans represent hierarchy. Even when the polarity expresses hierarchy, as opposed to symmetry, the higher level contains within it both the superordinate and the subordinate, as does the lower. The male side is weighted in that male direction and generally stands for or acts out that status or position, as does the female. The same can be said for superordinate and subordinate levels. However, it is expected that the male and the female may change sides or the hierarchical entity sink below the subordinate one, usually only for short periods of time. Through periodic and deliberate alternations of position, people must ensure that these polarizations are maintained in this dynamic balance or risk a dramatic and overwhelming shift, a pachacuti or world reversal, that will threaten the world as andean people know it. In a most prosaic example of the preventive efforts, clockwise circle dancing is common on ritual occasions, but dancers must momentarily reverse direction several times during each dance.

This kind of thinking is not unknown in the post-Enlightenment Western world, but it does not hold the privileged place. Separating right from wrong, or male from female, or white from indian, and using these decisions as the basis for further conceptual constructions is the favored goal. Significantly, the familiar duality of good and evil that means so much to the worldviews developed in interaction with the great religions originating in the Middle East—Judaism, Islam, and Christianity—is much less central in andean thought. In fact, while evil has indeed been a culturally valid concept in the Andes since the introduction of Christianity, a more common duality is that between good, *ali*, and bad, *mana ali* (literally, "not good"). Like the polarities considered above, they tend to be conceptualized as a nested series. There is no absolute good and no absolute bad; good includes some bad and bad contains some good, and they may briefly change places. Their existence is both complementary and conflicting. Would sexual desire be as pleasurable without fear and desire for domination? Or can the effort for economic improvement be far away from greed? All of these taken together mean that the indigenous and hispanic cultures can interrelate in complex and shifting ways, again recalling Isbell's kaleidoscope of mirrored images.

For purposes of this exposition, this kind of thinking could be called Shaya logic, for the upper and lower moieties of Otavalan communities, although Shaya focuses attention on the spatial positioning. Dean recently proposed a term focused more on the dynamic, time-oriented dimensions—the Quichua word *tincui*, which refers to the energetic encounter of two opposing entities, be they partners in a dance or two mountain streams (1999, 162). In either case, the ritual roles of the different shayacuna during calendrical festivals, which will be described in chapter three, clearly act out of kinds of separations and interpenetrations common to the relationships of symbols, of spirits and humans, and of human groups to each other in this andean cultural complex.

Despite the ancient history of binary conflicts and complementarities in andean conceptual structures, their current salience is also a product of the postcolonial experience. Just as drinking rituals took on an increasingly important role in religious observance in the post-conquest world of the andean natives in Otavalo and elsewhere as a response to forced Christian evangelization, this ancient conceptual scheme also takes on heightened significance as a result of the oppositions of European and native, civilized and primitive, dominant and dominated, clean and dirty (Colloredo-Mansfeld 1999) imposed by the colonial and postcolonial elite. All social dialogue engages contrasting perspectives, but the colonial situation makes the dual nature of the world seem even more convincing. There the vanquished must to some extent accept their reduced authority and value in the worlds of both action and meaning now directed by the conquerors and their descendants, while simultaneously struggling to bolster their autochthonous sources of value and weasel as much self-determination as possible out of their separation from or interaction with the dominant society. When we use this set of general interpretive expectations, what might have seemed like impossible contradictions in the meanings associated with Otavalan indigenous ethnicity, religion, and drinking practices become coherent and generative cultural assumptions. The kind of cultural and social characteristics often referred to as *hybridity* or *border lives* (Bhabha 1994, 1) in the current literature come to seem normal, while the more traditional theorizing about cultural essence and stability appears problematic. It is the world elite, who claim the power to define the world and impose their conceptual categories on others, who are more likely to favor absolute and static categories than are those over whom they exercise their hegemony (Gramsci 1971; Foucault 1983; Bhabha 1994).

Different parts of the book may hold more interest for some readers than others. For those seeking to learn more about the culture and social life of Otavalo, this account from the late 1970s of a more agrarian community than Peguche or the other weaving communities, which have attracted more studies (see Parsons 1945; Chavez 1982; Colloredo-Mansfeld 1999; Meisch 2002) may be a useful contrast. For others the topics of alcohol use and abuse, religion, or culture change may hold greater appeal. Chapters 1–5 read something like a traditional ethnography, giving us a snapshot view of family, leadership, religion, ethnic relations, and making a living during the late 1970s. Chapters 1, "*Huasichiy Boda Huasi*: A Ceremonial Open House," and 2, "*Ufyapashunchic*: Let's All Drink Together," describe runa culture almost as if it existed in some kind of pristine seclusion, understandable exclusively on its own terms. Relatively little reference will be made to the dominant society of Ecuador that plays such an important role in the lives of indigenous people and their cultural understandings. Chapters 1 and 2 contrast with each other in that the former expresses more of the negative consequences of festive drinking, examining it at the level of individual families, while chapter 2 outlines a generalized and highly idealized culture of alcohol use. Despite the incompleteness of this presentation, it has a place in local life. In their everyday existence, runa people often like to think that they are living this simplified version of reality, this exclusively runa *causai*, or indigenous lifeway.

Chapter 3, "*Taita Dios* and *Taita Imbabura*," is an exploration of the indigenous Catholicism of the 1970s. It takes the argument a step further than chapter two, since it begins to examine the inevitably two-sided nature of all power, whether social or spiritual, which can equally harm and help human beings. This chapter also presents a transition to a fuller portrait of the interplay of the indigenous and hispanic roots in contemporary runa culture. It explores the syntheses and juxtapositions that make up indigenous religion but still overemphasizes the creative role of indigenous thinkers and practitioners, as if the Roman Catholic and hispanic influences were passively arrayed in a cultural supermarket for the indigenous people to sample and rearrange at will.

Beginning in chapter 4, "*Cantina* and *Boda Huasi*: Local Bar and Ceremonial Open House," the contemporary interplay between the runa and mishu worlds in the creation of the culture of drinking, religious life, and ethnic identities and relationships will form a new contrast and set of interactions to explore. Chapter 4 looks at interethnic drinking and chapter 5, "*Curagacuna* or *Viejos Chumados*: Native Lords or Drunk Old Men," the forms and processes of indigenous leadership, which are poised between defending and promoting indigenous self-determination and directing the necessary accommodations to the fluctuating demands of the dominant society.

For those most interested in understanding the traditional culture of alcohol use, alcohol-related problems, and the swift change of both norms and behaviors, chapters 1, 2, and 4 are the most important; chapter 1 outlines the challenges getting drunk was presenting to the family and community, chapter 2 the traditional domestic rituals of drinking, and chapter 4 the interplay of the hispanic and indigenous venues for drinking. Chapter 9 is the most significant for the analysis of drinking. It presents an overall model of risk and protective factors of alcohol use and how they changed in the last decades, taking into account the cultural meanings of drinking to intoxication described in earlier chapters. Here it should become clear how intoxication could have been holy and unifying at one time and then become devastating with a later set of conditions.

Those most interested in the religious aspect of drinking and ethnic identity formation may find chapters 2, 3, 8, and 10 the most enlightening. Chapter 2 outlines domestic ritual and chapter 3 the andean/ Christian spiritual system. Chapter 8 looks at the inroads made by evangelist Protestantism and catequists in the Catholic Church on religious belief and practice in Huaycopungo over time. Finally, chapter 10 is the account of a fiesta sponsorship, once organized with the help of the San Rafael Catholic church and mestizo elite, that was planned and carried out with much fanfare by the leaders of the evangelical church for the benefit of the whole community.

Since this is a study of cultural change, readers with that particular focus will be most interested in the data and arguments presented in chapters 4, 6, 7, 8, and 9. Chapter 4 describes the effect on indigenous drinking of the community's embeddedness in a wider society dominated by mestizos. Chapter 7 looks at the changing regional and national economic, educational, and political environment of the past few decades, and chapter 8 examines conscious efforts to change indigenous culture and interethnic relations by missionaries and political activists. Chapter 6 is particularly significant because it uses a newer model from rational choice theory, most commonly found in economics and political science, to explain how drinking norms could change so quickly and radically. Chapter 9 takes the ethnographic information presented thus far and weaves it into a more focused analysis of alcohol abuse and alcohol-related harm to provide a model of change.

A CHAPTER OUTLINE

Part I immerses the reader into a novel world of meaning, with special attention to drinking, before the earthquake of 1987, and part II describes and explains the changes that took place in indigenous behavior and explanatory themes after the earthquake. This neat boundary between before and after provided by the earthquake is something of a fiction, since the ideas represented in part I continue, although in somewhat attenuated form, today, and the changes discussed in part II have roots that stretch back long before 1987. What people said they did and believed they should do changed more than what they really wanted to do. Actual behaviors also changed, but perhaps a bit less than the acceptable interpretations of those behaviors. Perhaps the metaphor of a seesaw's swing will be helpful here. The seesaw image allows us to see the point of view of a single rider as switching from a downward trajectory on the first swing to an upward thrust on the second, while the perspective shifts in reverse for that rider's partner. Both perspectives are separately accurate and together necessary for the fullest experience of the situation. Likewise, we can see the community's path at each point in time as characterized by both advances upward and reversals back downward, while at the same time recognizing that the plank on which the riders sit can be experienced as an enduring plane. This search for interpretive continuity in a period of intense change is important for ensuring the longevity of the local transformations.

Part I begins with chapter 1, "*Huasichiy Boda Huasi*: A Ceremonial Open House," a story from the early years of my research that

North American readers will find ambivalent at best. It tells of a family struggle during a ritual event that became painful to the main participants, laying bare contradictions in their personal lives and their shared ideals. This chapter also introduces the expectations held by the people in Huaycopungo in the 1970s about what made good persons, moral families, productive kinship relations, and successful households within a constricted set of available options. In the particular case presented, the cooperative and ritualized building of a house for a young married couple in 1978 led to considerable family conflict and drunken misery. Obligatory drinking during the celebration of this major life-cycle event was supposed to enhance the union among participants and between the humans present and the supernatural powers that could determine the future. However, it seemed only to intensify the internal conflicts among individuals and families. The resulting suffering challenged my understanding of what getting drunk together meant to the people in Huaycopungo, and only after exploring that subject in depth was I better able to appreciate the productive combination of good and bad they were attempting to achieve in their behavior. And in chapter 1 I struggle to lead the reader away from the easy generalizations that are part of our North American cultural repertoire so we can interpret drunken behavior from a strikingly different cultural view. Nonetheless, ambivalence about the event was experienced by the native participants as well as by me, and years later this house-building story became an example of how their traditional drinking rituals had failed to achieve the proper mix of harmony and combustion that would ensure them a satisfying present and improved future.

Chapter 2, "*Ufyapashunchic*: Let's All Drink Together," considers different sets of polarities. Whereas "*Huasichiy Boda Huasi*" concerns ritual behavior in one household, highlighting individual histories and personal decisions in a celebration that produced much anger and sadness, "*Ufyapashunchic*" examines human interactions with other people and with nonhuman powers in a highly symbolic and idealized universe designed to bring as much joy and contentment to the sad lot of runacuna as possible. In the movie *Smoke Signals* (1998), a film based on a collection of short stories (1993) by Sherman Alexie, a Coeur d'Alene indian, the narrator, Thomas Builds-the-Fire, is asked by someone about to tell him a story if he wants the truth or a lie. "Both," he replies, and it is left ambiguous which is which. While this chapter may approach a lie in the sense of being too good to be true, it is as true as a more objective account in the sense of its power to shape people's hopes and dreams. This describes who they wanted to be and knowing *that* is as important as knowing who they really are. Going beyond the creation of persons and households that we examined in chapter one, here we trace the interrelationships of households with one another to create the community, seen idealistically as a web of interdependent relationships that make it like one organism. Ritual drinking will be revealed as a symbolic currency for the creation, exchange, and store of value, both social and spiritual.

Since ritual drinking is embedded within traditional runa religious practice, chapter 3—"*Taita Dios* and *Taita Imbabura*"—examines the complex combinations of elements counterposed from Catholic and native traditions that constituted the whole of indigenous religion until the 1970s. In the late 1970s people in Huaycopungo considered themselves real Catholics, although their practices included many elements nonexistent in majority Catholic practice or formal church doctrine. From the local indian viewpoint, runa Catholicism was true indian religion, despite the fact that its origins in the distant past included so much that was brutally imposed by the Spanish conquerors and hispanic-Ecuadorian church authorities. One side of the polar inter-pretations available to them was that the elements they considered nonnative were the necessary counterpart of a whole runa Catholicism, which was nevertheless overwhelmingly runa. Alternatively, when trying to convince the priest, the obviously runa elements were a small but essential part of a truly hispanic Catholic whole. Unless our discussion is confined to the pre-Columbian era, it is impossible to identify and study some kind of pure indigenous practice or belief (Abercrombie 1998). Nonetheless, in chapter 2 we will continue to downplay the contemporary mishu-runa polarities and we will, as yet, postpone the consideration of the changes after 1987. We will pretend, for the sake of clarity, that runacuna are in charge of their own existence in a world of their own making and that the idealized peasant adaptations they value are in fact efficacious and productive of a satisfactory pres-ent and improved future for all. People in Huaycopungo, like people everywhere, do sometimes pretend this when justifying their values to themselves and to others.

Chapters 2 and 3 present a kind of world that people would like to live in but usually experience only in ritualized events. The disturbing fact is that while peoples who are in a dominant position in the world system and in their own societies often have the power to tell the idealized stories of their lives—even to teach them in their schools—but these same peoples find the portraits of the less fortunate to be realistic only if they concentrate on how the poor individuals, communities, or countries fail to attain the ideals of the dominant—themselves. The idealized portraits that the dominated create of their life are as unrealistic as any of their supposed betters. Nonetheless, they are important to examine in order to achieve a richer understanding of people's motivations and goals and the sources of their occasional satisfactions. So we will begin like children understanding our own culture, learning first the sugar-coated version of who we are and how our parents conduct their lives, before examining the more disturbing realities of the fault lines in our culture and society and our relative powerlessness in the face of pressures from local, national, and world system forces.

Chapter 4—"*Cantina* and *Boda Huasi*: Local Bar and Ceremonial Open House"—introduces the polarities in drinking behavior and worlds of meaning attendant upon the mishu/runa dichotomy. This is not intended as a portrait of nonindian Ecuadorian life; rather, I analyze the incorporation of reworked images of mishu culture by indians and the forms of interrelationship between indians and mestizos that indians experience. By andean logic the indigenous would always contain some of the mishu. In addition, the extent of cultural mixing by those who wish to remain indigenous has been far greater than that of those termed mestizo, or mixed. Although the term *mestizo* explicitly refers to the genealogical and cultural mixing of indian and Spanish that is supposed to characterize the majority of Ecuadorians, it continues to suggest inferiority to the elite, sometimes called *blancos*, or whites, who remain supposedly free of the indian taint in ancestry and tradition. If one is elite, one is more likely to be light in skin tone and if one is light in skin tone, one is more likely to gain some social advantage. But not all elite are white, nor are all light-skinned people elite. Mestizos try harder to eschew the phenotypical traits and most recognized cultural characteristics of the stigmatized indian identity than the indigenous people do to avoid the nationally valorized characteristics of the hispanic majority. The chapter, then, will be skewed to the indian side of the conjuncture.

Chapter 5—"*Curagacuna* or *Viejos Chumados*: Native Lords or Drunk Old Men"—examines traditional indigenous leadership and the heavy obligatory drinking it entails. We begin again with examples from individual lives and personal decisions in an exploration of the careers of forward-looking leaders of the earlier period who became, for the next generation of leaders, the "drunk old men" that *mishucuna* had always accused them of being. While they carefully nurtured particular forms of cultural resistance and interchange, they became, within their lifetimes, known for their rigid—and mistaken—cultural conservatism. This last chapter of part I will serve as a transition to part II.

Part II is entitled "After the 1987 Earthquake." There, starting with chapter 6—"Pachacuti: World Reversal," we begin to discuss the changes that are, in fact, continual in the period under discussion, but that are conceptualized as if the events of 1987 made them suddenly fundamental and God-given. The symbolism of the earthquake creates a kind of hinge that allows a reversal of direction without a complete disarticulation from the trajectory of the past. Despite the periodic welling up of dissatisfactions and disputes over elements of the normative lifestyle and its justifications over a long period, and despite the occurrence of a natural event that could be interpreted as a message from God, the fact that public opinion made a 180° turn almost instantaneously still demands explanation. If they had been able to go on for so long supporting the ritual drinking regardless of perceived costs, and if they had been able to interpret other natural disasters as messages to people other than themselves, and if the strictures of ethnic solidarity still kept individuals committed to satisfying the expectations of their fellows despite personal suffering, then the quick shift in direction was not inevitable. Something further is required for a complete explanation. Toward that end, chapter 6 introduces the recent literature on *norm cascades*, an addition to rational choice theory in the work of economists, political scientists, and legal theorists. Of special interest is how the cumulative thresholds for maintaining or discarding a public position given strong personal opposition to it on the part of a social group can change suddenly, resulting in "revolutionary" changes in public belief and behavior as chronicled here.

Chapter 7, "*Runa Gente, Gente* Civilizada: Uniting the Contradictions of the Indigenous and the Fully Civilized," focuses on the comprehensive changes occurring in Ecuador during the last quarter of the twentieth century, including the social, political, and economic relations between the country's majority and its indigenous people. Therein lie some of the institutional factors that altered the cost-benefit analysis that individuals made in deciding how to live their lives. Some of the resulting shifts, and contradictions, to be traced include those between agriculture and business, community insularity and community openness to the world, monolingualism in Quichua and bilingualism in Quichua and Spanish, and illiteracy and education.

Chapter 8, "*Evangelistas, Catequistas,* and *Activistas*," takes on a different set of changing institutions in which the people of Huaycopungo are embedded and which demand that they alter their worldview and corresponding behavior. The change of direction in the symbolic casting of the universe that publicly engaged the majority after 1987 was given additional forward momentum by a new sacred dichotomy between evangelical Protestantism, as brought by local missionaries, and a revolutionary Catholicism. From the beginning of the twentieth century, evangelical missionaries in Latin American made the complete abstention from alcohol a central behavioral symbol of their new religious message, and the new Catholic movement also tackles the problems that intoxicated worship presents for the national integration of indigenous people and the well-being of native families. Both the new Catholic and Protestant movements are conceived, in part, as movements of protest, and their relationship to more typically political forms of protest is also explored.

Chapter 9, "*Yapa Ufyadur Carcanchic*: We Drank Too Much"[8] takes a different approach by addressing the effects of alcohol consumption directly in the lives of Huaycopungo's people and their individual assessment of cost-benefit. The institutional changes in the encompassing society of Ecuador affected the impact these drinking rituals had on people, which in turn facilitated the quick change in majority opinion in Huaycopungo: from treating ceremonial binge drinking as a centerpoint of indigenous religious life and ethnic identity to judging that the community was drinking too much and suffering because of it. Not only had alcohol consumption increased, thereby occasioning a rise in such problems as accidents, domestic violence, and alcoholism, but other behavioral and interpretative alternatives became both advantageous and feasible, such as the growing hispanicization of indigenous culture and the Protestant and Catholic religious alternatives discussed in chapters 7 and 8.

Chapter 10, "Transnational Corazas 2000," however, brings us back to where we began with an account of a major ritual celebration, resuscitated in 2000 after a hiatus of about fifteen years, that shows a unique and self-consciously indigenous world still alive in Huaycopungo. From the more material concerns of the previous chapters, we look again at the ways people creatively interpret their place in the universe within the context of this real-world environment. These imagined worlds have deep consequences, particularly in the political negotiations of the indigenous and nonindigenous people of the region. Chapter ten presents the transformation of this densely symbolic ritual of traditional culture, which once included days of intoxication in the service of native Catholicism, with the result that indigenous poverty was deepened and poor local mestizos contrived to finance the escapes of their own children into a more socially acceptable future. Today it is becoming a community ritual of moderation that includes both Protestants and new Catholics. This modern transformation of tradition manages to preserve the best of the past and serve the needs of the future in ways today's leaders had long envisioned. Here we finally enter the new world in which presenting a case of Coca-Cola while ritually enjoining one's social partners to join one in surrendering to drunkenness makes perfect sense.

Finally, the conclusion, "*Que Viva Runa Causai*: Long Live Indigenous Culture," considers more generally the nature of cultural persistence and change in andean Ecuador. Continuing the theme introduced in the introduction, we note how contemporary negotiations of ethnic and more general power relations in Ecuadorian society may intensify the significance of indigenous cultural themes of seeming antiquity. What seems most astonishingly ancient can be recognized as a reflection of current events and processes. Then we make some limited predictions about the continuity of the cultural patterns and concerns presented in the book as a whole. After the passage of one more generation, what of this account will still be recognizable in the culture of Otavalo's indigenous people?

The Place and the People

Before plunging into the clouds of dust raised by the feet of the participants during the *huasichiy fishta* (house-building party) of 1978 chronicled in chapter one, I would like to introduce the physical landscape and the people within it. An outsider usually begins by following the curving Pan-American Highway up and down the precipitous hills north from Quito. If you are lucky, halfway there Cayambe, the eternally snow-capped volcano rising 19,000 feet high just off the equator, will appear from out of its screen of clouds to accompany your travel. Depending on the time of day, it is either dazzling silver-white, shadowy blue, or rosy pink. In local lore, Cayambe is a very wealthy and beautiful woman mountain who sometimes flirts with Mount Imbabura, the ever-present mountain backdrop in Otavalo, almost never hidden by clouds, who is Otavalo's spiritual patron. Taita Imbabura's wife, Mama Cotacachi, faces him across the valley and shows her disapproval of his philandering with the distant Cayambe by unleashing terrifying lightning bolts and deep rumbling thunder from deep within her craters. At lower altitudes you, the traveler, can't see Imbabura's dark and glacier-free slopes at the same time shining Cayambe is visible to you. Still, the two mountains are facing one another, which you can see only when you yourself are high up in altitude where there are few fields and fewer inhabitants. The distances that humans can see, considerable in these deforested mountain valleys and passes, are still restricted in the extreme, compared to the mountains themselves. This preoccupation with multiple visual perspectives is commonplace in the Andes, as is the idea that the landscape perceives us more thoroughly than we do it. Evidence of a long and growing presence of humans is apparent everywhere in the landscape, but the largest mountains loom above human endeavor, reminding us of our insignificance. In the andean way of thinking, these peaks are reference points for both spiritual and geopolitical territories that stretch well beyond the parochial concerns of home.

To reach the valley of Otavalo from the valley of Cayambe, one must climb up the flanks of Mount Mojanda and go through the chilly pass at Cajas. There, indigenous neighbors of the native Otavaleños struggle to grow potatoes, quinoa, and barley in their high-altitude plots, received from haciendas during the land reforms only thirty years ago. The women's bright-colored *centros*,[9] or circular wool skirts, swirl about them in the cold winds as they work, providing a welcome contrast to the men's much-mended and dirty clothes. There are few trees and the patchwork of fields displays a different set of colors in different seasons: the palest green on dark brown in the winter, when fields have been recently plowed and seeded, and a blazing color spectrum from yellow to red to purple in early summer, when the quinoa, a high-protein Andean grain, is in full bloom. As you begin to weave down from the pass to the Otavalo valley, lakeshore Huaycopungo and its uphill counterpart on Mount Mojanda's lowest slopes, Tocagon, are the very first Otavaleño communities you pass on the Pan-American Highway. In fact, speculation is that the name Huaycopungo, literally

Fig. 3. The imposing *Taita* Imbabura
(PHOTO BY AUTHOR)

Fig. 4. The glittering *Mama* Cayambe
(PHOTO BY AUTHOR)

Fig. 5. The fiercely demanding *Mama* Cotacachi
(PHOTO BY AUTHOR)

"ravine door," refers to its position as entrance to the ancient chiefdom of Caranqui, the town of Sarance, and its sacred lake Imbacocha. Today, the municipal center of the valley is the town of Otavalo, not on the lake, and it is world famous for its large and colorful textile market specializing in the tourist trade and foreign export and run by indigenous Otavalans. The people of Huaycopungo and the valley as a whole today belong to a large ethnic group of Quichua speakers, usually called Otavaleños for the cantón of Otavalo, of which they are the majority. Native Otavalans proudly display their ethnic distinctiveness in hairstyle and costume, whether at home or abroad. Huaycopungo is the largest legally recognized indian community, about 1,800 people, in the cantón, and is situated in the southernmost part of the parish of San Rafael.

The nearest neighbors in the parish of Gonzalez Suarez further south are of a different ethnicity, although they also speak Quichua and share many aspects of culture with Otavalo runa. They are reputedly descendants of the pre-Columbian chiefdomship of the Cayambes to the south. Like the women in Cajas, Huaycopungo's nearest neighbors wear *centros*, sometimes called *puendos*, and not the double *anacos*, wrapped skirts long ago copied from Inca royal dress, favored by Otavalo runa. This neighboring group used to be called Puendos, using the name of women's typical garb to refer to the ethnic group. Otavalo men traditionally wear one long braid, although the youthful male fashion these days is for long but unbraided hair pulled back with an elastic band.[10] Their southern neighbors have cut their hair short for generations and so Otavaleños often use the term *Mochos*, people with cropped hair, to refer to this ethnic group. In Huaycopungo mocho is a mild insult. While Huaycopungo has long owned its own land, these Mochos had almost all been owned by haciendas[11] and given tiny plots to cultivate, but not own, until the land reform freed them from their servitude and gave them individual or cooperative title to the redistributed land.

The town of San Rafael is the parish seat. San Rafael parish was founded in the nineteenth century to divide the by then over-large parish of Otavalo into smaller segments. While Otavalo was a cantón in the civil government, administered by the municipal authorities in the town of Otavalo, parishes were simultaneously religious and civil administrative units of territory within the cantón. The town of San Rafael was designed to be a hispanic geopolitical center of a smaller region inhabited by indians, which had previously been part of Otavalo's enormous indigenous hinterland. In particular, the new parish would relieve crowding in Otavalo's churches, attract new indigenous parishioners, and employ a greater number of priests. Some civil functions, like that of police services, could also be localized in the new parish. Five *comunas* surrounding San Rafael—Tocagon, Huaycopungo (the most populous), Cachiviro, San Miguel, and Cachimuel—are part of the parish.[12] San Rafael was traditionally the home of mestizos who had moved into the town during the last hundred years to establish stores and bars, man the clinic and the police station, assist the priest and nuns at the church, and so on. Free indians, as were most Otavaleños, provided a great resource for poor mestizos in the province of Imbabura. Like the five communities surrounding San Rafael, they provided cheap or free labor, a source of confiscated produce during lean times, and a market for mestizo-produced commodities. Each comuna also has named sections and each section must be a focus of attention in religious processions in the typical andean practice of combining communalism and differentiation. In fact, people in each section would each prefer to field their own ritual sponsor during the major fiestas, although this goal is rarely achieved. In the late 1970s Huaycopungo contained Langaburo, Villagran Pugru, Huaycopungo, and Huaycopungo Chiquito.[13] In the past, sections that grew sufficiently populous could behave as separate communities and eventually achieve public recognition as such, by organizing their own *mingas,* or communal work parties, fielding their own fiesta sponsors, and other such communitywide activities. Therefore, traditionally, the divisions have been somewhat malleable and continue to be a source of contention. However, the legal registering of indigenous communities with the cantón authorities in the last few decades has made changes much more difficult.

Until recently, the indians of San Rafael had a reputation for being very conservative and old-fashioned (Espinosa Soriano 1988a, 138), in part for their lavish religious festivals. About twenty years ago, the first few families experimented with long-distance peddling of clothing in small, relatively isolated towns, particularly in Colombia; now most families in Huaycopungo combine this trade with the earlier occupations. Long-distance trade has been a specialty of the Otavalo area since pre-Hispanic times (Salomon [1973] 1981; Espinosa Soriano 1988b), although up until twenty years ago indigenous people from San Rafael had confined their trade to agricultural products.

Finally, the traditional arrangement of houses among these andean people was to spread out houses among small garden plots. The Spanish tried to impose a pattern of nucleated settlements upon the native peoples, with only mixed success. While Ecuador's mestizos uniformly believe that nucleated living arrangements are a quintessential mark of civilization, indigenous people still prefer to have their houses separated from each other by cultivated fields. Nevertheless, the cobblestoned Pan-American Highway used to run through Huaycopungo and that stretch of road has long been more densely settled than the rest, especially at the southeastern end. Although the newer paved highway now runs between Huaycopungo and Tocagon as you travel north, the rapid population growth has given Huaycopungo a more suburban than rural character today. The garden plots and rows of planted eucalyptus trees can still be seen as you stand at the elevated corner in the northwest known as Jurubi and survey Huaycopungo, sloping gently to the Itambi River and Lake San Pablo, but they are filled in with more and more houses every year. The Taita Imbaburapac mesa, "table of Taita Imbabura," a ceremonial mound unused today but a remnant of pre-Catholic forms of religious worship, used to stand silently, surrounded by fields of corn and quinoa, facing Taita Imbabura across the lake. Today, its edge has been filed away to provide one wall of the new "stadium," or playing field for soccer and volleyball. Its flat top has not been planted since 1999, since Huaycopungo is trying to acquire it as communal property from the two hereditary owners, but people still occasionally climb the steep slopes to glean useful wild and self-seeded cultivated plants.

Between the corner, good for surveying the whole village, of Jurubi, and the Pan-American Highway, my assistant and her husband were, in the summer of 1978, finally beginning to construct a house so they could move out of her parents' home, the scene of my inaugural binge. My assistant's mother had contributed the plot of land, which was conveniently located but lacked any flat surfaces near the road. Her father had saved up roof tiles for a number of years, and her husband's

Fig. 6. *Mesa* of Taita Imbabura from Jurubi
(PHOTO BY AUTHOR)

mother gave them a few mature eucalyptus trees from her land to use
for rafters. With the mixture of high hopes and nameless anxieties that
so characterizes young couples in their early twenties, they embarked
on this major adventure of their lives, which they expected to finish
in a couple of months. Relatives and neighbors were recruited to help,
as was I. From the *alpa pascai*, the day we ritually "opened" the earth
and asked permission of the spirits to build, until we completed the
house took a scandalous six months. Manually digging out the slope
to provide a flat place on which to erect the mud walls and a number
of major family quarrels stretched the time out endlessly. Numbed by
day after day of ritually consuming asua and sugarcane brandy with
the workers, in November 1978 we made it at last to the *huasichiy
fishta*, house-building party, that is the subject of the first chapter.

PART I

Before the 1987 Earthquake

Huasichiy Boda Huasi
A Ceremonial Open House

A True Story

THE HOUSE WAS BUILT, with the impressive two-story mud walls properly molded and dried to form one big room. The rafters were in place and the roof tiles laid upon them, but neither the door frame nor the door was yet installed. Nor had a proper yard been dug out of the hill immediately behind the house, and the door, once installed, would open inauspiciously toward the winds off the mountain, rather than away from them. Nevertheless, all the family, relatives, compadres (ritual co-parents), neighbors, and construction masters who had participated in the house construction were feting each other and its completion. The new house was a *boda huasi*, the house (*huasi*) where a special festive dish (*boda*) is served, and, more loosely, a house where people are celebrating by eating and drinking in a ceremonial fashion. The young couple for whom the house was built, and their parents who had helped them build it, were ritually thanking all those others who had donated labor and goods to the project. Simultaneously they were petitioning the local and transcendent spirits for a peaceful and productive future for the house and its residents. More personally, we were all thrilled that Larka José's efforts to spend more money and build a bigger house faster had just resulted in a collapsed wall. The belief that unspecified evil always followed money quickly acquired had been justified.

The couple, who would soon move into the house with their two young children, had made the final important step into full adult status. Both had a spouse, a child and, now, a house. José Manuel Tituaña Amaguaña was *huarmiyuc* (a wife belonged to him),[1] *churiyuc* (a child, literally a son,[2] belonged to him), and *huasiyuc* (a house belonged to him); Isabel Criollo Perugachi was *cusayuc* (had a husband), *huahuayuc* (had a child), and also *huasiyuc* (had a house). Their parents had contributed what land, food, labor, and materials they could, fulfilling the responsibilities that gave them elder status for the first time, since the young husband and wife were both eldest children. This step produces intense anxiety in an ambitious senior couple since its successful completion is so significant for their continuing reputation, but both signals and is enacted through a reduction of their control over their material resources and adult children. In their joint efforts to build

Fig. 7. New house (far left),
with roofers finishing tile, 1978
(PHOTO BY AUTHOR)

Fig. 8. *Boda huasi,* 1978
(PHOTO BY AUTHOR)

the house, both sets of parents and other relatives (*ayllucuna*) of the young couple had demonstrated a productive cooperation that they hoped would now take precedence over the mutual suspicion characteristic of families related by marriage in the early years of a couple's union. The completion of a house marked major transformations of the living earth on which the house was built, of the community, which now had a new constituent household, and of the couple, who now had become responsible for participating in world-perpetuating and regenerating activities.

Isabel's cousin and his wife, home for a visit from Quito, were happy to serve as sponsors for the cross representing San José, who was the lead spirit being asked to bless the house, a mediator to God and to the lesser localized spirits. The couple would serve as godparents, *padrinos*, to the house and thereby become co-parents, compadres, with the homeowners. The hosts expected to tax their energies to the breaking point in a several-day marathon of serving guests. The most

Fig. 9. Isabel Criollo, 1978
(PHOTO BY AUTHOR)

Fig. 10. José Manuel Tituaña, with daughter
Maria Susana at left and baby son Luis Ricardo, 1978
(PHOTO BY AUTHOR)

potent ceremonial activity would be the required sharing of asua (corn beer) and *tragu* (sugarcane brandy or aguardiente), as well as the serving of special ceremonial cooked foods. Offering drinks would serve several functions. The ritual sharing of drinks included payment for the donation of labor, a celebration of the countless mutual exchanges that have bound the participants into a family and a community, and a public commitment to continued social and material obligation among the major participants. At the same time as these acts of payment, celebration, and commitment were made to fellow community members, they were offered as well to nonhuman spiritual agents, whose many manifestations could be subsumed in the Christian concept of God. Drinking ritually expressed gratitude to the spiritual forces that allow life to continue through the birth and maturation of the community's crops and children and constituted a pact between humans and nonhuman agents to continue in reciprocal exchange of benefit. Everyone claimed that the shared alcohol would enhance the feelings of union and happiness that the successful completion of this important life-cycle transition should bring. *Cushishsha, alishsha cashunchic*, they said with the strung-out sibilants (-*sh*-) and in the high-pitched voices that express superlatives. "We will be really, *really* happy, really good."

Yet, while every participant, to the best of his or her ability, went through the motions of celebrating these accomplishments and honoring their moral underpinnings, the events were marked by the same conflicts, despair, frustration, and lack of fit between what was expected and what resulted that had characterized the entire building of the house. For example, during the festivities Isabel's father, Antonio Criollo, would not enter the house when his son-in-law, José Manuel, was present. A proud community leader at the time, he bitterly complained that José Manuel never acted the proper son-in-law with him, neither helping him with agricultural tasks nor accompanying him in drinking. He claimed that by not meeting the expectations of what a proper son-in-law should do, José Manuel was expressing a lack of love and commitment to his wife, children, and family by marriage. By the same actions José Manuel was also implicitly claiming that Antonio's role performance as father and father-in-law was unworthy of his love. People feel loved when members of their family behave as they should toward them, given their position as son, wife, or father. Equally, each person expresses love to another by behaving as would a model daughter, husband, or mother. Loving words or gifts could never measure up to a superlative role performance, even among courting couples, and even less between parents and children. "Am I not a father who supports my children?" cried Antonio tearfully every day after he had been drinking. Painfully aware of the resource deficits that made the house building stretch out over three months and into the planting season, he kept claiming his contributions to the couple were under-recognized. His continuing responsibility to support his six younger children, who would all need grants of land and materials for a house someday, limited his ability to be generous. His fear back then was well founded, since competition over insufficient resources bitterly alienated his children from one another a decade later and estranged him from his eldest daughter.[3] In part, those complaints may have represented an excuse to safeguard his other children's futures, despite his love for his eldest daughter, his desire to gain public recognition of his stature through the building of her house, and his daughter's own ambitions for a prestigious future. By publicizing this set of generally acceptable justifications and an ungrateful son-in-law, he could restrict his resource contribution to this house, however much that galled him both in his role performance at home and in his competitive endeavors to prove his material and social worth in the community as a whole. To be a good father to his six younger children, he had to be a less than stellar father to his eldest child, the one whose passage to full adulthood signaled his own passage to elderhood. And so he wept and bemoaned his fate to all those who would listen—including, maybe especially, the visiting anthropologist. While it was not generally recognized yet, Antonio had developed alcoholism after years of frequent drinking.

José Manuel's mother, Emilia, was a widow and a recognized alcoholic who went on long periodic binges.[4] She countered with her own sense of pain and injustice; since her husband was dead, it was left to her to justify the fact that José Manuel and his wife were not going to receive the best of everything from her hands. In fact, they would receive not much of anything. She too would theoretically, if never in fact, be responsible for her three younger children's futures. But her household lacked the resources and status of the household headed by Antonio. The pathos of her real and publicly dramatized pain, unlike Antonio's frustrated ambition, was of her tragic adulthood marked by widowhood, alcoholism, and lack of resources. Everyone was criticizing her for having secretly sold trees from the land her mother had said was going to be José Manuel's in order to buy booze. The loss was discovered when we had gone as a house-building party to cut rafter poles. But she too suffered, she keened through her tears, having been left a widow with four children even before her husband actually died. He became ill and died in a Quito prison after serving thirteen years of his sentence for killing a drinking companion in a drunken brawl. She too claimed to receive no recognition for trying to help her children.

Isabel's mother's youngest brother, also José Manuel, one of whose nicknames was Chunda Fucu, had offered to be the master roofer, a job that also entails directing the house building as a whole. The nickname means "Chonta Palm Blower" and refers to time he spent living in Santo Domingo de los Colorados, where the famous local shaman among the "Colorado," or Tsachila, indians use chonta palm tubes in their curing rituals. Dolores and Antonio had also become Chunda Fucu's godparents at his wedding, which obligated him to work for them when needed, just as they should support him materially and morally throughout his life. Antonio and Dolores, and José Manuel and Isabel, would pay him for his expert services. As soon as the other houses he had agreed to supervise were done, and before the end of the long season of harvest, festivities, and house building, from roughly late April to early October, he would start his niece's house. He offered to work on credit, as a kinsman and godchild, and he was one of the few workers who stayed until the house was completely erected.

But Chunda Fucu's wife became extremely bitter about the time and money he had wasted on *his* ayllu, to the detriment of her, their children, and her own ayllu. It was not a happy marriage, since it was arranged hastily and secretly to prevent Chunda Fucu from going back to Santo Domingo. She spent the several days of festivities drinking and screaming insults in the near distance wherever the celebrants happened to be. It was acceptable for her to drink because of the boda huasi; in turn drinking gave her license to speak her mind bluntly, which would not have been the case had she been sober. Still, as a woman, her complaints were personal and came from the middle distance but were not directly addressed to the participants in a group. During the last few days, the voice of one rational person or another could be heard at all times over her exhausted croak, exhorting an infuriated fellow celebrant to ignore her rantings, rather than carry the fight any farther.

When drunk himself, José Manuel claimed he would never live in that house. It belonged not to him but to Antonio, who had never wanted him as a son-in-law and whose goal was to maintain control of his daughter and thwart José Manuel's own future plans. He claimed that as soon as the house was built, his wife would kick him out anyway, in order to consort with other men. During the house building José Manuel had several times escaped to Quito, the capital city, leaving his wife Isabel to supervise the work and worry about whether he would return. Responding to a tip about where to find him in Quito one night, she arrived at my house in Otavalo after midnight and begged me to accompany her on the next bus. Arriving in Quito just before it got light, we entered a construction site and knocked on the door of a caretaker's hut, surprising a whole line of sleeping people, huddled together to escape the cold. Asleep next to José Manuel was a woman with her skirts askew. Sleeping next to one another in a line is not in itself an indication of infidelity, but, everyone agreed, she would not have opened her two wrap skirts (anacos) had the encounter been innocent. To top it all off, Isabel made sure everyone knew that the subsequent gastrointestinal complaint of the visiting anthropologist and godmother to their second child was due to the fright sickness, *susto*, received at the discovery.[5]

In the last month of house building, José Manuel occasionally vomited blood, which everyone, included a doctor he consulted, attributed to the effects of continual drinking on his stomach. Although he tried to avoid advanced intoxication with the rest by feigning more drunkenness than he felt, he could not stop sharing drinks with the workers. I will never forget the afternoon when José Manuel, Isabel, and I finally relaxed because everyone else was stretched out on the ground, dead drunk. Giving up our pretend state of extreme intoxication, we straightened up, stopped weaving about and slurring our words, only to be overheard by the seemingly comatose neighbor and

Fig. 11. Pata Luchu, Larka José,
and Chunda Fucu at a *cantina*, 1979
(PHOTO BY AUTHOR)

maternal first cousin to Isabel's mother, Pata Luchu. He rose up, got
another bottle and poured us large shots of trago, determined that we
join the unconscious crowd. We never underestimated Pata Luchu's
capacity for alcohol again. On another afternoon of these celebrations
José Manuel raged drunk around the neighborhood, ripping off his own
new shirt and sweater and throwing them into the brush, climbing up
a rival neighbor's ladder despite his drunken lack of balance, and joining his own screaming voice to that of Chunda Fucu's wife. When he
was finally coaxed down to rest by his mother, he insisted in sleeping at
Pata Luchu's neighboring house, rather than enter his own new one.

   The day that the house-building party, led by José Manuel and
Isabel and accompanied by a musician playing his flute, proceeded ritually to the house of Isabel's cousin Chunda Fucu, the master roofer,
in order to present him with the traditional completion gift of alcohol
and cooked food, *mediano*, they met him walking toward the highway.
In a rage, Chunda Fucu said he was fleeing town. He and his wife had

fought bitterly, and he absolutely refused to be led or dragged home to receive the group. After some discussion, the procession proceeded to his house, where they presented the mediano to his weeping wife, who had a puffy eye and a missing tooth. Although she continued to cry and complain for a while, everyone went through the motions of cheerfully celebrating with her, in her husband's place, his contribution to kin and community continuity. That is, everyone got drunk while exchanging stories and gossip. Later in the afternoon, Chunda Fucu, also drunk, stumbled back into his yard and more fights broke out between the unhappy participants.

Trying to Understand

Before we proceed any further with our understanding of the lives of people in Huaycopungo in the 1970s, let's examine our own diagnoses of this situation. I know that my students have had a tendency to see everyone in Huaycopungo as an abusive drinker or alcoholic when they encounter this story. Despite the cases presented above, the vast majority of people in Huaycopungo were not alcoholics. Whether or not they could be said to "abuse" alcohol is difficult to say, since it is usually judged by such culturally bound criteria. We will return to this question in chapter 9. But it is important to remember that the opportunities for most people usually—and for young women almost all of the time—to drink were few and of short duration during the year. Children were never served alcohol. It would only be during the most festive seasons, during major life-cycle celebrations or Catholic feast days from April to October, when a majority of people would be given the opportunity to drink at all. The symbolic importance, to community members and outsiders to the community, of the indigenous use of alcohol is so rich and deep, and the impact of too much drinking on a few individuals' lives is so devastating that we may be tempted to see their lives as one drinking party after another. But daily life was in fact far more prosaic, filled with work and simple obligations to household and family.

Secondly, I suggest that we see in this story the common plight of the very poor everywhere—an inability, due to lack of resources, to accomplish the goals they set for themselves as individuals and to satisfy the moral guidelines for a good life set for them as members of a community. This should be a familiar scenario to anyone acquainted with the disadvantaged in any society.

However, in this case, there is a further historical dimension to this lack of fit between expectations and outcomes. Social forms that have worked in the past for Otavaleños are no longer working as well, in part because of a reduction in traditional resources relative to population. While the indigenous people have indeed long been poor and disadvantaged by Ecuadorian standards, they have felt themselves, as owners of land—the means of production for both the present and the future—as far more advantaged than landless Ecuadorians. Despite the fact that nonindian ethnicity provided wage laborers with an opportunity to lord it over them, Huaycopungo runa have comforted themselves privately that these upstart mestizos, with no resources but their own backs to sell to owners of the means of production, were deluded about their own superiority. But in the late 1970s it had become increasingly common to find that parents could no longer provide sufficient land resources for their adult children's futures even as they had in the recent past. Nor could young adults afford to owe a substantial portion of their own labor hours to their parents in exchange for future land inheritance, rather than using it to directly support themselves and their children. The webs of reciprocity they were trying to celebrate were unraveling. The old patterns of living did not seem to fit the new circumstances. It was not yet acceptable to purchase food, especially for ritual occasions, for that would mean succumbing to dependence on the outside economy. But did God truly deserve such loyal and generous thanks for such a poor harvest? Should such an expense be made to the spiritual forces if their generosity in return was as pitifully small in the future? As outsiders, we might immediately suspect that the money being spent on alcohol and other consumable goods for this housewarming celebration would be better directed toward less social and spiritual aims and more for a material investment in the future. The local mestizo schoolteachers and others certainly tried tirelessly to convince the local people of the superiority of this type of thinking. As we will see in what is to follow, there were both real and imagined barriers to making these kinds of investments.

Furthermore, from the point of view of the AODA professional and popular culture in the United States, we might suspect that heavy drinking is interfering in people's ability to achieve their goals and maintain self-respect and public prestige. Nor are they able to respond adequately to the changing world around them. They are stuck in old patterns of behavior, drinking so as not to face up to the fact that these patterns no longer work (Shkilnyk 1985). Terms like *dysfunctional families*, *alcoholism*, and *denial* spring readily to mind. The family and friends are wondering what is wrong and they don't see the elephant in the living room, an image that refers to the fact that while heavy drinking is negatively affecting everything they do, they refuse to recognize that drinking is a problem. I would not entirely disagree with either of these assessments, from my point of view as a North American with a master's degree in social work, work with AODA professionals on a North American indian reservation, personal experience of alcoholism in my own family, and ten years of Al-Anon. These are stories with powerful explanatory power; however, they are neither the whole truth nor the only truth. Understanding how my friends in Otavalo talk about and respond to these situations has challenged me to see the world in a very different way. I have been learning more about my own folk philosophy concerning how the world works as I begin to understand a quite different set of expectations about the world. Unless we explore these different cultural patterns and symbols, our understanding of our selves and others will always be partial at best. To do so, we must move away from the consideration of decisions made by individuals and groups about how to behave and consider, for a moment, a more abstract level: how those decisions are informed by the structures of meaning that Otavaleños learn through daily living and ritual participation. The available explanatory and motivational norms and schemas passed down and modified through the generations form the repertoire from which individual choices are made. Furthermore, individuals are strongly pressured to conform their choices to those they expect from their fellows in any social group to which they are committed.

Central to our understanding of the world is the concept of good and bad. In the great monotheistic traditions originating in the Middle East—Judaism, Islam, and Christianity—good and evil are established in the world only after the advent of humans. The common origin myth from these traditions about Adam and Eve tells that God created a world that was entirely good. But humans, being inferior to God, disobeyed God and were banished from paradise and exiled into a world where evil always threatens to overwhelm the good. Christianity has especially elaborated the ideas about how this dual form of the universe engenders continual conflict, both social and spiritual. God is good, and evil is personified by the devil, a fallen angel. Human responsibility is to try to vanquish evil from the world, and God promises that should humans behave in a satisfactory fashion, the kingdom of God will someday return to earth. In the meantime, upstanding humans who follow God's will can be with God in heaven, an entirely good place, only after death. Good and evil are always inimical to one other, always separate entities, always in conflict, and we can only hope that the conflict will end when evil is vanquished and the world will be one, and all good, again.

These perspectives on the world's fundamental dualism are not just a myth from the past, but a foundational statement of a folk philosophical position to be applied to living in general. With this perspective we are directed to judge behaviors, beliefs, events, and so on as good or bad. An argument about whether something like, say, sexual desire or the profit motive is fundamentally good or fundamentally bad is entirely reasonable, although we may have differences of opinion about the answer. It is all well and good to pick apart the nuanced mix of good and bad in any situation to be judged, but in order to decide on an effective plan of action, we need to decide what must be eliminated. Applying this particular Western perspective, we know that the huasichiy fishta above has gone bad, despite people's best efforts. The reason the participants kept celebrating the master roofer despite his absence and the tearful complaints of his puffy-eyed wife was denial—they did not want to recognize what was right in front of their faces. It was easier to get drunk together and pretend that they were in fact *cushishsha, alishsha*—superlatively happy, content and morally upstanding—than to recognize that their best efforts had been in vain. For Western observers, it is thinkable, but unsatisfying and ultimately unproductive, to consider this huasichiy fishta at least partially successful, especially if we want to act in regard to it. Something is wrong and should be eliminated so that harmony can be restored. That is our folk philosophical position, and that is the foundation of our dominant approach to alcohol use and abuse.

But as we read in the introduction, native andeans are far more comfortable with such paradoxes than we are. We Westerners recognize that categorical statements logically imply their opposite and consider this simultaneous perception of opposites as an inevitable product of cognitive processing that is, nonetheless, problematic in the real world where opposites cannot both be simultaneously true. In contrast, andean thought more commonly holds that the inevitable linking of categorical opposites is a principle of the real world outside of human minds, not just the uncomfortable product of human mental processes. Opposites are *more* likely to both be true than are two unrelated concepts. Furthermore, opposites are particularly likely to interact, overlap, and change position.

The conflict between oppositions, as in the case of the Western notions of good and evil, is acceptable not because of the continuing potential for good to triumph, but because conflict is the inevitable complement to cooperation. This last statement is nonsensical with regard to good and evil in the Western tradition, unless we substitute the more common andean positions on good and bad for Western good and evil. In the cosmic sense, the terms—ali and mana ali—are best glossed in this context as good or helpful for humans and not good or harmful for humans. The powerful forces in the universe are always both, although some are weighted more heavily to one side or another most of the time. Human responsibility is not to work toward the permanent elimination of the bad. That may be desirable, but not in the least bit realistic. Since power has both potentials, if the harmful side is repressed completely and too long, there will be an inevitable shift to a period where the helpful is continually overwhelmed by the harmful. Human responsibility is to properly recognize the balance and maintain reciprocal relations with the powers of the universe in general, and thus to maximize their own experience of the helpful and minimize their experience of the harmful, particularly in unleashed and chaotic form.

In fact, gender relationships are much more likely to express the fundamental nature of oppositions than are good and evil. The world is profoundly gendered and the combination of opposition and symbiosis that characterizes sexual relations and reproduces living things serves as a template for most social and other processes. The genders are supposed to enact their linked potentials for fiery conflict in sexual relations, on the one hand, and collaborative interdependence as a linked pair heading a household and family on the other.

To return to the huasichiy fishta, the conflicts experienced during this ritually significant time were expectable and acceptable up to a point. For example, marriages are frequently sources of strife, especially in the early years, although they ideally become warm and intimate collaborations as the years go on. The same can be said for interayllu relations established through marriage. They begin with a prickly opposition between unrelated families but are desired to result in lifelong cooperation between large groups of relatives. In addition, drinking is a supremely powerful ritual activity, and as all such generators of potent forces, it could as easily harm as help people in their quest for harmony with the universe. The question in their minds was: had their ritual behaviors become ineffective in keeping the proper relationships to the spiritual realm? And had this ineffectiveness shifted the balance so that the impacts on their lives were now predominantly harmful rather than maximally helpful? Were the failings experienced individual or did they reflect a community crisis? Was it the case that *this particular* family was behaving badly in ways that should have been dealt with a long time ago, and therefore surfaced explosively while drunk, or was drinking itself causing the hard feelings and threatening their source of spiritual comfort? Among the participants in 1978, these were only questions, and perhaps the private assessments of many contradicted what they were willing to proclaim in public. The answers continued to be sought publicly, more often than not, from among traditional explanations.

What follows will demonstrate the faith of people in Huaycopungo that given the clear warning, they can find a new way of life that will restore the balance between unity and conflict. Life lived within the proper moral and spiritual guidelines will continually reproduce growth and unity for runa people not just despite but indeed because of the dynamic forces released in the ever-present conflicts. The memories of that house-building ceremony would be a good example to the people involved of how human life got off track, producing only more and more conflict and less and less unity. After all, *Ñucanchic llactapura shuclla shungu canchic, shuc shungullatami charinchic* (We people of the same place are one heart, we have but one heart), a fiction of daily life, is experienced as real in ritual events and thus retains some power to shape lived reality.

The Good Life in Huaycopungo and Barriers to Achieving It

What José Manuel and Isabel and their families were hoping for and how they expected to achieve it can be understood only with some more understanding about family, household, gender relations, and the ways of making a living, which together comprise the traditional baseline of anthropological studies. By telling and interpreting some of the early life stories of the main characters in this huasichiy fishta, I will sketch a general outline of what was necessary to achieve a satisfying and moral life for most people in Huaycopungo during the 1970s.

Above all, everyday life should be characterized by long hours of hard work and constant attention on the part of all family members to making life better for everyone. No one ever serves himself or herself a drink after a hard day of work and alcohol is never used just for recreation. In fact, alcohol for consumption can be received only from the hand of another during the periodic ritual occasions that dot the year—from festivals of the ritual calendar to individual life-cycle ceremonies—particularly in the harvest months from April through October. Despite the fact that fiestas interrupt this productive work cycle and provide some recreational relief, they too are considered a responsibility, a burden undertaken to enhance the spiritual foundation of ties among the community's families and between the people and the world of spirits, in which is included the earth, the mountains, the springs, and many other aspects of the environment.

Let's start with one of these moments in the life cycle, marriage, when individuals undergo a major transformation. Marriage begins a new life stage, one that is expected to lead to a new household within a few years. All households carry on the work of community, but with luck and skill, the process can result in the founding couple being remembered as the founders of a several-generation ayllu after their death. The problems during the building of José Manuel and Isabel's house can reasonably be traced to their decision to marry.

Ayllu is a term with many referents in Quichua and a term about which anthropologists have long argued. Family member, relative, family, kindred, descent group, and place where most of the residents are related to one another are all possible meanings. Andean social relationships enjoin continual reciprocal exchanges of real and promised aid of a material, social, and spiritual nature among members of an ayllu. I will consider the people who actively engage in this continual reciprocity to constitute an ayllu. The people linked by such intense reciprocal aid can be as different as a number of unrelated neighbors or a grouping of close consanguineal kin or a mix of both. This definitional inexactness likely developed to accommodate the fluctuations of populations relative to other resources over time, giving people rules by which they can exclude outsiders when resources to share are in short supply and the flexibility to treat outsiders as insiders when their labor or other resources are in demand (Rappoport 1999, 130).[6] Still, an ayllu, like other group terms such as *comuna*, or community, is often discussed *as if* it were any group of people with a fixed type of kinship relationship or territorial membership.[7]

Furthermore, an ayllu can be visualized something like a set of Russian dolls. Like many terms in Quichua, it refers to an entity at many segmentary levels. The smallest level of ayllu, like the smallest Russian doll, is contained by the next larger one, and so on until one reaches the most inclusive set of relationships characterized by reciprocal exchange. The exchange is most intense at the smallest level of inclusion and least intense at the widest.

The easiest referent of the term ayllu to understand is ego-centered kinship, where ayllu refers to all of those relatives, individually and collectively, related to one equally through either one's mother or one's father. One's ayllucuna, relatives, can be closer kin, ayllu, or more distantly related kin, *caru ayllu*. Otavaleño kinship is as bilateral as American kinship, with no greater weight given for ordinary purposes to one's father's side over one's mother's side.

At the same time, Otavaleños sometimes act as if there is an enduring group identity among the descendants of an important ancestor or ancestral pair, usually only a few generations deep. Ayllu may also refer

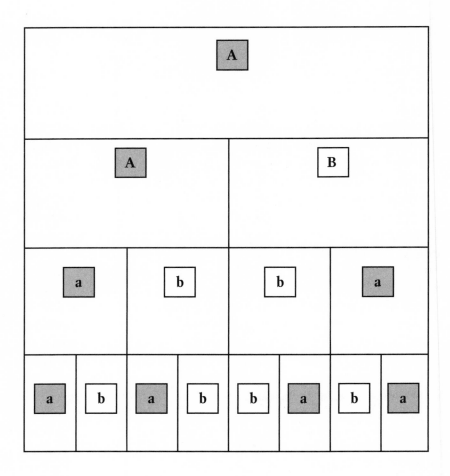

Fig. 12. Russian dolls

to this unstructured group, formed from the field of dense reciprocal relations among some of those who can claim to be the descendants, or close relatives of the direct descendants, of this illustrious person or couple. Since each person traces kinship through both mother and father, each person also has a large number of distant ancestors from which to trace his or her identity. In practice, people will claim membership only in one ayllu, in this descent group sense, if there is a compelling reason of prestige or material resources to do so. The descendants of an individual or pair whose household has become powerful enough to exert leadership over the comuna will attempt to perpetuate the rights and privileges of this elevated status after their death.

Finally, because of community endogamous marriages, community residents are all so interrelated, however distantly, that it is possible in the right contexts, with respect to other like communities, to emphasize the way the community as a whole is like one enormous ayllu, the descendants of one founder. In fact, Lebret (1981, 14) claims that one surname dominated in each Otavalan indigenous community during the eighteenth century.

At other times, not the least of which are those when marriages or land inheritance are being considered, it is more important to distinguish one ayllu, including the descendants of one ancestor for several generations, from other like groups within the same community. Kinship, while providing a schematic for uniting individuals into dyadic and group relations, also embodies a number of important oppositions. The act of defining people or relationships as similar to each other defines others as different from them. Individuals treat their network of kin on their mother's side as both complementary to their network of kin from their father's side and in conflict with it. This use of dyadic relations to bond people into an encompassing whole, while simultaneously separating and opposing them as component parts, is a recurrent symbolic theme in andean cultural life. In a similar example from a Peruvian andean society, Urton (1992, 231) claims that a "link is forged between social organization and cosmology" in the "constant dialectical relationship" between *communalism*, which directs people to think of property as jointly owned and to accomplish tasks communally, and *differentiation*, which divides communal property into segments under the care of subsets of the community and mandates that communal tasks be done in these smaller groups, which work side by side with others like themselves.

Marriage repeats this theme of communalism and differentiation. It joins two people profoundly opposed in gender and family loyalty in order to create the union of a married couple, *jari-huarmi*, literally man-woman, from which children are born and society replenished. The introduction suggested that gender traditionally serves as a key trope for the workings of the world. Men and women are very unlike and equally capable of generating sparks of conflict that can either be harnessed to light the warming fires of the hearth in an interdependent household or that can burn away domestic contentment. This adds a special dimension to the ayllu, considered as both an egocentric kindred and as an ad hoc cognatic descent group. On the one hand, daughters and sons have equal claim on the genealogical, social, and material resources of both their parents. There is simultaneously a suggestion of a special bond between males linked patrilineally and women linked matrilineally. A man's father's ayllu and a woman's mother's ayllu has a special role in creating and sustaining a person's identity. Some people suggested to me that the man in a couple made a male fetus and the woman made a female fetus; others argued for an equal contribution of egg and sperm. At the ontological level, male and female are separate principles of the universe but have come together to create known reality. A man's patrilineal identity and a woman's matrilineal identity connect them to this spiritual foundation of their being.

In Otavalo, each married couple starts a new household and will ideally live in their own house, huasi. One cannot see inside a traditional house from the curridur, or veranda for receiving guests, because of the absence of windows, and the interior, *huasi ucu*, seems especially dark in contrast to the equatorial light outside. This sunless interior, only dimly lit and warmed by a cooking fire, is valued by the inhabitants as a womblike protection from the cold and dangerous winds that sweep down from the mountains. The huasi ucu is ideally heated and animated by the continual work of a woman, who tends the fire, cooks the food, and prepares the asua that warms her family inside. The animating heat of her work is further extended to the curridur when she unobtrusively brings a bowl of soup or a gourd of asua to serve the guests sitting there (Allen 1988; Weismantel 1988). The walls around the house compound set that comforting domain apart from the wider world.

From outside the high mud wall that surrounds a house compound, visitors call out *Alabadu*,[8] *mingachihuai* or "Hello, give me permission," holding the last vowel for several extra seconds. Men raise the pitch of their voices slightly and women tighten theirs into a falsetto, which projects over a distance what should sound like a humble plea. A return call of *Yalipai* or *Shamupaichic*, "Please proceed" or "You [plural], please come" allows visitors to enter the doorway to the yard, which may be flanked by small kitchen gardens and animal corrals, and approach the *curridur* or sometimes a small front room used for receiving guests. Visitors must stop and ask permission to move forward at two or three places before they are free to converse with their hosts. At the entrance to the curridur, they again call out *Mingachihuai* and usually receive instructions to please come, *Shamupai*, and please sit, *Tiyaripai*, by someone who has come out to receive them. If not already in place, a clean reed mat will be dragged out for the visitors to sit on and, if any male visitors are formally dressed, a tiny stool is provided for them to sit on, so that their pants can remain the dazzling white for which Otavaleños are internationally famous. Quite rarely, visitors may be called forward once again to the door of the huasi ucu, where they again must pause and ask permission to proceed.[9] Only huasi residents enter the huasi ucu freely. The huasi may be visualized from the front as three concentric rings, with the central ring the most intimate and the outermost ring the most public. The huasi ucu protects the resident family alone, while they use the curridur to work where there is more light and to seat guests, and the yard is best for standing work and for accommodating the overflow of guests during a boda huasi. Enemies or suspicious strangers would rarely be allowed past the yard, although mestizos with official business usually walk right into the house without asking permission.

The domestic group consisting of those people who live together in a house and who are united by close kinship is treated as a basic unit of indigenous communities. Each household is a productive unit, with the members contributing their labor toward meeting all of the household's needs. When the main subsistence activity is agriculture, food is planted, tended, harvested, stored, processed, and consumed in large part within the household, although webs of reciprocity and trade unite households with many others. Each household is also a political unit, having one vote in community decisions, one quota for communal labor projects, and a joint responsibility for religious festival sponsorships.

The roles of husbands and wives within the household are quite distinct, although men can do almost all tasks women do on occasion without any stigma and vice versa. Individual men and women both derive personal pride from their gendered contributions to society, which is believed to spring from the joint, and distinct, foundations of male and female sources of strength. Men more often work away from the house and women in the house. Women are in charge of the food supply, including storing, preparing, cooking, and serving food. They do the laundry, tend any domestic animals they may own, from guinea pigs to cattle, and mend the clothes. Adult men rarely tend smaller animals but they may look after cattle or horses. They do more of the agricultural work, although women assist in planting, weeding, and harvesting. Men and women both weave, but men weave on the upright loom of European origin and women used to weave only on the backstrap loom, which very few people use at all anymore. When they travel together, men walk slightly ahead of their women, relatively unencumbered by things to carry. Women follow, carrying the loads. Very heavy bundles are shared, with the men hefting the greatest weight, which is generally, if mistakenly, interpreted by Hispanic Ecuadorians to prove the lower status of women among indigenous people. In their eyes, women are not protected as they should be but made to carry the heavy loads. Women dress, feed, bathe, and care for children more often than do men, but both parents equally discipline them.

In many respects Otavalan gender roles correspond to the public/private distinction between men's and women's realms so frequently seen cross-culturally. And since this public/private distinction is so embedded in an associated hierarchy in many Western traditions, with the private far below the public in value, it is almost impossible for Western outsiders to see these domains as equal or even ranked in an exceedingly shallow and reversible hierarchy. But in most contexts, such is the case among indigenous andeans. In a telling anecdote from Allen's study of rural Quichua-speaking Peru, a man tells the ethnographer, "In February when there's no agricultural work, I'll be a woman and go around knitting" (1988, 78). When a man does women's work, he is activating the female side of himself, and the same holds for a woman doing work traditionally allocated to men.

As a North American, I was initially surprised that, if there was no woman around when I offered to take a Polaroid picture of the family to repay participation in a small survey, the fathers would competently wash and dress the children, including the little girls, so that they would look their best for the photo. The men did not act embarrassed, nor did my female assistant think it at all unusual. I always expected her to rush in and volunteer to do it for him, as would happen in the United States. She helped only if he had so many children we would have been waiting around too long, and she seemed to pick the closest child regardless of gender. Fathers not only knew where the children's clothes were, they chose good outfits for the picture, contrary to the U.S. stereotype of fathers hopeless at dressing their girls especially. The task most associated with women's power in society is serving food; therefore men are extremely uncomfortable about trespassing on this right. Equally, men's roles are encapsulated by a man's responsibility to represent the household in formal events. Women scrupulously resist taking on this role unless their husband is not present or dead.

Indigenous men's special role in the public arena overlaps enough with hispanic gender conceptions that indigenous gender roles have frequently been misinterpreted in Ecuador. Indigenous peoples themselves sometimes overly equate the two. Indigenous people today are not clear in what ways they are similar and in what ways they are different, and often assume, in a woman's case, or assert, in the case of a man, a stronger male dominance than is in practice the case. In the Mediterranean, women's power in the domestic arena can parallel and equal men's power in the public arena, but that is both rarer in practice, and almost absent in ideology, than is a gender hierarchy, with men assumed to be generally superior and socially dominant. The public arena is simply considered much more important than the domestic one. Andean gender hierarchy is much more equivocal. A strong parallelism between the genders exists at the ontological level, and a tendency toward the social dominance of males seems an addition to, rather than an essential component of, the essence of the sexes. Since women's sexuality leads to motherhood, a form of absolute responsibility for nurturance quite different from men's, women's sexuality before and after marriage is considered far more problematic than men's. Women are more confined in the home and their opportunities for agency as individuals outside the domestic arena, until roughly the age of menopause, are very limited compared to men's. Nonetheless, men are considered far more dependent on the services of women than vice versa. This adds to women's political agency in less obvious ways. Women's opinions, given freely at home to their husbands and other close male kin, are listened to carefully. When women sit together in a mostly silent group at public events, the men are well aware of them there, since the collaboration of these women represents at least half of what men will need to be able to accomplish their goals. Unlike hispanic men in Ecuador, indian men would never promise their wives' labor or other contribution if in fact they were not already assured by the women that they would willingly cooperate. Husbands and wives are morally enjoined to help each other, but they both retain the right to act independently.

Women own productive property just as do men, and both men and women, as well as children, can decide how the money they earn from their own labor is spent. Men will likely say that a particular household is headed by a man, although he may say it is headed by his sister rather than his brother-in-law. By the same token, women are most likely to claim that the head of a particular household is a woman, although she may consider her brother, not her sister-in-law, the head of the household they share. A man may refer to a particular agricultural plot, *chacra*, that one household cultivates as belonging to the male head of household (and a woman may say it belongs to the woman), but either one could be corrected by someone who knows the actual source of inheritance for that particular plot, if such specificity is relevant to the discussion. Chacras belong properly to the sibling set or individual who inherited them, not to the household as a whole, and those inheritors will decide to whom they will leave them in the next generation. In some ways, the chacras are owned by ayllus, not by households at all. Still further, though less likely activated in the 1970s than before, the community as a whole, represented by its *curaga* or *curagas*, semihereditary leaders, retained some rights over all the land (see chapter 5). The curaga serve as the court of last resort for resolving land disputes, providing resources to the landless, or allowing outsiders to settle in the community in the name of everyone. Still, for most everyday practice, land is treated as household property; the male household head cultivates, with the help of his wife and family members, in the chacra inherited by either one.

While men officially undertake ritual sponsorships and political offices to gain prestige for their household, women provide essential ingredients for household and ayllu success. Although everyone recognizes public competition for success as a predominantly male pursuit, women are by no means deemed irrelevant or uninterested in the competition. Every successful man has a strong woman working with him, and some relatively ineffectual men are heads of prestigious households because of the skills and efforts of their powerful wives. A respected household whose founding couple we will meet in chapter 4, Mama Juana's, fits this pattern. While all but the close relatives of the husband would usually name Mama Juana first as household head, no one would find him a pitiful or laughable figure because the stature of his household depended more on his wife's skills than his own. Likewise, the death of an ambitious and highly competent wife can ruin a powerful man's career, as we will see in an anecdote about the curaga Rafael Otavalo in chapter 5. During parts of every ritual or political event, and especially when the man is absent or the woman's family is more prominent than her husband's, women's achievements in the household competitive endeavors are formally recognized. Men may claim more power and authority than women, just as in the hispanic households around them, but the differential in power is much less in indigenous households than in hispanic ones.

Sisters and brothers expect to inherit equally from both parents, and most of their inheritance is cultivated jointly even after their parents' death. Splitting the plots is such a divisive and difficult process that many siblings delay it until their own children start needing resources. Siblings are ranked hierarchically by birth order, but the privilege is very slight and the sibling relationship serves as a common model of equality. But despite being one of the most structurally linked relationships, it is perhaps the most commonly competitive, since each sibling inherits a portion of the same resource base, which they must one day divide. Before their deaths, parents must begin to devolve some inheritance to each individual child, so that each one may begin his or her own household. However much the parents struggle to make these gifts equal, a child can always feel slighted. The ideal of each couple forming its own domestic group creates conflict between parents and children, since the resources the older couple has at its disposal must be stretched to support the families of their younger children as well. Still, the joint interest of both generations in maintaining and expanding the larger family resource base also unites them. Youngest children traditionally care for their parents and post-pone building their own house until their parents have died; then the roof tiles and rafters of the parental home are removed and divided among the siblings. The house lot becomes a chacra again, and the house's mud walls are left to crumble slowly as the active influence of the deceased couple fades away.

In this pattern, which has since changed, marriages are generally endogamous to the community, which keeps the land resources inher-ited by both husbands and wives within the traditional land-owning community. They are also strongly endogamous to the ethnic group, with marriages to nonindians being the least desirable and marriages to other indigenous groups only slightly better. But since everyone wished to marry close to home, such cross-ethnic marriages were seldom a worry. From the individual point of view, households formed by endogamous marriages could more easily manage their joint land resources than those with inherited fields in distant comunas. From larger perspective, cross-community marriages knit ever-larger kin-ship networks together, expanding the number of individuals with claims to community resources. In my sample taken in 1978–79 of eighty-two marriages, seventy-five (91.5 percent) were endogamous. Nevertheless, politically powerful people have always broadened alli-ances by marrying outside the community, emphasizing a higher level of unity—intraparish or intraregion as well as intracommunity—and a higher level of conflict, intercommunity as well as interayllu.

All marriages are exogamous to the ayllu, with first and second cousins being unacceptable marriage partners. Parents and their chil-dren investigate shared surnames very carefully. In the 1970s most marriages were still arranged by parents, who wanted to ensure that their new son- or daughter-in-law would be a skilled and dedicated worker and that a productive cooperation between the two families would result. Some families arranged marriages when their children were still quite young; others considered the young people's own inclinations when they became old enough. Trial marriages were not uncommon, where the young couple would live alternately with both sets of parents for a few months to see if the couples and the fami-lies could live and work harmoniously before undergoing a formal cer-emony. Nor was it uncommon to hold a native wedding ceremony

before a more binding civil marriage or, in some cases, a civil ceremony before submitting to the most serious rite, that in the Catholic
church. The process of marrying could thus take a number of years,
although it was considered desirable to have completed it by the time
a couple of children were born. The poorer the family, the fewer the
steps of marriage they could afford. Well-off but frugal families would
have to decide between saving money and losing face.

Once children were young teenagers, boys and girls were kept apart
most of the time, with particular emphasis on teenaged girls staying as
close to home and family members as possible. Nonetheless, despite
this care to protect girls and the preference for arranged marriages,
young unmarried people were given license to meet, flirt, and even
engage in sexual experimentation during major festivals. Attachments
made at that time could be channeled into trial marriages, which might
become longer lasting after the birth of a child.

For the time (1974), José Manuel and Isabel's marriage was unusual,
if not unique. It was neither arranged nor endogamous to the community or even parish. José Manuel's family came from Pivarinsi, an
indigenous community in Eugenio Espejo parish, about six miles north
of Isabel's community of Huaycopungo in San Rafael parish. And they
met because the subsistence patterns of José Manuel's family were
completely atypical in Huaycopungo. In the late 1970s, the people in
San Rafael still thought of themselves as peasants. They either grew or
traded for most of the food they ate and looked down upon people who
had to buy food. They commonly ranged on foot as far as Cayambe,
twenty miles to the south, and Ibarra, twenty-two miles to the north,
to meet trading partners, who might also be compadres, trading their
labor or agricultural products for food they could not grow themselves.
Sometimes they went much farther. They also traded, or more commonly sold, mats woven from *totora* reeds, grown on the shores of the
lake or cut in other highland marshes. Money was used for expenses
other than food, such as clothing, roof tiles, or fiesta sponsorships.
Alternatives for making money included work on coastal plantations
or entering domestic service for urban housewives in Quito. During
the 1970s construction boom, one could sell one's labor at the weekly
unskilled construction labor roundup in the Quito park called La
Carolina. Unlike the agricultural work described above, these wage

labor jobs were not considered a way of life but an unpleasant necessary supplement, particularly before or after a major expense—such as a fiesta sponsorship or the marriage of one's child—for those who could not meet their expenses another way. However, the population was growing, land parcels were getting smaller, and agricultural production was less and less adequate for subsistence. People were conscious of eating increasingly poorly but defended their poor diet, even glorified it, as the representation of their self-sufficiency and independence from the wider Ecuadorian world. They were not irresponsible gluttons like the mishucuna.

José Manuel, however, had very little to recommend him by these traditional standards. Pivarinsi was his mother's native community. His father's parents had lost all their lands in Monserrate to mestizos from the encroaching town of Otavalo, and his landless father had made his living by occasional weaving and ambulatory sales, mostly in Colombia. During a drunken quarrel in a *cantina* (storefront bar), he killed a drinking buddy and was sentenced to prison in Quito. He died

Fig. 13. *Totora* harvest
(PHOTO BY AUTHOR)

Fig. 14. *Esteras* waiting for transport
on the Pan-American Highway
(PHOTO BY AUTHOR)

in prison after serving thirteen years, when José Manuel was still in his
teens. José Manuel's mother, Mama Emilia, lived with her mother, also
a recent widow, who butchered and sold meat from her home. Mama
Emilia took the meat house to house to sell in communities around
the lake, accompanied sometimes by the teenaged José Manuel, who
had left school after second grade to scrounge a living in ambulatory
sales. There he saw and fell in love with Isabel, who was very pretty,
intelligent, and as ambitious for a different future as he was.

Mama Emilia dedicated much of her widowhood to drinking
heavily. Although sympathy is extended to those who drown such
tragic sorrows in drink for a time, she continued year after year to
live a life unrespectable by anyone's standards. Her father, a heavy
drinker himself but one who nevertheless managed his affairs well, had
refused to give her land inheritance to her, fearing she would squander
it on drink. Emilia's mother, who drank only for the rare obligatory

ceremony, as was proper, held to this resolution after her husband's death, giving one-half of the land to her younger child, the frugal and abstemious son with whom she lived, and stating her intention of saving the other half for José Manuel.

José Manuel's younger brothers and sisters were increasingly neglected by their mother, sometimes farmed out to mestizos in the local area and in Quito to serve as servants in exchange for their upkeep. José Manuel, as eldest son, felt obliged to succeed economically so he could help his siblings and redeem their future, despite the tragedies of their past and present. He struggled to keep his youngest brother, who early on demonstrated an unusual intelligence, in school, but with only periodic success. Otavaleños who lack both parents, one parent, or even a land inheritance are called *huaccha*—which means both an orphan and a destitute person. It is one of the most poignant identities in the culture, frequently finding its way into common rhetoric and popular song. Only when he is very sad and drunk will José Manuel make reference to his huaccha status, although his younger siblings refer to their own much more frequently.

José Manuel knew almost nothing about agriculture, which was the measure of a man in Huaycopungo at the time of his marriage, nor did he have the education that was such an important resource in the mestizo world. Nonetheless, he treasured two resources inherited from his father; he had a loom and had learned from his father the arts of weaving and ambulatory trade to Quito and Colombia. While traditionalists in San Rafael felt that land ownership was the measure of a family's wealth and standing, many of those from communities to the north of the lake had begun to see weaving and sales as the basis of a good life, with agriculture as supplementary. Many Otavaleños in Otavalo and in the most powerful weaving towns of Peguche, Ilumán, Quinchuquí, and La Companía to the north were becoming increasingly wealthy in the production and sale of textiles for the tourist market and international export. Their increasing, if imperfect, ability to retain their profits, rather than lose them to the local mestizos who had traditionally controlled all local wealth and power, made it seem plausible to the people of Huaycopungo that opportunities for making a living beyond the peasant community were now possible for indians. Although indians still had to ride in the back of the bus, get off the sidewalk for an approaching mestizo, accept only the worst-cut and half-rotten meat for the same price from the Otavalo butcher, be last in line for any public service, and endure verbal harassment, they were increasingly able to compete in the market, particularly as entrepreneurs. Now the rotten meat is still sold more commonly to indigenous people, but the reasons behind it are largely economic. Racial and ethnic prejudice in sales is now but the background rather than the foreground. Whereas in the early seventies, an Otavaleño with money could not buy good meat, today the poor still eat it because it is all they can afford. After the meat markets close Saturday night, trucks take the spoiled remains out to the poorest indian communities. While those who can afford good meat, like Isabel, are revolted by the stench of rotten meat, she and I have sadly watched a steady stream of impoverished customers carrying it home in the dark.

José Manuel was convinced that he could join the new entrepreneurial elite of Otavalo given support and good luck, and thereby change his own fate and that of his family. Like many of the early entrepreneurs, he sensed that his lack of a strong geographic base in land, ayllu, and community offered some advantages; it was not solely the lamentable extension of his huaccha status as it seemed to traditionalists such as his father-in-law. Antonio figured that José Manuel had no choice but to become his supporter, since his own ayllu was poor in land, far away, and alienated from him because his parents had not been available to defend his interests. However, if he chose this strategy of becoming embedded in the reciprocal obligations of Huaycopungo as the *masha*, or laughable gofer, as the word for son-in-law implies, of the ambitious Antonio, José Manuel would have found any resulting prestige going to his wife's ayllu—specifically, to his father-in-law. If he could use his unaffiliated status to increase the resources of his own household rather than become a supporter of his father-in-law's ambitions, he could have more control over how he spent whatever wealth his was able to earn. If he were lucky, he could help his siblings and cousins and regain the status lost by his own parents among their kin. Events have in many ways vindicated José Manuel's stubborn rebellion of those years. Following his lead, ambulatory trade of clothing in Colombia has surpassed *estera* (reed mat) manufacture as the most important economic specialization of

Huaycopungo today besides subsistence agriculture. Relatives on his father's side, who had ignored him all his life, now visit regularly. And he is respected in Huaycopungo as well. His sons are referred to by *his* surname, Tituaña, which did not occur in Huaycopungo before he came, and which no one could ever remember at first, referring to him as Isabel's husband or Antonio's son-in-law.

Otavaleños expand their network of people with whom they share obligatory support and assistance beyond blood relatives to include neighbors and ritual co-parents, compadres. In the relationships between neighbors, it is important to recognize that kinship and place identification overlap to a great degree because siblings inherit contiguous plots and their children, cousins to each other, also inherit contiguous plots. Some of these plots then become the sites for a new house, so neighbors are frequently first cousins. But in addition, andean people derive a significant portion of their identity from their geography. They identify themselves as from places in a nesting series, often starting with the specific field, hill, or ravine edge where they grew up, or even where one of their parents grew up. Even if they are not related by kinship, neighbors share a number of interests (or conflicts) over the carrying out of daily chores, use of local natural resources, supervision of fields and animals, and road improvements, among other things. While Otavaleños now most often use the Spanish word for neighbors, *vecinos*, to refer to these individuals, even when they are kin, the more complicated Quichua term *llactapura* also expresses this relationship. Again, the referent for *llacta*, territory or homeland, can be quite small or larger and more inclusive depending on whom one is addressing. When people and the land they live on engage in reciprocal relations over time and jointly undergo events, they begin to take on some of their identity from each other. That process makes neighbors more alike.

Chunda Fucu, the master roofer, owned a piece of land two plots down from José Manuel and Isabel's new house, which he had inherited from his mother, just as his sister Dolores had inherited the piece she gave to the young couple. Later Chunda Fucu helped his son, Isabel's cousin, build a house on that plot when he got married. The plot that separated Chunda Fucu's from the new house belonged to the son and wife of another sister of Chunda Fucu and Dolores. An older brother's daughter, Isabel's maternal first cousin, was already living in a new house on the other side. Next door to that was Pata Luchu, Dolores's maternal first cousin, representing the land division of the preceding generation. Because of his exogamous marriage, José Manuel did not have the advantage of close kin who were also neighbors. While he could become llactapura with time, he would for many years be an affine, a son-in-law or masha, a role that is the butt of jokes, since a masha is seen as eager to please but inept, and he must take on the jobs no one else wants among his wife's ayllu. Only as his own children matured into adulthood would he largely replace the masha identity with one as *taita*, which means both father and elder.

More important are those fictive kin called compadres. One's compadres are the godparents of one's children, chosen for baptism, confirmation, and marriage. Compadres can also be chosen for the dedication of a new house, a church, or any ongoing institution that needs social and spiritual support over time. One's own compadres, those one chooses to serve as godparents to one's children or house, are compadres to everyone in one's ayllu. Likewise, the compadres of one's relatives are one's compadres as well. It is both an intercouple and an intergroup relationship. At the time of the house building, god-parents and compadres were most often kin, like Antonio serving as his brother-in-law's marriage godparent or José Manuel's cousin serving as his housewarming compadre. They were chosen to celebrate and further strengthen an already close relationship of material and labor exchange. Although the relationship is ritually created and thereby unbreakable in name, in practice the intense mutual exchanges may last only a few months or a few years. The relationship remains and can be rekindled socially at any time. Choosing compadres to reinforce ties with nonkin, noncommunity members, and nonindians who may be helpful in the future or who have been helpful in the past is also common. Relationships of *compadrazco* are expensive but potentially very rewarding as well. The conflict in the relationship is similar to that of the marriage relationship, also one involving choice. One must give so much, both in goods or money and trust, to someone with fundamentally separate interests in the hope of receiving something of equal, but less personally accessible, value in return over time. Compadre relationships can be both extremely intimate and open to coercion. They can also be more or less hierarchical or symmetrical, depending on the relative social or material resources of the parties involved.

Again, José Manuel and his mother were at a disadvantage in calling in labor from compadres, since they were so far from home. Nor had Mama Emilia managed to maintain a household of her own. She lived with her mother, who would not relinquish any long-term productive resources to her, and was estranged from her children, who were trying to make a living on their own mostly away from Otavalo altogether. Who would ask her to be comadre? Nor did she have any reason to ask someone to serve as godparent and become her co-parent.

While José Manuel was huaccha with respect to his paternal ayllu, Isabel's paternal grandfather had been called curaga, native lord or village headman. Her father, Antonio, was well off, with a salaried job that he had inherited from his father, as laborer on the railroad, and with chacras (garden plots) in several choice microecological zones of his own or shared with his two siblings. He also had several cows. Although neither he nor his siblings inherited the title curaga, Antonio was also a community leader, serving as one of the early presidents of the *cabildo*, or community council, on several occasions.

Because of his job, he had acquired a rudimentary command of Spanish, which was a community resource for dealing with the nonindians in the parish capital. Besides allowing Isabel to enter high school, he arranged with some difficulty for mestizo railroad employees to teach his first son (second child) the craft of telegraph work. In addition, he chose to have his second son (fifth child) dress like a mestizo, wear his hair short, and learn good Spanish, which was a common strategy at the time for ensuring a tie to the mestizo world within the family. Isabel's mother, Dolores, also had access to a respectable number of varied chacras and dedicated her efforts for her children's future to raising and selling animals and selling her inherited coral jewelry, like those long *rinri warkuna* (earrings) described in the preface, in order to purchase more land.

Isabel had been the best student in the San Rafael elementary school while she attended, and so had earned the grudging respect of many local mestizos. A priest pleaded with Antonio until he reluctantly agreed to let Isabel be the first person from Huaycopungo to attend high school. She completed the first two years (seventh and eighth grade in the United States) at a school run by Italian nuns in San Pablo across the lake. During high school she was actively recruited by indigenist political groups as a consequence of her literacy in Spanish, and she made a name for herself as an activist. She also served as secretary of the cabildo, which was unusual for a woman and one so young.

In 1964, a major land reform had affected the region, and another period of indigenous and rural proletarian activism began. At the end of the decade, the first school for indians was started, with Yolanda Hidalgo from San Rafael as the teacher in Huaycopungo, although a few students, like Isabel, had been permitted to attend the mestizo school in San Rafael before that. In general, the hegemony of the nonindian civil and religious authorities of San Rafael and Otavalo were slowly reduced, giving the people of Huaycopungo a right to interact with the national government directly, a strategy that indigenous people had attempted, with varying success, since the colonial period. One of their first acts in the early 1970s, with the help of regional peasant and indigenist unions, was to thwart a government attempt to put a military base on the shores of the lake. The local mestizo political authority in San Rafael had made a deal with the armed forces in which the indian families with rights to the lakeside land would be paid a pittance for the alienation of all rights in perpetuity. Isabel was a leader of the movement and, along with others in Huaycopungo, faced soldiers' guns with sticks and stones to safeguard the community's land. As a result she spent time in jail while pregnant with her first child, earning a reputation as something of a local hero that persists to the present. (Land titling by community members increased substantially following this incident, preserving the land from nonindian encroachment but reducing some of the earlier communal control over land inheritance.) Isabel's activities added fear and hatred to the respect she inspired among San Rafael's mestizos, and she received several death threats. Finally, the year before she met José Manuel, she had been chosen to serve as Sara Ñusta, Maize Princess, an honor reserved for indian girls, during the Otavalo mestizo Festival of Yamor. By some standards, both traditional and modern, she was a catch. However, one concern was that her independence and proactive stance might make her difficult to integrate into a family as daughter-in-law. Nor were her domestic skills ever a major selling point. By her own admission, she could never learn to spin, which luckily was no longer a necessary skill, but more significantly she never much enjoyed cooking and felt her own dishes generally lacked flavor. But her skills at forging bonds of obligation and commitments to aid were impressive.

Isabel had been influenced by a number of people who advocated a changing future. They included those of her teachers who believed Otavaleños could be civilized into proper mestizos if they really tried, those *campesino* (peasant) leaders of the time who also advocated literacy in Spanish, for example, believing that such resources of civilization would allow indians to compete more successfully with mestizos for political and economic power in Ecuador, and the small, elite group of other educated Otavaleños in the cantón at the time.[10]

So both Isabel and José Manuel believed they had a mission to effect change: for Isabel, to improve the lot of her community and for José Manuel, to better the situation of his family. Charmed by José Manuel's fervor, his now-legendary sense of humor, and his vision of a new future free from toadying to the local mestizos, Isabel ran off with him. Besides, she found her parents' marriage candidates repulsive; in later days she pointed them out to me, shuddering.

Antonio and José Manuel therefore were at odds from the very first. Exogamous marriages were then chosen either by the very poor, who were willing to bargain away their own status for a secure subsistence, or by the very powerful, who were wealthy and connected enough to assure their interests despite the distance. When not working for local hacienda owners in their Quito homes, Isabel and José Manuel lived in Huaycopungo with Antonio and Dolores. Despite José Manuel's pleas, Isabel would not leave her mother, to whom she was close—a traditional and thoroughly understandable reaction—nor did she want to give up her work as community leader in Huaycopungo, a more radical choice.

For his part, instead of acting with the humble deference expected of such a nonprepossessing son-in-law, José Manuel insisted on following his own economic strategies. He denied Antonio the only traditional advantage of marrying one's daughter to a poor man: to receive the labor of someone who could never be a competitor. What never failed to provoke an argument was José Manuel's devotion to Huaycopungo's first soccer team, which played every Sunday. It had been organized by the first evangelical missionary but continued long after most of the team had left the church. Antonio wanted José Manuel to help with agricultural chores and then join him in celebrating some event with kin, compadres, or workmates by drinking. A new son-in-law, the supposedly toadying masha, is considered a perfect substitute for one's wife, if she is too busy, to accompany a man in drinking—but to drink moderately and see that the elder man gets home safely. Despite the requirement for all important middle-aged men to drink heavily, Antonio was already getting the reputation of manufacturing reasons to drink and too often searching out the nearest boda huasi, a house in which chicha and trago were being served to guests. His father before him was said to have died an alcoholic, and much of Antonio's later life until his death in 2000 was dedicated to drink.

The basic conflicts between Antonio and José Manuel were in some ways mirrored between José Manuel and his wife. Isabel's ambitions to be a community leader in Huaycopungo were also at odds with her husband's plans for a more restricted entrepreneurial strategy that would assure his own and his siblings' future and wipe out the memory of their recent past. Her strong attachment to and reliance on the large ayllus of her mother and father threatened the future of his own. Sexual attraction and fidelity are so closely associated with the proper cooperative marital role behavior that sexual jealousy is inflamed by role conflict, just as conflict in other spousal roles is exacerbated by sexual jealousy. A man's justification for considering an extramarital affair can be the absence of a hot meal when he is hungry; a woman's justification might be her husband's refusal to participate in the household's community labor obligation, leaving it to the wife and children alone. José Manuel's drunken complaints that Isabel would invite in many lovers as soon as the house was built was an expression of his legitimate worry that his family did not have the social or economic resources to command respect and interdependence from Isabel and her family. Antonio correctly interpreted José Manuel's infidelity as a challenge to examine his own role performance. Perhaps José Manuel's failure to behave as a husband and son-in-law should was the proper reciprocal response to Antonio's inadequacies as father and father-in-law, which he questioned tearfully and obsessively when he was drunk.

José Manuel and all his siblings were particularly insecure about their affective relationships, perhaps because their early needs for nurturance were not met because of their father's imprisonment and their mother's drinking. However, the acting out of sexual conflict—jealousy and infidelity—is a common way to test or coerce the proper loyalty in all marital cooperation, only one aspect of which is sexual.

The story of Isabel's uncle José Manuel, Chunda Fucu, the house-building maestro, also involves many of the same themes. The youngest of five children and thus least favored in competition for land inheritance despite his family's relative prosperity, this José Manuel ran away as a teenager to work on the coast and did not return for many years. Succumbing to local pressure in the boom area around Santo Domingo de los Colorados, he cut his hair and wore mestizo clothes, the only ones he could buy there. Many Ecuadorians persist in the belief that an indigenous man's long braid must be unwearable in the jungle, although they never say that about women's long hair. José Manuel was a good worker and became, in his words, attached like a son to the hacienda owner he worked for—his *patron*. Occasionally trusted by his patron to take the hacienda's products to the Santo Domingo market to sell, José Manuel would see people there from Huaycopungo, but he enjoyed allowing them to pass him by, mistaking him for another mestizo. One fateful day, however, he decided to approach someone from home. As everyone had been primed for years to do if they ran into José Manuel anywhere in the country, the person he approached told him his father was dead and his mother dying. As predicted, he took the next bus home. Walking home from the Pan-American Highway where the bus had left him, he passed his older married sister Dolores but she did not recognize him. After the family had all recovered from the shock of his return, Chunda Fucu's perfectly healthy parents had a party to celebrate his homecoming. As I was told a number of years later, when he was completely drunk, they led him to the church and married him off to a local girl, rightly convinced that marriage would anchor him to the community. Although he tried to leave a number of times, after the birth of his first child, he became resigned to his fate.

At the time of the house building, Chunda Fucu's hair had grown in again although people still called him mocho, which means cropped hair and by extension, those who throw away their indian heritage in order to pass as mestizo. Mocho Jusi Mali was his other nickname from the Santo Domingo days. He was trying to make a traditional combined strategy of community embeddedness and occasional outside labor work for him and his family. That festive and house-building season, he had charged for the use of his carpentry skills, as house-building master. Still, his involvement in several house buildings meant he had also drunk ritually with many families, thereby extending his ties as well as receiving food and money wages. Helping his sister, his influential brother-in-law and godfather, Antonio, and his important niece was part of that strategy, although it entailed giving in order to get later—in the form of labor, portions of future harvests, cooked food and drink, or cash—in a more traditional labor-exchange arrangement. The risks that his short-term losses of labor would not be adequately repaid, especially after the house building dragged on so long, were more than his wife could countenance, especially since it was not her ayllu that was benefiting from his work.

The Subsistence Ethic Is Challenged

In summary, then, traditional conflicts between men and women in the marital relationship, between the ayllus related by marriage, between different communities, between generations, between siblings, and between strategies for dealing with the mestizo world were illustrated in this particular boda huasi. In addition, we saw the struggle between drinking as a pleasurable way to achieve social and spiritual union in this world and the next and as a means to coerce others into giving up their own labor and other resources, employed particularly by the older generation and the mestizos of San Rafael.

However, these conflicts were pushed to an uncomfortable limit for a number of reasons. First, traditional resources have become too scarce for parents to be able to provide all their children with sufficient land inheritance.[11] New opportunities have arisen for Otavaleños to participate in the market economy, and Otavaleños from other parts of the county have become quite wealthy as a result. The market economy challenges the traditional reciprocal economy, with its strong moral and spiritual pressures and rewards. While Huaycopungo's pressures in this direction lag behind those of the northern communities of the cantón like Peguche or Ariasucu, whose weaving specialty so thoroughly changed the peasant adaptations at an earlier date, in Meisch's words, "There is no doubt that many Otavalos are experiencing a conflict between the values of entrepreneurship and those of harmony and reciprocity, with the balance tipping toward entrepreneurship and individualism" (2002, 248). As Colloredo-Mansfeld puts it: "No longer united by poverty or a common agrarian livelihood, native Otavalenos sometimes seem to be going their separate ways" (1999, 224).

In the interim period in Huaycopungo, however, the pressure to invest money into social-spiritual spending resulted in more drinking for more days as access to money increased. The breakdown of the subsistence ethic threatened a whole way of life and no one was sure what the ritual underpinnings of the new one should be. Whereas the communal use of alcohol had bound community members together into a moral economy separate from the nonindian world in the past, both symbolizing and enacting their most precious moral values, the prescription to conspicuously spend and share all resources today, especially money, is not consistent with the growing entrepreneurial economy. Younger relatives, now believing that some of the elders were alcoholics—such as José Manuel's mother, father, and maternal grandfather; Isabel's father and paternal grandfather—see this as another squandering of resources, both material and human. Antonio was an alcoholic by anyone's standards in his later years and may have suffered some resultant brain damage. Alcohol intoxication contributed to Dolores's death in 1994. Chunda Fucu repeatedly, but unsuccessfully, tries to stop his binge drinking, when he succumbs to violence toward all with whom he has a conflict—his brother, his wife, his eldest son. Emilia remarried, to a first cousin of Dolores from Huaycopungo who is another violent alcoholic. Although she frequently discusses quitting and has gone up to a month or two without a drink, in general she drank regularly with and without her husband until their divorce in 1999 and she has binged every few months since. Drinking, far from being the currency and symbol of mellow unity when José Manuel and Isabel built their house, had become a catalyst for the enactment of supreme anger and despair, for the expression of unbearable, rather than regenerative, conflict.

Chapter 2 will again emphasize the importance of an unending exchange of drinks among members of the community, but this time in the idealized and deeply religious portrait of themselves the local people cherished, but only rarely lived. Here we linked a particular story of one family's house building to the social expectations of a traditional society based on kinship—consanguineal, affinal, and fictive—and characterized by continual reciprocity. The next chapter, "*Ufyapashunchic*: Let's All Drink Together," takes this topic a step further into an explication of how alcoholic beverages shared ritually created the bonds of reciprocity that made a community, one that could claim to be "of one heart." Ritual took reciprocity beyond the bounds of a material economy, of how needy people accessed some part of the labor and resources of their fellows, into the realm of moral and even cosmic significance. We will answer the question of how the properties of alcohol, the ways it is produced, the symbolism of its effects, and the protocol for its consumption taken together serve as means to express and create the desired society. Sometimes a metaphor of blood circulating through the bodies of a nested series of communities seems most appropriate, since alcohol may be seen as an ever-flowing liquid that animates the living organism. At other times alcohol seems to act as the connective tissue that binds the separate organic parts, each with its own goals and requirements, into a living community.

CHAPTER TWO

Ufyapashunchic
Let's All Drink Together

Dancing, Weaving, Leaving,
and Returning—Metaphors for Life

ALMOST EVERY MORNING when I got off the bus in Huaycopungo in 1978, an eight-year-old girl waited for me in the doorway of her widowed mother's house on the corner of the Pan-American Highway. I remember her grinning from ear to ear and almost bouncing with anticipation. ¿*Maymanda shamujungui*? "Where are you coming from?" Or ¿*Mayta ringui*? "Where are you going?" she would call to me, loudly and slowly, trying to smother her giggles and willing me to understand and reply. Every afternoon when I left, she tried to catch me again and would repeat those questions or ask, ¿*Otavaluman tigrajunguichu*? "Are you returning to Otavalo?" She wasn't being nosy; these are the customary greetings used in Quichua Otavalo.[1] One can answer literally if one wants, or one can use the equivalent of "Fine" to the American query "How are you?" such as *Chaillaman,* "To just over there," or *Chaillamanda,* "From just over there." When I would struggle to respond with O*tavalumanda shamujuni*," I am coming from Otavalo," or *Ñuca comaripakman,* "To my comadre's," Margarita would correct my pitiful Quichua and laugh with pleasure. This feisty and mischievous little girl, now an assertive and humorous mother of three,[2] seemed oblivious to the usual expectation that extreme deference be shown to a white person—she was trying to make me human. White people speaking Quichua there is still so rare, children and even adults sometimes stare at me in astonishment as if an animal has begun to speak. To myself I start humming the theme song from the 1960s TV show about the talking horse: "I Am Mister Ed."

Despite the routine nature of these greetings, Margarita's childish mission calls attention to a major theme in the workings of both everyday human life and of the timeless cosmos in native andean America.

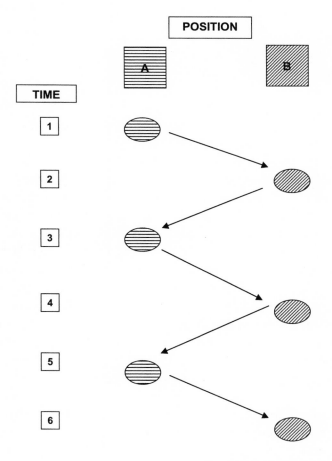

Fig. 15. Zigzag through time

Her greetings, like everyone else's, paid continual attention to movement: to and fro, up and down, back and forth, which is a proper preoccupation of people, sacred geographic places, and other, less localized cosmic forces. This concept is more than a customary pattern; it is a basic cosmological principle that is acted out in ritual and observed in such diverse things as the alternation of generations, the back and forth movement of the shuttle in weaving, and the obligatory reciprocity of people, communities, ecological zones, and spirits.

On any ordinary day, given the bird's-eye view that can be obtained from high points in Huaycopungo's hilly terrain, the people of the comuna can and do watch other men and women go about their daily tasks on the paths and in their yards. When I first brought my binoculars, used for bird-watching, my friends immediately trained the lenses on distant houses and offered a detailed interpretation of the inhabitants' activities. They watched men in their navy *ruanas* (ponchos) and women in dark wool *anacos* (wrapped skirts) and *fachalinas* (shawls) circulate in ones, two, and threes along the dusty footpaths outside the walled houses, trading goods and labor among themselves, their help attracted and reciprocated through the food and drink ladled out to greet them when they arrived at another's household. Women's arms moved gracefully back and forth between the pots at the fire and the bowls held out by their daughters and daughters-in-law, who themselves glided between the hearth and the guests in repeated crossings.

Of course, the people of Huaycopungo are interested in the goings-on of their neighbors in the nosy way, too, and they especially direct their gaze to espy out of the ordinary activities, including elaborate, but immediately interpretable, preparations for a ceremonial event or visits that they suspect the inhabitants would like kept secret. Beyond that, however, a proper family is one in constant and reciprocal production; a healthy community is one crisscrossed by people moving between their homes and their fields and between their own and others' houses and fields; and a living cosmos is also marked by continuous exchange between the mountains and the valleys, between the past and the present, between people and spirits, and between sources of water and dry land. Movement in a zigzag (*quingu-quingu*) form, like the whoosh and thwock as a shuttle is thrown back and forth across the warped threads in a handloom, represents life. Careful attention to the movement in alternating directions of ordinary life and a commitment to ritual action to connect spatial and directional opposites must be made to ensure life's healthy continuance for the whole universe. Processions of dancers during the major fiestas of the ritual calendar, which both encircle the community and weave across its major paths, are the most dramatic examples of this preoccupation with reciprocal motion.

In the early years of my research in Huaycopungo, nothing better symbolized and actuated that reciprocity, interchange, and animation than the offering and acceptance of gourd bowls or wooden shot glasses of alcohol. Alcohol is a sacred substance given by the gods to humans in the beginning times. Like coca leaves (Allen 1988) and the *cuy*, or guinea pig (Morales 1995), alcohol carries a special capacity to mediate between humans and spirits, containing and activating the life force. Sharing drinks initiates and invigorates the continuous reciprocal aid that, in the ideal model, characterizes the relationships of humans with each other and with the spiritually animated world and even with

Fig. 16. *Pendoneros* procession
(PHOTO BY AUTHOR)

God. The best of all possible worlds initiated by such sharing is never still, but in continuous motion.

When a particular household is sponsoring a life-cycle ritual or a public ceremonial sponsorship, the household attracts large numbers of people at a time, and asua is supposed to flow in an endless supply. Navy blue ponchos make little tents around the sitting men spread out around the yard, one at a time leaning forward to sip from the gourd bowl (*pilchi*) of asua they hold, cradling the pilchi in one hand well away from their white pants so as not to drip, and then passing it back to the waiting server. The server then scoops another pilchi from a pail and passes it to the next. This scene, along with the huddles of well-dressed women in a corner, whose turquoise *rebozos* (shawls) and strings of golden glass beads enliven their outfits of black or dark blue anacos and fachalinas, signals from afar a boda huasi. Resident women and their helpers glide silently in and out of the huasi ucu or outdoor kitchens set up for the special event, with steaming bowls of *api* (ground maize soup) or chicken soup, followed by the mediano: a washbasin heaped with white *muti* (hulled corn) and boiled potato and topped with glistening brown *cuy asado* (roast guinea pig).

During a major calendrical fiesta (*fishta*) like San Juan/Inti Raymi or Corazas, an outpouring of people can be seen on all the paths. The flow of people is periodically clotted in certain spots, such as the entrance to a house, for the sharing of beverages. These temporary gatherings are especially concentrated at crossroads, springs, the dance ground, or the plaza in front of the church, where processions stop to offer ritual prayers, dancing, and toasts to the resident spirits and to each other. Asua and home-baked bread rolls, *tanta*, or cooked finger foods, *cucavi*, change hands wherever women relatives or neighbors meet each other. The sponsor's male assistants circulate among the participants, pouring trago into a wooden or plastic shot glass for each one. While one needs to be inside the house compound on an ordinary day to smell the cooking food and pungently sour asua, during a boda huasi one can hear localized music from afar and smell the typical odors from the *chaquiñancuna*, or footpaths. The smells of dust, asua, and trago permeate the air wherever you go, and the sound of music comes from so many directions it is often hard to pinpoint it or to unravel one tune from the other. It is like the community's paths become the curridur of a giant boda huasi, the scene of circulating food and drink among all who are present.

The culminating moments of festivals, when humans and spirits are heated and intoxicated by the cacophony of sights, sounds, and odors emanating from everywhere, and exuberantly joined together by the exchange and consumption of an overabundance of food and drink, express a major theme of andean religiosity. Humans, animals, plants, lakes, springs, rocks, earth, sun, and stars—all desire

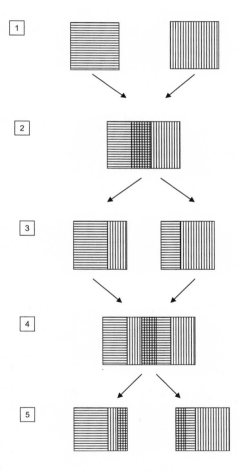

Fig. 17. Intersecting oppositions: the contra dance

infusions of animating energy to maximize their active force. Those elements we Westerners would consider inanimate—like rocks and lakes—or animate but lacking in a spiritual dimension—like plants and animals—are all considered both living and infused with spirit. And all the components of the world are nurtured best in an atmosphere of continuous reciprocal interaction with one other. These moments of heightened relationship ignite, animate, entertain, and feed the material, social, and spiritual elements of the world, so that they, in turn, release their plenty for human benefit. The animating effort was supposed to be both total—in other words, not restricted to certain particular spiritual entities contained in certain localities— and excessive—demonstrating an ideally infinite human capacity to give in the hopes of a never-ending return of those things that make human life rich and productive. In this interchange, humans and non-humans would each incorporate some of the other, transforming their separateness into symbiosis and even into a partial union of interests and essential states. Like a seesaw or pair of circling dancers at double speed, the speed and multiplicity of the interactions would make momentarily imperceptible the differences between up and down, him and her, inside and outside, kin and nonkin, human and spiritual, distant and close. Another image sometimes used is that of the contra dance, which highlights the moments of maximum opposition, the moments of maximum unity, and the exchange of substance that ensures a long-lasting effect of a heightened interdependence and sense of union beyond the ritual moment.

A Chapter Guide

During the ceremonial season of the year, the continuous flow of alcoholic beverages among houses and along the paths is the single most important exchange that serves to bind people and spirits into a meaningful world. This chapter will trace that flow—the history, symbolism, and rules for the exchange of alcoholic drinks among people and between people and the spirits, inside and outside, forward and back. This is what I call domestic ritual; it is part of religion but quite removed from the orthodox practices of Roman Catholics, as the majority of Huaycopungo claimed to be in the 1970s.[3] It is removed in two senses. The first is that despite this proclaimed loyalty to the Catholic faith, religious beliefs and rituals have evolved over five hundred years into a complex juxtaposition and synthesis of ancient andean religion and the Christianity introduced after European conquest. Secondly, it corresponds to religion as worldview or *cosmovision*, the term chosen by my compadre Francisco Otavalo, who is an expert in bilingual and bicultural education, rather than as an established international institution. Geertz's famous definition of religion as a cultural system best encapsulates this former sense: "Religion is a system of symbols which acts to establish powerful, pervasive, and long-lasting moods and motivations in men by formulating conceptions of a general order of existence and clothing these conceptions with such an aura of factuality that the moods and motivations seem uniquely realistic" ([1966] 1973, 90). From this perspective, one finds religion in ordinary life as much as in formal ritual—in underlying, and frequently unspoken, assumptions about the world as often as in myths about the origin and order of the cosmos or in formal theology. This symbolic complex is best understood through its ritual enactment, by which the symbolic systems become clothed with their special aura of factuality. In Rappoport's terms, ritual is "the foundry within which the Word is forged" (1999, 21).

Reciprocity is both a basic social process in local conception and, even more profoundly, a foundation of Otavalans' thinking about form and process in the world in general, what have variously been called *cosmological axioms* (Rappoport 1999, 263), *cultural schemas* (Ortner 1990), or *dominant metaphors* (Ohnuki-Tierney 1990). While culture is never still, these cosmological axioms have real staying power. In fact, it is these mental complexes that people in groups use to help them interpret real changes in a way that preserves a sense of meaning and continuity in a changing society. That reciprocity occurs both between equal partners and those unequal in wealth, power, or prestige, between insiders and with outsiders. Both result in shared interest and an unbreakable connection, one that theoretically transcends the individual will, becoming a part of the self that springs up from within (see Carpenter 1992).

For the purposes of this chapter, we will neglect the world of spiritual forces beyond the human into which the community is embedded

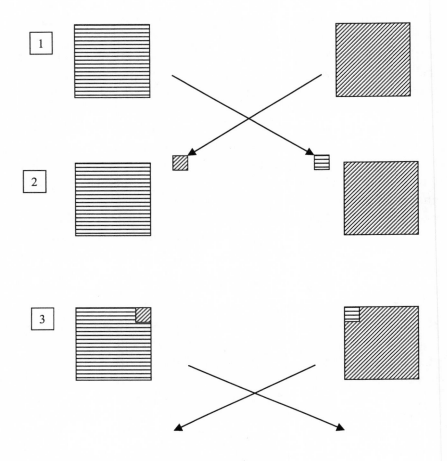

Fig. 18. Reciprocity between equals

in order to concentrate on social relations. Chapter 3, "Taita Dios and Taita Imbabura," will take us beyond human social life to delve into the role of drinking rituals in the relations of people and the spiritual forces, both Christian and of andean origin. Furthermore, here we will continue to treat as real the ideological barriers that runacuna sometimes erect to claim that Huaycopungo is an autonomous society, free from the constraints of the hispanic-mestizo world created by the descendants of their conquerors. Chapter 4, *Cantina* and *Boda Huasi*, takes Huaycopungo out of the relative isolation asserted for ideological purposes and reconnects it to the reality shared with the local mestizos. This chapter is a highly idealized account, but ideals are motivators for real human beings and it is well for us to be as aware of what people think they are doing or hope they are doing as we are of what we can see and count, and of our own culturally biased interpretations.

A major goal of this chapter is to present the generally acceptable guidelines for the behavior that ritually spins the webs of significance in which the people of Huaycopungo are suspended, to use Geertz's famous metaphor again. As such, it requires an attention to ethnographic detail that is important for the record and should reinforce the main points, but may be a bit more elaborate, and therefore tedious, than some readers may find necessary for the purposes of understanding the story and following the argument. This is especially true in the sections entitled *"Hayca Cai Asuaguta, Taitagu*: Take This Little Corn Beer, Dear Sir" and "Who Can Get Drunk: The Logic of Consuming Drinks." Such readers may find reading the introductory and concluding paragraphs of those sections and skimming the body to be sufficient for their purposes.

Asua and *Trago*: A Natural History

In the 1970s two forms of alcohol were most common in indigenous Otavalo—asua, home-brewed corn beer, and trago, distilled sugarcane alcohol. Asua is frequently referred to in Spanish by the word chicha, and trago is more formally referred to in Spanish as aguardiente. While asua is often thick and sour, with a relatively low alcohol content, trago is clear and very potent, with a medicinal taste that most people prefer to disguise with something sweet like soda or juice, unless they are already drunk and intent on getting drunker as fast as they can. The two forms of alcohol differ also because asua is native to the Andes, and trago was brought by Spaniards to the New World and is still produced almost entirely by nonindian Ecuadorians. In Otavalo, maize and the products produced from it play a powerful role in life as lived and as represented in their cosmovision.

Early colonial chronicles suggest that at least by the late sixteenth century, maize was the staple food in northern interandean valleys of Ecuador, such as in Otavalo, then known as Sarance, the center of the Caranqui chiefdom (Salomon [1973] 1981). In contrast, in the pre-Columbian central Andes of Peru, according to Murra, maize was originally used mostly for chicha, with potatoes providing the staple food (1973, 383). In the Otavalo of the 1970s, corn was the central food item; one could eat without sufficient corn, but it would be an unsatisfying meal. With enough corn a family had plenty for both subsistence and ceremonial needs. *Camlla* (toasted maize), *muti* (hominy), *chuchuca* (corn first cooked and then dried in the sun), *chugllu* (sweet corn on the cob), *api* (cornmeal porridge), and asua are still among the most common preparations. No wedding or other major ceremonial can be held if muti and asua are absent. A cucavi without camlla is incomplete because there is no crunch to complement the soft texture of the boiled potatoes or beans. As I spent more time there, the sight of healthy, ripening cornfields ceased to mean picturesque rural peace and summer's welcome warmth to me, as I had learned growing up in the northeast United States. I began to feel hungry at the sight of waving yellow corn silk and dream of future meals. Asua, then, is not just a convenient form of alcoholic beverage, but one of the staffs of life.

Asua can be used as both a food and as a ceremonial beverage, somewhat like wine in the Mediterranean countries of Europe. Early Spanish colonists rarely recognized the similarity, although there was some debate in Peru about whether asua could substitute for wine in the mass. They decided against it. As one chronicler in Mexico put it in 1692: "If the Indians drank *pulque* the way Spaniards drink wine (which is not the case, nor has it been, nor is there any hope of their ever doing so) it could be permitted . . . but these are Indians and it is proven that their custom is to get drunk, and it is for that reason that they drink" (quoted in Taylor 1979; 41). The Spaniards in Peru felt the same way about the drinking habits of the natives there.

Research suggests that fermentation and additives associated with the fermenting process increase the nutritive value of the grains, or tubers in the case of the Amazonian lowlands, used in the production of asua. Among the Amazonian Canelos Quichua, lightly fermented asua—made more often from *yuca* or sweet potato than from corn—until recently functioned as a daily foodstuff. It is reasonable to suppose that such was the once the case in Otavalo. Asua's alcohol content varies greatly. Lightly fermented asua is *mishci*, sweet, and asua fermented longer is *jayaj*, or sour/bitter and strong.

More highly fermented asua was used as a ceremonial beverage and the intention of drinking it was to feel the effects and to reach intoxication, as it still is in Otavalo. The Canelos Quichua drink lightly fermented asua all day long, while Otavaleños are more likely to consume mishci asua during communal work parties than during religious festivals. Until recently, the production of asua was still a favored way to use agricultural surplus, most particularly maize. In the late 1970s in Huaycopungo, asua was made in large *pondos* (pottery jars) or barrels for major ceremonies as well as to celebrate the social and religious values underlying any minga, joint work party, such as a house building or the repair of the cobblestones on a community road, even though the national government made the home brew illegal. Served in the early morning at a house building, it could be thick and filling; or at noon after a hard morning's field work high up the mountain, it could be light, cool, and thirst-quenching, like a barely hard cider. At other times, the sour liquid packed a kick like ale and the point of drinking it was to get very drunk.

In contrast, trago was purchased with money, another kind of surplus to subsistence requirements, since food was properly obtained through agricultural production only. People preferred to use all surplus for the creation of social and spiritual value, rather than for economic investment, for at least two reasons. This use of money deserves some explanation. First, the goal in Huaycopungo to maintain their limited autonomy by producing their own subsistence had kept them marginally involved in the consumer society in the first half of the twentieth century. Without a consumer orientation there was little motivation to acquire any durable possessions beyond tools, houses, and clothing. Once subsistence needs were met, the usually small surplus was transformed into nonmaterial resources, valued relationships and states that would spiritually ensure surplus or at least allow people to endure scarcity in the future. A second reason for investing surplus in social and spiritual, rather than material, resources, was the political and economic control over the indigenous peasantry exercised by the dominant society. In order to keep a peasantry as a self-reproducing source of cheap surplus labor, the nonindigenous elite prevented Otavaleños, like other indigenous people in Ecuador, from investing in their own community or regional infrastructure, since that would challenge the elite's political and economic control. They enacted rules to limit indians' economic freedom, subjected them to unfair pricing in the market, or confiscated the results of new and successful economic investments. Self-sufficiency was both a source of strength defended within the community and a severe limitation on productive potential imposed from outside. While an outsider observer may see this as an example of getting a lemon and deciding to make lemonade, the creative capacity of humans to find and develop the advantage to themselves in those situations that are disadvantageous in the first instance allows people to survive and even flourish somewhat despite oppressive circumstances.

Trago's alcohol content always surpasses asua's because of the distillation process. For that reason, it has partially taken over the role that highly fermented asua has had in signifying the most important, most ritually effective, most symbolically powerful alcoholic beverage. It is produced from sugarcane, which is grown only at altitudes lower than Otavalo. While the geographically distinct origin of trago makes impossible the symbolic symbiosis created in the interactions of people, land, and plants in the local production of asua, it contrarily invests trago with some of the special spiritual powers generated in the tropical lowlands (see chapter 3). Finally, while national and regional governments have frequently sought to reduce or eliminate the brewing of asua, trago production, in contrast, is government licensed and its sale subject to luxury taxes. In theory, that meant that the government made money on every bottle sold. In practice, this rule resulted in a flourishing illegal production and distribution of moonshine.

Asua has long been a substance of high value in the Andes, associated with sources of power both secular and sacred. As suggested above, trago has been partially assimilated into the symbolic complex created for asua, in which strong alcohol is favored by humans and spirits for its animating, boundary-erasing, and contractual properties. During the precolonial period and since, more highly fermented asua was a favored offering to the supernatural forces, its communal consumption a central part of ceremonies at sacred times of the year or the life cycle, and its greatest production and distribution directed by hereditary leaders. The Incas, most likely only elaborating upon an already existent cultural base, made the steady production of chicha and its distribution to loyal native lords within its far-flung empire a central part of its administrative structure. Archeologists have identified certain buildings in ritual centers as halls specialized for the group consumption of asua. Specially chosen virgins, *acllacuna*, housed in an *aclla-huasi*, brewed this sacred imperial asua. An aclla-huasi was established in Otavalo in the very last years of the Inca Empire. Both the political and the religious significance of shared alcohol are still common throughout the Andes.[4] However, as indigenous politics have been substantially reduced to the activities of community leaders only, since the regional, national, and international arenas of political control are in the hands of the encapsulating nonindigenous society, the imperial practices are no longer relevant. The political significance is seen most in the more frequent drinking by curagas, successful elders, fiesta sponsors, and native healers and in the competitive serving of drinks to recruit personal supporters.

Asua is produced in the dark huasi ucu, where the good indigenous woman (Allen 1988; Weismantel 1988), round and warm, sits by the fire ladling out the food that is always ready to warm her family or any visitors waiting in the curridur. Women are in charge of the family's maize harvest. The female household head decides which corn is to be converted to asua and makes it with the help of her female relatives. The male household head may tell her when to make it, but the ultimate control should be hers, since she is responsible for making sure the family eats until next year's harvest. In Otavalo there is only one maize harvest a year. While it is easy to concentrate on the dominant male role in offering and accepting drinks, it is well to remember asua's origins in this symbolically very female realm that make it a gift from the female side of a household's resources. Asua is properly served by a woman—wife, daughter, daughter-in-law, or mother—who unobtrusively brings it out to the curridur and serves it by the gourd to each person in turn, or presents a pail to whoever is hosting the guests—her husband, her daughter and son-in-law, her father or mother.

In contrast, trago is purchased, served, and consumed properly by men. Men are disproportionately involved with the outside world, where one finds sources of money and where trago is purchased. Women keep control of any money they make. But since women were necessary for the proper huasi, and were less likely to leave home for seasonal or other labor opportunities unless their families were exceptionally needy, they had less access to money than did men. Although they might spend their own money on the brown sugar cakes, *panela*, used by some to make asua ferment more quickly, they are less likely to spend it on trago. In the nonindian world that produces trago, its consumption is believed to be more properly a masculine activity and this is certainly repeated within the indigenous community. Finally, while asua is most often consumed in the house where it is made, trago is more likely to be brought to a home by male visitors.

While chapter 4, *"Cantina* and *Boda Huasi,"* further contrasts the symbolic and behavioral consequences of drinking asua versus trago, the rest of this chapter treats the two forms of alcohol as equally important, and, to a certain extent, equivalent. During the late 1970s the ritualized sharing of drinks at a boda huasi always featured both.

Shared Alcohol Creates and Validates the Ties That Bind

Offering a drink is a way to request or repay a favor, to ritually create or sustain a relationship of marriage or fictive kinship, for ordinary people to pay their respects to those in superior positions, and for leaders to recruit or repay the support of their followers.[5] These acts were not simply polite gestures that accompanied the creation of obligations, they were what anthropologists call perfomative: they had the power to transform events, causing the pledge of mutual responsibility to become an unbreakable bond. Each of these social agreements would remain only potential and without substance unless each individual of the interacting pair drank from a cup handed to him or her by the other. The ritualized sharing of alcohol is therefore obligatory for a marriage to be finalized or a favor repaid. Shared drinks did often symbolize and perpetuate active reciprocal exchanges among people in equal or hierarchical relationships, but more importantly they created and activated those relationships in the first place.

The role of alcohol is thus similar to that of money, which is frequently used in the creation and circulation of value. And in Otavalo, money and trago are often treated as substitutes for one other, as illustrated in Barlett's account of an alcalde in Agato (1980, 120): "Since he was no longer allowed to drink, but still wished to hold a traditional house-warming for his new house, he gave his guests money instead of alcohol." In valued social relationships, alcohol acts as a medium of exchange, when one's labor is "paid for" (the Spanish word *pagar* is used) by alcohol, and as a store of value, when relationships that could lead to labor or material aid in the future are kept active through the sharing of drinks. Drinks given to guests are like money in the bank, to be withdrawn in the form of labor or material support in the event of some future need. However, alcohol does not serve as a universal standard of value, which is a third characteristic of general-purpose money. The worth of most other things cannot be measured by an equivalent quantity of alcohol. And unlike money, asua and trago are not just tokens of value but gifts from the gods with their own intrinsic worth.

Shared drinks also resemble oaths made to seal a contract. Because of its role as a communicator between this world and the embracing world of cosmic space/time, the acceptance of drinks in *this world* is immediately perceptible in *the other*. One does not drink alone; spiritual forces may be deliberately invoked or may simply be attracted by the presence of this valued drug. Therefore the relationships pledged while drinking no longer exist simply as human promises but have a spiritual existence as well, and are theoretically unbreakable. In Rappoport's terms (1999), the public acceptance of the conventional order in ritual makes the private dispositions irrelevant and constitutes individual support for the social order over and above the individual's future actions. Engaging in the ritual of accepting a drink and thereby pledging support publicly creates specially interdependent relationships, although it does not prevent people from breaking these promises and violating these relationships in practice. In fact, they do so rather frequently in cases, say, of insufficient resources or where an interayllu feud makes a compadrazgo relationship difficult to pursue. Nonetheless, the consequences of having ignored the contract may be faced by the lax household when the general traffic among community members, interrelated in complex ways and engaged in continual reciprocal aid, becomes snarled due their inconsistent participation. Worse, a family may find itself off the highway of reciprocity altogether, impoverished both socially and materially in their isolation. Ultimately, one may experience spiritual sanction, if only when one meets these ill-treated compadres in God's presence after death. As I was told repeatedly when I divorced my first husband, should I make it to heaven, I would be united with him there for eternity.

When we examine below the individual application of the rules for the social sharing of alcohol, a game of great complexity is revealed, with goals that seem both complementary and conflicting. At the most ideal and inclusive level, individuals try to maximize their own benefit in the cosmic webs of reciprocity at the same time that they increase the reward for the nested series of groups to which they belong—their household, their ayllu, their neighborhood, their community, their parish, their region, their ethnic group. In practice, of course, the interests of these groups may be in sharp conflict, but the ideal exists nonetheless. With a high rate of community endogamy, people's crosscutting ties to a number of potentially opposed groups does in fact dampen the fires of conflict between them. These webs of reciprocity contracted through shared drinks symbolically create a community where everyone shares the obligations and love of close kinship, each with an equal claim to a community's joint resources.

At the same time, the careful calculation of drink offers and acceptances reveals a competition for individual and family advantage in the acquisition of material and labor resources from each other and, most importantly, in the attendant social ranking of households in the community. Those who are able to give the most, and therefore receive the most, demonstrate their superior economic performance and can thereby attract the larger number of supporters necessary for authority in community decision making. Competition for household advancement and prestige may seem to be contradictory to generous redistribution by community leaders. In an economy of scarcity, largesse by the better off may well impoverish them once again. However, as Rappoport (1999, 204) claims, "That prestige as much as or even more than wealth is among the chief rewards of life properly lived in societies in which reciprocity prevails also encourages vigorous, valorous and generous fulfillment of obligation."[6]

If her family is wealthy enough, the woman of the house proudly keeps a ready supply of asua in the proper stage of fermentation bubbling away in the pondos (large ceramic jars with pointed bases sunk into the dirt floor), or nowadays in plastic barrels, to offer visitors. The important business of the household will be better served if this social lubricant, honor for the recipient, and means for sealing promises is readily available. In the recent past, curagas were offered asua or trago when visited with a request and were expected to drink communally with other community elders when conducting political or judicial business, particularly regarding land claims, on behalf of the community. This willingness to consume alcohol communally indicated their seriousness and willingness to take as binding any joint decisions made. A curaga's wife, who always has assistants, must never run short of asua to share, but when any household serves as a boda huasi, that house resembles a curaga's. Special assistants, drawn from the personal network of the female head of household, are appointed to ensure that the barrel of asua never runs dry.

When a person visits a household for any reason, particularly in the festive season of May–August when maize ripens, he or she may be offered a drink of alcohol, as I learned to my chagrin in early fieldwork. The household heads may be found at home precisely because they are honoring someone in their exchange network. Since it is highly insulting to refuse an offered drink and thus repudiate the status of the relationship proposed by the offering person, people who don't want the responsibilities that acceptance would bring try to avoid being in a position where drinks will be offered to them.[7] Children, who do most of the casual messenger work between households, are not served. However, if a man or a woman enters when asua is already being shared with others, he or she may be offered a portion. While a man must accept, a woman would be expected to decline the offer politely and accept, with an extremely embarrassed air, only if pressed. If the offer were to be made seriously, she would be reminded, usually with a mischievous smile, that she represents her household in the absence of her husband or father, with which this household is in an active exchange relationship, and she must therefore share in the festive moment. This is a good reason for women, or anyone, not to visit alone, so they might have protection should a legitimate drinking obligation be presented. Still, a woman's refusal to share in drinking would never be resented as much as a man's, unless there were no men to represent her household and reinforcing exchange relationships with her household were very important at that moment. Men and women wishing to make a casual visit but avoid drinking may verify with neighbors visible from the road or footpath near the house whether or not the inhabitants are sharing drinks before they announce their arrival at the entrance to the house compound. If they are espied from within, however, and their presence highly desired as a pledge of continuing material support, someone will rush out to laughingly drag them inside. It is an honor to be so sought out by other households, but one that can have a high cost, since one is so often pressured to neglect one's own goals for the day in order to drink convivially with others.

When one household seeks a pledge from another to help build a house, to serve as godparent, or to assist in a ceremonial sponsorship, the household heads will carefully, and indirectly, sound out the likelihood of acceptance before making an appeal and offering a drink. Nonetheless, a potential donor of resources may ostentatiously avoid members of the petitioning family for a while to indicate that their resources are quite limited and that their eventual acceptance will not mean unlimited generosity. This is one way in which the bird-watcher's binoculars are extremely useful to keep track of people's movement. The petitioners may then choose the approach very carefully. They make sure that the desired donor is indeed present, ask to come in without much fanfare, and, when least expected, whip a live guinea pig, a bundle of eggs, or a bottle of trago out from under a poncho or shawl and thrust it into the hands of their unsuspecting quarry before he or she has a chance to refuse. While the ritualized sharing of alcohol is necessary to complete the social contract, it is not required for the initial acceptance. Receiving an uncooked food offering seals a good-faith agreement. The more serious the obligation, however, the more the petitioners will feel uncomfortable until the two parties have actually consumed alcohol together. While the local people may use similar methods when requesting aid from the indian or nonindian elite, the elite recipient retains greater control over what, when, and how the honor will be (or even has already been) repaid.

Hayca Cai Asuaguta, Taitagu:
Take This Little Corn Beer, Dear Sir

In a boda huasi, where a large group of people is being served, the order in which drinks are offered represents the social ordering of the recipients. The guests who are more important are served first and drink more overall, and the least important are served last or not at all. Age and gender are the two most basic criteria for deciding who gets served first, with men taking priority over women, and senior men and women taking priority over junior ones. A senior woman may sometimes precede a junior man. As noted above, children are not served and young women are rarely served. The drinks presented to the first few individuals, or married pairs, are remembered honors for the recipients; subsequent drinks only recognize the relationship that brought them to the boda huasi. Furthermore, guests have a higher status than do hosts.

Would that were all one needed to know! While those general rules apply, usually there are a number of choices in drink order, type, and quantity that can be chosen to claim certain relationships. For example, the server can choose a plain or fancy serving cup; asua, trago, a mix of the two, or even a beer; a tiny sip or a large serving; an outpouring of flowery phrases of honor or a perfunctorily extended hand; and many other methods to enhance or downplay the offer. The distributing of drinks offers the opportunity for a complicated, and almost infinitely gradable, calculation of rank relative to the others present and relative to ego as well, for purposes of this occasion as well as over time. Nor is preexisting rank the only criterion for shaping the presentation. Every drink offered represents the desire of the server that the receiver agree to a certain state of relationship and thereby accept a certain level of responsibility for mutual aid (or the payment for such aid already received). Furthermore, Otavaleños would claim that they are offering and accepting love.

Furthermore, a junior person can be served before a senior or a woman before a man if he or she is representing a household that is being honored for a particular reason or with which close ties are highly desired. Sometimes drinks are served to a couple, rather than an individual. If the occasion is in honor of a particular household, such as the groom's family, then the couple that heads the household is served before anyone else. The remaining men will then be served, sometimes followed by the other women.

During a small family celebration, close kinship often results in honored treatment. The household members visibly thank those visiting relatives and compadres with whom they have shared a lot in the recent past and with whom they want to remain close in the future. In contrast, when the house serves as a boda huasi, close kin, affines, and compadres from other households will act as helpers for that ritual occasion. They become hosts rather than guests during the event. Compadres chosen from social equals and siblings are the proper helpers at a boda huasi. For the fulfillment of a boda huasi's role, household members do not constitute a sufficient workforce, and a larger personal network in fact provides the necessary labor. Beyond those who are repaying past favors or ensuring future favors through labor at the boda huasi, other men of the ayllu bring money or trago to be used by the host, and the related women bring food and sometimes asua for the hostess to share with the guests. In some senses, the ayllu, as an ego-centered kindred often extended to include consanguineal, affinal, and fictive kin serves as host, although the heads of the households lead the event and get more social credit. In fact, the larger the number of helpers a couple can mobilize to serve at an event that they host, the greater the authority over others they demonstrate, and the more prestigious they appear to their guests. That prestige trickles down to all those in their network as well.

The amount of alcohol offered to one person relative to another at the same event also communicates to everyone present the extent of the honor that is given and the strength of the relationship claimed. A couple can serve a fuller or bigger gourd bowl (pilchi) of asua or a larger glass of trago to someone they wish to honor above others. All drinks must be consumed in their entirety and the vessel handed back. Of course, if you want to mock a person's high status, such as that of a visiting woman anthropologist, you can offer a ridiculously large pilchi and then just die laughing, or you can kill a higher-status enemy with kindness by offering an amount just short of being unacceptably large in order to increase his intoxication and decrease his ability to exercise any political savvy.

In addition, asua and trago can be exchanged by the container or by the drink. For example, a pondo or pail of asua can be given to someone, who then directs the offering of gourd bowls or cups of asua to the other people present. Or the bottle, or even a case, of trago may be given to someone by the host, after he has shared a drink with him or her, for that person to distribute to the others. Each transfer of alcohol from one person to another is a way to honor the receiver. The honor of receiving a container is greater than the honor of receiving a drink. Just imagine the surplus wealth and redistributive power demonstrated by a household that can provide the resources for another couple to honor and recruit their own exchange networks at the boda huasi of the hosts. While the guest is being greatly honored, the ability of the host to so honor is publicly displayed as well. If a person who has been presented a container is very busy or of very high status, he or she will only begin the distribution, leaving it to a junior relative or someone in a similar position to finish. Put in other words, the right to decide distribution represents power, while the responsibility to physically distribute the drinks demonstrates a subordinate, supporting role in public events. The more levels of power and prestige represented, or claimed, among the participants on a single occasion, the more the distribution decisions and acts of distribution will be divided among a variety of participants, as guests and hosts vie to display the size of their personal networks. Even the extent to which the distributor can seem to flow continuously and effortlessly between each guest, calling as little attention to him- or herself as possible, represents a level of aesthetic excellence toward which individuals may strive.

Someone who is offered a drink has the additional option of accepting only if the server drinks first, thereby honoring the server at the same time and balancing the relationship. *Ufyapashun, ishcandin nishpa* is the phrase repeated in a superpolite near whisper while the speaker repeatedly points his head toward the drink: "Let's drink together, two saying it as one." Parenthetically, then, if someone tries the strategy of offering an overly large drink to a rival, he risks getting it back to drink himself. Not a skilled player myself, I repeatedly get caught in this trap, as I try to discharge my responsibility as quickly as possible. As a drinking occasion continues, drinks tend to become distributed in a circle, only beginning with the principle participants. Of course, the seating arrangement roughly corresponds to the ranking that is in operation for that occasion. If another important person enters the group, a more formal distribution begins again. Also as drinking continues, those who do not wish to drink and who are not among the principal participants will remove themselves physically from proximity to the circling drinks. One common ploy is to answer a call of nature just as the circling drinks approach, being careful to act as if one were too preoccupied by the conversation to have seen the gourd bowl or bottle approaching.

Relationships with important elders, those who are both senior and actively engaged in community affairs, are not characterized by equal exchanges of alcohol. Generational seniority always elicits the combination of respectful/intimate forms of speech and other etiquette that honor by trying to diminish the social distance between the subordinate and the superordinate person.[8] In practice, most senior community members also control more resources for redistribution and require more aid in labor than do younger people. In terms of alcohol offerings, senior men are more often in the position of hosting drinking occasions, of receiving containers to redistribute, of being owed favors rather than owing them, and of being served early in the line. According to these rules, senior men drink a far greater quantity of alcohol than do younger ones. Exchanges with them rarely, if ever, change the hierarchical nature of the relationship. However, time always will, as people age and die and once-junior men and women become senior themselves. The very old, while treated with respect and affection, are considered retired from the authority positions that give them the right to priority in drinking rituals; many cease to drink at all. So close to their own death, they have become overly vulnerable to alcohol's power, both material and spiritual.

Successful senior men, especially those who hold named positions of authority, whether short or long term, such as curagas, cabildo officers, fiesta sponsors, or curers, must distribute and consume even greater quantities of alcohol. Those who can engage in this dangerous behavior and continue to exercise their authority with wisdom and skill reconfirm the absolute rightness of their elevated position in a society that both reveres and fears hierarchy. "It is generally supposed that a man who drinks has money, is a good worker and is generous with his friends . . . the Indian likes to speak of him as rich . . . industrious . . . generous . . . and with plenty of friends" (Rodriguez Sandoval 1945, 44).

Nonetheless, most mestizos, and those fellow *indígena* who wish to challenge their authority, label these heavy-drinking leaders *viejos chumados*, "drunk old men." In fact, it is recognized that elders and officeholders *do* run a greater risk of developing a craving for alcohol, which can lead them to neglect their responsibilities. An alcohol abuser, whether a community leader or not, does not work or does poor work, gets into fights, and treats his family and other people in his social network badly. This risk of alcoholism is the burdensome side of drinking, and of assuming power and authority, for the benefit of the community. That the risk is greatest for community leaders is also an Achilles' heel in a system where alcohol availability is increasing.

Blancu (white) and mishu (mestizo) guests are also entitled to preference in the drinking rounds, since in the larger society they are always superordinate to indígena. Some indígena establish compadre relationships with high-status outsiders, and shared drinking is an integral part of those relationships. When low-status nonindígena or *cholos*, those people whose social identity is ambiguous although their self-identity is nonindígena, attend a boda huasi they may or may not be given this deference in practice. They are particularly likely to receive but humble treatment if they have been the recipients of conspicuous indígena help in the past. The following chapter more thoroughly explores the issue of interethnic drinking.

The sharing of alcohol creates a society composed of several essential processes, some of which seem contradictory on the surface. Symmetrical relationships of loving mutual aid that are the ideal for a community come to life, individuals and households are encouraged to compete for public recognition of their superior economic and political success over other households, and the hierarchical nature of relationships between ordinary people and the very powerful is both affirmed and denied. Beginning with symmetry, mutual exchanges of alcohol are supposed to symbolize reciprocity in the exchange of labor and goods that ensure subsistence in an economy of scarcity, where few would survive for long if they were dependent solely on their own household's resources. It begins with a gift from one person to another in front of an audience, publicly proclaiming the receiver's high value. Since to refuse the drink is to refuse the honor and to deny the relationship being proposed by the giver, once given and accepted, the gift of shared drinking places the giver in a more favored position. Nonetheless, it is a position of great anxiety, since a willingness to commit has been publicly declared and scarce resources have been invested; a refusal to reciprocate would mean that the giver's love and commitment is deemed not worth acknowledging at the same time as his or her assets have been depleted. However, in the best circumstances, the giver is now publicly pledged a relationship that involves aid in goods and services and can expect to be so honored by the public offering to share drinks in the future. If the drink is a partial payment for help already received, then the giver simply avoids falling into a greater indebtedness. Among people of equal or approximately equal status in the community, these gifts and debts—of drinks, of honor, and of aid—even themselves out over time. The goal and the result are to maintain both a relationship of even exchange and close, equal friendship. This is the ideal community, one composed of people in continual active exchange, both material and symbolic, whose reciprocal actions animate the members into the experience of love.

Nonetheless, every time alcohol is being consumed, animated nonverbal conversations about the state of relationships between individuals and households are being enacted, often competitively. There is often an element of coercion in offering someone else a drink. By attaining the position to offer drinks, and the accompanying food, to many people, a couple demonstrates that their household is rich enough to enter into exchange relations with all those people. What's more, they have more power to define the nature of the relationship by the size and timing of their offered drinks. The more a household can give, the more it will receive and the higher it will rise in the local prestige hierarchy. Certain households rank higher socially than others through a combination of generational seniority, current or past political officeholding, a history of ritual sponsorship, obviously greater wealth, generous gifts of time and other resources to community welfare, or esoteric healing specialization.

Less illustrious households will most likely engage in asymmetrical exchange relations with the heads of more prestigious ones, demonstrating in effusive words, higher-pitched voices, and self-deprecating body language their fidelity, respect, and willingness to be of the most humble assistance in exchange for protection, guidance, and largesse from their superiors. Weaving the high and the low together into a loving interdependence that will increase the social bounty for all is as important as fostering multiple and symmetrical bonds among ordinary community members.

Who Can Get Drunk:
The Logic of Consuming Drinks

Finally, let us examine who can drink to intoxication, with whom, in what locations, and on which occasions. When the community participated very little in the market, these opportunities were relatively few and highly anticipated for most people, who were not important leaders. As we have seen above, the combination of gender, age, and importance would mean that older, politically and economically successful men are the most likely to receive quantities necessary for intoxication. They drink greater quantities more frequently than do others. It is important to note that the success attributed to individuals and households can come from a combination of their own efforts and the prestige already accorded their ayllu, in the sense of the bilateral descendants of an esteemed leader. The categories of preferred drink recipients could be ranked as follows (leaving out nonindians):

Older, successful men
Older, successful women and older, less successful men
Younger, more successful men
Younger, less successful men and older, less successful women
Younger, more successful women

Young and unimportant women and old, retired men and women are least likely to participate in the rounds of drinking. They are either assisting others in the preparations or absent from the boda huasi altogether.

While ambitious individuals in search of personal prestige and community bounty seek to attain intoxication at the hands of others with some frequency, many others see heavy drinking as a source of pleasure only when spaced at long intervals—for their own children's life-cycle rites and attendance for a day or two at calendrical fiestas. On these occasions, too, they would prefer to moderate the time spent drinking and the quantity consumed. Still, two factors work against individuals' attempts to control the quantity they consume. First of all, religious ideology expresses the efficacy of offering excess (*yapata*) to the spirits scattered throughout the environment in order to provoke a maximum return generosity in the form of good weather, crop and animal increase, and human prosperity. Since nonhuman spirits share in humans' festive offerings to each other, they will be moved to excessive beneficence toward humans by the humans' lavish celebrations.

A second factor involves the competitive aspects of feasting each other, where households seek to motivate substantial future assistance from their exchange network by giving away a little more than they can afford in festive resources. Such outpourings of food and drink to guests help them develop a reputation for wealth and generosity sufficient to maintain a very large and active support network. Public recognition of these acts and expectations of more to come will increase the influence their household and ayllu can exercise in the community. Hosts want to offer as much as they can to as many people over as many days as they can afford, even though they may not wish to consume that much themselves, so as to increase their networks and their prestige. A couple's ability to cause a large number of people to end up passed out in their yard, the many blue-tented ponchos now deflated into twisted blankets and the once gleaming white pants stained with sticky asua, is an indication of their power that distant people can view from afar. While the guests may not wish to consume so great a quantity of alcohol, the fact that refusing is an insult often overcomes their desires.

The occasions people had to drink were numerous, although only those individuals who could delegate their work to large personal networks and receive generous contributions of trago from them as well, or those whose political responsibilities required interacting formally with others, took advantage of the range of opportunities. Life-cycle ceremonies, calendrical fiestas, communal work parties and, for elders and curers, the acceptance and carrying out of their duties were all occasions to share alcoholic beverages. When a member of one's own household or the household of a close relative, in-law, or compadre undertook a life-cycle ritual such as baptism, confirmation, marriage, house building, or funeral, or sponsored a calendrical fiesta, all married adults, except the youngest women, could be expected to share at least one drink with others. A large proportion of those would, in turn, be expected to get drunk at least once. The older, ambitious men would expect to become intoxicated several times during the event.

Throughout the several festivals associated with the Corazas sponsorship, described in the next chapter, or during the weeklong celebration of the summer solstice (San Juan or Inti Raymi), a wide array of the population could expect to share a drink, even if their own kindred network was not serving in a named position. Even visiting strangers from neighboring communities may be offered a drink. This is in keeping with the more regional focus of these fiestas. A substantial portion of men would expect to maintain a high level of intoxication, when not asleep, for several days. The sponsors themselves might expect a week or more of almost continuous alcoholic intoxication, a burden and sacrifice for the community to which no one looks forward with aplomb. Both life-cycle rites and calendrical festivals were most likely to take place during the months of harvest, from April through October.

During a communal work party, organized by cabildo officers or comuna section leaders, asua, and sometimes trago, would be available during work breaks for meals and at the end of the work. During the work, it was considered more desirable to drink beverages with less alcohol content and more thirst-quenching properties, but some male participants would look forward to drinking to intoxication after a day's work was through. It should be clear that such drinking removed communal projects from the realm of the merely instrumental and made them another support for the sacred interdependency of the community that was so desired. One may slog away at work in one's own chacra, perhaps with the help of some very close kin. But when one worked for the good of everyone, that sense of communion with one's fellows and the spirits could be helped along by the ritual implications of the shared drinks as well as the mind-altering properties of the drug itself.

Finally, as mentioned before, if someone petitioned a specialist for help, he or she might bring uncooked food or alcohol as an offering. If the petition were accepted, then the alcohol would be shared. Native healers, curagas, nonindians, and elders serving on the cabildo were always entitled to this treatment. Sometimes a wife or son or other close relative of that person would be pressed to accept the offering and pass on the petition in the official's absence. Furthermore, elders and curers were also expected to drink during the exercise of their duties. When elders met to discuss community business or lead others in a public project, they would be expected to publicly pledge their devotion to the community and solicit supernatural aid to that end by consuming alcohol. The same held true for curers during all phases of the curing rituals, from gathering and preparing medicinal herbs to divining and removing the offending illness with a candle, egg, or guinea pig.

On all of these occasions, there was no time of day that was considered more appropriate for drinking; any time that people congregated was as good as another, so you could find groups sharing alcohol at 8 a.m., at noon, at midnight, and in between. However, certain days of the week, like Tuesdays and Saturdays, were considered more dangerous than others, more likely to attract negative supernatural influence. The same held true for the hours after dark. Only those individuals most sure of having personal, social, and supernatural protection and resistance to harm would begin drinking during those periods and they would ensure they drank in a spiritually protected place.

However, if anyone expected to be involved in drinking to the point of intoxication, he or she would make sure to bring someone along who would remain sober and take care of the drinker. The dangers of intoxication were both human and supernatural. For one thing, theft was always a possibility and men would frequently wake up from a drunken sleep to find hats, watches, musical instruments, and ponchos missing. Women were susceptible to the risk of consenting to pressure for sex because of their impaired judgment or even to rape. In addition, drunken individuals often lacked the judgment or ability to avoid night travel or stay clear of spiritually dangerous places or even to make it all the way home. If localized spirits didn't harm the person, dangerous winds from faraway places of power could also harm the vulnerable drunk asleep on the side of the road with his head uncovered and exposed. For young, married men a common designated caretaker is his wife, although any subordinate person, such as a younger sibling or dependent niece or nephew, could take the role. Should harm come to an intoxicated married man left to sleep it off on the path, his wife may be held responsible. In the 1860s Hassaurek visited the areas and described the situation as follows:

> As soon as her spouse commences to be overpowered by the immense quantities of rum, or chicha, which he consumes, she is at his side and remains with him. A woman who would fail to comply with this most important of her marital duties on a great occasion like this would be despised by the whole Indian community, if not abandoned by her husband. I do not propose to say that she does not get drunk too; but never so drunk as to become unable to manage him. She clings to him with the utmost tenacity. She holds him back and rolls him off when his intoxication assumes a belligerous character; she prevents him from committing excesses; she makes him sleep on her lap, and finally leads him to his home. ([1868] 1967, 270)

In the case of one intoxicated man's accidental death while I was there, men and women both agreed that his wife had killed him by her neglect. Although older men also frequently rely on their wives, they have many other subordinates to take her place. A particularly popular choice is a son-in-law, masha. Older women who no longer have young children to care for may wish to join in the drinking and will find their own designated caretaker. In this case a daughter-in-law, jachun, plays the stereotypically subservient role.

Getting publicly drunk is both an honor and a burden, shared disproportionately by elders, both men and women, and adult men. Sleeping it off on the side of the path is not considered shameful at all, as long as the intoxicated people have protection from subordinates in their social network. When older men and women pass out alone it is considered very sad; either they have no children or other junior supporters, or these younger relatives neglect them. Worse yet, they may put themselves in harm's way simply to get a drink; they may be alcoholic.

However, when such excessive drinking is successful, large groups of people have experienced *communitas*, Victor Turner's word for the blissful feeling of union and communion when everyday social distinctions among members of a group dissolve. To participants, the group seems more like one organism, humming the same delightful tune, than a collection of individual people. During successful ceremonial drinking, individuals have successfully advanced their careers, but in the process of doing so have recommitted themselves to directing that success toward the good of the whole community. Both the burdensome aspects of heavy drinking and the pleasurable ones are essential to fully convey the meaning of the ritualized consumption. The good things in life—general fertility, household prosperity, large and active kinship networks, prestige among one's fellows—are achieved by hard work, personal sacrifice, and subordination to the groups, be it the household, the ayllu, the neighborhood, or the community as a whole. The short-term rewards of communal drinking—communitas, chemical intoxication, and festive foods—are followed, in the short term, by hangover and exhaustion, a reduction of ready resources, whether in the form of cash or uncooked food, and new or renewed obligations to others.

Drinking at José Manuel's and Isabel's *Huasi Fichai*

The story of José Manual and Isabel's dedication of the new house, a ritual "sweeping," *fichai*, of the house to clean it of harmful spirits, in chapter 1 illustrates some of these norms for mobilizing exchange networks through the offer of shared drinking. The discussion also highlights the ways that individuals can fail to honor them or can manipulate them to their own advantage. To recapitulate some of the structural implications of a house building, a house is built by the shared labor of all those people in one's personal network, whether they are returning a past favor or investing in the relationship for their own future needs. House building is the beginning of full adult status for a young couple. Up until this point, they have been able to cultivate exchange relations mostly within their own and their spouse's ayllus, trying to develop cooperative relations between the two families. In addition, they have begun to choose compadres for their young children, some of whom are kin and some of whom are not.

In keeping with their ambitious and nontraditional strategy, the first two birth godparents that Isabel and José Manuel chose were non-indigenous. Susana, their first child, was baptized in the arms of the local schoolteacher from San Rafael, who both founded the first school in Huaycopungo and served as head assistant, along with Isabel, to Berta Ares Quejía, the Spanish anthropologist who was doing research in San Rafael when Susana was born. Their second child's, Ricardo's, baptism *achi-Mama*, or godmother, is the author.[9] As the first educated woman in Huaycopungo, Isabel was staking a claim to that source of cultural capital—educated and light-skinned foreigners—in her person and for the benefit of both her family and the community. In both cases, the chosen women's positions as educator/anthropologist to indigenous people made them unlikely to use their ethnic superiority to exploit their indigenous compadres.

The process of building a house allows a young couple to add relationships with neighbors and to add new compadres. The house building itself is the first test of their ability to attract labor support. They are likely to accept labor that primarily represents their parents' networks, if it is forthcoming. But some ambitious individuals who do not see their parents' wealth as being sufficient to launch their futures in any secure way will compete to attract labor on their own strengths. Such was the case for José Manuel. The sharing of alcohol with all the men who work on the house during the labor is an essential part of the protocol. It attracts people to a pleasant social event, "pays" those who work, ratifies the social relationships between the sponsors and their personal networks, and obtains the blessing of supernatural powers.

This concept of "paying" is always expressed with the Spanish word pagar, and people often use it humorously or with an ironic tone. Since there was at most only an incipient money economy at the time of the conquest, the Spanish word was used to express this alien European concept. However, I would like to suggest that the use of the word today can include both the native and the hispanic concepts of exchange. The former concept demands a social relationship and mutual responsibility, and the European concept of payment denotes a nonsocial and monetary exchange of measured value. Both imply a very close accounting, rather than a diffuse expectation of return. These two meanings may be balanced or either one take precedence over the other. In their dealings with indians, the Spanish and their cultural descendants often violated both the native and the European rules of exchange/pay, promising mutual aid relations and payment for land and labor, neither of which materialized.

José Manuel and Isabel had difficulty attracting sufficient labor to their house building for several reasons: their exogamous marriage, the slope of the terrain chosen, which made site excavation particularly time-consuming (it was finished in 1996), and finally, the absence of young men, many of whom were in Quito earning needed cash in construction work during the building boom. Nor would José Manuel accept the option of having his father-in-law mobilize his kindred network and take the credit for the house, while José Manuel continued to play the role of obsequious and servile masha. José Manuel had already served his groom service in three years of residence in his in-laws' house. Despite his own lack of active ayllu networks, he was determined to establish a successful household through his and his wife's own efforts.

As a solution, José Manuel, long practiced in using humor to his advantage, would approach everyone who passed on the well-traveled path in the front of the house, which leads to the Pan-American Highway. Holding his pail of asua, he used teasing to try to force people to accept a drink and therefore a promise to contribute some labor time. It was a joke, a plea for help, and an attempt at coercion. A gift was offered—alcohol itself, shared consumption and thus social relatedness and spiritual blessing—in the hope of enticing an obligation—the obligation to work on this particular occasion and the acceptance of a preexisting and continuing obligation to pursue the mutual aid that comes with a social relationship. More idiosyncratically, José Manuel was offering a good time, with lots of joking and a relative lack of family infighting, since he was without family in the community. For many men, the pleasure of convivial drinking was enticement enough. Many other people tried, laughing, to say no, while being pursued assiduously. Some gave in, usually those who believed there was some basis for obligation in the family relationships, although many escaped for home as soon as possible. As an outsider, José Manuel could safely pretend ignorance of the fine points of actual relations over the years and focus on the structural guidelines. But the process of weaving this net of reciprocity began to transform him into a community member, llactapura, rather than the in-married stranger he had originally been. He is proud today of the number of people in Huaycopungo who know him and seek him out for a place in their personal networks. The downside, of course, is that he is likely to get repeatedly drunk during calendrical ceremonies, when he routinely loses valuable property, like his hat or his guitar, or becomes abusive to his family as they try to steer him free of danger during these episodes.[10]

What this example reemphasizes is the balancing act that such rituals represent and the challenge to participants to keep the balance from swinging too far into personal loss and violence, competition, and anger. A toast in front of an audience can be a remembered honor or a terrible obligation. Shared consumption is both a source of individual and communal pleasure and a source of misery. Social and spiritual ends can be served or can be submerged in favor of utilitarian ones. The offer of alcohol can be a genuine gift of love and a covert weapon in a competition for power. Finally, exchanging drinks can be sacred and funny at the same time. We will return, especially in chapters 7 and 8, to the question of how and why the people of Huaycopungo decided, with special fervor after the 1987 earthquake, that this plunge to one end of the continuum had in fact occurred.

Rituals of Integration
or Denial of Dysfunction?

Overall, the discussion of shared drinking in this chapter has been idealized. Another side to ritual drinking will be presented in chapter 4, "*Cantina* and *Boda Huasi*." While the Otavalans' theory of ritual efficacy in establishing productive relationships with people and spirits allows for, even takes pains to ensure, a significant cost to accompany any benefit, this account of drinking stresses how the social, spiritual, and material gains can be made to outweigh any increase in suffering. To repeat a theme, this is the Walt Disney or Sunday school model of social and cultural reality, a model that is extremely valuable for guiding, motivating, and justifying the lives of people who create and repeat these cultural myths, even though they recognize their ideal character. Like all myths, they are both powerful and true but not sufficient for a complete understanding of the social organization they purport to describe and mold.

In cases like these, such cultural formulations may seem like denial, as used in the alcohol and other drug abuse literature to label an individual's inability to see things as they really are and the largely unconscious determination to present a clearly dysfunctional situation in a benign or beneficial light. But the enactment of cultural canons through ritual action is not the same as individual belief and other psychological dispositions as demonstrated in, or inferred from, individual behavior. Denial, as used in the AODA literature, is an individual psychological state and thus cannot be applied to a community of people, whose private dispositions may be many, indeterminate, and variable, while the cultural myth continues to live in the group through the repetition of ritualized forms, such as sharing a drink (Rappoport 1999). As we will see more clearly in chapter 6, *private preference falsification* (Kuran 1995b) may be a more illuminating way of explaining a group of people's continuing choice to maintain behaviors that cause them harm. The advantages of group membership may outweigh the costs to individuals of continuing this traditional norm.

Nonetheless, at what point does such cultural mythmaking and its materialization in ritual action become at least comparable to denial in the dysfunctional sense meant in the alcohol literature? Said another way, can cultural forms come to serve individual and family denial more frequently than they promote a healthy community? It goes without saying that the ability of culture, largely in its religious dimension, to conjure a world in which flawed and frustrated humans can see themselves as efficacious and fulfilled is one of the crowning achievements of the human mind realized in social groups. Nevertheless, could the canons represented in ritual drinking in Huaycopungo have been publicly accepted out of social duty and habit, while also serving many individuals as a comforting fantasy to avoid facing the increased suffering that they were privately noticing and to delay undertaking the wrenching changes that they feared? Were the indigenous Otavalans in the latter part of the 1970s still exercising their power to create the most bountiful world possible for themselves in the context of political, economic, and cultural domination? Or were they in full-fledged denial; had the bounty become imaginary only, while ritual drinking did little or nothing to advance, and much to diminish, their social relationships and material well-being? We will return to this question in chapter 8.

CHAPTER THREE

Taita Dios and Taita Imbabura

Indigenous Religion,
Both Andean and Christian

ONE DAY IN THE LATE 1970S after a soccer match, my compadres and I were relaxing and talking on a grassy slope, where we could watch the shadows creep up the steep sides of Mount Imbabura as the sun sank behind Mount Mojanda at our backs. Taita Imbabura, a latent volcano, is the highpoint of the Otavalo cantón and the mountain guardian of the region, something like a patron saint. While only occasionally snowcapped, the mountain rises well above the tree line to 4,630 meters (15,279 feet). Its twin-peaked lava cone sweeping up from the shores of Lake San Pablo is the constant backdrop and visual reference point for life in Huaycopungo. *Taita* is an honorific that literally means father, used for people, ancestors, and male deities.[1]

José Manuel began to ruminate about Taita Imbabura himself, a personified deity who is said to reside deep within the mountain. Like tales of buried treasure, stories of the numerous people who have failed, and even died, in the attempt to enter the promised land, where the personified Taita Imbabura presides, endlessly fascinate and entertain runa people. For Taita Imbabura's interior realm is an endless patchwork quilt of agricultural marvels. Waving golden tassels top

Fig. 19. Taita Imbabura and Lake San Pablo
(PHOTO BY AUTHOR)

Taita Dios and *Taita Imbabura*   117

acres of ripening corn, each chacra, or field, encircled by stalks of blue-flowering lupines, fava bean plants with their pale green and velvety pods bulging with numerous plump seeds, and vigorous vines of *zambo* squash twisting up the stout stalks of *sara* or corn plants. These sara chacras are interspersed with fields of quinoa flowering in a blaze of orange, maroon, mustard, and purple, and bright green pastures where herds of wooly *llamacuna* (the Otavalo Quichua word for sheep; llamas are called *llamingocuna*) contentedly graze. The higher slopes are bursting with potatoes, *oca, melloco,* and other Andean tuberous vegetables; firewood is plentiful in the forests; and clear water bursts forth for people, animals, and plants to drink without threatening floods or droughts. Taita Imbabura himself sits surrounded by golden statues and resplendently dressed in the finest cloth, ornamented with feathers and gold. Inside the mountain is a paradise worth the dangerous feats undertaken to find the entrance, through which a lucky few have mysteriously disappeared in the past.

So half dreaming and half seriously, my compadre came to me for novel answers (as he did in those days to many things about which I had no idea, like how airplanes and telephones work), asking my advice on how we could make the attempt to enter the mountain.[2] When I reminded him that even if we could find the opening, I could not follow, because Taita Imbabura's empire deep within the mountain is closed to white people, he was momentarily speechless. Of course he knew that, but he had forgotten. Perhaps that choice, a perfect world that was nonetheless empty of modern opportunities, particularly those now more directly accessible from North America and Europe, was somewhat less desirable, once he had remembered. That world, a purely Andean one with foods and clothes and rulers and gods of entirely native origin, is gone. It is an idea, one that both indigenous people and outside observers like to think about. Both make finding the hidden entrance, flanked with innumerable dangers, into an adventurous game. But it is not a lived reality. Indigenous people are culturally mestizo, or mixed. The animals found in Taita Imbabura's paradise with the Quichua name, but whose round wooly bodies are of Old World origin, are just one pointed example of these five hundred years of cultural mixing.

Nevertheless, Taita Imbabura has not, for most Otavalans, become simply a figure in folklore and fairy tales, like Santa Claus or King Arthur in Camelot. Taita Imbabura and other mountain peaks are invoked at healing sessions, at the graves of loved ones, during religious processions, and at home altars during ritual sponsorships and life-cycle rites. A few people, mostly shaman, ritually climb the mountain to leave offerings at special old *Lechero* trees (in Spanish; literally "milk-giver," for its creamy white sap) at the specified times of the year. Different communities in Otavalo cantón preserve their own versions of ancient rites, which anyone can experience if their personal networks extend across the lake. People in Huaycopungo talk about doing it and discuss among themselves the unmistakable signs that others are moving up the slopes or the old offerings they have found. They do so with a mixture of curiosity, skepticism, and nervous wonder, as if they are torn between the dangers of ignoring a potentially significant source of supernatural power in their own neighborhood or risking a social judgment of being backward, or even the wrath of Taita Dios, God, for too directly ignoring the church's dictates on proper worship. Hair-raising stories told by locals and foreign climbers alike of difficult climbs and strange things occurring while on the mountain's slopes also contribute to Taita Imbabura's aura of fearsome power. Throughout the Andes, the mountains attend carefully to human doings on the earth, especially when people dare to cross their slopes, and frequently give careless people evidence of their cranky displeasure.

House walls facing Taita Imbabura almost never have an opening; the doors are cut into a wall on the opposite side of the house, so that people can feel protected from spiritual dangers sometimes carried by the cold mountain winds once they enter the dark and fire-warmed huasi ucu. The first doorway in José Manuel and Isabel's house faced the mountain because of the house's placement against a hill, which caused a lot of comment and concern. Nor did it have a closeable door for months after they moved in, because they couldn't afford to buy one. Coupled with their fear that the spirits of the land were not satisfied with the rituals of *alpa pascai*, when the first hole was dug for the house, and *huasi fichai*, literally house sweeping, when they hosted the housewarming *boda wasi*, the worry about the winds from Taita Imbabura entering their house had them scrutinizing every nightmare, every quarrel, every stomach upset, every meal one of the children refused to eat, during the first few weeks in their new house for signs that the family would never be accepted by the spirits. It wasn't until the Red Cross rebuilt their house after the earthquake that the door was placed properly on the opposite side.

Taita Dios, a version of the Christian God, does not spark a similar array of visual images, since he is a more remote personification of foundational power, presiding over all other manifestations of spirit. Strictly speaking, God does not parallel Taita Imbabura, despite the title of this chapter and their shared honorific. The Sun, Taita Indi, played a role similar to God for traditional andeans. The power of the Sun, as of God, was essential for the continuation of the world. That gift of world creation was the Sun's only gift to humans, assured for the future in exchange for tireless ritual effort on the part of the people and the other spirits below. In fact, another term for God is Achil Taita (Shining Father), a term long ago applied to Indi. However, the two terms are not exactly synonyms; they do not represent identical alternatives for addressing the supreme spiritual power. The first mixes a Quichua word (taita) with a Spanish word (Dios) and more clearly expresses fidelity to Christianity. The second term, all in Quichua, emphasizes the indigenous people's right to conceptualize spiritual power for themselves, but it most often refers to a syncretic deity with an indigenous name. Only some shamanic experts, small local cults, or young activists searching for their roots, however, would claim that Achil Taita refers to a native andean god, such as Taita Indi, Father Sun, to whom the term Achil Taita originally applied.[3] Nonetheless, the local practitioners do invoke Taita Indi in a list of spirits and sacred places when the religious context is most isolated from church control. In short, the contrast is maintained between the most distant and encompassing celestial power springing from Catholic or indigenous roots. The Christian God, however, has assumed a superior position overall.

The contrast between Taita Imbabura and Taita Dios that starts this chapter is meant to call attention to the two sources of religiosity among the people of Huaycopungo and the fundamentally juxtaposed nature of their relationships to the two great traditions that spiritually nurture them. Until the 1970s, Otavalans called themselves Christians and meant Roman Catholics. They believed then that Protestants were not Christians, although this has recently changed. The mixed elements of their spiritual life, whether of pre-Columbian, hispanic Catholic or more recent origin, could display differing structural relationships to one another. Some of the elements were mixed so thoroughly as to no longer be recognizable as different in origin, like the *llama*/sheep above, a process that can be referred to as *syncretism*. The use of candles, first rubbed on a petitioner's body or wrapped with a strand of the supplicant's hair or other personal item and then offered with prayers to Christ, the Virgin, or Taita Imbabura, is now as much a part of andean shamanic practice as it is a venerable element of folk Catholic worship in the church. I doubt if any shaman would believe me if I suggested the technique originated in Europe. Other religious beliefs and practices were *juxtaposed*, following a religious strategy that self-consciously seeks the best of both spiritual worlds, worlds that nevertheless remain conceptually distinct. Examples abound throughout ceremonial practices, such as the juxtaposition of hushed worship in the church with noisy devotion enacted in processions circling throughout the landscape and up the slopes of Taita Imbabura, or the ritualized serving of both chicken, the national luxury meat of European origin, and guinea pig, the indigenous luxury meat, during rites of passage. What is significant in these examples is that the contrast between the origins and associated symbolic complexes is highlighted in the ritual and that the counterposed elements are considered equally essential for religious efficacy. Finally, hispanic and andean elements were also *transposed*, where the form from one tradition is maintained but fleshed out with content from the other (Rueda 1981). For example, as we will see below, the Virgin Mamacuna, memorialized appearances of the Virgin Mary at specific places, substituted for geographically referenced expressions of Pacha Mama in earlier worship. As such, the Virgin Mamacuna reveal some of the characteristics of both. Although all these forms of combination take place, the andean region is particularly characterized by the salience of juxtaposition (Wachtel 1977).

People in Huaycopungo called themselves Catholics because from the time of the conquest it had been unacceptable, and sometimes mortally dangerous, to profess any other religion. But even if they had been allowed to profess allegiance to a religion with an andean name in the past, that religion would today still contain a mix of symbols, beliefs, and practices, both native and imported. Practicing a Catholicism that is solely defined and controlled by the priests and bishops of the local churches in the period under discussion here amounted to consorting with the enemy, leaving one's homeland, betraying one's parents, and becoming something else. In short, for most indigenous people pure andean religion represents a distant and ambivalently desired dream, like Imbabura's idyllic kingdom deep within the patron mountain, which implies the obliteration of the present world. At the other extreme, practicing only pure Catholicism promises a nightmare of erased identity, while the world goes on empty of indigenous presence. Indigenous people of Otavalo today consider their privileged access to superhuman powers from both heritages to be one of their greatest assets.

A Chapter Guide

The previous chapter examined domestic ritual, highlighting the social relationships desired for a moral community. Less attention was given to the relationships between humans and spirits. In this chapter, we turn our attention to this somewhat more formal aspect of religion, examining how human-spirit interaction in ritual activity beyond the boda huasicuna reflects and transforms the world for the benefit of people in this particular society. Nonetheless, the relationship between people and the spirits is still a matter of communalistic interactions, designed to reflect and ensure the beneficial nature of the cosmos, rather than one of individual belief or commitment to precepts established by church authorities. The domestic ritual described in the last chapter serves as a model for the form and goals of the ritual with regional and even cosmic implications in this one.

While introducing the extent to which indigenous culture is a hybrid one, this chapter stops short of engaging in the contemporary discourse between the people who identify themselves as indigenous and those who identify themselves as hispanic Ecuadorians. In that sense, we are still overemphasizing the power of the local inhabitants to shape the world they live in and giving more attention to the indigenous principles used to interpret Catholicism than to the ways more orthodox Catholicism has shaped indigenous society. Therefore the Christianity presented here displays a particular andean cast. We are laying the foundation for understanding the deeply embedded *cosmological axioms* (or *cultural schemas* or *dominant metaphors*) discussed in the previous chapter (Rappoport 1999; Ortner 1990; Ohnuki-Tierney 1990). These basic premises help guide the transformation of Huaycopungo that will be described in part II, as they have so many transformations of a smaller or similar magnitude in the past. So while this chapter does not explicate the sociological framework in which drinking behavior took place and changed, it does provide some of the models of thinking, shared among many Otavaleños, that helped interpret the behavior of others and generate their own.

These axioms are learned, enacted, and embodied during ritual, whether everyday or part of the ritual calendar, rather than taught explicitly. Ordinary Otavalans do not attempt to analyze their knowledge of religion abstractly and systematically. Religion is a three-dimensional and polysensual practice remembered bodily in the experiences of singing, dancing, physically tracing the community's paths in procession, and offering and receiving drinks (Abercrombie 1998), rather than the memorized or studied Word of God or any particular set of beliefs. Esoteric is the proper name for both the most general and most in-depth religious knowledge of the invocations and other verbal practices, since that is the domain of a few specialists. An advantage of religion practiced this way is that it seems part of natural reality, rather than a distinct kind of thinking that might contrast with other mental models.

We will continue this chapter by completing the pantheon of spirits presided over by Taita Dios. The next cast of characters to whom you will be introduced are the types of religious specialists, people who have esoteric knowledge and techniques to help ordinary people relate to the spiritual world. Then, following a brief introduction to the ritual calendar, we can examine the rituals themselves. The themes of (1) sacred space as it is marked and traversed in ritual; (2) ritual battle and its opposite, symbiotic union; (3) the polarity of humility and hierarchy, especially as it is enacted in the Corazas fiesta; and (4) world reversal, especially in San Juan/Inti Raymi guide our exploration.

The Spirit Powers

Despite the Christian form of the supreme deity, the argument for strict monotheism in the andean version of Catholic Christianity is even more tenuous than in the European one. Supernatural power is traditionally distributed among many personifications at several levels. In some sense, each lower level is a refraction of the more inclusive one, and the whole, represented by God, consists of the sum and interaction of its parts. While a whole at each level is gendered predominantly male or female, the parts are subdivided into male and female; each whole is both one gender, seen as a unit, and both genders, seen as a set of parts (see Allen 1988). In an alternate conceptualization to the one in which Taita Dios alone is supreme, Taita Dios and the Virgin Mary jointly represent the highest levels of power, as the linked and essential male and female principles of the cosmos. Although Christian doctrine would highlight the Trinity, it had little influence among most indigenous people, who conceptualized the Holy Spirit as a localized spirit that mediates between humans and the higher levels of spiritual power. Other older andean models of this rarefied spiritual level include the Sun, Taita Indi, and the Moon, Mama Quilla, Taita Indi's female celestial counterpart. Mama, Mother, is the female counterpart of Taita, serving as a common honorific for adult women as well as a title for female ancestors and spirits. While the traditional celestial realm was overwhelmingly male, its parts were male and female. However, the female counterpart of the male celestial realm conceived as a whole was the earth, Pacha Mama, an earth/world deity with a long history in the Andes. Though Pacha Mama was overwhelmingly female, some of her manifestations, like Taita Imbabura, for example, were in fact male.

To some extent, the Catholic Virgin Mary has taken over both the positions of the female side of the celestial realm and of the earthly realm that complements the celestial. However, Pacha Mama has also lost her prominence as a focus of worship, although her name still appears in the long list of supernatural powers invoked by shaman and other esoteric practitioners, like the Sun and Moon. In the 1970s people in Huaycopungo all tossed some drops of each gourd of asua or shot glass of trago onto the ground, which in other parts of the Andes was explained as an offering to Pacha Mama. In Otavalo, people said they didn't know why they did it, that perhaps the last bit of every drink was dirty. The concept of the supreme male power has become more densely concentrated and thus more closely resembles the Christian God. Pacha Mama, in her manifestation as the Virgin Mary, has been reduced to a subsidiary position relative to the all-powerful, male God. Still, she is both Catholic in her character as an all-forgiving virgin mother who mediates between men and God and andean in her multiplicity and her geographic and geological specificity. The Virgin Mary is frequently spoken of in the plural, Virgin Mamacuna, in reference to her many personifications, usually referencing specific historical appearances, around the world. Perhaps the two Virgins most invoked and visited in Otavalo are the Virgin of El Quinche in Pichincha province to the south and the Virgin of Las Lajas, just across the border into Colombia to the north. Unlike God, the Virgin Mamacuna are strongly linked to specific places on the earth and that location's special earthly characteristics, in a similar fashion to the guardian mountains.

At a level somewhat less distant to humans than that occupied by Taita Dios, we find *Jesusitu*, the saints, and the mountain deities represented at particular shrines, as well as the Virgin Mamacuna. They can serve as mediators between humans and the more distant God. For many people, Jesus has the same approximate status as the saints, although others more versed in Christian orthodoxy grant Jesus a more important status. Some people would find the inclusion of the mountain deities inappropriate in this list, aware that it conflicts with standard Catholic teachings, especially if the context was linked to the church. But the same individuals might see nothing amiss in the invocation of Taita Imbabura, for example, in an indigenous curing ritual.

Nearby hills, springs, caves, deep ravines, and waterfalls, which were once revered as openings into Pacha Mama, continue to receive prayers and offerings on their own by the older people, spiritual specialists, and in some other communities of the Otavalo region. Most adults in Huaycopungo will talk about that practice but no longer organize communal efforts to honor these spots. The closer spirits are to humans in space, the more potentially bothersome are they to humans on a daily basis. This nearby level of spiritual power has been partially assimilated to the hispanic concept of the devil or evil spirits. Neighboring spirits are frequently called demons and people shiver at the mention of them, but their powers are nevertheless considered potentially helpful to humans. People approach them with more ambivalence than they do Taita Jesus or any Mama Virgin, but they are as likely to be pacified as shunned or directly assailed. Perhaps the pressure of the church to deny local deities and label them demons and the resultant avoidance of them by indigenous people have increased people's fear. These spirits are now more frightening because they are no longer drawn into the webs of reciprocity with humans. Nor is this fear of supernatural forces emanating from earthly homes in specific places confined to indigenous Otavalans. Rural and less educated mestizos have long shared this preoccupation with their indigenous neighbors. Here is an example of syncretism on both sides of the ethnic boundary, where indigenous people made their local spirits more devilish in character in imitation of their more hispanic neighbors, and, in a corresponding fashion, those neighbors increasingly came to emphasize the geographic localization of spiritual power long so meaningful in the official religion of the andean region. Nonetheless, these views on the part of local mestizos exist outside of official Catholicism, as similar unorthodox beliefs have done throughout Europe.

Even saints are treated as ambivalently powerful among indigenous Otavalans. Some saints' actions most often demonstrate their warm and caring personality, and they can be depended upon to be kind to humans. Those saints represented in European iconography as well fed and sporting a beatific gaze are believed by natives to be generally benevolent. However, the power of these loving saints is sometimes suspected of being insufficient to solve a really difficult problem, such as the intractable illness of someone the family cannot afford to let God call home. In such cases, it is often worthwhile, if extremely dangerous, to approach those saints associated with death and destruction to see if their damaging power can restore the balance that will return a family to health and prosperity. Somewhat less innocently, those who would like more wealth and good fortune than is really their due might try to turn a close association with one of those scary saints into personal advantage, usually to the detriment of someone else. One recognizes these saints by their portrayal in painting and sculpture as starving ascetics who carry the instruments of death and gaze inward with a look of intense suffering.

In traditional pan-Andean cosmology, sources of water united the celestial and terrestrial domains. Both water and air, as mobile substances, have the power to mediate between realms and serve a similar place in andean metaphysics (Salomon and Urioste 1991). The dangerous winds that flow from distant geo-spiritual locations into the domestic realm exemplify this. The earth's crust encloses a body of water, dry land surrounds the ocean, and the highest peaks are crowned with frozen water reservoirs in the form of glaciers. Beyond these earthly and watery domains is the sky, from which flows the rain, hail, and frost. The great *amaru*, or primordial snake, and *cuichic*, rainbow, both spring from the lower waters into the sky, saturating it with the water that both falls to the earth again as rain and becomes the mountain glaciers that slowly melt into rivers, flowing swiftly back into the sea. The openings of the earth, especially those associated with water,

Fig. 20. *Potro Pogyo*, a spring in Huaycopungo
(PHOTO BY AUTHOR)

Taita Dios and *Taita Imbabura*　　127

like springs and waterfalls, dripping caves and flood-washed ravines, are especially sacred, and dangerous, as the doors into Pacha Mama's interior realm.

Similarly, the wet world of the steep cloud forests to the east and west and Amazonian rainforests and flooded plains to the east also provide access to the primordial and unifying power of the serpent. While highland Quichua speakers called the native human inhabitants of the rainforest *aucacuna*,[4] savages, they believe that these *sacha runa* (forest people) are owners of particularly efficacious medicines and mind-altering drugs, a special ability to approach the spirits directly, and other esoteric knowledge native to their dark and humid environment. The sacha runa may be precultural in the minds of the highland natives, but as such they are closer to the primordial sources of natural power. All highland shaman periodically make pilgrimages to the lowlands for purification and intensification of their own healing abilities.

Religious Specialists

People in Huaycopungo seek the help of all sorts of religious specialists, who may be indigenous or mestizo; native or foreign; entirely hispanic Catholic, almost exclusively removed from Catholicism and immersed in native spiritual knowledge, or a mixture of both. In fact, in recent decades all kinds of foreign missionaries, from Hare Krishna disciples to Jehovah's Witnesses, have attracted Otavaleño interest as well. Nonetheless, in this chapter we will be concerned primarily with the interaction of Catholic Christianity and religious beliefs and behaviors with a more native origin. The list of Catholic religious specialists is lead by priests and completed with the local bishop, members of religious orders, lay prayer leaders, and sacristans. Among the least Catholic of religious specialists are the *yachaccuna*, specialists in native esoteric knowledge who engage in shamanic practice. But even yachaccuna all include some conceptions or ritual behaviors drawn from Christianity in their practice. Other native healers, including midwives, herbalists, and bonesetters, must also learn to manipulate spiritual power in their practice, although to a lesser degree than yachaccuna.

Elders who have sponsored a number of calendrical festivals and who have demonstrated a special interest and ability in learning the ritual protocol are also recognized as masters of some spiritual knowledge. Among these are a few elders who specialize in a sort of clown role. They are expected to drink continuously throughout a ritual event, but always exaggerate any drunkenness they may actually experience, and act as deconstructors of any order that is displayed or enacted by the ritual's participants. If there is a procession dancing straight ahead, they weave in and out of the line. Wherever they are found, they attempt to insult or embarrass the mighty, make magnified and inappropriate advances toward little girls and young women, married or not, periodically shout obscenities or make lewd jokes, join in dance presentations and take drunken pratfalls when the dancers are executing an especially tricky move, tease children, and pick fake fights with other men. They look distinctly messy, like typical drunks, with uncombed hair, dirty old clothes, and imperfectly focusing eyes, in a group of people who pride themselves, and are known internationally, for the elegant simplicity and cleanliness of their clothes and hair. In fact, the phrase meaning messy hair, *uma sapa*, is used as a metonym for retarded or mentally ill. Like other sacred clowns around the world, their acting out of antistructure preserves the balance and allows humans a generally structured life in a world that inevitably must manifest both tendencies. This is a strange role to claim for a "religious specialist" since they embody a less desirable pole of the sacred, rather than acting to ensure a world that is beneficial for humans; nevertheless, their role is essential for a proper human relation with the cosmos.

Shaman, called yachaccuna, are healers, mostly consulted at times of personal crises, like illness or despair or the repetitive loss of productive resources. The ability to work with spirits successfully is believed to be inborn, a particular form of spiritual strength that, nonetheless, needs to be developed through discipline, practice, and guidance from more experienced spiritual specialists. In addition to yachaccuna, all native healers and lay ritual leaders, including midwives, herbalists, bonesetters, prayer masters, and elders who have completed a series of ritual sponsorships, are said to be *yachac* to a certain extent, through a combination of their natural powers, their efforts to learn, and their close association with the forces of life and death. If they did not become knowledgeable and skillful with esoteric power, they would be very vulnerable to supernatural harm themselves and more likely to worsen, rather than improve, the condition of their patients, clients, or the community as a whole. In Huaycopungo everyone recognizes the power of native esoteric knowledge but uses the few specialists in that knowledge on an irregular basis. Furthermore, while some individuals in and originally from Huaycopungo claim to be *yachac*, knowledgeable in the spiritual arts, they are relatively amateur and no one truly adept lives there. For powerful healing, one must range farther afield, to Ilumán in the north of the cantón, to the high mountain peaks, or beyond them to the tropical forests on the eastern and western slopes. Nor do the yachaccuna have any special role in the major fiestas of the ritual calendar. For these reasons, they will not be a focus in the examination of religious practice below.[5]

Priests are the Catholic religious specialists most frequently sought out, albeit with the same mixture of awe and fear in the pursuit of pragmatic goals as are shamans. Priests are rarely called to heal physical, psychological, or economic woes, most likely since they have rarely offered their services for such things. A few priests I have met may consider themselves to be pastors to their flocks, both indian and mishu, but their indian parishioners rarely see them in that light. However, people highly desire the priest's ritual skills for calendrical and life-cycle rites, although regular attendance at mass is extremely rare. Until recently, even confirmation in the church was a formality, since a proper catechism of children who spoke no Spanish was virtually impossible. Frustrated priests talked at indigenous children and taught them to recite meaningless noises back to them. Orthodox and institutional Catholic teaching was, if anything, even less understood and susceptible to analysis than the complex of indigenous-led efforts to influence the realm of the sacred space/time.

Since among mestizos, the priesthood constitutes a socially acceptable career for someone of relatively high status or a route to upward social mobility for those of more humble birth, local priests are likely to be part of, or desire to be part of, the socially distant and powerful mestizo elite. Indigenous people usually avoid such notables in everyday affairs, approaching them with great humility, familial feeling, and generosity when their material, social, or spiritual resources need to be directed to the runa world. The honorifics used on such occasions are all in Spanish, such as *Su Merced* (your grace), rather than the less distancing Taita.

All priests in San Rafael and in the larger towns of the cantón have an impossible role to play. They must mediate between the local traditions and the contemporary directives of the Mother Church; between the local mestizo elite, so lowly by national standards but so obsessed with raising their status in others' eyes, and the runacuna; between their own urban upbringing and education and the poor and uncultivated rural reality; and between their desires to live well but simply and the severe economic restrictions of an impoverished parish. No two priests that I have known in the last decades, a period of tremendous turnover, have chosen the same strategy for dealing with these conflicts. There have been priests who have catered to the local elite and derided the indians, while agreeing grudgingly, and for a hefty fee, to officiate at indigenous ceremonial events, and those who have struggled to release indians from what seems to them to be the linked bondages of poverty, mishu exploitation, and idolatrous false consciousness. There have been those who lived in splendor in Otavalo, usually supported by relatives, and those who lived in simple poverty in San Rafael.

Ritual Life

During the late 1970s in Huaycopungo, the ceremonial cycle began with the first harvests in the spring and ended with the last harvests in October, when preparations would begin for next year's planting at the start of the rains, usually in November. In this bipartite arrangement, so common among native agricultural peoples of the New World, the spirits withdrew from direct interaction with humans during the colder, wetter months of the year. Since we are hardly north of the equator in Otavalo, the division into cold and warm months of the year has little if anything to do with the position of the sun. In the highlands, it is colder in the rainy season and warmer in the dry season because the absence of daytime clouds allows the sun's warmth to be felt, but on Ecuador's lowland coast, it is colder in the dry season and warmer in the wet season when the clouds at night keep the day's heat from escaping. Between the fall and spring equinoxes, it is the wet season, and the spirits were preoccupied in their distant realms with maintaining their own fertility, which would, in turn, ensure the proper conditions of warmth and moisture for the growth of plants and animals in the months to come. During the warmer and drier months, the spirits moved into closer association with the humans who were invoking them to celebrate their bounty, beginning with the first harvests around the spring equinox and ending with the last harvests at the autumn equinox.

The most costly ritual sponsorship, Corazas, spanned the entire fiesta season. Easter, or Pascua Florida, signaled the first appearance of Corazas, officially in celebration of the parish's patron saint, San Luis. Although every fiesta seems to pack in as much diverse symbolic significance as is possible, one theme may tend to dominate. Hierarchy and humility, wealth and poverty, authority and submission are the central theme of Corazas. The outrageously ornamented

Fig. 21. The *Capitan de Corazas*
(PHOTO BY AUTHOR)

Fig. 22. The *castillo* for *Gallos Pasai*

(PHOTO BY AUTHOR)

Taita Dios and *Taita Imbabura*   133

sponsors, called *Capitanes de Corazas* or just *Corazas*, first presented themselves, and their many attendants, to the parish during Holy Week. On the eve of August 19, San Luis's day, the Corazas's next, and most elaborate, ritual performance began. Depending on the resources of the competing Corazas, this fiesta ended approximately one to two weeks later. Finally, the Corazas would sometimes appear again very briefly to close the ritual season in October.

In addition to Corazas, the ritual calendar included the summer solstice ceremony called San Juan, or Inti Raymi, celebrated for a week beginning on June 24. Gallos Pasai, the smallest fiesta sponsorship, could be undertaken during the week of San Juan. Finally, Pendoneros, another ritual sponsorship, took place in October. San Juan was and is a complex festival of many parts, but it can be summed up as a typical ritualized reversing of the world order and direction in order to renew it. San Juan clearly expressed the symbolism of ensuring the passage of the sun and moon through the sky as a metonym for the continuance of space and time as a whole. As it was played out in the last few decades, a temporary reversal of ethnic relations was also a major theme. Gallos Pasai aimed to stimulate abundance for the following year by the conspicuous offering of food and drink to the spirits during the current harvest season. Pendoneros literally means "flag bearers," this was visually represented by the red flag–topped staffs carried by the ritual sponsors and their assistants. Pendoneros was an inter-community battle for sacred territory. Regional unity through directed conflict was acted out in the competition between different communities, represented by this year's sponsors, to conquer a special chapel and the dance ground in front of it.

RITUAL SPACES IN MOTION

The stunning geography of Ecuador, with high mountains, temperate interandean valleys, deep tropical jungles, and coastal lowlands occupying a small east-west range, has been a rich source of symbolic material for interpreting the cosmos for thousands of years. No cursory examination here could possibly do justice to this topic. Nonetheless, the relationship of places nearby to visible but distant places in the mountains or down the length of a valley, the relationship of ecosystems at low and high altitudes that serve both as sources of production

Fig. 23. *San Juan/Inti Raymi*
(PHOTO BY AUTHOR)

Taita Dios and *Taita Imbabura*   135

Fig. 24. Victorious *Pendoneros* dance in front of chapel
(PHOTO BY AUTHOR)

and as a differentiation of the landscape into a multitude of micro-ecological zones all make attention to the geography highly compel-ling. For purposes of this discussion, we will concentrate on the uses of space in processions, the organization of people into various levels of the nested series of sociospatial units for specific events, and, most particularly, in the ritual division of the world into upper, *janan*, and lower, *urai*, moieties. More abstract directions such as up and down, inside and outside, in front and behind, here and there are all simi-larly elaborated in ritual action, particularly with reference to specific places. Familiar preoccupations with hierarchy and equality, conflict and cooperation, and unity and differentiation are all revisited with these directional symbols. Lastly, the ancient meaning of *Pacha*, or World, refers to Space/Time, rather than just the space itself; ritual in Huaycopungo continues that experience of space and time as indis-solubly linked, hence the centrality of movement in space, rather than just the places themselves.

In the previous chapter we saw how people crisscrossed the community on its chaquiñancuna, rounding the curve at Jurubi, following the old Pan-American Highway past the school, then speeding up along the ravine from which the community gets its name, down toward the stadium with the lake and Taita Imbabura as a backdrop, across again past the spring, past the pre-Columbian mound that sparks conjecture, and up the interminable hill toward Jurubi again, to share labor, advice, special events, and especially alcoholic drinks with one another. The chaquiñancuna fused the people and the land into an active and productive alliance facilitated by local and more distant spirits. The fiestas of the ritual calendar deepen and widen the sacralization of the geographic space of Huaycopungo's world. Common conceptualizations of social and spiritual space include (1) a center-periphery model; (2) a nested series as described in chapter 1; and (3) interacting polarities. The most Catholic and hispanic dimension of their world is the center-periphery dimension of the parish and beyond. Polarities of space mark the most native spatial symbolism.

In the 1970s the central plaza of San Rafael was a bare, dusty space where the observing eye would be quickly drawn away to the panorama provided by Lago San Pablo and Taita Imbabura to the northeast or toward the imposing buildings, perennially in need of another coat of whitewash, on three sides. On the upward-sloping side of the plaza, the church's tall blank walls dominate the view; steps lead up from the plaza to the ornately carved entrance of the sanctuary. On ordinary days, the plaza presented a sad, bedraggled, windswept countenance, but during fiestas it was alive with crowds in navy blue wool, outlined with white and accented with startlingly bright-colored shawls or scarves. Competing tunes on recorder and panpipes provided background to the dancing men, and a few women, adding to the pandemonium of voices lifted in song, excited greetings, and gossip. Fragrant wisps of smoke rose from cooking fires, while small groups of people passed gourd bowls of asua back and forth to a designated server. The culminating moments of the festival sponsorship of Corazas, which occurs during Easter Week and on San Luis Day, August 19, take place on the plaza, where each comuna in the parish had its own corner, from which they would begin processions and to which they would withdraw after interacting in the center.

Fig. 25. San Rafael Plaza during *Corazas*, 1978
(PHOTO BY AUTHOR)

The plaza was kept bare for these large indigenous festivals. In the local mestizo thinking, the indians would have wrecked any ambitious, but at the time misguided, attempts at an ordered and civilized park. The plaza was most suffused with the power of the Catholic God and of the institutional church. At the same time, it was centrally located in the social realm of the dominating mishu, a relic of the colonial imposition of an intertwined sacred and secular authority over the indigenous populations. Legend has it that San Luis, the patron deity of a major church in Otavalo proper, appeared miraculously one morning in the new church in San Rafael in the eighteenth century, and thus the new cult was built. It is likely that some such ploy as pretending the statue came by himself was used, or accepted, by the church in order to recruit parishioners into the new orbit and away from the services in Otavalo. San Rafael's plaza represented a place of superior social and spiritual power compared to the indigenous living spaces, accepted both as a public policy and an explicit truth by San Rafael's mestizos and as an unpalatable but nevertheless inescapable fact of life for the runacuna of the parish. From the point of view of the San Rafael mestizos, this was the only possible and acceptable reality. The few indigenous counterexplanations they were aware of were not considered to be principled resistance, but the befuddlement of the uneducated and unintelligent.

From the runacuna perspective of polarities, this plaza and the San Rafael church together represented one ritual pole of a spiritual continuum from the most Catholic to the most indigenous. At the other extreme of the runa-mishu continuum were the ritual dance grounds, also kept clear for periodic use, in each indigenous community of San Rafael. Near the lakeshore adjacent to Rio Itambi, a small but permanent river flowing into Lago San Pablo, lies the place where Huaycopungo's Cali Uma rituals were carried out. While *uma* is literally "head" in Quichua, in this context it refers to the masks that are worn to represent spiritually charged "others" who danced during fiestas. The most typical is called the Aya Uma in pure Quichua or Diablo Uma in a mix of Spanish and Quichua; the first literally means Spirit Head/Mask and the latter Devil Head/Mask. In either case they are meant to invoke fear, with the face on both sides, often with the features rearranged, the eyes but slits and multicolored medusa strands coming out of the head. The grass-covered ground near Rio Itambi is uneven and apt to have cowpats, so one must pick one's step carefully when crossing it, but the air seems fresher and sharper, perhaps because of the added humidity near the lakeshore. Here, away from streetlights, the quick changes of light and dark characteristic of the equator are more noticeable, especially with the altered sense of time achieved with continuous music and dancing. Taita Imbabura looms even larger and closer there as its slopes begin just across the lake. At a Cali Uma, festive behavior is carried out as freely as possible, although never entirely free, from mishu control and Catholic religious orthodoxy. It is also closer to the many sources of supernatural power, including God's, inherent in the animated physical environment, since it is distant from the town and even relatively distant from indigenous households.

The introduction presented an andean perception of the world as an entity that divides naturally into interacting polarities, whose conflicts and cooperations are the source of the world's dynamic

Fig. 26. Walking to *Cali Uma*;
boy lagging behind wears an *Aya Uma* mask
(PHOTO BY JACQUELINE PURCELL CALLISTER)

Fig. 27. Huaycopungo *Cali Uma*
during Levantimiento Indígena
(PHOTO BY JACQUELINE PURCELL CALLISTER)

continuation and also of many of its small- and large-scale changes. Basic patterns of thinking that are part of the Euro-American heritage place such ambivalence and paradox outside of structure, outside of domesticated or sacred space and practice, and attempt to confine it to the wild, the untamed, the liminal, the transgressing, and the transforming. In contrast, traditional andean thought seems to try to domesticate the paradoxes created by opposition, such as the equal potential of spiritual powers to help or to harm or the equal likelihood that gender differences will produce conflict or symbiotic cooperation. By "domesticate" is meant, for example, that ritual acts out and thereby channels and forms these structural poles for maximum human benefit, rather than trying to conquer or banish one of them, such as evil or gender conflict, from human society. In the andean worldview the paradoxes should be an integral part of thought and action within a society, rather than a threat to it. Allowing their interaction to unfold without human guidance would be hazardous, but even more dangerous would be attempting to eliminate one pole or the other. Too long or energetically suppressed, and the less desirable pole would spring back with an uncontrollable and devastating force.

Given this perspective that hierarchies must be periodically reversed for a proper balance, Cali Uma assumes a higher position than the plaza in San Rafael at certain moments in the major fiestas. Under Taita Imbabura's shadow, the most intense spiritual power, even the potential for a renewal of indigenous secular power, was concentrated, explicitly challenging the ordinary hierarchical structures. Both the church's power and the church's insignificance were celebrated in these yearly festivals. The summer solstice ceremony explicitly acted out indigenous numerical superiority and potential sovereignty over the local mestizos as well, warning the mestizos that their sustained oppression of indigenous people could lead to an inevitable future reversal of ethnic domination, or *pachakuti*.[6]

Even more important than the contrast between the ritual space at Rio Itambi and the park in San Rafael is the distinction between Janan Shaya and Urai Shaya.[7] This structural form has a long history and wide geographic spread in the Andes. In San Rafael, the dividing line cuts the central plaza in half. Huaycopungo and Cachiviro are part of Urai Shaya, and Tocagon, Cachimuel, and San Miguel represent Janan

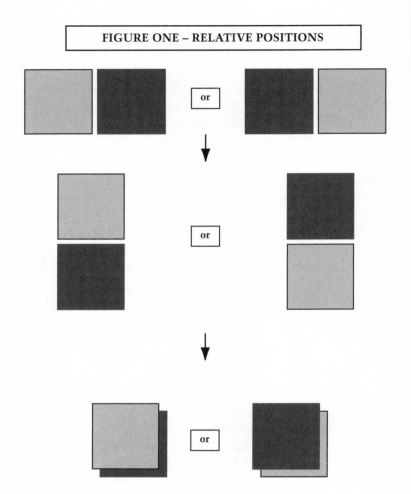

Fig. 28. Relative positions

Shaya. High and low have the metaphorical meaning of hierarchy, here in the sense of first among equals, like older siblings, so Huaycopungo and Cachiviro follow Tocagon, Cachimuel, and San Miguel. The choice of the word "follow" for this relationship is a translation from the Quichua verb *catina*, to follow, and it implies a dynamic interaction more than a static position relative to the other. Just as circle dances must periodically reverse direction, followers must regularly, if briefly, take the role of leaders.

However, when the shayas are not in interactive movement, they stand as complementary mirror images of each other. Tocagon and Huaycopungo are thought of as one cooperative unit of up and down. While Huaycopungo controls access to the river and the lake, with its water for domestic and agricultural uses, fish, totora reeds (so important in mat production), and watercress, Tocagon is situated on the border of the communal highlands up Mojanda's slopes, which are used for firewood collection, occasional pasture, herb gathering, and cold crop cultivation. While Huaycopungo used to be crossed by the Pan-American Highway and is now on its border, Tocagon is crossed by the railroad line. While Tocagon has high pasture, Huaycopungo has lakeside pasture. While Huaycopungo has more water and generally warmer temperatures, Tocagon has more land, and its fields have less early frost risk than the fields in Huaycopungo. Tocagon generally has greater cold crop yields—quinoa, potatoes, and barley, while Huaycopungo is superior in corn, bean, and squash production.

Ritual sponsorship should ideally be balanced between the sides, with an even number of sponsors from Janan Shaya and Urai Shaya, although there is no formal effort to ensure it and an exact balance rarely occurs. Nonetheless, people talk as if it always does. During the festival of Corazas, the different sides have different procession routes around the town, enter the plaza from different directions, sit on different sides of the church, and each have different days of preeminence in the plaza, with Janan Shaya's turn always preceding the turn of Urai Shaya. In anticipation of the event people love to talk about the rivalry and enmity between the two sides during Corazas, as if they were rival football teams. They claim that the reason each side has a day to predominate in the plaza is because otherwise they would fight to the death for preeminence (Ares Quejía 1988). But this talk of rivalry and competition is balanced at other times with cooperative unity.

During Pendoneros another territorial division that crosscuts the distinctions of up and down (Ares Quejía 1988) extends the symbolic space to the entire parish. Two sets of Janan/Urai pairs are opposed to each other, along another pair of directional oppositions, *Vichai Ladu* and *Urai Ladu*. Whereas the other calendrical fiestas utilize San Rafael's plaza for the church-oriented parts of the ritual events, the sponsors of Pendoneros attempt to capture small Catholic chapels with their associated plazas that are no longer in use, if they ever were. One chapel is to the southeast, or Vichai Ladu[8] and the other is to the morthwest, or Urai Ladu. The line that separates the more southern from the northern set of communities crosses the Janan/Urai line perpendicularly in San Rafael's plaza. This second opposition effectively splits the community into four sections. The Janan community(s) continue to compete with the Urai community(s), but they are divided into two groups, Vichai and Urai, who in turn compete with each other.

While the Janan Shaya/Urai Shaya communities are spoken of as being siblings, the Vichai Ladu/Urai Ladu communities are distinguished by gender. Vichai Ladu communities honor the Virgin at a chapel in Tocagon, Janan Shaya, and are therefore identified with the female sacred powers. In contrast, the Urai Ladu communities worship San Miguel at the chapel in San Miguel, also Janan Shaya, and are associated with male spiritual power. In contrast to the sibling-ship metaphor, which expresses similarity of nature and divergence of interest and which is sometimes used to describe the shayas, the use of symbolic gender for the ladus implies an ineradicable difference between the two, which in turn suggests both fundamental conflict and a greater potential for symbiotic union. Siblings are more alike, but the genders are more mutually irresistible and necessary to each other because of their difference.

In reality, contiguous communities, whether they belong to the same or different Janan/Urai pair, suffer real conflict over land use and boundaries, while communities without shared borders more rarely fight with each other. However, contiguous communities have more crosscutting kin ties and a greater history of cooperation as well, so they are not as likely to treat neighbors with the suspicion directed toward relative strangers as they do people from communities that do not share a border. The Urai Shaya communities of the Urai Ladu share a border, as do the communities of Janan Shaya and Vichai Ladu. However, Janan Shaya communities and Urai Shaya communities of both laducuna are relative strangers to one another. It is this symbolic marrying of strangers and extolling the benefits of close kinship that together ritually unite the entire parish, as indeed real relationships of this sort do in an endogamous community.[9]

Processions during the major fiestas linked the four major spaces reserved for large ritual events with an audience—the plaza, Cali Uma, and the chapels to San Miguel and the Virgin—but more importantly they stitched together a variety of places of major and minor importance throughout the limits of the community. Each house was a place with sacred importance for the resident family, and whether family members stopped their work to attend as participants or audience or whether they noted the processing dancers as they passed the gate of their huasi, they were joined into the webs of integration being woven by those who had undertaken sponsorship of the fiesta. During Corazas, San Juan, and Gallos Pasai, many households were indeed boda huasicuna as they also used this time of harvest to undertake the baptisms, confirmations, and marriages of their children. These more family-oriented celebrations were thought not to conflict with the public fiestas but to add to them. Not only were the human members of the community joined, the spirits of the places themselves were also brought into direct interaction with the participants during sacred moments. It is one thing to stand in the plaza of San Rafael and invoke Jurubi, a named corner with a long view of the lake, the surrounding communities, and Taita Imbabura, or Potro Pogyo, one of the springs. It is another to stop a procession at this spot to dance to special tunes, recite prayers, and share several cups of asua or trago, and thereby engage the spirits one-on-one as you would a human whose boda huasi you visited.

The movement through the landscape in each of these fiestas involves social and spatial relationships larger than the community and even the parish. Some of the activities during San Juan/Inti Raymi include neighboring parishes and to some extent the entire cantón of Otavalo as well. As we will see, a bigger dance ground than the one at Rio Itambi sits across the lake in Araque and hosts thousands of visitors from around the lake for the Cali Uma during one day of the week-long summer solstice festival.

RITUAL BATTLE AND SYMBIOTIC UNION

The theme of battle runs through all of the fiestas, since it ensures both the activation of the energy necessary for future production and the reversal to harmony and cooperation that will be required to harness that energy for human endeavors. The most dramatic enactment of battle is probably the struggle to capture the opposed chapels during Pendoneros. Ares Quejía gives us a vivid account of rituals that took place at the chapel of the Virgin during a Pendoneros observed and recorded by her in 1976. The participants are from Huaycopungo, Urai Shaya and Urai Ladu, and Tocagon, Janan Shaya, Urai Ladu, but they refer to previous events involving themselves and the participants from Vichai Ladu. "Entonces se reúnen todos los Pendoneros delante de la capilla y colocándose enfrente comienzan a andar lentamente hacia ella, en un momento dado se vuelven bruscamente y comienzan a besarse y morderse en las orejas, hombres con hombres y mujeres con mujeres, diciendo 'Ya somos hermanos, ya hemos separado a la Virgen de Dios'" [Then all the Pendoneros gather together in front of the chapel and facing it, they begin to walk slowly toward it, then at a given moment they turn quickly and begin to kiss and bite each other on the ears, men with men and women with women, saying, "Now we are brothers and sisters; now we have separated the Virgin from God" (1988 78; my translation)]. In Ares Quejía's analysis the last statement refers to the joining of the opposed Janan/Urai southern pair into brotherhood and sisterhood, in contradistinction to the northern Janan/Urai pair, from whom they have separated. That northern pair are celebrating in the same manner at the Chapel to San Miguel.

The alternate biting and kissing during this example is as clear a representation of the linked nature of conflict and cooperation, enmity and love, violence and tenderness as one could imagine. But other forms of conflict also take place during Pendoneros and the other fiestas. Pendoneros, Corazas, and San Juan all contain enactments of battle, in which it is desirable to draw blood. During the mock battles to capture the dance ground of Pendoneros, the participating sponsors and their attendants strike at each other with their flag-topped staffs, attempting to inflict shallow wounds. During a part of the Corazas fiesta, the *limai*,[10] the Corazas's costumed assistants, the *Yumbos*, named for the native peoples of the western cloud forests and lowland rainforests,[11] are required to chase the Corazas on horseback around the plaza and through the streets of the town throwing hard candies at their faces. While the Corazas dodge the candies and try to avoid a direct hit, they must not cover their faces. The chase ends when "the Coraza is wounded in the face and bleeding" (Ares Quejía 1988, 57;

my translation). Similarly, throughout the weeklong festivities for San Juan/Inti Raymi, men from neighboring communities would ambush and fight each other. In the 1970s, the communities at the northern end of the lake, in the parish of Eugenio Espejo, were especially known for their San Juan rock fights, where the combatants competed to inflict a bleeding wound on their rivals and to demonstrate their superior prowess over their neighboring rivals. San Juan fights have occasionally ended in deaths, usually as the result of real conflict between individuals over sex partners or between families, comuna sections, or comunas over land boundaries.

While lay and professional observers alike have most often interpreted this orchestrated violence as the unfortunate side effect of continuous drunken revelry, in fact they are a necessary part of maintaining the proper balance of conflict and cooperation in the world, according to the traditional worldview. Furthermore, the blood spilled during these ritual battles once undoubtedly served as a blood sacrifice

Fig. 29. *Yumbos* attempt to wound *Coraza*'s face with candies
(PHOTO BY AUTHOR)

to the spirits. In the Incaic and pre-Incaic past, religious sacrifices included domestic animals and even people. It is most likely that a blood sacrifice was once a fully recognized part of the rituals, while now the behavior remains with an attenuation of meaning. Today no one says that the spilling of blood during fiesta conflicts is a sacrifice to God or Pacha Mama. Nonetheless, the violence is still considered a traditional part of these ritualized events. Even without the significance of blood sacrifice, violent conflict as one kind of interaction between pairs of opposites makes perfect sense. The power unleashed by the clashing of opposites—whether the flame of sexual desire between humans, which they think of as a kind of war, or the lightning, provoked by the anger of the mountain gods with each other, that opens the skies to release rain—can be channeled by humans, in reciprocal obligation with the gods, into forms of increase: children or fertile, well-watered fields. An avoidance or suppression of violence would deprive the world of a source of energy for its healthy continuation. The word *tincui* still refers to this kind of generative conflict. Such things as a dance form where men and women flirt by trying to inflict wounds on one another (Allen 1988), the powerful confluence of two mountain streams, and ritual battles have all been called by this term. The kissing, biting ritual in Pendoneros described above could be called a kind of tincui.

For decades, the mestizo authorities made a special effort to control and end the San Juan fighting, so this is an extremely sensitive and contested area of ritual behavior. It is interpreted from the outside as the result of heavy drinking and intercommunity rivalry, and certainly those factors do play a part in the events. But the deeply metaphysical interpretation of rivalry and fighting and the expectation of supernaturally proferred gain from such ritualized, and sometimes deadly, violence are completely ignored. Humans have a responsibility to recognize and honor conflict, with the hope that by their behavior, they can minimize the negative impact on themselves. With the goodwill of Taita Dios and other spiritual forces, they can turn what might otherwise be chaotic and terrifying violence into a structure of ordered competition and choreographed bloodshed. But rather than seeing a way to socially and supernaturally control ineradicable intercommunity rivalry and direct it toward regional unity, mestizos have interpreted it as unbridled license to engage in violence and destroy regional harmony. The reason for this lack of understanding is not only the differing metaphysical principles underlying the runa and mishu worlds, but the need on the part of the ruling group to control all licit violence in their domination of minority groups. Therefore, they could not acknowledge the disparate principles even if they had understood them thoroughly.

Across the lake from Huaycopungo is a larger dance ground at Araque, where people from several parishes come on Wednesday during San Juan. There the dancers are not all Otavaleños; some are indigenous people of another ethnic group, locally known as Puendo(a)s, for the huge pleated wool skirts worn by the women, or Mocho(a)s, for the cropped hair of the men or, most recently, Cayambis. The unsupervised competitions often resulted in fights, and a level of intergroup rivalry and male violent reaction is an expected part of the whole event, though by no means the only one. The atmosphere of a union interwoven from many atomized parts predominates despite the expectation of rivalry and some violence. Secondly, soccer matches were introduced in the late 1960s and have become common throughout the cantón. San Juan often features intercommunity or interparish soccer competitions. In the 1970s I was repeatedly told in Huaycopungo that their community was trying to avoid the intervention of the mestizo police in their celebrations by avoiding overtly violent conflict.

RITUAL HIERARCHY AND HUMILITY

Hierarchy and humility, the main themes of the Corazas fiesta, are similarly represented as a search for balance between an acceptance of the ineradicable fact of power inequality with an attempt to maximize its benefits to the less powerful, and a desire to limit hierarchy and redirect the flow of excess resources from the mighty to the weak. Great inequality in the social sphere occasions more resentment and attempts to limit its scope, while spiritual inequality is embraced willingly so long as humans have the ability to stay in the good graces of the potentially overwhelming sources of power. While this results in the kind of paternalistic politics that political scientists decry as characteristic of an immature social order and devastating to human dignity, it can provide sources of agency to those who have been left out of the more democratic civil institutions, as long as the honor, or social capital, they are able to offer the powerful is regarded by the recipients as a sufficiently attractive resource.

During Corazas, the sponsor, or Capitan de Corazas, volunteers to symbolically represent the highest possible power positions, sacred and secular, for both personal and communitywide benefit. The personal benefit for the Coraza himself (rarely herself) is mostly symbolic capital at the expense of economic capital, while the community expects to receive and increase in material resources from the grateful spirits. The Coraza is challenged to expend an excess of resources— from physical energy to social skills to money and stored food—and to go beyond what is simply possible or imaginable to the point of causing awe among the observers. While prestige is won by a surpassing performance, part of the effort of the other participants is to push the Coraza too far—into drinking too much, sleeping too little, spending more than he can afford, and demonstrating an overweening pride that calls for an orchestrated fall. On the social level, the Coraza sets himself up to be admired and honored, as well as mocked and stripped of resources. On the spiritual level, the Coraza's spectacular expenditure of resources in the name of the community should so impress the sources of power in eternal space/time that benefits flow unceasingly to all. There has long been a controversy in the literature about these ritual sponsorships, whether they are an economic leveling device or whether they help build up the symbolic capital of those who maintain a high level of economic capital, thus reinforcing their power over others in their own and subsequent generations. It is an empirical question in any particular case whether one or the other outcome dominates, but the system makes both possible and the indigenous communities struggle to maintain some form of balance between the two competing interests.

Remember the imaginative description of Taita Imbabura presented at the start of the chapter, with his clothes of fine cloth and ornaments of gold and feathers. The Capitan de Corazas too has a resplendent outfit ornamented with shiny glass jewels, brass chains and pendants, dyed feathers, and multicolored sequins. Ares Quejía (1988) attempted to locate the origins of the figure represented and found the closest match in the reenactment of a colonial military honor given to a special cavalry regiment. Putting aside the origins and concentrating on the contemporary symbolism, the Coraza in his finery clearly represents extreme hierarchy, whatever the original forms, be it military, divine, ecclesiastical, or royal. The Coraza's costume seems to be a pastiche of a variety of wearable symbols of power. While mestizos told Ares Quejía that the costume resembled a king's, I also see a parodic version of the heavily decorated surplices that bishops may use at mass. Ares Quejía also examines in depth a hypothesis that one hears among indigenous participants that Atahualpa is being represented but discards it, only after identifying items of the Coraza's attire that are also described in accounts of the last, and part Ecuadorian, Incan emperor.

The Capitan de Corazas wears a tunic with a large mantle and a pair of pants, all made of white satin. But the mantle, the bottom of the tunic, and the pants below the knees are heavily encrusted with lace, embroidery, appliqué, and sequins of many colors. Strings of pearls lie on the Coraza's chest and, during the formal parts of the festival, his face is covered by what is called an *uma*, literally "head" but signifying "mask" in this context. Golden chains strung with medals, pearls, glass jewels and pendants completely cover his face, painted white. The chains hang from a hat shaped by sewing two highly decorated felt half-moons together at the rounded edges. It is worn over a blue handkerchief tied on his head. From the crown of the hat waves a line of dyed ostrich plumes. When he does not don the uma, an ordinary felt hat, decorated in front with sequins and feathers, tops the blue kerchief. His long hair is carefully formed into ringlets, called *churros* for the tiny land snails that are a festive delicacy. He wears decorated shoes and socks, instead of the sandals that make up both everyday and dress footwear for runa. In his gloved hand he carries a golden staff decorated with paper flowers and a black umbrella that he uses to shade himself from the sun. He rides on horseback and is called patron, or "master." The origins of these items are so diverse, from both hispanic and indigenous traditions, that a contemporary attempt to represent an overabundance of wealth and power from all available sources best encapsulates its symbolism. They in every way contradict the ordinary appearance of a runa man, from the white face to the gloves, from being mounted on horseback to wearing shoes, from the decorated clothes made of neither wool nor cotton to the surfeit of jewels. In addition, in a strikingly similar way to the costumes assumed by Inca elite in the early colonial period festivals in Cuzco, Peru, described by Dean, they represent the attempt by contemporary indigenous people to craft their own identity and power out of a variety of sources, rather than allowing themselves to be confined by the definitions of others. Allow me to quote her description at length, since her analysis of colonial costumes worn by the elite so clearly applies to Corazas in twentieth-century Otavalo as well.

> Although in daily life, Inka *caciques* commonly mimicked elite Hispanic fashion, they crafted a transcultural costume that underscored their mediative role between Inka past and Christian present, Hispanic colonial authorities and native constituencies, in order to participate in Christian festivals. In "voicing" two visual rhetorics, a third was created and, through it, mediativity was pronounced. This third voice is heard not by listening for pre-Hispanic Inka utterances and separating them from European sounds, but by attending to the cadence of the interstices. By examining the costume worn by Inka nobles for Corpus Christi . . . we come to see that colonial Inka elites understood how, being compelled to cultural hybridity, they could fashion their own bodies as empowered sites of cultural confluence. (Dean 1999, 122–23)

The Capitan de Coraza's mounted attendants include two or more Yumbos and at least one *Loa*. The Yumbos are costumed in a slightly less elaborate version of the Coraza's costume, but in pink or blue rather than white. Their faces are painted white like his, but they do not wear the uma. The Loa is usually a mestizo child, dressed with ribbons crossing his chest and a cockaded hat, who, at key moments in the ritual, recites from memory a long praise poem in Spanish. The Capitan de Coraza's wife or other female counterpart accompanies him on foot, dressed in her best clothes, topped with her husband's felt hat when he is wearing the uma and carrying his decorated staff while he is on horseback. Other assistants include the ritual counselors; the caretakers of the mask, the Coraza's person, the horses, the alcohol supply,

Fig. 30. Two *Loa*s in San Rafael's church
(PHOTO BY AUTHOR)

Fig. 31. *Yumbos* and *Corazas* await mass for San Luis
(PHOTO BY AUTHOR)

Taita Dios and *Taita Imbabura* 153

and the fireworks; the cooks; the indigenous musicians; the mestizo band; the mestiza dresser who rents the costume; and water carriers.

It is not immediately obvious how this pageant fits into religious practice, whether Catholic, indigenous, or some mix of both. This opacity probably results, in part, from the necessity for indigenous people to adapt to the requirements of the missionizing church, disguising rituals that the priests would not approve in forms they would deem acceptable. Little by little they might incorporate elements of meaning to themselves in pageants the priests or secular authorities directed them to enact.[12] In honor of San Luis, the patron saint of the parish, the indigenous people stage a pageant that reenacts a secular triumph of power, combining the power of the state and the church that was a fact of life during the colonial and early national eras. Given this secular/sacred conflation, it is not surprising that the liberal reform era of the beginning of the twentieth century resulted in 1918 with an attempt to outlaw the indigenous fiestas.

In this reading, the Corazas fiesta is a way for ambitious runa to stake their claim to prestige and power. However, as it is a parishwide event, the mishucuna did everything they could to monopolize the resources necessary for fiesta sponsorship and to encourage indians toward ever greater expenditure to the point of incurring great debt to themselves, as a way to short-circuit the process of runa socioeconomic ascension and fuel their own. Ambitious runa might acquire prestige among their fellows but become ruined financially, transferring their excess into the hands of the local mishu elite, themselves desperate to enhance their own pitiful socioeconomic status beyond the parish boundaries at the expense of the indigenous people. Looked at this way, it should become clear that the Corazas fiesta, far from being an indigenous tradition passed on intact from the grandfathers, was the locus of ongoing social and economic contestation between the subordinate indigenous majority and the superordinate mestizo minority as well as a battle for making and interpreting the meaning of life in this world and its connection to the sacred. The display of such lavish symbols of power, far greater than anything presented during the year by the mestizos of San Rafael, the unstinting generosity with food and drink, and the occupation by a thousand runacuna of the streets of the tiny parish capital must all be read as a momentary overturning of the everyday power balance. San Rafael runacuna seized symbolic wealth and power from the hands of their poor mestizo neighbors in a religious ritual sponsored by the hispanic Catholic Church, if only in a symbolic gesture that could be read simultaneously as a joke, a warning of their potential might, and a relief from their feelings of oppression. Looked at this way, it may be closer to contemporary performance art that highlights and destabilizes issues of race and ethnicity, such as the performances of John Leguizamo, rather than some solemn religious rite staged by an orthodox cult.

In the religion fashioned by indigenous people from both streams of the sacred, the Corazas festival served other functions as well. Like agriculturalists worldwide, the people of Huaycopungo offered their first fruits and late harvest surpluses in thanks for this year's production and in a plea for the rain to plant the next year's crops in the fall. Celebrating runa made offerings to the spiritual forces at large throughout the landscape, from the church in the town plaza to the

Fig. 32. *Corazapac Huarmi*, the *Coraza*'s wife, dances with native musicians at Jurubi

river and natural springs of the comuna. Prayers and mass were offered to Catholic deities in church by the priests and their assistants, and invocations to both Catholic and andean spirits at *misacuna*, or altars, set up in the Coraza's boda huasi and at ritual stops in the Coraza's processions. Resources for a surpassing offering were amassed through competition, rewarding individual households and ayllucuna in prestige, for the benefit of all.

During the 1970s these competing and complementary goals envisioned for Corazas were continually contested. Some priests and San Rafael's other mishucuna supported this fiesta out of some combination of an appreciation of the traditional entertainment and a deep need for the boost to their own income. Others fought it as a combination of superstitious nonsense and source of indigenous impoverishment. Still others derided and promoted it simultaneously, finding that a negative evaluation of the fiesta supported their belief in indigenous inferiority, which, in turn, justified their treating indigenous people as a naïve resource to exploit. It also enabled the priests, like other mestizos, to avoid manual labor and the accompanying stigma themselves and reserve it for the indigenous population. When indians are so self-destructive, why not enjoy the fun and reap the profits? The challenge for runacuna was to balance their attempts to reduce mishu contempt and control, with their efforts to increase their own acceptance of alternative standards of value and their social separation and economic independence from the outside world. Neither was completely achievable, but there was always the possibility of gaining ground by adjusting the balance in one direction or the other.

RITUALS OF WORLD REVERSAL

San Juan/Inti Raymi provides a stunning contrast to the Corazas fiesta's dependence on the local mishucuna. Not only is this fiesta self-consciously removed from mestizo control, it also includes a theme of temporary reversal of the normal interethnic relationships. Huaycopungo residents participate in the weeklong festivities throughout their comuna, at other places in their own and neighboring northern lakeside parishes. The places characterized by the greatest density of participants are in locations relatively distant from the parish centers that mestizos inhabit and control. A world-renewing summer solstice festival, it includes such typical rituals of reversal as a license to mock, ignore, or even insult mestizos in their presence. Mestizos flinch, but politely accept the ridicule and resistance as long as it stays within limits. Presumably they tell themselves that San Juan/Inti Raymi will end in a few days and indigenous people will return to their usual circumspect humility. Again we see the general principle of great hierarchy being upheld by moments of reversal; while it is a fiction, indigenous and hispanic people in Otavalo momentarily agree that the state of things is a mutual agreement that could be reversed at any time, as in Taita Imbabura's paradise.

Like Christmas in the United States, San Juan in Otavalo is an omnipresent focus of the year. Otavaleños everywhere try to come back "to dance," *bailangapac*,[13] they say, even though San Juan is much more than just dancing. While dancing is the central symbol of the fiesta, in andean culture dancing is always accompanied by drinking, and Inti Raymi was also the earliest part of the year when a sufficient surplus of maize could be available for the home production of asua. San Juan/Inti Raymi involved one week of almost continuous movement of people in festive dress to the accompaniment of music, dance, shared food treats, and cups of alcohol from home to home, on every path to the dance plaza on the lake, and to other communities and their dances. Like Christmas in North America, it was inescapable.

Preparations began in the huasicuna, where families brewed asua and, if they had access to an outdoor oven, baked bread, tanda. Starting well after dark, individuals would form and decorate a few bread dolls and animals and then work as a group to produce as many bagel-shaped and barely leavened rolls, called *roscas*, as they could before dawn. Tanda was made to hand out to guests at home or to relatives, compadres, and neighbors met on the paths or at a dance during the week. Families were expected to be at home, rather than in the fields or working elsewhere, so that they could receive guests from their personal network and make visits to the same relatives, compadres, and neighbors. The bread and fresh asua were special treats that attracted visitors, and much discussion revolved around who knew how to make really good bread that was not so tough as to break teeth, or asua that would be well strained and neither too sour to be appetizing nor too fresh and sweet to give a buzz.

If a family could afford it, everyone got a new set of clothes for San Juan/Inti Raymi. People showed off their new outfits during the fiesta and thereafter reserved them for special occasions. Last year's good outfit became this year's daily wear. Traditional clothing is quite expensive, since only the very poor or elderly have worn homespun since the early 1970s. The search for a good but affordable *ruana* (poncho) and *muchicu* (felt hat) for men, a blouse, two *anacos* (wrap skirts), one or two *chumbis* (woven belts), and jewelry for women—not to mention the tailors and seamstresses who could do the finishing work—occupied a good deal of frantic energy right before the holiday. Only a very bad husband would not help his wife purchase something new, and a only a very neglectful wife would not make sure her husband's best pants were as white as snow to start the days of visiting and dancing. The Saturday market in Otavalo buzzed with greater than usual indigenous activity in the beginning of June as couples came to purchase the desired finery; mestizo shopkeepers beamed at them from across the counter with grateful contempt.

Throughout the San Juan of the 1970s the whole comuna was animated by tunes played by small groups of young male musicians and dancers day and night. San Juanitos run to a simple measured tune from house to house for the entire week, demanding in falsetto or low raspy voice to enter, where they dance in a tight circle while playing the songs, also called *San Juanitos*. The men are said to dance twenty-four hours a day for all seven days, and the dancers do make a point of stretching their stamina to the breaking point by continuing to dance and drink for long hours. However, all groups stop and sleep a while and then continue again. Each group may sleep for a few hours at any time of the day or night, so that there are always groups of dancers making the rounds at all times. Older men sometimes join them, and openly admire those who can keep it up for days, but it is generally thought to be the privilege and responsibility of the vigorous young.

San Juanitos are not ordinary humans, although people usually do recognize the costumed dancers. They often wear masks or other clothes to indicate evil spirits, overseers, gringos, or women and they alter their voices accordingly. The people at home, who are sometimes groggy with sleep when the San Juanitos arrive, treat them with a fearful respect, alternating with humor, as if they were visitors from the

Fig. 33. San Juan bread dolls and finery: author's daughter,
Marisa Rivero, and Isabel Criollo's daughter Maria Susana, 1978
(PHOTO BY AUTHOR)

other world. As they finish dancing, the San Juanitos beg for a treat
and threaten a trick if it is not quickly and respectfully forthcoming.
The treat they expect is a drink of asua or trago, although they also
accept food. If denied, they make mocking attempts to steal something
valuable from the home. Not only do San Juanitos violate ordinary
norms of visiting among indigenous people, but, even more than anyone else during the fiesta, San Juanitos egregiously insult the powerful,
including local mestizos, while aggrandizing the humble. They play-
fully violate other taboos as well, such as those against sexual teasing
between a man and his comadre, a man and a little girl, or a man and
his mother-in-law. The efforts made by San Juanitos are called "working," and receiving them in one's house is frequently considered a
burdensome responsibility.

In addition to the house-to-house dancing of the San Juanitos, most
comunas host a public dance at their dance ground on one of the days of

the fiesta. People from all over the region of neighboring parishes come, especially if they are members of the local hosts' social networks. The women bring food and drink, and they make sure it circulates continuously hand to hand. Not only should a woman honor all her families' compadres, kin, affines, or neighbors with something she brought, but she can choose to share a special treat, *wanlla* (Weismantel 1988), received from someone else in recognition of a debt owed or in solicitation of a future favor. The excitement of receiving an endless array of snacks, even if your own family brought only cooked beans and roscas of bread, gives a special appeal to the dance. Mestizos also come, some as spectators but more with hopes of making money by selling soft drinks; candies; fish grilled on portable charcoal fires, or *llapingachos*; cheese-stuffed potato patties, sauteed and brushed with annatto oil from a green-onion brush; or tropical fruits such as oranges, sugarcane, and bananas. The poorer families eye these appetizing treats wistfully, while those with some resources try to share at least one purchased luxury food with those closest to them. Mestizos share one portion of their merchandise with their indigenous compadres, who pass them a handful of toasted corn or a rosca of bread in turn, although they sell to those who are not fictive kin. In fact, their comadres receive one portion free but then most feel obligated to buy several more to share with their families, if they can afford it.

Groups of San Juanitos come to dance competitively, and people sit and watch them, commenting on the costumes, the quality of the music, and the skillfulness of the dancing. Men and older women may join the groups of San Juanitos to dance for a while. In the non-Otavaleño comunas to the south, both men and women dance as San Juanitos, causing great interest and titillating pleasure among the Otavaleño hosts, as only elder women can dance without embarrassment in Huaycopungo. For ambitious men, the shared drinking can be competitive and the female family members keep an eye on them, so they can stop any explosive arguments and carefully escort their male relatives home. The largest dance at the south end of the lake is in Araque, where hundreds of people, both Otavaleños and Mochos, gather lakeside in the same way. In addition, some people from Huaycopungo travel to other large towns to the north, famous for their lively dances and good costumes.

Fig. 34. *Mishu* merchants at *Cali Uma* during San Juan
(PHOTO BY AUTHOR)

These large group events are not choreographed and often seem quite chaotic, with several competing San Juanito tunes being played right next to each other, so that no song can be heard distinctly. The atmosphere of competition, the presence of many drunks, and the traditional expectation of intercomuna violence keep people vigilant as they try to protect their relatives and keep out of trouble themselves. But overall this chaotic conflict can be seen by the spiritual forces above and felt by those within the earth below, who must surely become sated with the food, drink, music, colorful clothing, and dancing and feel positively inclined toward the people congregated at the very end of Imbabura's slopes and on the shores of the lake, two direct access points to the spiritual worlds above and below. Nor can the experience be captured by chaotic conflict alone, because this one-sided activity inevitably elicits the opposite experience, of an interwoven unity of equals who compete and cooperate in equal measure. Given the proper synergy between all these excited and dancing bodies, the whole region can momentarily seem like one pulsating organism. The participants ritually act out their hope that life properly lived will lead to the same conclusion—a generative balance of conflict and interdependence between social relational fields arranged in nested series. These nested series can be seen both from the ego-centered view of individuals, huasi-familias, ayllus (as kindreds), and their different social networks, and from the more hypothetically bounded perspective of ayllus (as descent group), comuna sections, comunas, parishes, and ethnic groups.

During San Juan a family can also choose to sponsor Gallo Pasai. The distinctive symbolic behavior of this fiesta sponsorship is the public displaying of a *castillo* and two staffs, one strung with live guinea pigs and the other live chickens, and both carried horizontally. The castillo is made by lashing poles together into a roof-shaped structure, which measures about three feet long and two feet high. Tied to the poles are luxury items including tropical fruit, chili peppers (*uchu*), money, panela (raw brown sugar in blocks), cigarettes, roscas of bread, bottles of trago, and green onions. Even in the 1970s the luxury items displayed an overwhelmingly nonandean origin; they were luxuries in part because they were purchased. Only the green onions and uchu were luxury items in the preconquest period, although the other items may be mestizo forms of pre-Columbian items, such as corn bread (*chugllu tanda*) or tobacco leaves.

Assistants to the sponsor carry the castillo in processions through the comuna. Other assistants carry the poles onto which white and black guinea pigs and white and black chickens are tied by their legs. Female assistants dance behind the musicians in the procession, also carrying decorated live chickens, bound at their feet, in their hands. These are offerings to the spirits, who can take only their spiritual essence. At the end of San Juan, visitors to the boda huasi of the sponsor are given license to grab the chickens, guinea pigs, and luxury items from the castillo and poles in a competitive rush. But whatever they seize this year they must multiply by a factor of two or more and offer during next year's fiesta. Theft is thus transformed in the following years into remarkable generosity.

Like Christmas, San Juan/Inti Raymi is a solstice ceremony. On the equator people experience both the summer solstice and the winter solstice as times when the sun is at the greatest distance from them, while in the Northern Hemisphere the sun is maximally distant at the winter solstice and maximally close during the summer solstice. However, the winter solstice in both geographic sites marks a time without any agricultural production. In Otavalo, people have finished planting but are beginning to run low on the food stores from last year, while people in the Northern Hemisphere have a long wait to begin planting but still have stores from last year's harvest. However, in Otavalo the summer solstice, the time of San Juan/Inti Raymi, is the heart of a long harvest season, which begins during Holy Week and dribbles to an end by September. While people in Huaycopungo considered the Sun and San Juan Bautista both recipients of special honor during this time, they pay little attention to San Juan besides a quick mass attended on his day, and could not have analyzed the obvious sun symbolism in such things as the behavior of the San Juanitos. While Inti Raymi has had many variations over space and time, one motivation for continuing the ritual was to ensure the continuation of the Sun's trajectory around the earth, a traditional preoccupation of andean religions. During San Juan people act out a controlled reversal of time/space and social relations, a man-made pachacuti, in order to ensure their continuation on the usual path. San Juanitos act out the Sun's responsibility to continue without cease. They overdo it, thus priming the pump of solar energy, by dancing from house to house night and day, rather than disappearing on the western horizon at night. Like the Sun, they circulate the comuna, arriving at a home from one direction, leaving in the other, and returning from the original direction. When they dance, their tight circles start in a clockwise direction; at a signal from a leader they reverse directions briefly, and then return to the clockwise direction. By preempting the inevitable switch in direction to the opposite, they make it possible for the Sun to remain on the direction, from east to west, which is its default route.

Similarly, in the familiar worldwide pattern, San Juan/Inti Raymi is a fiesta where world reversal ensures world renewal. San Juanitos costume themselves as nonindian, not male, nonhuman, not subordinate, not Ecuadorian—and any other negations of their usual identity they can find or imagine. Mestizos do not direct but assist at the sidelines. They have certainly tried and have sometimes succeeded in controlling or changing some part of the festivities or in trying to make them their own, such as curbing the intercomuna rock fights. But in Huaycopungo, overall the understanding by both runa and mishus is that San Juan/Inti Raymi is an indigenous fiesta first. The powerful, especially mestizos, can be ignored or insulted with impunity. The center of ritual action is not the church and plaza but special sites beyond the bounds of homes and fields in the runa communities themselves. People with a powerful work ethic do not work. People who live far away, who have formed satellite communities (Lund Skar 1994) in the city or the jungle or on some faraway lake where totora reeds are plentiful for reed mat production, return "home" to dance.

Although San Juan/Inti Raymi, like all rituals of world renewal, may seem essentially conservative, undergoing temporary reversals in order for long-term reproduction of society as it is to continue, it is nonetheless potentially revolutionary. The reversal is not, like the counterclockwise dancing of the San Juanitos, simply a controlled enactment of the least favorable swing of the pendulum, but in some ways represents the short-lived enjoyment of the longed-for paradise of indigenous prosperity and autonomy. The fact of mestizo political, economic, and social domination makes everyday reality troubling. In San Juan people can act out a "return" to a greater share of the land's bounty. The potentially destabilizing character of this large-scale indigenous mobilizations has long been recognized by local mestizos and has been the focus of attention during the indigenous-led *Levantimientos*, or Uprisings, of the 1990s, as will be seen in part II.

Finally, the theme of a year's renewal is also seen at the start and at the end of the week's activities. Everyone should take a purifying bath in a natural spring to start the holiday, then don his or her new clothes. San Juan ends (and San Pedro begins) when people sweep the house and yard and burn the resulting garbage on the path in front. Small plumes of smoke can be seen up the hills in every direction, as people cleanse their houses for the start of a new year.

Weaving the Threads of the Past into a Brighter Present

Taken together, this set of symbolic resources acted out through the ritual calendar has implications for the reproduction and evolution of society in periods of stability, in slowly changing conditions, and, as we will examine in part II, in situations of rapid transformation. Although any examination of scholarship on the precolonial period suggests a deep root for this kind of conceptualization, it has been further elaborated and reinforced in the context of a postcolonial situation, where being able to embrace two sources of culture that are kept somewhat separate has served as a resource for indigenous pride and persistence. Therefore it is a particularly rich source for understanding the creation of an indigenous religion with clearly bifurcated roots in the context of an ethnically divided society. It is also a potent model for remaining the same, while changing dramatically.

In the late 1970s, the major religious fiestas in Huaycopungo asserted the benefits of separate ethnicity and continued the struggle to widen the envelope in which Otavaleños in general were confined by virtue of being an ethnic minority in their native land, dominated by a society whose most powerful myths of origin, dreams for the future, and measures of worth were crafted abroad. Nonetheless, that ethnic

Fig. 35. Walking home from *Cali Uma*
(PHOTO BY JACQUELINE PURCELL CALLISTER)

Taita Dios and *Taita Imbabura*   165

separateness did not exclude the dominant society's spiritual sources of honor, power, and plenty from the indigenous world but combined them together with other beliefs and practices believed to be autochthonous, in a union that included both the sparks of struggle and the warm embrace of collaboration. Spirituality was lived by individuals every day in their bodily experience of interactions with each other, with their animated environment, and with the humble objects of daily life (Colloredo-Mansfeld 1999), but the group events of the ritual calendar argued larger questions. These took on the well-being of the community as a whole, of the interrelated indigenous communities in a parish and a region and, especially, of the relationships between the dominant society and the Otavaleño runa, a numerical majority at the local level but a minority in the nation. The calendrical festivals explored how the institutions that dominated religious and secular power in their universe, the Ecuadorian government and the Catholic Church, could be religiously explained and simultaneously forced to render whatever material and spiritual advantage to indigenous people that it could. This religious adaptation helped indigenous Otavalans to brighten their present and spiritually craft their own more prosperous future.

CHAPTER FOUR

Cantina and *Boda Huasi*

Local Bar and Ceremonial Open House

The Symbolic Contrasts in
Different Drinking Venues

THE CATHOLIC CHURCH IN SAN RAFAEL, the largest building in town, looms over the open central plaza, with a spire that soars even higher above the dusty streets. One must climb many steps from the plaza to reach the door to the sanctuary's hushed, dark interior, where candles light altars to richly garbed saints, virgins, or Christ. Such images lead into very different symbolic domains from those described in the previous chapter. There religiosity's central images were of cacophonies of the senses—dust clouds from dancing feet, plaintive songs overlapping from competing recorders and panpipes, the pungent smells of asua and cucavi, the cracks and sparks of fireworks, and the swirl of colored woolens—all circulating along the paths of the comuna, from one boda huasi to another, illustrating deep religious sensibilities. While the Corazas brought this tumultuous worship from the boda huasi to the central plaza, when they were blessed inside the church, the Corazas and their entourages sat in silent humility.

The storefront bars, cantinas, that dot the side streets away from San Rafael's central plaza, near which can usually be heard loud male laughter and the snick of pool cues on wooden balls, and from whose doors burst drunk and aggressive men whom the sober try to avoid, represent another domain that contrasts with both the church and the boda huasi. But all three symbolic complexes are intersecting parts of the world of the Otavalo runacuna and have been for five hundred years. This chapter takes us beyond the inward-looking and runa-focused life of chapter 1, which focuses on real people failing to live according to their own ideals, and chapter 2, which presents the extremely generalized and idealized patterns of runa social and religious behavior. We will extend the exploration, begun in chapter 3, of the symbolic runa-mishu boundaries and their intersections. This chapter looks more closely at how social interaction between local mestizos and indigenous people leads to cultural changes that many of the latter would like to prevent. Drinking behavior is not just ritual in service of a religious worldview, but much more. Runacuna are not fully in charge of who they are, who they were, and who they are becoming; they must respond to the dominant culture around them.

Let us begin with the contrasts between the two cultural complexes before we investigate how they intertwine. Exploring the symbolic complexes suggested by the three previous examples—the tallest and most silent building in the central plaza as the focus of religious worship; the small, dark, and noisy cantina dedicated to irreligious and questionable moral behavior on the side streets; and worship characterized by drunken dancing on the paths that unite all the inhabited and uninhabited spaces of the comuna—leads to quite different ways of conceptualizing the human and spiritual relationship to the environment. The relationship of center and periphery and of high and low, both literally and as a metaphorical representation of hierarchy (Levi-Strauss 1963), are two key areas to explore.

Mediterranean and Andean Themes of Spiritual Responsibility

Civilization literally means, in its derivation from Latin, the "coming to be of cities," and in the Mediterranean world, where the concept originated, human action designed to construct a symbolic world that is both socially and spiritually meaningful has a direction—from the periphery toward a civilized center. The civilizing and sanctifying process moves from outside to inside, from the wilds to the town plaza, from outdoors to buildings' interiors, from the natural light of the sun to the dim, restricted flames of the flickering candles, and from the chaotic to the hierarchically ordered. In this common interpretation, it is within the centralized, human- constructed and -controlled environments of the city and town that people can most approximate God's perfect labors in creating the world and can become most near to God in the sacred spaces dedicated to his worship.[1] This ordering and purifying endeavor was God's charge to humans as well. For example, it is the controlled, sanctified use of wine that makes it sacred, a triumph over but not a surrendering to its boundary-erasing and mind-altering properties. As one leaves the center toward ever more distant peripheries, one moves further away from civic value in the sociopolitical sense at the same time as one leaves behind God's sure protection to enter the realm where evil has freer rein. The wilds of mountains, forests, swamps, and other relatively uninhabited spaces stand in sharp contrast to domesticated and consecrated spaces of the center. Chaotic forces loose in these untamed places threaten the order that represents both civilization and, indeed, God's dominion on earth. Outdoor processions can be an important part of religious practice, but they repeat the centralizing and civilizing acts that link all inhabited space to the increasingly interior and sacred places of central plaza, church, sanctuary, and central altars, each suffused with a greater divine presence and control. Still, the forces of evil from beyond the margins of civilized space may always reinvade without the presence of walls and icons and human activity to guard the sacred in protected interiors. While this Mediterranean perspective has progressively less sway in the Western-influenced world as a whole, and is diminishing in Ecuador as well, as we reprioritize the wild as the repository of God's goodness, it has had considerable influence in Ecuador until the present.

In clear contrast, in andean cosmology a movement toward the wild and the distant leads to sources of ever greater supernatural power, neither entirely good nor entirely bad. In Otavalo, as is nearly universal in the Andes, the sun- and snowcapped mountain peaks frequently symbolize divine power at the highest levels. It is true that the domesticated and interior space of the huasi ucu is similarly protected from outside forces of evil, as are the hispanic home and church. However, the sanctifying movement is not unidirectional, from periphery to center. In fact, it is both back and forth and circular, from the most distant and uninhabited sacred places, around all inhabited space, to the domestic realm of the huasi and back again. The sacred is found in continuous movement and exchange, not in stillness.

Home and the wild, the ordered and chaotic, the sacred and spiritually dangerous, the near and the distant, like many key paired concepts, derive their meaning and their power from their relationship to each other. Up and down, high and low, back and front are paired categories; each is a "relational term, like 'here' or 'there,' which changes according to the speaker's point of reference" (Weismantel 1988, 197–201). In Quichua *ucu* is inside, and outside is *canlla.* In one sociogeographic application, ucu refers to the moist forests over the mountain ranges either to the east or to the west. In this sense it captures an idea of inside as primordial or autochthonous openings into the earth's spiritual essence. Humans in the Andes exist at a mediating point between the forces of the earth's inside and the sky's divine realms, while their counterparts in the jungle live closer to the earth's origin point. Ucu can also be applied to social territory in a nested Russian doll sense. The smallest and most exclusive of the inside spaces is the huasi ucu, while the limit of perceived social/geographic inclusion is most commonly the northern half of the country, although theoretically it can be extended much further. In English, the inside and outside of concentric circles are naturally transformed into the concept of center and periphery, carrying with it an implicit hierarchical dimension, with the center taking priority over the larger periphery. Inside and outside in both English and Quichua can be equally applied to concentric circles or to mirrored contrasts facing each other, but in Quichua ucu and canlla apply preferentially to the latter. According to Levi-Strauss (1963), this linked pair formulation is more often symbolically egalitarian or hierarchically neutral than are the representation of concentric circles. In Quichua thought, the emphasis of inside/outside in concentric circles is more likely to be on their status as opposed pairs with equally valuable back-and-forth movement than as center and periphery.

One key locus of social production is the huasi ucu, which offers protection and from which ideally springs forth a morally enjoined generosity. But to fully exploit the potentials of the world, humans must work to extend the characteristics of the home to the most distant and feared places and to bring the dangerous but infinitely powerful resources of the distant mountains and jungles into the home as well. The relational interplay of all aspects of the physical, social, and spiritual environment is foremost, not the raising of one above all others in value and attempting to either convert what is outside into the civilized and sacred interior states or exclude it once and for all.

That said, both hispanic and andean religious symbolism suppose a hierarchical arrangement of spiritual power. In both traditions, distance from humans is used symbolically to represent a greater degree of supernatural power. The exaggerated height of the church spire and the elaborate decoration of the altars of its interior all express a scale of power, inherent in the spirits, which is greater than anything an ordinary human will ever experience on earth. A similar concept of overwhelming greatness is expressed in the effort to dance longer, drink more, share more food—in short, approach infinity in the pouring forth of sensual stimulants as an offering to the spirits. The distance of heaven from earth parallels the remoteness of the sun, the highest mountain peaks, or the ocean deeps.

Nonetheless, a substantially different relationship toward hierarchical power, related to the contrast between the concepts of center and periphery discussed above, guides the religious behavior of those immersed in the hispanic traditions from those who have been taught the indigenous practices. While the Euro-American Catholic model requires the exaggerated reinforcement of the social and other symbols of hierarchy and distance in religious practice, indigenous Catholicism applies the general principle of offering an elaborate intimacy as a way to demonstrate respect. This is a hard concept to describe or grasp, but the Quichua bound morpheme "-pa-" provides an example. It is a polite form, added to verbs and used to demonstrate high esteem. Although one may use it with social equals and social superiors alike, it is optional for the former and obligatory for the latter. The use of "-pa-" represents a kind of meek intimacy, something like how we think of children behaving with their parents, expressing affection and vulnerably seeking it in return. Rather than representing respect through social distance, the subordinate seeks to decrease social distance as a means to honor the person of higher status. It is not an attempt to overthrow hierarchical power but to momentarily erase it with intimacy and thereby increase the long-term benefits for the less powerful. Or, if not to erase it, it serves to cast such power into the idiom of kinship hierarchy, with its implications of mutual responsibility and love. This clearly fits with what we call paternalism, a form of hierarchical relationships we deplore and consider more primitive in form than our own.

It is no accident that people who have suffered oppression in their homeland for the five hundred years since their military conquest value this form of hierarchical relationships. The Spanish conquest and colonization resulted in the decapitation of the highest levels of political power in the indigenous world. In the centuries following the Spanish invasion, economic and political power became concentrated in the hispanicized world, and Quichua-speaking indigenous people were confined to a relatively uniform level of powerlessness. Of course, even within Huaycopungo, shallow levels of hierarchy can be found in the statuses ascribed by age, gender, and sometimes ayllu prominence and achieved by relative success in subsistence activities and religious sponsorships, which together lead to political influence. While in the early twenty-first century, Huaycopungo could be said to encompass at least two socioeconomic classes, this was not the case in the 1970s. Gender hierarchy was limited, most often overshadowed by gender parallelism; age-related advantage could be obtained just by getting older; and achieved status was highly ceremonialized and subject to pressures that strongly limited its continuing growth.[2] Nonetheless, outside the indigenous comuna and indigenous world as a whole lies the vast power of the state. The greatest secular hierarchical boundary exists between the indigenous and nonindigenous world. There could be no socioeconomic mobility for indians in Ecuador as indians. While this has changed in recent years, indians were not, as a group, the lowest, or even second lowest after rural Afro-Ecuadorians (Whitten 1976), in the idealized social hierarchy in Ecuador—they were outside the social hierarchy. While runa extend to the powerful mishucuna the same exaggerated respectful intimacy as they do to the powerful spirits as a way to overcome their monopoly of resources and redirect some of that wealth toward themselves, the problems of cultural comprehension complicate that process and reduce runacuna expectation of success.

Lastly, there was a significant contrast in the conceptions of the creation of cultural identity through time. Both runa and mishu have incorporated material and nonmaterial aspects of the other's culture, although mishu recognize very little of this mixture in their present, preferring to consider it an unconscious holdover from a more primitive past. Any contemporary sharing of culture with the stigmatized indigenous other, beyond folkloric music or a taste for roasted guinea pig, would make mestizos stigmatized as well.[3] To be modern is to forsake the primitiveness of the ancestors and to follow the world leaders into the future. This emphasis on progress allows mestizos to accept their stigmatized past as both indian and hispanic but claim a stigma-free future in the modern world, a future that indian people seem to inexplicably reject.

For the people who identify themselves as indigenous, the future is never so detached from the past, since the past never recedes into the distance but is both ever-present and the direction we face, while moving backward into the unknowable future. We face what we know and can use to orient ourselves, because to face the future is to face the void, which we must fill with knowledge from the past. Faith in tradition represents the preservation of a separate standard of human value, with which indigenous Ecuadorians have been able to fend off the dominant society's judgment of them as vastly inferior people for hundreds of years. Furthermore, intercourse with the hispanic world does not necessarily convert indians into mestizos but can be a means for the indians and mestizos both to reinvigorate themselves with the power of the other, while remaining overwhelmingly distinct. In the meantime, in-depth knowledge of the dominant society is highly valued, since only by acquiring it can indians hope to find the loopholes that could lead to an their advantage. This chapter will try to capture the complex combinations of actions and reactions in the interface between mestizo and indigenous drinking behaviors, when drinking is a powerful symbol of the ethnic boundary between them.

Let's examine the boda huasi and cantina in the context of these two tendencies—the first, which maximizes the difference between high and low, wild and domesticated, sacred and profane, modern and traditional and so on, and the second, which encourages a dynamic interchange between such fundamental oppositions that may momentarily erase or reverse them, and in doing so propels them into extreme intimacy.

The *Cantina*

The Spanish brought with them to Andean America the local bar, called cantina throughout Ecuador. It refers to a room in a building or a small building specialized for the consumption of alcohol, but not food. The word cantina in Spain originally referred to a wine cellar. In that sense, it probably partially mirrored the rural Andean pondo (large ceramic jar) full of asua at every prosperous house. But it has come to mean a place where alcohol is sold by the owner and purchased by the mostly male clientele. The drinking usually occurs inside, although in small cantinas overflow indian drinkers often gather in front. Therefore, those neighbors and others who wish to watch the drinkers from afar can do so only as they stumble home. Nondrinking runacuna and mishucuna alike expect the worst of cantina drinkers, and the bars' owners deride their drunken clients while simultaneously counting their profits.

Cantinas are liminal places, within the public and civilized spaces of town but freed somewhat from the restraints that civilization brings. Like the wild landscape beyond the town and fields, the cantina's atmosphere of license can give free rein to the forces of darkness.[4] While consecrated wine served in church can represent Christ's blood and its consumption bind men and women to the realm of God, the trago or beer served in the cantina can bring out the devil in anyone, turning even the good Christian into a sinner. The cantina and the church are two interior, human-made spaces where alcohol consumption takes place, but they stand in complete opposition to each other. At best the cantina is religiously neutral; at worst temptation turns all men and women away from God.

Cantinas are also public places where, in the pan-Mediterranean pattern the Spanish brought to the New World, behavior is expected to differ markedly from that in either the more protected and intimate spaces of home or in the carefully controlled and sacred recesses of the church. First of all, public spaces are more properly the domain of men, which means that the expected behavior is more competitive and more aggressive, where men pursue the esteem of other men. Domestic spaces are ideally more feminine, nurturing, and egalitarian. The church, in contrast to both the cantina and the home, is hierarchical. Distinctions of gender or personal and family honor that are important in the domestic and public spheres are subordinated in the church to the authority of God and the leaders of Mother Church. More generally, public behavior is instrumental and goal-directed, while both domestic and sacred interactions are ideally motivated more by love, commitment, self-denial, and faith.

In the cantina men release themselves from their everyday social constraints and responsibilities, combining camaraderie and competition to talk, argue, sing, shout, and cry together, individually, in pairs, or in larger groups. Emotions, usually kept under conventional control to ensure success in their daily goals, can be released more freely in the cantina. Cantina drinking is often spoken of as a way to vent emotions for better general health and sustained masculine strength in everyday life. An exaggeration of both male rivalry and male intimacy while under the influence is considered a safety valve that enables men to remain coolly and instrumentally competitive in sober public life. People forgive drunken behavior that would be unacceptable outside of a drinking context, since a major responsibility for the poor judgment lies in the properties of alcohol, not the person.

Young adult men, roughly between the ages of eighteen and thirty-five, are expected to frequent cantinas much more frequently than boys or the middle-aged and elderly. Cantina drinking is just another arena for the restlessness, insecurity, and competitiveness of men who are in the process of establishing their social positions. For those whose established position is relatively high, more formal and domestic forms of drinking become the norm, where the men themselves can either control the amount consumed or the consequences of their drinking themselves, or rely on their supporters to provide that control. Total surrender to drunkenness, at least on a regular basis, would be dangerous to their social goals and responsibilities.

In this Euro-American model, one that should be relatively familiar to North Americans, sexual inhibitions are also conquered by drinking, especially in a bar. Bar drinking inevitably increases lust between men and women, such that even conventionally ugly women begin to appear bewitching to the drunk. This lust may masquerade as love or may even lead to real love, but love cannot be created in a bar alone. Friendship may result, but only between men. We often engage in drinking in bars in order to plunge into the excitement of flirting with lustful and mildly antisocial behavior, behavior that nevertheless should normatively fall short of serious social transgression.

Finally, increased violence is an expected consequence of cantina drinking. It follows the loosening of inhibitions, the venting of intensified feelings, the masculine competition, the increase in sexual desire, the expectation of satanic temptation, and the excuse provided by alcohol's chemical properties. When young men start a fight in a cantina, it is considered understandable, if not actually desirable. But when women become involved as aggressors or the mighty behave with the destructive abandon of fledgling men, then it is considered a tragedy.

The greatest demonstration of masculine prowess is to drink great quantities and release tensions without losing all physical and emotional control. Like the violence that is presumed to follow drunkenness, the loss of psychomotor control is accepted but not desired. And it is accepted more in males than females and more among young adults than among children or the elderly, more among the socially inept than among the mighty. It is not only accepted but also expected among society's rejects. The bourgeois look upon them with either contempt or pity. A complete surrender to intoxication would signal to others that one had forsaken the duties of the civilized to exercise control over oneself and one's environment and thus stave off the chaotic forces of evil that linger impatiently in the periphery. The vision of a stooped, white-haired granny weaving unsteadily home and singing out loud is considered a horrifying sign of the collapse of all moral underpinnings. An important community leader passed out on the side of the road indicates a disturbing vacuum of control at the top. These are common sights in the indigenous community.

Contrarily, in the boda huasi, surrendering to drunkenness is the morally enjoined duty of all who strive to uphold and further the social and spiritual order, especially the middle-aged and elderly. Vulnerability, rather than self-control, signals respect. Within the indigenous world, the most ambitious and respected leaders should publicly demonstrate their vulnerability to members of their comuna and to social and supernatural superiors outside.

Unlike the cantina's largely male-segregated environment, symbolically contrasted to both home and church, the boda huasi ideally extends the values and expectations of home into the more public arena. Women's roles are different from men's in the boda huasi, but equally important. Otavalans hope that shared drinking at the boda huasi enhances platonic love between individuals as part of families, although they recognize that unbridled lust may be a danger of heavy drinking. The continual and uncalculated exchange of goods and services for the benefit of all that is characteristic of the family that lives in the huasi, and ideally extended to members of the close ayllu, is enacted in the boda huasi by the ceaseless flow of offered and accepted gourd bowls of asua and api, followed by heaps of muti and glistening roast cuy, as guests come and go over several days and nights.

Such generalized reciprocity becomes increasingly ceremonialized as kin become more distant genealogically, or as a relationship is extended beyond the bounds of kin and community to strangers, mishucuna, or *gringucuna*. Nonetheless, the strategy is to give generously as a means to draw strangers into a web of reciprocity much as one entices distant mountain spirits, since receiving a gift means accepting an obligation for continuing a relationship of exchange in the future. Flowery gestures and phrases accompany the gifts to strangers and higher-status individuals with whom one wants to have a relationship of obligatory exchange. While the community is ideally characterized by its impenetrable web of these exchanges, indian people also try to extend them to mestizos and strangers, both near and distant, whether socially equal or more powerful, when they think such a relationship will be beneficial. These relationships are *in fact* more instrumental, but it is desirable to try to convert them into, or at least imagine them as, something far more morally charged, rather than simply accepting that public encounters are goal-directed and competitive and reserving moral commitment for domestic and sacred relationships. Nor is competition incompatible with commitment, as we have seen the contest of wills involved in the offer of a drink and the acceptance of a commitment in the boda huasi.

In the Otavalo area, cantinas themselves fall on two ends of a continuum; one end is maximally similar to the boda huasi and the other is maximally distinct. They vary from a seemingly simple extension of the woman-warmed house where relationships between indigenous households, formed by the partnership of a married couple, are ideally made and strengthened in all their personal, spiritual, economic, and political dimensions. These indian-run cantinas serve both asua and trago. The indian drinkers may bring beverages to share as well as purchase what is offered by the house. Offering surplus for purchase, rather than exchanging it for political and religious power in the service of the community, is the major innovation. In the 1970s, this innovative behavior was considered both a respected rebellion against mishu economic domination and a dangerous precedent for indigenous exploitation of their own people.

At the other extreme, some cantinas are local bars where men, almost exclusively mestizo, conduct personal, economic, and political business in a very different idiom, that of competitive machismo, over beer and trago (other alcoholic beverages are available but more rarely consumed). These are characteristic of urban mestizo-run cantinas. Both the indian-run urban cantinas and the rural mestizo-run cantinas, which were common until a decade ago, take on a decidedly mixed character. In general the indian tradition in Otavalo is a rural one, while the hispanic is urban. This has resulted in part from the processes begun at the conquest, when the Spanish and their descendants monopolized and transformed indigenous urban centers, like Quito, or began new cities of their own, like Lima, in their desire to replicate the centers of social and spiritual worth so important in the Mediterranean. At the same time, they hoped thereby to more easily control large territories of indigenous subjects. Indigenous urban centers, with their associated urban cultures, ceased to exist.

The most positively regarded Huaycopungo cantina was, and is still, Mama Juana's home, on the old Pan-American Highway, now the main street of Huaycopungo. Somehow Ravil Juana Mama and her mild-mannered husband have managed to drink every day with their customers, as tradition requires here as in other parts of Andean and

Middle America (see Eber 1995), but remain capable of carrying out all their responsibilities, including the curing in which Mama Juana specializes. They are not community leaders, but they are respected elders and Mama Juana demonstrates her unusual dignity, courtesy, and sense of humor to everyone who uses her services. When a younger couple needs asua to serve to honored guests but have not had the resources to make it, they can buy some from Mama Juana's or invite their guests to join them in drinking in Mama Juana's front room. Those who temporarily exhaust the supplies at a boda huasi can continue at Mama Juana's. If you were looking for one of the community's known alcoholics, one of the stops in your search would be Mama Juana's. He has either found a legitimate celebrant whom he may accompany in drinking, or he has manufactured a flimsy justification for inviting others to join him.

Although Mama Juana clearly serves chronic alcoholics often, in general she does not tolerate drunken fights in her house. She and her husband both seem to achieve the mellow effects of drinking so

Fig. 36. *Mama* Juana Otavalo and *Taita* José Manuel Otavalo
(PHOTO BY AUTHOR)

locally desired. Drinking there usually proceeds with relative decorum. Native decorum does not imply the absence of weaving or falling or slurred speaking; those are positive signs of surrender, not instances of antisocial lack of self-control. Decorum means restraining strong emotions and continuing to treat others with the gentle respect they deserve, relative to their personal relationships or public standing in the community. However, if people drink long and hard enough, long-standing individual and family quarrels rise to the surface, resulting in loud arguments and fights. Then, in the best of all possible worlds, the drunken revelers are led home, protesting vociferously, by their more sober caretakers.

Nonetheless, Mama Juana's house, which looks so traditional today, bore signs of a rapprochement with mestizo values twenty-five years ago. The house, of packed mud walls, *tapia*, had been built on the old Pan-American Highway, which was later rerouted further up the hill toward San Rafael. The house sat in a close-packed line of houses that looked more like the urbanized mestizo pattern than the indigenous one. Another building, which in the visual iconography of the late 1970s so clearly said cantina or storefront because of its non-indigenous and more modern look, today appears to be neither old nor modern, but just pitifully small and poor.

Until recently, the people in Huaycopungo also frequented cantinas owned by mestizos within the boundary of Huaycopungo or in San Rafael's town center.[5] Easily available credit and almost inexhaustible supplies of alcohol attracted runa to these cantinas. Top-heavy and open-sided delivery trucks would regularly grind their gears negotiating the steep, rutted slopes and deep potholes to grumble to a halt in front of one Huaycopungo's mestizo-owned storefronts. Drinking in mestizo-owned cantinas contrasts strikingly with drinking at Mama Juana's. Again the front rooms of houses are used, but in this case they are set aside for business purposes. Most of them function as small convenience stores as well. While Mama Juana uses her front room as both personal and professional space, this is very rare in San Rafael and would be considered shameful by the owners. By mishu standards, one should have enough rooms to be able to separate family life from commercial life and to keep both drunks and indians from entering and defiling the nonindian family's personal space. Family members, most often the women, control the beverage supply as they also go about their regular daily chores, but they only rarely share drinks with their customers as Mama Juana and her husband do, since bars are not proper spaces for women in hispanic Ecuadorian culture. Women other than the owners and their families are usually considered morally compromised should they enter the cantina.

The women cantina proprietors most often act haughtily removed even when they are physically present, while their husbands and fathers are more likely to be jovial. While both mestizo men and mestiza women are likely to protect their class and ethnic reputation in the eyes of inferiors, peers, and any superiors who may come around, women have the added burden of maintaining their reputation as good women. Nevertheless, both men and women can be astonishingly verbally abusive to indigenous customers with impunity. Even when they are being friendly, they expect to be addressed with the formal "you" *(usted)* and respond with the informal *tu* or *vos*. They address the native people regardless of age by first name or by such locally common term for indian as *longo(a)* or *huangudo(a)*, considered affectionate, if demeaning, by mestizos. In turn they are addressed as Sra./Sr. or Doña/Don and their own first name.

San Rafael's mishu inhabitants are cursed with a low status in Otavalo—indeed, in the nation as a whole—for living cheek by jowl with Quichua speakers. As a result, San Rafael's mestizos most often exaggerated their social distance from Otavalans. They cultivated fear in their tiny children, claiming that the indians would steal them if they strayed too far from their parents and got too close to indians.[6] San Rafael's mestizos would not share a bench with indigenous people, or sometimes even the same side of a room, and always insisted on sitting in the front seats of a bus. They did not respect the boundaries of Otavalan houses, marching right in rather than calling out for permission at each boundary—the entrances to the compound, the *curridur*, and, for a few intimates, the house's interior—as indigenous people expect of each other. Nor did they wait to be invited to sit, but grabbed any available bench or stool. They rudely stared straight at indigenous people when addressing them, pulled them aside by their clothes, and used authoritative voices, while expecting lowered eyes and heads, high-pitched voices, and automatic cession of space on the path, sidewalk, room, or doorway on the part of their indigenous neighbors. An assumption so deep-seated as to be quite casual was that indian people were the natural means by which status-conscious mestizos could avoid the debasement of manual labor themselves. Nor was it always necessary to pay for this labor; it was owed to the mestizos, as the leaders of the parish. When they felt like it, high-status mestizos could enter runa yards and select indigenous chickens or guinea pigs, stores of corn or potatoes to take home. More menacing still, pubescent girls caught pasturing sheep or gathering watercress at or beyond the borders of the comuna were considered fair game for rape.

While most indigenous residents of Huaycopungo, especially its women, took pains to go into San Rafael as little as possible, some people knew the inhabitants there almost as well as they knew their own indigenous neighbors. They sometimes successfully recruited the cantina owners to symbolic exchange relationships in drinking, or even longer-lasting exchange relationships through godparenthood. However, a financial motive generally prevailed in mishus' dealings with their indigenous clientele. The financial benefits were not limited to the money paid for alcohol, but also included harvested crops, animals, the services of indigenous children, hand-woven reed mats to sell outside the region, captive customers for machine-embroidered blouses, glass beads, or sundries, and even plots of land. Anything and everything was taken as collateral in credit payments. The most unscrupulous doubled the debts as they recorded them, especially if the debtor was too drunk to notice. Crops and animals might be taken in better quantity or quality than what was owed; land held in collateral was registered in the lender's own name and thereby stolen.

Sometimes indigenous children were taken in payment of debt. If parents tried to protest that their children, who were working as servants, suffered beatings or lack of food under the cantina owner's care, the children would be whisked away to Quito or Guayaquil to work at the whims of the owner in locations kept strictly secret from the parents. A few particularly abusive employers would hide valuable property and then unjustly accuse an indigenous child-servant of having stolen that property, so as to exact from the collaborating authorities a judgment of guilt and a punishment of a decade or more of free labor.

Those cantina owners who specialized in the provision of ceremonial paraphernalia as well as asua and trago did indeed make impressive profits, especially since they charged exorbitant rents and multiplied the replacement prices of the paraphernalia, sometimes by a factor greater than one hundred (Villavicencio 1973). Nowadays they brag to all who listen, including, with breathtaking insensitivity, their indigenous acquaintances, about their own children's professional education and careers in Quito, financed through years of exploitation, often illegal, of their Otavalan neighbors. They expect admiration for their accomplishments.

In the 1970s, Otavalan women's talk of cantinas was uniformly negative. Cantinas, especially in San Rafael, were seen as a kind of trap where unlimited alcohol supply and unlimited credit would keep men and even some, usually older, women drinking beyond their physical, emotional, and financial capacity. While young women accompanying drinkers, who are usually their husbands, are always expected to be relatively withdrawn and shy, in San Rafael's cantinas they are downright sullen, trying to hide their anger and frustration with mute determination. By accompanying their husbands, they will be subject to criticism for neglecting their duties at home, but they *must* do so, because if they left their husbands alone and something should happen, they would also be criticized. In 1978, one young woman whose husband became sick and died shortly after spending a night drunk, passed out, and unaccompanied on the road home from a cantina was accused in very public gossip of murder. While it is customary for mourning women to get drunk and publicly sing/chant of their grief, their own spousal shortcomings, and the hopelessness of their future as widows as they traverse the comuna's paths, it was particularly poignant to hear this woman's voice approach and fade as she wailed about her act of fatal neglect.

The young wives in cantinas gather up their husbands' watches, ponchos, and hats, because these are easily lost or stolen when their husbands are drunk, then sit on the edges of the room and wait. They fear drunken violence between their husbands and other men while in the cantina and violence against themselves when they go home. They try to come between the combatants, as a group, in the cantina and only hope there will be others to defend them when they are home.

Helplessly, they watch their household's disposable income sliding down their husband's throats.

It is difficult for them to respond with the requisite humble politeness when spoken to by the mestiza owners, who are happily watching their own incomes grow, and they sometimes pretend not to hear or understand any Spanish in order to avoid social contact. When their husbands drink in a Huaycopungo boda huasi, they are cultivating exchange relationships that may pay off in the future, relationships to which the wives can often contribute as well as benefit from. Furthermore, the women are more likely to have relatives present or nearby who can help them stave off fights or other undesirable behaviors. But those who provide the alcohol in San Rafael owe them nothing and are paid only in money. In fact, the cantina owners' own relative social esteem rises as they see their indigenous neighbors fail in civilized behavior or ensure their own continued poverty.

Those few indigenous women who frequently join in the drinking at cantinas are the objects of particular concern, particularly if they are still young enough to bear children. Women become sad watching a drunken woman relative dance with abandon to the cantina's recorded music. Gently and respectfully, they offer to accompany the woman home or to fetch her children to get her. Like as not, the inebriated dancer brushes them off with a string of profanities in Spanish,[7] at which cantina owners either laugh or convey their own disgust at such depraved conduct on the part of a woman, even if she is an indian.

As with drinking, women in Huaycopungo must be pressed to dance and they must not do it too often, although it becomes more acceptable as a woman gets older (see Eber 1995 for a similar observation from Mayan Guatemala). A woman whose children are now adult either shares more ritual responsibilities with her husband or has the time and resources to relax and enjoy the social networks they spent so many years building up. When dancing, Otavalan women frequently appear to be drunk, whether they have consumed any alcohol or not. Music, dancing, and alcohol consumption are such traditionally linked offerings to the gods that one implies the others. It is only for serious, shared ritual goals that a woman would consent to join in the dancing. A woman who would dance without the ceremony of shared alcohol to mediate and partially erase the spiritual boundary between the secular world of today and the universal space/time calls into question her moral character.

Younger women also complain of drunken men's unwanted sexual attentions, especially their husbands,' and blame unwanted pregnancies on ceremonies that led to heavy drinking, especially in cantinas. However, some men brag that when everyone left in a boda huasi has succumbed to intoxication, sexual intercourse can be had with women too drunk to resist or even know they are being violated. The woman who stayed and put herself in that position would bear more responsibility in local thinking than the man who took advantage of it. As described by Eber (1995) for Mayan Guatemala, the women who run comuna cantinas win some income and independence but lose the status of a good moral character. Or they may turn an already soiled reputation into a source of income for their children. Mama Juana is long married and has successful adult children with her husband, but some women cantina operators indeed have children by more than one man and no stable marital partner.

Fig. 37. *Yumbo*'s wife dances drunkenly as appropriate
(PHOTO BY AUTHOR)

These scenes of violent drunken men and sullen or drunken women are also played out in Huaycopungo's own cantinas, but more social pressure is brought to prevent or end them. In San Rafael, the indigenous people feel relatively helpless; every drink sold is money in one family's pocket alone. It is not a liquid glue between neighbors and relatives and between people and their gods. The mestizo families of San Rafael have no vested interest in Huaycopungo's moral health. In fact, they have a vested interest in believing that the Otavalans are insufficiently civilized or even morally degraded to the point that they cannot help themselves. From their vantage point, indians slide helplessly into alcoholism, enriching on the way those nonindians who are wise enough to take advantage of the situation they believe they had no hand in making.

Drinking in the town of Otavalo's cantinas or in cantinas in other large towns or cities in the province plays out these themes a little differently. Because of their greater physical distance and therefore presumed social distance between mestizos and indigenous people in Otavalo, mestizos in Otavalo who desire economic relationships with Otavalans are freer to cultivate friendly, if shallow, social relationships with them. This friendliness was more marked in verbal interchange than in any physical closeness.

Until the 1970s, Otavalans from outlying communities walked, with their backs heavily loaded, to Otavalo's Saturday market once a week or once a month, and sometimes only once a year. Today, Otavalo has a substantial indigenous population and may be visited daily by high school students and even Huaycopungo's few remaining subsistence agriculturalists. Before the arrival of cheap public transportation, Otavalo cantinas were often the arrival destination for indians visiting from the surrounding towns, much like the role taverns served in other Euro-American traditions. As among relatives, neighbors, and exchange partners within indigenous communities, many generations of Otavalans and cantina owners shared alcohol, made business deals, and ate and slept in the same household compound, although the owners used beds in their bedrooms and the indigenous guests slept on the patio floor. It was both a business and a personal relationship, at best only somewhat more professional and hierarchical than one between genuine fictive kin. At their worst, cantinas run by mestizos for indigenous people were exploitative business ventures run in a transparently false idiom of hierarchical, but nonetheless morally enjoined, exchange relationships (see Montes del Castillo 1989). For cantina owners, having indigenous clientele who would come to sleep, store their goods or, even better, leave their goods to be sold meant a business advantage. Their social standing was reduced because of the proximity to indians, but they could claim to their peers and those of higher status that the relationship was strictly business, with their friendliness only feigned to coax the childlike indigenous peasants into yielding substantial profits to them. These town mestizos also frequently served as godparents to the children of their indigenous clients, thereby becoming the obligatory recipients of a portion of each harvest. While the mestizos most often took advantage of the lack of sophistication of rural dwellers and the indigenous people's lack of Spanish-language skills (or, indeed, the ability to read and write in any language), the indigenous people sometimes reaped the benefits of an urban advocate against those who would cheat them in the market, abuse them in the streets, or prosecute them for disorderly conduct if they got drunk in town.

Some of these cantina relationships began between indigenous families whose ethnic orientation slowly shifted to mestizo. See Butler (Rivero) 1981 for a description of how spatial mobility can, over a period of generations, begin a process, often hastened by intermarriage or economic mobility, of ethnic mobility. Some migrant families from Huaycopungo in San Pablo and Quito continue to benefit economically from close ties to indigenous people and the manipulation of skills and symbols of nonindigenous identity. They remain low in the national status hierarchy, but their children and children's children have different kinds of options from the children of people thoroughly identified as indigenous.

Long-distance trading has been a specialty of Otavalo since well before the Spanish and Incan conquests. In order to obtain shelter, food, and protection in the distant places to which they traveled, one can guess that Otavalans in the past, like those today, attempted to establish a relationship that in some ways mirrored the warm interdependence they wish to create with relatives and neighbors at home. Charm and a sense of humor are an Otavalan's best business assets.

With it he, or she, can begin a friendship that becomes characterized by ceremonialized mutual exchange—of food and favors and alcohol. In June of 1996 a friend and long-distance trader told me that his Pasto customers said that they are buying only from him now because they have developed a friendly relationship over the years, despite the facts that Otavalan traders are now a dime a dozen in their neck of the woods and the local economy is undergoing a severe slump. If the demand for the products of each region is strong and the relationship is expected to be long term, then relationships of compadrazgo are made and intermarriages jokingly discussed. Such exchanges include Otavalo's corn for a higher territory's potatoes or totora reeds from a distant marsh for mats, esteras, woven from them; Huaycopungo's esteras, other Otavalan handicrafts, or affordable manufactured clothing for money. While men are usually the long-distance traders, they feel disadvantaged if they do not have the help of a woman, especially their wife or older daughter.

Replacements, Juxtapositions, and Syntheses of Two Symbolic Worlds

The above examples demonstrate the by now somewhat commonplace observation that rural indigenous people are not just the passive recipients of hegemonic ideas and practices issuing from the dominant local and international elite. The benefits as seen by Otavalans in the establishment of intercultural fictive kinship relationships are not just in the realm of symbolic social capital but can be quite practical as well. After my first godson, an infant, and I together experienced the ritual transformation in church that created our indissoluble bonds, much discussion ensued about whether he would have a natural facility for English. They did not argue that he would be exposed to the language through time spent with me, but that our spiritual union would make us like kin, likely to share certain capacities and characteristics.[8]

I would agree with Montes del Castillo (1989) that such positive interpretations of relations are frequently a fiction maintained by nonindians in order to obscure the exploitation at the heart of the relationship. I would also add that Otavalans themselves use this fictive kinship idiom for quite pragmatic purposes, much as did the Inca in his attempts to tie the disparate parts of the empire into a hegemonic belief system supporting his rule. Offering exotic friendship represents the search for that marketing edge that will allow a profit in a crowded market. Nevertheless, indigenous actors are inserting their own idiom into the dominant culture, rather than simply engaging it on its own terms. These behaviors and their interpretations represent the inter-twined interculture asserted for the Andean area by Abercrombie (1998). Indigenous people offer such relationships and mestizos accept them, for it reduces uncertainty in the market transactions for the poor buyers and sellers alike. But each learns something of new cultural idioms as a result. For a few years after beginning traveling sales in the hinterlands of southern Colombia, friends in Huaycopungo would analyze in detail the etiquette of coffee drinking and how to engage in proper social behavior with their customers without ending up walk-ing the streets between houses with jangling nerves and a perpetually full bladder—much as I had been concerned in conducting house-to-house interviews during the boda huasi season.

The cantina and the boda huasi have remained quite distinct ven-ues for drinking, with behaviors proper to each well understood by the indigenous people who employ both. Nonetheless, the fact that the boda huasi is interpreted by the hispanic outsiders with the idioms of drinking proper to their own culture blurs the picture for the out-sider considerably, eventually affecting the Otavalan view of their own situation as well. How does a child exposed to this viewpoint since kindergarten avoid thinking it at least partially true? While in the previous paragraph I emphasized the indigenous agency in resisting and even modifying the dominant culture, in all its diversity, here we must reverse the perspective and recognize the extent to which the domi-nant society, with all the power of the state behind it, has sought for years to acculturate and assimilate the indian in the name of national unity (Stutzman 1981; Whitten 1981). Ecuadorians do not all passively accept as given the assessment that pathological indigenous drinking is inevitable and inescapable. Many groups and individuals at all levels of society have long initiated social reforms to alleviate the problem. Even those indigenous people most isolated by monolingualism and avoidance of mishu spaces are aware of alcohol abuse as a supposed reason for indians' position as outcasts from the social hierarchy.

Let us recapitulate some of the significant differences. When hispanics see drunken middle-aged and elderly indians, they don't assume that alcohol is preferentially consumed by the socially prominent. Instead they take for granted that indians remain forever immature, never outgrowing the tendency of youth to overindulge. When these elders are women, they assume that indian men lack the level of civilization necessary to treasure and protect their women, and that indigenous women have so little concept of their own honor that they fail to guard it themselves. Hispanic Ecuadorians do not know that Otavalans often exaggerate the ataxia resulting from their drinking, since total surrender is prized, so they judge the weaving, stumbling indians as particularly susceptible to drink, unable to maintain the physical control that is the mark of a truly admirable man. That men, and even older women, may sleep off their intoxication on the side of the road is nothing short of bestial. Even sitting on the ground in urbanized places is taboo for those who wish to be considered civilized. When a wife sits patiently besides her comatose husband, shielding his head from the elements, nonindians clearly perceive the exploitation of indian women by their society and a corresponding female lack of self-esteem. The surrender to total intoxication, a customary goal with religious implications, is seen as the monumental venting of emotions, where indians seek to escape the burdens of their impoverished and hopeless daily existence in the pleasurable oblivion guaranteed in a bottle. The prevalence of alcoholism is perceived to be great, since so many people can be seen demonstrating signs of problem drinking—ataxia, unconsciousness, public spectacle, intoxication at an inappropriate age or by the wrong gender—as designated in nonindian culture. From this point of view, indians are so far gone that they no longer even attempt to hide these signs of trouble (Rubio Orbe 1956).

Where, then, lies the overlap in hispanic and indigenous perspectives about drinking among Otavalans? Specifically, the ideas that young men may rebel through mildly antisocial behavior, like drinking to intoxication; that women are responsible for protecting an extremely vulnerable sexual reputation, which alcohol consumption will always damage; and that drinking represents a release of negative emotions, which has short-term costs but long-term benefits are all ideas that are becoming more common among people in Huaycopungo. While these judgments are much more likely to be made about cantina drinking than about sharing asua in the boda huasi, they can also be applied to drinking in general. Certainly, it is reasonable to expect that indigenous people have always derived short-term pleasure from a loosening of inhibitions and a temporary freedom from ordinary responsibilities and constraints, as they believe the spirits have done as well. But it is one thing to judge that unrestrained pleasure opens the door to temptation and serves as an escape valve for those whose benefits from society's strictures have yet to equal the costs, and quite another to consider it the moral responsibility of society's leaders, who hope thereby to achieve a positive union with spirits that stimulates them to respond with generosity toward humans. Drinking to intoxication is supposed by Otavalans to support the social order; to hispanic Ecuadorians it is supposed to potentially undermine it.

Otavalans had at least two systems of beliefs, practices, and symbols from which to judge behavior and guide their own actions. These systems were not monolithic; each contained a number of inconsistencies and choices. An example cited above is the widespread disagreement in Ecuador about whether indian inferiority, including that demonstrated by their drinking, is theirs by nature or the result of environmental factors, specifically the facts of conquest and domination. Cantina drinking can be considered spiritually neutral or positively evil. Admirable men of substance can be seen drunk in properly controlled settings or should never be visibly intoxicated at all. From the indigenous side, in the 1970s the interchange with spiritual forces, only vaguely differentiated by their Christian or pagan origins, can be seen as powerful and real or can be seen as traditional pageantry in problematic relationship with the orthodox teachings of the church. Some people may believe that asua is the central ceremonial beverage of the expected pair, while others find the more potent trago the preferred form. Drinking in the cantina may act for some as a simple extension of toasts at a boda huasi, particularly for those men who seem to enjoy the drunken conviviality, while for others it represents a worrisome break in the morality of home.

When the *Boda Huasi* Resembles the *Cantina*

In summary, the people of Huaycopungo had, from childhood, a number of ways to approach the drinking of alcohol. Because of their specific history, none of the alternatives were either spiritually or politically neutral. Acting in one way had consequences for the relationship of runa to the secular and mestizo powers of Ecuador and to the spiritual powers of the universe, however hispanic or andean Catholic. But differing behaviors and their associated symbolic meanings could be juxtaposed, transposed, or mixed in different ways for different purposes (Amselle 1998). The challenge was to reap as much benefit in this world and with God as possible, while not jeopardizing the indigenous people's special status in the eternal animated environment of the Andes nor sacrificing the separate moral economy that defended their worth against the value judgments of the dominant society. While the effort to maintain an obvious and meaningful social boundary between mestizos and indians has continued undiminished, and perhaps increased, until the present, many daily and ceremonial practices have become more assimilated to the Ecuadorian mainstream over the years, as we will see in part II. Then, it seemed, the distinctions between the boda huasi and the cantina began to blur a bit too much. Today's curagas soon became known as viejos chumados, drunk old men.

CHAPTER FIVE

Curagacuna or *Viejos Chumados*
Native Lords or Drunk Old Men

Curaga

ONE LATE AFTERNOON Taita Rafael Criollo was laboring on the railroad line above San Rafael when he spotted a hawk, made suddenly visible in the new shadows as the blinding equatorial sun began its quick descent behind Mount Cotacachi. Excitedly he pointed it out to his fellow workers, saying, *Anga, anga* (Hawk, hawk). Perhaps they were all so tired and bored that Rafael's excited call seemed completely out of proportion to the event and they laughed themselves silly. Whatever the reason, he was permanently nicknamed Anga Rafael, and he passed this nickname on to his children, grandchildren, and now, great-grandchildren. People in Huaycopungo have had registered surnames in the Spanish system for a long time, taking both their father's and mother's patronymic, in that order. For given names, in the 1970s a small pool of hispanic names served everyone, so that Juans and Juanas were everywhere, but other common hispanic names, like Ricardo, were treated as if in a foreign language. Despite this international naming system, adults were most often identified by a Quichuaized version of their given name, like Jusi instead of José, preceded by a nickname, which they inherited from their mother or father or acquired on their own. If no catchy nickname has been inherited or acquired, the first name of a parent was often used to distinguish one Rafael or Mercedes from the others. When asked, people often can't remember their relatives' and neighbors' official surnames. Rafael Criollo, Anga Rafi, was Antonio Criollo's father and the paternal grandfather of Isabel Criollo, whom we met building the house in chapter 1. People refer to father and daughter as Anga Andu and Anga Sabila. Nicknames survive several generations only if the original bearer was important enough to be remembered as the founder of an ayllu.

Anga Rafi was called curaga, village headman or native lord (Salomon [1973] 1981, 1986). The outlines of his career, and that of other curagacuna, provide a good introduction to the subjects of the limited, but treasured, political and economic autonomy and agency within the indigenous community in the 1970s. While Huaycopungo is embedded in a regional, national, and even international political and economic system that effectively, and often brutally, constrains the possibilities of its residents, individuals try to wrest as much advantage as possible for their families and the community and to establish a space of autonomy, even if it is largely symbolic. Poor indigenous communities may gain only a bit of wiggle room by their efforts, but whatever little advantage can be gained provides people in the community with the sense of some control over their destinies. Autonomy is a value, a goal, and a very rare achievement in political and economic arenas, although it is a very real accomplishment in symbolic culture as explored in chapter 3. While early Marxist doctrine claimed that symbolic autonomy, through religious beliefs, simply constituted a barrier to achieving real political and economic autonomy, since it engendered complacency, here it is emphasized that such symbolic agency may provide a reservoir of hope and pride that can be mobilized in continuing or future social struggles for political and economic equity. Like the hawk, Huaycopungo's leaders can soar in their own minds far above the petty machinations of the poor but haughty mestizos in San Rafael and look down on the land where the numerical dominance of the indigenous people suggests a more desired reality.

Mestizos and Indians in the Regional Economy of the 1970s

The indigenous people of San Rafael parish were particularly known for their production of esteras, reed mats from the totora reeds gathered, in part, from the marshy lakeshores. Before dawn every morning, each family would spend a few hours weaving the treated reeds into mats that they would then sell to middlemen, each individual keeping the money from the mats they made themselves. Regional and intraregional differentiation by occupation or craft has a long history in this part of the Andes. Buitrón, the native ethnographer who studied Otavalo in the 1940s and 1950s, described a pattern of handicraft production that could still be seen in the 1970s and to a lesser extent today.

"Cada parcialidad tiene su nombre, su tradición, su especialidad. . . . Los indios de Punyaro son tejedores de cestas y sombreros de *zuro*. Los de San Juan son tejedores de lienzos de algodón. Los de Peguche e Ilumán son tejedores de casimires y chales. Los de Carabuela tejen ponchos y los de Quinchuquí cobijas. Los indios de Pucará tejen esteras y aventadores con la *totora* que crece en las orillas del Lago de San Pablo y los de Calpanquí son alfareros"

[Each native community has its name, its tradition and its specialty. . . . The indians of Punyaro weave baskets and hats of *zuro*.[1] Those from San Juan are weavers of cotton rope. Those from Peguche and Ilumán are weavers of fine woolens and shawls. Those from Carabuela weave ponchos and those in Quinchuquí blankets. The indians of Pucará weave mats and fans from the totora that grows on the shores of Lake San Pablo and the people of Calpanquí[2] are potters (n.d., 21; my translation)]. He goes on to say that each family added these specializations to their main job of tilling their small fields, at least for the majority of families that were lucky enough to have inherited land.

Mestizos and runa alike were also accustomed to an ideal and traditional division of labor between them, where manual labor was the duty of runa and value-added labor was the exclusive privilege of the mestizos and blancos. In general, all but the poorest mestizos did avoid manual labor for the cultural capital they could then acquire, and because indians and, in some regions, the descendants of Afro-Ecuadorian slaves and freedmen were available in large numbers to do it for them. Although the rights to certain activities were always contested and no traditional pattern achieved total compliance, this division of labor was quite influential. The pattern stemmed, in part, from colonial relations of production and generally favored the mestizos over indians. Nonetheless, indigenous people sought to wrest whatever benefit for themselves they could out of the productive activities to which they were confined, especially access to agricultural plots. The native worldview that exalted man's relationship to geographic space and physical landscape was preserved and intensified by this consequence of conquest. At times the indigenous people boldly defended their special rights to these restricted niches. And, of course, indians also exerted whatever pressure might be reasonably expected to increase their economic freedom and access to resources.

However, the most destitute mestizos could not afford this strategy of employing others to farm and living apart from indians, particularly if they had migrated in to the area in search of opportunity. From his research in Punyaro, on the outskirts of Otavalo during the 1950s, Rubio Orbe (1956, 133, 219) describes the similar lifestyles of the impoverished runa and mestizo cultivators. Nor did nonelite mestizos always support this division, since those who could obtain sufficient productive land and who could stay isolated from urban beliefs about the degrading quality of physical labor did sometimes farm. Still, the corollary of the expectation that mestizos would not do manual labor was that indigenous people would do only manual labor, as well as provide for their own subsistence. Secondly, as much as practicable, indians did not constitute paid labor. As a way to restrict a small money supply to the higher-status mestizos, labor arrangements that bypassed monetary compensation were preferred when using indigenous labor, such as in the provision of meals, alcohol, rights to huasipungos, rights to harvest totora, and the like, instead of pay. Indian children, especially girls, were often given to mestizo families as unpaid servants in payment for debt.

Well into the 1980s the Otavaleños continued to pay taxes to municipalities and to the churches in labor and sometimes in a portion of their harvest. When city streets needed to be swept or the jail scrubbed or the church whitewashed, indians were forcibly set to work. Such labor restrictions were often illegal, and sometimes unsuccessful, but nonetheless mestizos frequently tried to make these expectations become reality, while indigenous people either tried to resist them or to turn them to their own advantage. As Rubio Orbe (1956, 162) points out, the church could refuse to provide essential religious services, including denying the dead burial in hallowed ground, to those who did not comply. Similarly, the secular authorities could refuse to register a land deed or to jail a thief if the request came from someone who had declined to work on command.

The establishment of local monopolies in the production of rope, woolens, shawls, reed mats, pottery, and other basic goods for sale by Otavaleños constituted a combination of both an acceptance of an ethnic division of labor and an arena of contest for resources. If indigenous family production and sale of handicrafts became financially profitable, then mestizos would try to control the retailing of these items. The same holds for any surplus agricultural production, which mestizos purchased wholesale from the indigenous producers. Mestizo marketing often increased the volume of indigenous sales. However, marginal profits rarely improved for the producers, who were now working longer hours in production, because of the percentage taken by the middlemen.

Finally, mestizos preferred to make their homes in the commercial centers, whether Ibarra, the capital of the province; Otavalo, the capital of the cantón; or the many parish centers, while the indigenous people were expected to remain in the peripheral areas of the city or in the rural communities scattered around them. If the city expanded into a traditionally indigenous community, all native landowners generally lost their land in a very few years through a variety of legal and illegal means. For example, the current Otavalo neighborhood of Montserrat used to be a satellite indigenous community. While few indigenous people could afford urban real estate or dared to leave the insurance of their chacras so far behind, those who did attempt urban living were subject to subtle and not so subtle harassment. The advantages, however, were greatest for textile weavers, who could and did take advantage of the commercial opportunities of the city from the 1940s (Parsons 1945).

It is tempting, and partially accurate, to see these patterns as simply an extension of colonial relations between indians and nonindians. However, it is perhaps more accurate to recognize that rural and poor urban mestizos were often caught between the blancos, the landholding elite who owned the vast majority of fertile land, and the poor indians, who had tenaciously held on to their more marginal chacras. Lower-ranking elite, often termed blancos only locally, owned small commercial enterprises whose few hired help labored in the most precarious conditions. A lucky and educated few made their living through positions in the government or the church. But the majority of mestizos were landless in an economy dominated by agriculture and lacking industrial development. While they had their own labor to sell, industry was very scarce and agricultural labor was extremely degrading. Commercial activities in the informal sector were their one traditional opportunity and they guarded it zealously from competition.

The growing tourism of the latter half of the twentieth century challenged the ethnic economic divisions even further. In the 1970s Otavalo was a major tourist destination for international travelers, mostly for the Saturday market. In 1972 when I first visited the Otavalo market as a tourist, the explosive growth of handicraft production, especially textiles, for the tourism market had already begun. Based on his fieldwork in 1946, Otavalo native and ethnographer Anibal Buitrón described the Otavalo market as an outlet for indians and mestizos to sell to each other but hardly mentions tourism (Collier and Buitrón 1971). Rubio Orbe (1956) mentions North American tourists buying some weavings but speaks little of them when describing the Otavalo textile market.

While it may make sense to set the beginning of the growth period in indigenous marketing of weavings to tourists to the late 1960s and early 1970s, the roots, both real and imaginary, stretch deep into the past. Even before the Incas conquered the area, Otavalans wove cotton obtained from the eastern slopes of the Andes and marketed it in all directions, sometimes as far as Central America, along with other goods. This was so even though Central Americans grew both their own inferior cotton domesticates and some Andean strains (Vreeland

1999). Unlike in the Incan and other central Andean empires, where colonies were established to obtain goods from distant places, northern Ecuador had long-distance traders. In Imbabura, long-distance traders enjoyed freedom from labor and food tribute to the local chiefs, since they could provide the luxury goods—like gold, feathers, and beads (Salomon [1973] 1981)—that so enhanced their majesty. When the Incas consolidated their rule over this part of northern Ecuador in the late fifteenth century, after many years of struggle, they brought wool as a raw material for weaving, and Otavalans quickly added it to their repertoire.

After about only forty years of Inca domination in Imbabura, the Spanish arrived. Having assassinated the Inca emperor Atahualpa in 1532, they founded Quito in 1534 on the plateau high above the scorched cities, towns, and fields left by the Ecuadorian general Rumiñahui in his final desperate attempts to repel the Spanish invaders. In Imbabura province, Ibarra and Otavalo were also founded during the early years of empire, like Quito near the sites of pre-Columbian urban centers but also slightly apart from them. In the first hundred years after this conquest, the Spanish were not particularly interested in textiles as tribute, being more concerned with gold and other resources that would lead to instant wealth. Still, one presumes that weaving continued in Otavalo in order to satisfy local demand, even through the significant disruptions of fighting, disease, migrations, and the tribute demands of the Spanish. One hundred years later, however, Otavalo again became involved in a boom of textile production, directed by the colonial powers and destined for foreign export. While some of the Ecuadorian textiles were exported to Europe, they were in particular demand for the feverishly expanding mining industry in Peru and Bolivia. While the international market for Sierran textiles again fell precipitously a hundred years later, it is reasonable to suspect that, once again, enterprising people in Otavalo continued to seek new outlets for these skills beyond the provision of their own clothing. As Meisch recently said, "For 450 years it has been traditional for Otavalos to make nontraditional cloth" (2002, 21).

Perhaps then, as now, the traditional clothing and hairstyles of Otavaleños served as a kind of product logo, a guarantee that their textiles were genuinely Otavalo-made and therefore of the expected high quality. Pride in clothing themselves well also seems to have a very long and distinguished history. William Bennett Stevenson, an English visitor to Otavalo in the early nineteenth century wrote, "I never saw a finer looking people than an assembly of Otavaleños on a Sunday" (Salomon [1973] 1981, 420).

Even this emphasis on preserving indigenous traditional clothing has not prevented continual innovation, at least in the last fifty years or so. While anaco colors and embroidery styles have changed over the period, they still seem very like drawings made by Guaman Poma de Ayala in the late 1600s. But the colonial Spanish-type blouses have almost completely replaced the tunics worn by women almost exclusively up until forty years ago. And the ponchos distinctive of Otavalo have changed from red to blue, from handwoven to machine-woven, from one-sided to reversible, and have added a collar.

Nonetheless, the ease with which hindsight allows us to follow a thread of specialization in weaving and international trade backward in time for so many generations is a good reason to suspect that this ethnic specialization in local, national, and international trade in textiles is partially imaginary. People living at any time in the past would likely see the current elevation of these activities to the status of symbol of ethnic identity and blueprint for an indigenous future as exceedingly peculiar. Other occupational specializations and cultural symbols from times past have probably disappeared with barely a trace in the present.

Saturday morning was Otavalo's *feria*, or traditional market day. In the 1970s, the Plaza 24 de Mayo, the food market, was open daily, but on Saturday it overflowed with local vendors and purveyors of tropical produce from the coast or low-altitude mountain valleys. The textile market, the Plaza de Ponchos, opened only on Saturdays. Before dawn, the mostly indigenous sellers would carefully arrange their wares on ponchos spread out on the ground and sit behind them, awaiting the approach of the mestizo wholesalers who would compete with each other to buy the very best goods at the lowest price. Especially right before San Juan, prosperous indian couples would carefully finger the quality of the wool in the ponchos and anacos or count the number of strands of golden glass beads being sold for *hualcas* (necklaces) before buying themselves part of a new outfit.

The years of the 1970s involved a competition between the mestizos of Otavalo and the indigenous people of the region to reap the major benefits of the growth in tourism. Fortunately for native Otavaleños and unfortunately for the area's mestizos, it was the exotically dressed indigenous weavers the visitors came to see. Mestizos tried but ultimately failed to control the sales, the restaurants, the transportation, the public phones, the tours, and everything else involved with the tourism industry. Here the native people found a big loophole in the net that restricted them from full economic participation, which they struggled to make ever bigger and bigger.

The commercialization of weaving by individuals from the traditional weaving towns of Peguche, Ilumán, and Quinchuquí in the northern end of the valley helped spur the rise in tourism. Rosa Lema, a trailblazer from Peguche, moved her family into Otavalo and began a textile business there. She led the wave of successful entrepreneurial expansion of weaving for export and for the tourism market. Rosa Lema's legendary stature in the community only grew when a similarly pioneering young woman, the American anthropologist Elsie Clews Parsons, published her remarkable story in 1945. During the 1970s, Peguche and other neighboring towns were undergoing the 1970s version of some of the changes that only affected Huaycopungo ten to fifteen years later. Some communities were considered more prosperous than others, with Peguche, Ilumán, and Quinchuquí leading the way in the 1950s (Rubio Orbe 1956), as they still did during the 1970s. However, in practical terms, the indigenous families were class stratified within their communities, with the most prosperous buying land as a result of private sale or land reform (Rubio Orbe 1956, 165), building large homes, or moving into Otavalo.

During the late 1970s Huaycopungo was generally considered backward by indigenous people living in Otavalo or in the towns engaged in commercial weaving, since everyone there still relied primarily on agriculture for most of their food. Nonetheless, the interaction of individuals from both regions in the indigenist confederations, and the opportunities for people from Huaycopungo to witness the interchanges with tourists on Saturday, increased their references for thinking about their place in the world, even though it offered few economic opportunities. The reed mats, esteras, were marketable to the runa and mestizos of Ecuador and Colombia only, since, even should they want to buy them, tourists could not fit them into their luggage. However, during this time, antique jewelry and even some antique religious paraphernalia were sold to tourists, who would pay prices unthinkable in the local market. Isabel's mother, Mama Dolores Perugachi, sold the long strands of native coral beads that she, like many other women in San Rafael, hung from her ears, where they dangled to her shoulders. Mama Dolores, again like most other women, turned the profit into the purchase of land or animals rather than spending it on fiesta obligations. Almost all local coral was sold off at that time, and ten years later prosperous young women began to buy much cheaper coral imported from India.

Political Authority in Huaycopungo

Despite the changes going on in Otavalo in the 1970s, Huaycopungo still bore some resemblance to the "closed corporate peasant community" originally described for Mexico by Wolf (1955, 1957). A large number of monolingual residents had almost no personal contact with the outside world, and most of the leaders asserted an image of their community as separate and independent from the national society. But this was more an ideological stance than a factual state, and it was becoming less real all the time. Money was a necessity for such important expenses as a wedding, a baptism, a house building, a fiesta sponsorship, the purchase of land, or paying fines imposed by the local authorities, and money was earned in the mestizo economy all over the country. The municipal and provincial governments would frequently try to enact development schemes, improved tax collection programs, or more stringent and universally applied social control measures for the cantón, to which the indigenous communities had to respond, usually with some mixture of compliance and passive resistance. Only rarely did they try active resistance, since despite their greater numbers, in all other forms of power they were at a distinct disadvantage. On the most regular basis, the local runacuna had to accept some level of intrusion from their mestizo neighbors in San Rafael, who had administrative authority over them and who had so few economic resources of their own that squeezing free labor or foodstuffs out of their inferior charges often proved irresistible, as was collecting unpaid fines in the form of confiscated land. If the indians had a dispute with their neighbor that could not be solved internally, the *teniente político*, the highest parish authority, was always a potential recourse.

However, the ideology of autonomy kept people searching for whatever means they could find to squeeze a bit more local agency from the wider society, even if that meant only making a virtue out of necessity—we don't need to eat as much meat as the mishu because we are not gluttons. However illusory the victory, it could keep the community from despair. Many of these compromises in the name of preserving the belief in autonomy had high costs. The cost of the pride in a largely vegetarian diet was a decreasing adult height over time. But the lemonade they made from the lemon they had received was sometimes sweetened with unexpected benefits. For instance, the stance that "we have few material possessions because we are not greedy but put a higher value on social and spiritual forms of wealth" meant that they owned very few, and generally homemade, material goods. While this is commonly held to be a personal tragedy and a drag on a modern economy, the indigenous people in Huaycopungo held the significant problems caused by increasing amounts of nonbiodegradable garbage at bay for a lot longer than did their acquisitive neighbors.

Seen from one side, this adaptation involves asserting a separate identity and separate source of cultural capital that can make individuals symbolically rich, but on the other side it nevertheless requires a continual negotiation at the margins. The best curagas are poised at this juncture, supposedly perpetuating an ancient tradition of full indigenous autonomy but actually exercising their position in the overarching social system that extends beyond the socioeconomic boundaries of the indigenous communities in order to gain advantages for their families and their community, particularly as regards land resources. Mirroring the previous chapter, we will explore what the cultural interchange at the ethnic boundaries means for the production and perpetuation of indigenous culture and ethnic identity, here by examining the lives of the leaders of the 1970s.

From the time of the Spanish conquest, the Spanish-speaking authorities also recognized the shifting potential of curagas to do one of three things—to represent their interests in the indigenous community to the detriment of the indigenous citizenry; to oppose the authorities in the community's name; or to mediate between the hispanic outsiders and their indigenous subjects. While the first alternative is more desirable to colonial or national authorities in the short run, it is recognized that in the long run, such blatant toadying to the dominant society on the part of the curagas would cause them to lose legitimacy within their community. The best long-term strategy from the point of view of hispanic outsiders and indigenous insiders is the latter, trying to find a balance that satisfies the local power elite while minimizing the harm and maximizing the benefit to the local community. That leaves hispanic and indigenous leaders the leeway to occasionally try for a more radical advantage to themselves. Nevertheless, as much as nonindian leaders needed native middlemen to administer the usually monolingual and recalcitrant indigenous masses, they were always afraid that those middlemen would cheat them or, contrarily, become so associated with nonindian interests in the eyes of the indian majority that they would be ignored by their constituents, expelled from their home territories, or even suffer mysterious and fatal accidents. An indigenous leader who too brazenly worked with others to resist their domination could easily fall prey to an accident, as Isabel was threatened by local mestizos in the early years of her activism.

A mirror image of the same calculus held true for the indigenous people themselves. Indigenous leadership came to signify a dangerous double game. If it was too effective at uniting the indigenous community and increasing its strength and well-being, it would capture the negative attention of the mestizo minority, whose interest lay in keeping the indigenous people subordinate and disorganized. Perhaps for that reason, a soft-spoken, humble, self-sacrificing, and self-deprecating style of individual leadership came to prevail in the indigenous community, so these individuals would not appear to represent a challenge to outside authorities. Nonetheless, a local leader had to be able to deal effectively with the outside world as well. And as much as the natives prized those leaders with the necessary skills to deal with the Spanish, and later the Ecuadorian, authorities, they feared that these same persons would go too far, would be seduced by personal gain to represent the wishes of those colonial and national authorities over those of the community. These political realities have led to an extremely two-sided political strategy—indigenous communities are both integrated into the wider nonindian society and resolutely separate from it. In Huaycopungo curagas and other local leaders are respected and also despised, relied upon and mistrusted. Hierarchy is both glorified and mocked. Skills in the outside world are both desired and feared. The wealth and power of the Hispanic-Ecuadorian society and culture are simultaneously envied and scorned.

At the same time, this kind of double view of curagas as potentially selfless symbols and mobilizers of community unity and as self-aggrandizing exploiters of their people is not as unpleasantly paradoxical in Huaycopungo as it might be in a society with a different philosophical orientation. As we have seen, it is the nature of power of all kinds, whether political, spiritual, or economic, to be as easily directed toward the support of people or toward their harm. Nor is the outcome of the deployment of power necessarily under the direct control of the leader himself. His interventions on behalf of humans in affairs of the greatest consequence risk directing the negative attentions of superhuman powers toward the community in ways that may favor the mestizo community. The familiar nature of this folk philosophical position can be seen here to both spring from ancient cultural roots and to be given tremendous reinforcement by the dual reality in which the people live as a dominated ethnic minority in their native land. The way to ensure the best outcome from the curagas' actions is by continual ritualized interactions, such as the humble offering of alcoholic drinks, which obligates the mighty to reciprocate with generous aid.

Curaga is a very old term in the Andes, so I was initially surprised to find that the position still existed in Huaycopungo, which is not some isolated indigenous village but situated on the Pan-American Highway and only about one hundred kilometers from the national capital. Later I realized that the use of the term had most likely been reinvigorated in the recent past by social activists who believed that the *Ley de Comunas* of 1937 went too far in integrating indigenous communities into the national and political legal system, thus reducing indigenous autonomy. One of the founding policies of Ecuarunari, the first modern organization established by and for indigenous people in the Ecuadorian Sierra, in 1972, was to promote curagas and other traditional forms of community organization.[3] The indigenous people in the valleys of Cayambe and Otavalo were close enough to be targets of this political organizing. The founding of Ecuarunari was followed by the establishment in 1974 of the Conféderación Campesina (CC) in Imbabura (which became FICI, Federación Indígena y Campesina de Imbabura in 1984). The Conféderación Campesina held as important goals the recuperation of communal lands and the reestablishment of the authority of curagas (CONAIE 1989). The CC rejected the elaboration of bureaucratic laws driven by a different political culture and authority, such as the encouragement of legally registered cooperatives or the election of governing councils[4] in favor of the more flexible rules of communal land tenure and authority relationships to be rediscovered in the native past. The organization was trying to prevent such problems as the increase in the number of microchacras as a result of the registering of individual ownership rights to land.

In the late 1970s, when I asked people in Huaycopungo what *curaga* meant, they always began by saying that curagas were the "owners of the land." Although use rights to most land parcels are acquired through maternal or paternal inheritance, the curaga retained a role as the caretaker of all community land and had a (normally latent) responsibility to monitor all land distribution. If new land was obtained, or if landowners died without heirs, the curaga could redistribute it to the land poor or landless. Contrarily, if instead of land without owners, there was a person without land, the curaga should try to remedy the situation by redistributing any surplus, perhaps from his own reserves. In addition, curagas represented the community as a whole, acting as community power brokers and dispute mediators both to the outside world and among community members.

Ideally, curagas inherited their positions and passed them on to their children and children's children, making certain ayllucuna a kind of hereditary noble class. However, becoming a curaga required the demonstration of the right stuff along with some kind of kinship tie with a previous curaga. A lineal relationship with a previous curaga was neither necessary nor sufficient for someone to be recognized as a curaga. Nor were consanguineal kinship relationships presumed to be the only kinship ties capable of facilitating the transmission of particular traits. The ritual acts that create spouses, in-laws, godparents, and compadres were also thought to make possible the passing on of the special abilities that a curaga displays in abundance, such as generosity, economic success, wisdom in speech, humility, diplomacy, genealogical memory, unflagging energy, and selfless dedication. Another asset that kinship of all sorts represents for the curaga is the provision of an ayllu in both senses—the cognatic descent group and the ego-centered kindred—which provide sources of political support and legitimacy in the community, particularly if both are sufficiently large. The right stuff, in this case, is a big, powerful, and well-connected family. Furthermore, a child growing up in the house of a curaga receives excellent training for future responsibilities that might make him seem more qualified than someone without that childhood experience. However, in fact, a curaga gains social recognition as much by his demonstration of his personal abilities as through the right genealogy.[5] As with the concept off ayllu, as discussed in chapter 1, it might be better to define curaga by concentrating on the behavior that is characteristic of a curaga than on fixed eligibility criteria, even though the latter seems to natives and observers alike to be primary because it is supposed to be the source of the former.

In addition, curagas extend the meaning of endogamy, and homeland—for them *llactapura cazaranchic* (we marry among those who share our territorial home)—includes neighboring communities, making neighboring communities related like affinal kin to their own. Whereas endogamous marriage was the rule in Huaycopungo—92 percent of marriages were endogamous in my sample in 1977–79—the three living Huaycopungo curagas had married women from neighboring parish communities (Rafael Criollo was dead). The children of curagas often marry each other, particularly if they aspire to the position themselves. However, other wealthy men may succeed their fathers-in-law as curagas. Since all curagas have very large kindreds and considerable land resources in their native community, they only increase their social ties by adding physically distant affinal kin, always of some importance in their own community. Ordinary people, with fewer social and material resources, find that the physical distance between the houses and chacras of their kindreds would work to diminish their labor efficiency and sources of support. Perhaps more importantly, curagas then obtain usufruct rights, as a member of a married pair, to land outside their own community. Since one of the functions of curagas is to administer, defend, and even increase the land resources of the community, this territorial expansion is to their advantage. Their own children will then inherit land from their mother in that neighboring community as well as in their father's.

Anga Rafi—Rafael Criollo

Anga Rafi attained his position by leading Huaycopungo in a successful challenge against the very large Hacienda Cusín, stretching from the eastern end of the lake and way up Mount Cusín behind it. For decades Huaycopungo residents had supplied labor to the hacienda during peak times of the agricultural cycle as *yanaperos* (according to a traditional labor contract in which peasants owed an obligation to work when summoned in exchange for specific and restricted usufruct rights). In return they were given the right to harvest totora reeds on hacienda lands. Totora is the essential raw material for the reed mats that all children and adults wove and sold for cash to middlemen, who then peddled them all over Ecuador. The arrangements of *yanapa* did not restrict the economic rights of indians as much as did those for huasipungos, the labor pattern whereby the members of a permanent and resident hacienda labor force were given a small plot on which to live and cultivate their own food in exchange for their services in house and field. Nonetheless, the extent of the freedom of the free indian communities, like Huaycopungo, was relative, since the economic and political power of the large landowners was so overwhelming in the rural counties. Indigenous people tried to ensure that their relationship with the hacienda owners was personal, constrained by the same reciprocal and moral bonds that characterized their other hierarchical social relations. Just as they struggled to ensure that the curagas' power was used for the communal good, they endeavored to include *hacendados* in this andean Christian moral community in which all prosper, despite unequal access to resources. However, when the absentee hacienda owners left the management of their indigenous labor to hired managers, these overseers most often seemed to be motivated entirely by their pay, having no personal stake in the welfare of the land and its people. It stood to reason, in local eyes, that the overseers saw the traditional arrangements as a license to abuse the indigenous workers for personal profit. They would call for labor from Huaycopungo on very short notice, when families were busy with their own crops, and threaten a loss of the right to harvest totora if the laborers showed up late. They did not feed their workers, as customary law demanded. The laborers were worked longer, harder, and in more jobs than was considered fair, and access to totora could be unduly restricted. What Taita Rafael and others fought for was a legal contract specifying the responsibilities of both parties, so that there could be legal recourse if overseers overstepped the bounds of the contract. Fifty families signed up to form a legally registered cooperative, Cooperativa Preñadilla, which has continued until the present. It was this use of legal opportunities newly present in the national system, since the *Ley de Comunas* of 1937, to improve the access to resources and protection from outside abuse that gained Rafael the title curaga.

In addition, Rafael added a paying job to his agricultural work and the weaving of totora. After the rail line construction was completed, he was offered and accepted an opportunity to work in rail line maintenance. While large numbers of indigenous men had responded to calls for labor in the railroad construction, most of Anga Rafi's permanent workmates were poor mestizos and cholos. The standard definition of cholo in the highlands describes someone with recent known native heritage who embraces the cultural heritage of the hispanic national majority. However, the term is often used as a pejorative social label for the rural poor, with little regard for racial/ethnic specificities. Some of Rafi's coworkers were not recent converts to hispanic identity but were humble enough economically to be treated as if they were. Other "nonindians" with whom Rafael worked were indeed cholos in the strict sense. Many were men who had been termed "surplus" on the haciendas where their parents had huasipungos, such as Hacienda Cusín. They were surplus because their younger siblings would inherit their parents' huasipungos, and the hacienda could not or would not set aside more land for a larger labor force. When extra labor was required, it could easily be found in free communities like Huaycopungo or from among the huasipungo's surplus children, without entailing any year-round responsibility on the part of the hacienda. These young men and women were allowed/forced to leave home and, most often, to abandon their ethnic heritage to try to make a living on the margins of nonindian society (see Crespi 1968), where their presence depressed labor costs in general. So, while Antonio was working with people who had various spatial, genealogical, and cultural connections to indian ethnicity, he would not have considered them literally his people or potential relatives. They were, however, acceptable fictive kin.[6]

Cholos with indigenous parents and siblings as well as those with more distant ties to an indigenous community both find themselves frequently torn between embracing the ideologies of the economic/ethnic classes above them, which their chosen cultural affiliation usually directs them to do, or developing alternative ideologies that denigrates those below them less. With the first strategy, they are obliged to accept their own extreme lowliness in the overall social hierarchy, unless and until they can achieve upward socioeconomic mobility, an unlikely scenario. With the second, they can raise their own relative position in their own and social inferiors' eyes in the absence of economic gain, but will remain forever despicable in the eyes of the dominant classes. Many aspire to a double game, which is frequently subject to discovery, making them seem inherently shifty and untrustworthy. The dominant national ideology gives cholos credit for choosing the future of progress over the degenerate and primitive past to which indian people so thoughtlessly cling, although this indigenous past taints them still. However, indigenous Otavaleños overwhelmingly judge that cholos suffer from deficiencies in both sources of cultural capital, the indigenous and the hispanic.

With these workmates Rafael learned to speak what was often called *chaupi lengua*, literally "half language." Chaupi lengua aptly uses one Quichua word (*chaupi*, "half") and one Spanish (*lengua*, "language") to refer to a kind of pidgin mix of the two languages. Many local mestizos were able to communicate in chaupi lengua, which they considered to be a very ignorant Spanish, the best the simpleminded indians could achieve. Calling chaupi lengua a kind of Spanish allowed them to claim no knowledge of Quichua themselves while deriding the communication skills of indians. In fact, at this time Quichua was most frequently referred to as Yanga Shimi, which means Worthless Language, by mestizos and indigenous people alike. The number of mestizos who knew Quichua is hard to judge accurately, since only the most nonconformist would admit to knowing all but the few words necessary to order their servants, field hands, or load carriers in the market. Rafael's ability to communicate with non-Quichua speakers increased his usefulness to the others in Huaycopungo. Like any leadership recognized by the local nonindian authorities, however, this language facility was considered a double-edged sword, since he could as easily help exploit his fellows as help defend them. Many of these workmates also became drinking companions, and Rafael would spend hours in the local bars with them, participating in nonindian drinking practices and learning more about nonindian views of proper civilized life (see chapter 4).

Anga Rafi was a heavy drinker, and retired from the railroad in the late 1960s when he began to miss too much work due to his being drunk or sleeping off a drunk during work time. Anga Andu substituted for his father until the boss suggested that Anga Rafi retire so that Anga Andu could take his place permanently. Although I never knew him, people tell me that Anga Rafi dedicated himself entirely to drink after he retired. In her late teens, his granddaughter, Anga Sabila, was trying to lead him safely across the Pan-American Highway when he was very drunk, but he broke away from her and was hit and killed by a passing car.

Anga Rafi would have been pointed out as a perfect example of the stereotypes that outsiders used to such effect to prove the social pathology of the indian community—*viejo chumado* and *indio mana vali* ("useless indian" in chaupi lengua). Although Rafael was often publicly drunk and most likely an alcoholic, his life is not accurately summed up by the phrase *viejo chumado*, which connotes a drunken bum whose current public intoxication is a sign of his sodden and wasted life. By national reckoning, a publicly drunk elder man has never managed to control the unruly behavior thought to be acceptable only when one is young. Nor could Rafael's life represent the typical path of men in Huaycopungo, either in his success as curaga or his eventual alcoholism. People in Huaycopungo find his end very sad, since drinking eventually overcame his ability to work, to cooperate with his family, to successfully represent the community to the outside world, and even to protect himself from danger. But Rafael's career was highly successful for many years, and his ability to drink socially and ritually was a tool in the creation of that position. First, sharing drinks with his work fellows at the cantina enabled him pursue social relationships in which he could learn how to best negotiate the nonindian world, a skill he used to advantage in the creation of the Cooperative Preñadilla. At the same time, as curaga, his central position among the circling gourd bowls of asua and shot glasses of trago at a boda huasi, and his many receipts of a bottle in a contractual acceptance of a plea for aid from needy community members made him a power broker. He was a creator and mobilizer of many of the webs of reciprocity between gods and men, between ayllucuna and between runa and mishu, which could, if properly maintained, improve the life of everyone in Huaycopungo. Politically, spiritually, and socially, Rafael's drinking activities lifted him up and gave him the personal power to attempt real change in the impact of the dominant society on his community. Anga Rafi operated on the margins, learning chaupi lengua, taking a job, and fighting the system through legal means, and in return was called, at home, *curaga*, a term that calls to mind a long-defeated indigenous nobility in an autonomous political system. Contrarily, mishucuna called him the term—viejo chumado— that absolves themselves of their responsibility for the consequences of conquest and lays the blame for current indigenous political and economic marginality on useless drunkenness.

Anga Andu—Antonio Criollo

Anga Rafi's son, Anga Andu, continued a similar strategy, although neither he nor his less gregarious older brother was ever called curaga. As a result of his railroad job, Antonio acquired a plot of land in Tocagon, as well as compadres there, and added these resources to those he had in Huaycopungo. Antonio was several times president of the Huaycopungo cabildo, or community council, and head of the Padres de Familia committee, where he served as liaison between the parents of school-age children and the mestizo schoolteachers. He was long-term president of the Cooperativa Preñadilla established by his father. Despite the legal founding of a cooperative, the relationships between the hacienda owner and the indian workers and between the indians and the managers remained characterized by a mix of traditional and

Fig. 38. Antonio Criollo Criollo, Anga Andu *Taita*
(PHOTO BY AUTHOR)

Curagacuna or *Viejos Chumados*   213

modern, exploitative and paternalistic practices. Antonio was able to use that paternalistic relationship to his advantage, too. His arranging for Isabel and José Manuel to work as domestics in the hacienda owner's Quito house after their marriage is one example.

Antonio, in partnership with his wife Dolores, was an aggressive and intelligent cultivator, livestock breeder, and trader of agricultural products throughout the region. A staunch upholder of the runa work ethnic, he would awake his family every morning before dawn and set them to work weaving esteras, when the totora reeds were at their most pliable and before the coming of light made agricultural work possible and school open its doors. He would compete to be one of the earliest houses from which could be heard the regular thump, pause, thump, pause, thump that characterized early morning hours all over Huaycopungo, as the reeds, damp from morning dew, were crossed over each other and the overlap pounded flat with a river rock held in the palm of the hand.

In addition to drinking regularly with his workmates in the taverns, as a politically active community member, Antonio was also a frequent participant in drinking in community mingas, life-cycle ceremonies, and religious festivals. Dolores frequently made asua to share when Antonio celebrated with new compadres. However, he did not undertake a major ritual sponsorship when his children were young, although his oldest son, Cipriano, did serve as Loa for a sponsoring Coraza. Later he was quite frustrated by his inability to convince his adult children to undertake a ritual sponsorship with his help. This made him the target of humiliation when his competitive neighbor would return home drunk, stand in the middle of the path between the houses, and shout for all to hear that Antonio was a *mucusu* for his lack of ritual accomplishment. Mucusu is a Quichuaized version of the Spanish *mocoso*, meaning "snot-nose," like a little kid too young to know to wipe his nose.

Antonio was proud of his large family of seven living children when they were young; they were a measure of his ambitions. Only a very successful person could expect to provide the resources for so many children to become independent adults themselves. If he did, they, along with their spouses, their children, their godparents, would swell the ranks of his own supporters during the years of his greatest potential political authority. Dolores was more worried about their futures than her husband and concerned that her own inner resources would not be sufficient to see her seven living children through adulthood: the seven pregnancies that had ended in the infants' deaths and the care of her seven living children had so depleted her. But she continued her own economic efforts to increase their land resources, including selling the long strands of native coral she wore hanging from her ears and around her wrists, when the price for antique jewelry skyrocketed in the Otavalo market.

Antonio and Dolores were very concerned about ensuring that their children had every traditional and more modern benefit they could for the future. They were lucky in that the combination of agriculture on good plots each had inherited, rights to sufficient totora production for producing and selling esteras, and a paying job on the railroad were frequently enough to meet their needs for cash. Rarely did Antonio go himself or send his sons with *enganchadores*, labor contractors, to haciendas on the coast. Most often, the laborers would spend more time paying off their debts for food, clothes, and tools than making any money to bring home. Nor did his family have to seek jobs in Quito during the construction boom there in the 1970s, during which many impoverished agricultural families were able to gain the money for a decent wedding, fiesta sponsorship, house building, or school fees.

At the time the southern end of the Otavalo valley was undergoing a major change because of the boom in the tourist industry. Otavaleño weaving entrepreneurs were acquiring the economic power to challenge their lack of access to middle-class benefits such as schooling, residence in Otavalo, multiroom houses, cars, and respectful treatment in public places. People in Huaycopungo were proud of their continuing, though relative, self-sufficiency in agriculture and defiant separation from the mishu world, especially after Huaycopungo and Cachiviro had successfully repelled plans to build a military base on the lakeshore. Still, they began to envy the economic advances in Peguche and Quinchuquí and to fear the increasing insufficiency of land resources for their growing population.

Like many ambitious families of the time, Antonio and Dolores pursued different strategies for the preparation and education of each child. If they hedged their bets by preparing some children to play a larger role in the national economy, though this might disqualify them for manual labor, and let others take their place in Huaycopungo's subsistence economy, perhaps the whole family would come out ahead. Isabel was sent to elementary school in San Rafael, one of the few indigenous children among the mishu majority. She was a superior student, and the priest pressured her parents to send her to a junior high and high school for girls run by missionary nuns from Italy. Her parents' acquiescence made Isabel the first person from Huaycopungo to attend any high school, although she completed only two years. Antonio used his railroad connections to get his second child, Cipriano, trained as a telegraph operator for the railroad company, a white-collar job more prestigious than the work he had done himself. He sent his third and fourth children, daughters Asciencia and Rosa Maria, to school but was relatively lax in pushing them forward. However, Asciencia married the son of a curaga who was one of the community's first high school graduates and later went on to complete her own high school education. Rosa Maria trained as a practical nurse. When Antonio's fifth child, Oswaldo, was very young, his parents cut his hair so he would look like a mestizo, rather than let it grow long to be braided in the traditional fashion. This mixed mocho identity could be an advantage in some places where he would not be so readily typecast as a traditional indian. In contrast to Oswaldo, Cipriano was proud of his long, thick hair and would spend a long time ostentatiously brushing it in the sun when he was a teenager. When Oswaldo became a teenager, he too let his hair grow and continues to be proud of his thick and healthy braid. José and Juana, the two youngest, had less distinguished childhoods and young adulthoods. Like many younger children of important families, their histories became more like the average poor young person of their generation, struggling with little success to find the key to economic security.

When I first knew him in 1977, Antonio was well respected and influential in Huaycopungo. However, he had a reputation for drinking too much, for stretching the culturally appropriate reasons for drinking to an absurd point. He was frequently violent at home, attacking his wife or his domestic property, and verbally abusive to his children, his neighbors, and his relatives. They continued to respect him, tending to his needs when drunk, although his belligerent behavior and his bottomless self-pity challenged everyone's emotional resources. Nonetheless, he maintained an active work life, although perhaps spending more on alcohol than was desirable, and remained an active force in the community. He supported the efforts of the generation of young adults, including his eldest daughter, whose improved knowledge of Spanish and nonindian etiquette gave them an edge in negotiating for better treatment, even though at the same time he worried that their new methods undermined the exercise of his style of authority. While not approving of his behavior while drunk, few people criticized his drinking, since that was part of his legitimate role as a community elder and leader.

Like his father before him, Antonio's middle-aged years on the railroad were plagued with alcohol-related absenteeism. Dolores and her children did everything they could to ensure he put in enough days to be able to legally retire. With Isabel's help he was able to complete the paperwork necessary to get a retirement pension, which he collected monthly till his death. These benefits, while "ensured" by law, actually required substantial Spanish-language skills, obstinacy, courage, numerous costly trips to the national capital, small bribes, and even hired legal help to obtain. Ironically, while its annual monetary value was worth the tremendous effort in the 1980s, the value of the pension has since become negligible.

If I was around when he came home drunk in those years, Antonio would always get maudlin, beating his head against the house wall, weeping and shouting over and over again that his head was empty, that he was a stupid indian and knew nothing. Perhaps I represented a particularly challenging contradiction in terms for him. Because of my white skin, my relative wealth, and my high level of education, I was a representative of the highest social level they recognized, even though (or maybe because) I was also a foreigner, albeit married to an Ecuadorian with a hispanic last name. In contrast to my position in the local and national status hierarchy, in Huaycopungo I tried to insist on egalitarian relationships, even stressing the junior aspects of my gender, age, and stage in the life cycle (only one small child). Two drunk old women once said in my hearing—believing that I did not understand Quichua—that I was like the Virgin Mary come back to earth, much to my embarrassment. As this woman explained to her companion, I resembled the Virgin by representing the contradictory, but spiritually ideal, extremes of power and prestige, generosity and humility in one person.

At the same time, Antonio was engaging me in a kind of runa guilt trip, lowering himself to raise me up, offering me homage to compel a return gift of my personal resources to improve the conditions for him and his family. When he was drunk, it seemed he could not stop himself from either belittling or defending himself to me. His use of the Ecuadorian social cues of extreme humility—falsetto voice, lowered head, avoidance of eye contact, whining repetition, self-deprecatory references, and multiple honorifics directed at the listener—approached an exaggerated caricature. Similarly, I may have behaved as a stereotypical liberal American who came of age in the 1960s, reaping a windfall of moral superiority from my offer of equal relations to people almost universally judged to be my social inferiors. When I saw Disney's *Snow White and the Seven Dwarfs* several years later, I was haunted by the fear that in some senses this was the game I had been playing in Ecuador, being oh so sweet to the shorter, darker, barrel-chested andean natives that I patronizingly treated as my friends. One of the points of this book is to demonstrate how we are influenced by the stories that we have available to interpret our lives, so I have to recognize the Sunday school and Disney influences on my own utopian thinking. However, I do not have to judge anyone's motives as entirely pure or impure. What seemed so familiar about *Snow White* was not just my own sense of entitlement, but the efforts of people like Antonio to get me to accept my role as the bleeding-hearted, Snow White Princess among the canny dwarfs. In retrospect I see that he treated me to the same pressure applied to hacienda owners, designed to tug at the heartstrings and activate religious teachings about Christian charity. It can now make me laugh that I likely stimulated Antonio's ever more frantic efforts to humble himself in front of me. I idealistically offered to take the role of junior runa huarmi, which, in my lack of skill and physical endurance, I could never in my wildest dreams have pulled off. In turn, Antonio, when drunk, indirectly begged me to take the role of the rich outsider so he could reap the real benefits of my superior resources rather than the dubious advantage of my egalitarian friendship. We both thought we were making an offer the other could not refuse.

In addition, Antonio's enthusiastic pursuit of friendship, paternalistic relationships, and indebtedness with those who were not indians exposed him constantly to the prevailing Ecuadorian view of the base inferiority, indeed primitive immorality, of his person and his culture. Since he was actively trying to improve the life of his family and community by engaging in a limited way with the national world, he could not afford the luxury of a totally separate identity and cultural strategy. Drinking ceremonially as part of his native leadership role and recreationally as part of his culture broker role simultaneously anesthetized and exacerbated the pain of these conflicts.

In the late 1980s, Antonio built another house on his land in Tocagon, and he gave a house plot there to his son Cipriano. His youngest son, José, stayed in the house built by his parents in Huaycopungo, as was traditional for the youngest child. The main stated reason for the move was that it was safer for animals. Antonio and Dolores, like many others, had been plagued by theft of cattle and pigs in Huaycopungo. In addition, Huaycopungo had become so crowded that there was no food for animals anywhere near the houses anymore. Although his main pasture was still on the shores of the lake, Antonio now pastured animals for short periods around his new house as well. Another result of Tocagon's lower population was that there were more plots for planting and lesser chance of crop theft than in Huaycopungo. However, this move also resulted from Antonio's recognition that his political authority had diminished in Huaycopungo, which had become wholly converted to education, engagement as equals with the Ecuadorian authorities, and nonagricultural pursuits for the younger generations. All of these changes were in some sense inevitable, and all of them Antonio himself had helped to promote. Nonetheless, his way of life has been consigned to the distant past, long before he was dead.

Antonio became an alcoholic. In his later years, he drank when he woke up. If he didn't have something hidden in the house, he excused himself, saying he had to pasture the cow, and stopped at the nearest bar to get a drink. His talk, even when he was sober, didn't always make sense anymore. He continued to care for his animals and even to plant, but he no longer played a leadership role. He retired from the Cooperativa Preñadilla. In the last few years before he died of what appeared to be a massive heart attack on his way home, we repeatedly stalled a reenactment of his father's drunken death on the Pan-American Highway by running and grabbing his Antonio's poncho as he headed thoughtlessly into the traffic.

Curaga Rigurio—Rigurio Andrango

Antonio was never a curaga, since he never increased land resources for the community. However, in 1977–79, there were three men known as curagas in Huaycopungo and two in Tocagon. Isabel and other young adults always said that one of them, Taita Rigurio Andrango, was an old-time curaga, more interested in consolidating his own power, whether that meant collaborating with San Rafael mestizos or setting one indigenous kin group against another, than working for the good of the community. The reference to "old time" probably did not represent historical reality so much as an explicit contrast between the new leaders, like the Angacuna—Rafi, Andu, and Sabila—who were change agents, influenced by the various civil rights movements from the 1930s onward. Rigurio Andrango originally gained his title by arranging the expropriation of nearby hacienda lands, which he cultivated with a group of other community members. Many came to him with requests that he rectify their land shortage, as was the traditional responsibility of curagas. After he consolidated his power, however, it is said that he forgot his people and began thinking only of himself. In fact he defended his large tracts of land in part by aiding or condoning the systematic abuse of indigenous land rights by San Rafael mestizos. Nonetheless, as a powerful man from the point of view of people in Huaycopungo, he could be very useful if you had him on your side, even if you did not trust him. And since I never knew him myself, the stories I heard may represent only the suspicion of those people not in a leader's orbit of aid.

His son Luis, Curaga Lucho, married the daughter of the curaga in Tocagon and concentrated his attentions on Tocagon over Huaycopungo. Many people complained that, like the authorities in San Rafael, he assumed a kind of ownership over the belongings of his quasi-subjects and was as likely to commandeer a chicken or a sack of harvested peas as were mestizo authorities. He actively confiscated clothing and tools so that the local people would clean San Rafael's streets, town hall, jail, clinic, convent, and so on, as was expected of him by the nonindian authorities.

Ila Rafi and Ila Jusi—Rafael and José Otavalo

In contrast were the brothers Rafael and José Otavalo, Ila Rafi and Ila Jusi, both nicknamed for their father, Ilario (Ila). Rafael Otavalo is a contemporary of Antonio, both born around 1930, but Rafael's brother, José Otavalo, was born in 1946. Rafael became curaga from his father-in-law in Curaga-loma, a section of Tocagon. José also married a woman from Tocagon, although not a curaga's daughter.

In 1977–79, Rafi Taita's house was constantly full of people—asking

Fig. 39. Rafael Otavalo, Ila Rafi *Taita*, second from left; son Francisco on far left, son-in-law and daughter with new calf in center, 1978

(PHOTO BY AUTHOR)

Fig. 40. José Otavalo, Ila Jusi *Taita*,
at center, during *minga* on land he acquired
for a cooperative; Isabel Criollo sits to left, 1978
(PHOTO BY AUTHOR)

him favors, repaying favors, and receiving the largesse of his household.
Wherever he went he seemed to be offered drinks of asua and trago. In
my observation, he frequently seemed to be drinking but only infrequently exhibiting culturally specific drunken behaviors. He served
as president of the cabildo on several occasions and was active in defending community rights, cultivating communal lands, making community improvements, and standing up for dignified treatment from
local mestizos.

He had arranged the marriages of his first two daughters, and his
third child, a son, was studying in high school when that was still rare
for Huaycopungo's children. Two younger sons were in elementary
school, and the youngest daughter was still at home. But as he began
to enter the potentially rewarding years of his children's marriages,
when his labor and social resources would grow to fulfill his political
ambitions, he suffered a major setback. His wife died suddenly, and he

was left without his indispensable partner. His daughters and sisters attempted to help, but he was not able to recover his momentum.

Ila Rafi Taita eventually remarried. While it solved the pressing problems of being without a partner—and widowers almost always remarry, whereas widows with older children frequently do not—it led to another predictable problem, of alienating his former in-laws and the children of his first marriage. No longer were his children and grandchildren assured of inheriting either his or their mother's land, nor could any of the parties count on the mutual aid and support otherwise expected in a continuing relationship.

After his second marriage, Ila Rafi, like Anga Andu, moved to Tocagon, where he was freer to pasture his animals. Watching him bring his animals to the lakeside pasture at dawn or return them home at dusk in the 1990s, Isabel remarked that he had become dedicated only to drinking, just like her father. When pressed, she could give no details, and the several other people I asked, including his son, gave contradictory responses. When I was there, I saw Antonio obviously drunk almost every day, but I did not see Ila Rafi drunk except at a boda huasi. It seemed likely that Ila Rafi Taita had succumbed not to alcohol itself but to the new ethos that the elders of the past were living a destructive life, for which alcohol was the symbol, at least in the eyes of some people.

Ila Jusi Taita's story contrasts with that of the others who were then called curagas. Although it was said that José Otavalo was trained to be curaga by his brother, who in turn was trained by his curaga father-in-law, in fact, more than any others José was helped by the efforts of the Conféderación Campesina (now FICI). By the combined efforts of the Conféderación, José Otavalo, and others from Huaycopungo, the community managed to get control over a plot of land on the slopes of Mojanda that had previously been communal land for the parish. It had come to be controlled by San Rafael mestizos, who nevertheless did not cultivate it. By the land reform laws, uncultivated land in areas of population pressure could legally be expropriated. Thirty-five families initially cooperated in cultivating the plot.

Ila Jusi devoted part of his life to seeking out those opportunities and making others aware of them in his own community. He did not finish elementary school, but he continued to improve his reading and writing skills with every opportunity he got, and has a lively mind, continually preoccupied with those issues he feels are crucial to his own life and that of the indigenous community. He has served several times on the community council. In 1978, I witnessed him win an election and maintain his dignity, despite the concerted efforts of the mestizo teniente político and secretary of San Rafael to direct the election toward their own candidate. They tried to pull him aside by his poncho, but he snatched it back and continued his soft-spoken and heartfelt address to the crowded schoolroom.

Like his brother, he makes his living in traditional agricultural pursuits—growing corn, pasturing cattle, raising chickens and guinea pigs, and weaving reed mats. He is a member of several cooperatives. As youngest child, he has experienced difficulty obtaining legal rights to the land resources that would improve his economic position, nor has he had an economic opportunity outside the community.

His other interest besides the political and bureaucratic part of community improvement has always been religion. At age nineteen, as befitting a future leader, he undertook to sponsor Pendoneros in October. Thirteen years later, in 1978, Ila Jusi sponsored a celebration of Corpus Christi, for which he cooperated with a mestizo religious society in San Rafael. He was apologetic about sponsoring the fiesta then, since he had promoted the Conféderación Campesina's claim that fiestas were solely a means of mestizo exploitation. He explained that Corpus Christi took fewer resources and less time than Corazas. At the same time, this represented an apology for not taking the ceremonial responsibility consonant with his leadership status, such as the Coraza sponsorship. He was torn between traditional and evolving expectations for community leadership and for the religious devotion that so interested him. During that Corpus Christi celebration, two mestizo girls, dressed as angels and guarded by their mothers, decorated the six altars that were set up around the plaza. There were also costumed indian participants. José himself had rented a part of the Coraza costume from the local mestizo women to visually indicate his sponsorship. Finally, he has long served as sacristan in the Catholic Church and was one of those responsible for having a separate Catholic chapel built in Huaycopungo Chiquito.

The Progressive Leaders of Today
Become the Reactionaries of the Past

The examples of Anga Rafael and his son Antonio, of Rigurio Andrango, and of Ila Rafael and Ila Jusi together embody some of our themes. Two of the five, perhaps from some personal predisposition, became alcoholics despite their long careers as community leaders. The two brothers did not. Two out of five seems a large percentage, but the total number is too small to make statistical generalizations about. Yet all of the older leaders have now been relegated to the category of viejos chumados, because of a now outmoded lifestyle and approach to leadership. All of these leaders are lightning rods for controversy as people, deeply suspicious of their high profiles, scrutinize their lives for evidence of malfeasance, but only one was generally considered to have succumbed to exploitation. Only one, Ila Jusi, has straddled the transition that the watershed events of 1987 represent, and that is because he has searched his soul and his Bible and social activist messages for ways to face the future. And it has meant drinking very little. None of these men were called curaga in recent years. Ila Rafi and Anga Andu retired as community leaders. None are rich by modern standards.

From one perspective, all heavy alcohol use has now been designated abuse and relegated to a dysfunctional past. For instance, Antonio was criticized not only for his behavior while drunk but also for the drinking itself. At the same time that the younger generation began to agree with each other that alcohol abuse was a problem, the basis of economic and political authority also changed radically. That authority had rested on shared consumption of alcohol as a means to celebrate connection, compel reciprocity, and ensure ethnic separatism in resistance to the dominant society. But Antonio and Rafael had sent their children to school beyond the one or two grades that were common at the time. And Ecuador was changing rapidly. Huaycopungo became more and more integrated into the national society, as we will see in part II. And the spiritual bases of leadership, or even an ordinary runa life, changed radically as well.

After the 1987 Earthquake

CHAPTER SIX

Pachacuti
World Reversal

The Earth Shakes

IT WAS MARCH 5, 1987. In March the stored harvests are usually gone, and the first food won't be harvested from the chacras for about another month. The sun, after a day hidden by clouds, had gone down behind the mountains and it was dark. Susana, almost fourteen, had served the supper—probably a thin soup of store-bought noodles or a dry roll and some coffee—to her father, José Manuel, and her four younger brothers. It was an especially cold and sad family, since Isabel, who normally warmed the household (despite her greater gift for public service than homemaking), was serving a sentence for cattle theft in an Ibarra prison. She had purchased a slaughtered animal so that she could sell the meat; however, the animal had been stolen, which she says she didn't know. In any case, she did not steal it herself. However, community members with a long-standing grudge against her pursued the charge of cattle theft until she was convicted. Prison authorities had allowed her nursing baby to stay with his mother for a few months, but by March he had been ordered home with his father and siblings. That night José Manuel and the three older children were probably preparing for bed while the two little boys, Fernando and

Antonio, slept soundly. Throughout his childhood, the youngest, called Llullicu, or Baby, until he was a teenager, never could stay awake long enough for the evening meal, and he was still only about a year old.

At about 9:00 p.m., the earth shook for twenty seconds and José Manuel, Susana, Ricardo, and Alberto grabbed the sleeping little boys and ran outside. In that first shock, the house we had spent so many months constructing back in 1978 was spared, sustaining only a few cracks. After a while, the family decided it was safe to go back in. They had all settled into bed, though sleeping like cats, when at about 11:15 another quake began, this one shorter but far more powerful. As pieces of the roof started to fall in, the family fled outside again, meeting their panicked neighbors in the road. Huddled together against the cold, these families spent the rest of the night outside waiting and watching for the aftershocks. By morning, when José Manuel inspected the damage, it became clear that the house was uninhabitable, as were Isabel's cousins' houses on either side, and would need to be replaced. More than half of the houses in Huaycopungo were damaged, and about two-thirds of those were beyond repair.

The two shocks registered only a 6 on the Richter scale, but were fifteen kilometers deep. Overall, the damage in Ecuador, mostly in the northern interandean valleys and in the eastern lowlands, was significant. It is estimated that eight hundred people lost their lives in the Amazonian province of Napo, mostly indigenous people living on the banks of rivers, which crumbled into the water. There the oil and gas pipelines were also destroyed, causing Ecuador to lose an estimated $600 million (Ayala Mora and Villegas Domínguez 1988). Six venerable churches were leveled in the city of Ibarra north of Otavalo. About three thousand homes in the provinces of Imbabura and Pichincha were completely demolished, while another fifteen thousand were badly damaged. Fewer deaths were registered in these highland provinces than in the eastern forests, since the first shock had alerted people to the danger before the second, more damaging shock began more than two hours later. Many people continued to sleep outdoors a month after the quake had occurred, afraid to risk sheltering under unstable walls.

God Sends a Message and a
Norm Cascade Is Precipitated

People in Huaycopungo quickly interpreted this disaster as a punishment from God, as was conventional. But this time, in contrast to earlier disasters, after some days of informal discussions they came to agree
that the divine censure was intended for themselves. Previous natural
calamities, such as floods and eclipses, had frequently been blamed on
mishu sins. However, since the community had been engaged in heated
dialogues about spiritual change—introduced by Protestant missionaries, Catholic reformers, and political activists alike—for over a decade,
the particular failings for which God was punishing them were generally agreed upon quite quickly. Public drinking to drunkenness, having become a problematic behavior for many individuals, was thus
available to become a symbol of the more general social, economic,
and spiritual problems that characterized indigenous life, just as it had
so recently been a symbol of the separate moral economy that made
indigenous life worthwhile. In the developing interpretation, if they
could manage to change drinking behavior properly, then the solutions
for a better future, both concrete and spiritual, would fall into place.
They would join the majority Ecuadorians and the first world in a jour-
ney of progress.

God had engineered a pachacuti, literally a "world reversal,"
which Sánchez Parga characterizes as "simultáneamente un violento
cambio de la realidad del mundo, una destrucción reconstructora, y la
instauración de una nueva época" [simultaneously a violent change in
the reality of the world, a reconstructing destruction, and the installa-
tion of a new epoch (1988, 163; my translation)]. The seeming paradox
is that this terrible destructive event gave people the confidence to
give up behaviors of the past without the fear that they were betraying
their heritage and its sacred sanctions. God himself had told them that
indigenous people had gotten off track and had given them license to
reformulate their values, although he left no specific guidelines.[1]

This change took me by surprise, since I had seen the problems
associated with alcohol growing, but the responses were continuing in
the old patterns that were leading to the trouble in the first place. I had

heard people complain bitterly about the costs of drinking yet vigorously defend the culture that demanded the continual flow of shared drinks. One theoretical model that seemed to shed light on what I was seeing at the time was the description of culture contact and schismogenesis from Bateson's *Steps to an Ecology of Mind* (1972, 61–152). In a complementary relationship between two groups, when the first group behaves in a certain typical way toward another, the second group responds with a different set of behaviors that constitute its normative reply. The first group then repeats and escalates its original behavior in response to the move of group two, which replies in turn, creating a positive feedback loop that Bateson called schismogenesis. Unless somehow restrained, he suggested, schismogenesis would lead to "a breakdown of the whole system" (68).

The schismogenesis taking place in Huaycopungo seemed to be taking the following form. The more mestizos criticized indigenous people for their drinking habits, the more the runa asserted their right to a different moral economy, which included drinking for social, moral, and spiritual benefit. Rather than accept the stigmatizing judgment, they claimed the right to a separate standard of value. Additionally, the more runa suffered from the tragedies of existence—such as poverty, family violence, and alcohol-related accidents—which they attributed equally to the oppression of the dominant society and to God and other spiritual powers, the more they increased the ritual behavior designed to reinforce the webs of reciprocity within the community and with God and other spirits in search of relief. While access to money was increasing but homegrown means of subsistence decreasing, money was preferentially diverted to ceremonial purposes rather than spent in the outside economy for subsistence needs, since material self-sufficiency and austerity were central community goals and other economic initiatives were strictly limited by the encompassing mestizo society. And the more heavy drinkers imbibed, the easier it was for them to pretend, under the influence, that they were in fact achieving their goals rather than squandering their potential. What would break this feedback loop? And when would it happen?

In my attempts to understand and analyze the rapid switch that had seemed to occur so miraculously by 1987, I made the assumption that the actors were making rational choices within the usual limits of rational choice. That is, their information may be imperfect, their understanding of the situation may be flawed, their norms about what kinds of benefits to seek and what kinds of costs to accept may conflict with each other or with an objective outsider's calculus, and their willpower to change may be insufficient, particularly when it comes to the use of a mind-altering drug. However, given such constraints, individuals will generally seek to achieve the highest quality of life that is available for themselves and their families. Otavaleños, with their well-known entrepreneurial ethic (Chavez 1982), certainly talk that way, too.

Applying models of rationality, however hypothetical, in the analysis of the behavior of ethnic minorities is critically needed, since majorities so easily read minority behavior as irrational. The economic, social, and psychological pressures of minority status often radically alter the cost-benefit calculations of people living in what otherwise seems to be the same environment. An assumption of rationality on the part of indigenous individuals might yield the observation that a great benefit—ethnic self-justification in the face of oppression, for example—could significantly outweigh some substantial deficits associated with drinking norms. By the same token, the benefit of a safety net of reciprocity in goods and services among one's fellows, created through shared drinks, might outweigh the costs of giving up one's own or family's profits, especially when those profits are so vulnerable anyway to loss from theft, illness, weather, and expropriation by nonindian outsiders. But this divergence between minority and majority costs and benefits can become invisible to the majority. Their prevailing belief in their own superiority can short-circuit any potential empathic understanding that they may have otherwise been capable of developing for the contrasting situations of the minority. Furthermore, most actual empathy on the part of individuals will be censored publicly in favor of majority opinion, which holds that the irrationality of the minority is patently beyond question.

Thus began my search for the changes in the analyses of the costs and benefits of the traditional norms for drinking, changes that prepared the ground to the extent that the divine signal of an earthquake precipitated a watershed in the culture of drinking. The specific history of what led to the altered calculus of risk will be the subject of the next two chapters, chapter 7 taking up the economic and educational factors that altered the lives of natives in Huaycopungo and chapter 8 summarizing the religious and political movements for change. While the preparation of the ground was necessary for an explanation of the pachacuti in values, it was by no means sufficient. The reasons for the reversal in publicly proclaimed drinking norms do not themselves explain its timing and speed. Some of these changes in lifestyle and ideological pressures had been developing for decades. While the occurrence of the earthquake may partially account for the revolution's timing, since it providentially presented a means of justification for a radical change in beliefs and behaviors at that particular moment in time, its message could as easily have been read as something irrelevant to drinking and the general way of life it symbolized.

In order to specify *how* the change happened when it did and so quickly, our attention must be directed to the interplay among individual assessments of costs and benefits, individual decisions about personal behavior, and public norms. What happened in Huaycopungo is what Cass Sunstein termed a *norm cascade* (1997), wherein behavior that was normative in both the statistical and sociological senses—that is, what most people did and what most people agreed they *should* do—was abandoned by an increasing wave of people until it became uncommon and deemed unacceptable practice among the same people who had, until recently, loyally espoused and practiced it. Such changes are not in fact uncommon. A few dramatic and well-known examples include the change from 99 percent of Chinese families in Tinghsien binding their daughters' feet in 1889 to virtually none thirty years later (Mackie 1996), the rapid disintegration of the Communist regimes in eastern Europe in 1989 (Kuran 1991), the cascade of public opinion in the former Yugoslavia from a position of support for a multiethnic state to a platform of vicious ethnic separatism (Somer 2001), the partition of the former British Raj in the Indian subcontinent into India and Pakistan and the subsequent bloody migration of Indian Muslims to Pakistan (Kuran 1998). As one can see from these examples, the changes can as easily be for the better as for the worse.

Behavioral norms that have a high potential for personal cost, such as the accidents, interpersonal violence, and squandering of resources needed for survival that frequently accompany drinking heavily during fiestas, may nevertheless have tremendous symbolic value. In certain situations, as we have seen, particular behaviors may be used to signal loyalty to a group (Posner 1998). The value of these norms to individuals lies in the clues their acceptance by their fellows supplies about their fellows' intentions, specifically as regards the generally accepted and reciprocal responsibilities of the group members to each other. If their fellows are not willing to pay the price of the symbolic norm, then they cannot be expected to provide future material support to others in the group, either. Without that expectation of material reciprocity from their fellows as the reward for engaging in the symbolic behavior, it will become too costly for these individuals, in turn, to perform. Symbols of commitment to cooperation broadcast by others, then, become critical sources of information for individuals deciding what their own behavior should be.

Furthermore, if the benefits of cooperation are sufficiently great, the cost of symbolically signaling cooperation will be correspondingly high in order to discourage potential free riders—those who would like the benefits of group membership but who wish to avoid paying any of the costs, and who would be more likely to pretend to cooperate if the pretense was cheap. In such a case, such symbolic behavior as engaging in reciprocal drinking rituals to intoxication has such an important charge because it signals to one's fellows a willingness to sacrifice one's person and one's "surplus" resources to maintain group cohesiveness. The belief that alcohol ritually shared created unbreakable social ties sanctioned by God and other spirits served as a warning against the likelihood of new compadres receiving the benefits and refusing the enduring obligations of the exchange relationship to which they had publicly committed. Ethnic pride as a group is a treasured and hard-won benefit, and shame and humiliation only the first of a long list of the costs for seeming to thwart it, which could include social isolation and sometimes even direct legal, economic, or physical sanctions. In an ethnic community so intent on maintaining internal unity and boundaries against the depredations of the outside world, avoiding social isolation can mean the difference between survival and starvation.

Nonetheless, individuals usually have choices beyond a simple yes or no, choices that, furthermore, are made anew over months and years. Each individual decision whether or not to drink in support of traditional drinking norms is based on one's personal assessments of the costs and benefits of drinking to oneself and to one's family at that time. To repeat, some of the costs, such as alcohol dependence, waste of resources, interpersonal violence, neglect of one's children, or insults by mestizos, and the benefits, such as a time-out from everyday activities, the experience of communitas, the enlistment of spiritual aid, detachment from or defiance to mestizo harassment, and new or strengthened pledges of reciprocal support from one's fellows, are *intrinsic* to the value of the act itself. Intrinsic value can be symbolic and cultural or based on the chemical effects of the drug itself. Others, however, relate to the effects on a person's *self-conception* of having engaged in the normative behavior (Sunstein 1997, 39). If someone in Huaycopungo disagrees publicly with too many of his or her fellows, he or she may feel shame or experience humiliation. In the way the term is used here, *shame* does not refer simply to the internal emotion resulting from one's own recognition that one has strayed from one's values. What is key here is the affective state brought on by appearing publicly to be too far from mainstream values, acting as a free rider rather than a true group member. Finally, a person's *reputation* may be enhanced by drinking in support of traditional norms and reduced as a result of public resistance to those norms when the majority of people advocates them.

For reasons of personal disposition and history, the humiliation of doing something about which others express disapproval is relatively low for some, for others the cost is relatively high, and for a third group it would fall in a middling range. Balancing the particular costs and benefits of doing either determines the stand an individual takes, and any community can host a great variety of individual balances. The very personal judgment about the wisdom of engaging in normative behavior can be termed a *private preference*. However, prevailing norms that enjoin indigenous people to suffer the costs in search of the benefits, and to drink as a loyalty oath to their ethnically distinct moral economy, meant that *public preferences* might have been quite different, and more traditional, than private preferences (Kuran 1995b). For those people whose private calculation of risks and benefits caused them to disapprove of the traditional norms of drinking, the weight of a potentially humiliating and impoverishing alienation from one's fellows led to the public attachment to, even an exaggeration of, the traditional culture of drinking in the late 1970s. My impression at the time that people in Huaycopungo were "protesting too much" in the Shakespearean sense was, in retrospect, well founded. They were more committed to claiming their ethnic loyalty in public through their verbal and behavioral support for the drinking norms than to expressing their own views of the practical costs of doing so, since that could be interpreted as disloyalty and an immoral potential for ignoring reciprocal obligations. More accurately, although they would express their disapproval behind the scenes, at a boda huasi, many felt they could not afford to do so more publicly. When people privately prefer one alternative but publicly support another, it is called *preference falsification* (Kuran 1995b).

Since people tend to infer other people's private preferences from their publicly stated ones, a majority of people may commit publicly to a norm that they, in fact, deplore privately when preference falsification is both widespread and generally large in magnitude. Everyone is lying publicly about his or her true assessment of the value of drinking norms, but everyone assumes that he or she is the only one, since that is the least risky assumption. Given the speed with which people changed their public allegiances in Huaycopungo, transforming traditional leaders into drunken bums in public discourse almost overnight, it is reasonable to hypothesize that people with a private preference for a change in the drinking culture constituted the majority, although they had been unaware of that fact about each other or at least unwilling to be the first to test the waters.

Here we identify the key element in the precipitation of a norm cascade. Private calculations and preferences may be pushing ever more powerfully against the dam erected by public norms, leading to a trickle, a flow, and finally a cascade of individuals publicly espousing what they kept to themselves or confided only to their most intimate associates in the past. Still, what starts that trickle?

A desire to be true to one's personal beliefs can be a benefit of publicly upholding a minority norm, potentially overwhelming the costs of opposing the majority for a few individuals (Kuran 1995b). Some people act as extremists by publicly backing an unorthodox point of view, in part because of their powerful need to be true to themselves.

The intense desire to conform to what they perceive to be the majority opinion or the fear of sanctions that motivate others are vastly outweighed by their need to express their private opinions publicly or test the limits of how much they have to invest to belong to the group. The religious and political activists bent on bringing progress to indigenous life in Otavalo could be called the *norm entrepreneurs* (Sunstein 1997) whose early public disavowal of traditional norms facilitated the later trickle and eventual flood. Their challenges to the prevailing norms resulted in a small group of people, known as a *norm cluster* (Picker 1997), uniting against the majority on the overwhelming costs of shared drinking. Their courageous denial of the costly symbol of group loyalty constituted their new loyalty oath given to each other. In Huaycopungo, early Protestant converts, who officially forbade the consumption of any alcohol, constituted this norm cluster, suffering significant blows to their community reputation in the process. Their support for each other in opposition to the prevailing conventions was instrumental in providing a self-sustaining group of sufficient density to attract new renegades when a relatively small change in the generally recognized cost-benefit analysis occurred. As Picker pointed out in a classic article that used simplified computer simulations to model what he calls *informational cascades*,[2] a small destabilizing effect, which he calls a *norm perturbation*, can shift allegiance from one game move to its opposite in a remarkably few iterations. The cascade resembles the fall of a line of dominoes, as each individual change in position alters the environment of the next to the point that it, too, topples.

Not surprisingly, the list of norm perturbations in Otavalo is long. A series of alterations in the material circumstances of life and the contemporary ideological debates made the people of Huaycopungo ripe for a norm cascade. While the earthquake itself—or, more accurately, the need to make sense of the earthquake's damage—may have had a tipping effect, the inadequacy of previous ways of making a living and the search for new alternatives, a civil rights movement, efforts by both Protestant and reform-minded Catholic missionaries to alter worldviews and everyday practices, a new right to public education and a resulting increase in bilingualism, the spread of broadcast media into both rural and indigenous communities, and government policies to use education and the media to acculturate indigenous Ecuadorians

(Stutzman 1981) all had the potential to destabilize previous norms.[3] People's private preferences, or at least their internal debates, were more and more frequently challenged to reject the traditional drinking norms, even though a perceived need for group support and solidarity demanded they demonstrate their public preference for them ever more visibly when someone in their personal network baptized a child or built a new house.

To recap, when there is a fragile balance between private judgments and public norms supporting a status quo, a norm cascade can quite easily be precipitated. Small changes in the cost-benefit analysis can cause one or a few people for whom public shame is less personally costly, or for whom adherence to personal preferences is more valuable, to change their public discourse and behavior. Their threshold for reversing allegiance to the norms can be said to have been lower than the threshold of someone more generally dependent on the goodwill of others. However, in turn, that first person's switch in publicly expressed views changes the risk of social alienation perceived by those whose susceptibility to shame is just a little higher. The next least sensitive person or persons know that, should they go public with their disapproval, they will no longer be completely alone. With a norm cluster of individuals who have long stood out as the public renegades in favor of an altered moral compass, such as the Protestant teetotalers, the requisite number of fellows necessary to attract those who are most likely to switch norm allegiance is achieved ever more quickly. If the balance between private disapproval of the norms and public support for them is similarly precarious among other people, more and more of them will be swayed precisely by the increasing number of community members who have already publicly rejected the traditional norms, which guarantees them a reduction in the risk of shame and other social consequences. The numbers disapproving of the traditional drinking norms will now rise exponentially and there will be a rapid shift—a *bandwagon effect* or *norm cascade*—such that, in what seems to be the blink of an eye, what was recently the minority opinion becomes the opinion of the majority. The censure for violating public norms will rapidly shift from those espousing one opinion to those expressing the opposite. Only those most comfortable as iconoclasts, or those who cannot change their behavior because of other factors, will continue to act out the norms of the past. Thus they become drunks rather than self-sacrificing and upstanding models for others.

Gender and Private/Public Preference

The dimension of gender and public opinion is critical here, since men and women may experience significantly different costs and benefits from traditional ceremonial drinking. In Otavalo, men paid the highest personal costs but also reaped the most benefit. Women's costs were often lower than men's but were significantly greater than the benefits they received, since their consumption of alcohol was so much lower than men's until they were well into middle age. As in many cases around the world—the temperance movements in the United States or on the island of Truk (Marshall 1979; Marshall and Marshall 1990) or among the Highland Maya of Guatemala (Eber 1995)—women's views on alcohol in Otavalo were significantly more negative than those of men. In the event of an incipient norm cascade, this half of the population would be expected to shift its public loyalty rather quickly to the side it had been privately supporting for a long time and precipitate a wave of transformation.

Even before the earthquake, almost all women were privately critical of drinking and its costs to their families and society as a whole, especially when it came to the trago purchased with family money. However, the definition of *private* I would use here might be a bit different than used by Kuran (1991) or Somer (2001), who refer to what people keep to themselves or share only with their closest family members or friends. In this case from Otavalo, women were free to speak their minds in their homes and to other women; they were free to articulate their disapproval when drunk or grief stricken or otherwise released from the strictures of proper everyday behavior. Only in events of public significance, if they had an official role in a boda huasi or during a fiesta procession, were women expected to support the public view about drinking rituals in word and deed, as they accepted a series of offered toasts. For example, women expressed their personal sympathy for the 1978 Coraza's wife, who hated drinking, but also expressed their approval of her self-sacrifice as they watched her intoxicated processions around the community. However, in accordance with traditional andean culture, women's opinions about public issues were more private than men's by definition. Their views could have an informal but not a formal impact, as we have seen in the examples of women talking "privately" but loudly among themselves during public meetings to make their opinions known, or of women taking care to inform their male family members of their views before and after meetings but rarely addressing men and women publicly in meetings as men were expected to do. This gender division of labor allowed women to say what they believed more openly without it causing them as much public shame as it would men, although women did use this actually public, but ideologically private, complaining to shame their men, as we saw with Chunda Fucu's wife in chapter 1.

Nor were women the ones who had to decide to drink or not, except on rare occasions. It was men whose failure to drink reciprocally would lead to family social alienation. Women who hated the drinking practices made it possible for their husbands to participate, brewing the asua necessary for household participation in rituals and in the process reaping some enhancement of their own reputation as providers. Of course, as seen in chapter 4, women's greatest censure was reserved for cantina drinking.

Privately, in their homes and among their closest social contacts, many men may have felt free to articulate an evaluation of costs and benefits that did not support traditional norms. Many men even did so to me at least some of the time, since, as a member of the outside world, I was presumed to condemn the high level of indigenous drinking. Unless they were the staunchest evangelist supporters, they could later be seen engaging in ritual drinking. Publicly, they had too much to lose, so they routinely engaged in private preference falsification. And since men's private views were known only to a few intimates by definition, and women's views were assumed to contrast with men's most of the time by definition—most people did not have a good grasp of what their fellows really believed. They may well have assumed that women overstated their semipublic opposition to traditional norms against their own private views and in keeping with their position as the opposing sex. And in some cases, that assumption may have been correct. Certainly, most people overestimated the private allegiance to traditional norms, assuming that most men's private views coincided more closely with their publicly stated preferences than in fact was the case.

Not a Reversal, a Restoration of Continuity

Part II presents a period in Otavalo in which the ground has shifted to such an extent that the people in Huaycopungo respond with a dramatic reinterpretation of their culture and of how they fit in the social and spiritual environment, almost instantaneously altering their basic orienting narratives. The native metaphor of pachacuti is particularly apt here, and not only because it provides a productive indigenous theory of transcendent events with which to counter the dominant society's explanations, which feature indigenous failure and victimhood. Even more significant, perhaps, is that while the concept of pachacuti first brings to mind a terrifying vision of world reversal that mirrors the beginning of time, when the sun did not rise and human ancestors lived under the ground, planting their crops to rot in the dark and eating their children, indigenous religious ritual has always sanctioned controlled pachacuticuna, in which a short-term reversal of direction ensures a long-term continuation of existence. Once the transformation caused by the earthquake had taken place, it came to seem to the locals that they had always believed what they currently espoused. In a sense they were right, since, in the recent past, many people's private preferences presumably contradicted their publicly espoused beliefs. They did "believe" these things, they just could not express them openly or act upon them. And those other people whose private preferences had, in fact, been in tune with their public positions in the past, would be constrained in the present by their fear of social isolation against openly supporting the discredited traditions. This rapid acceptance of a long and seemingly inevitable history to an unanticipated, revolutionary change is a common and, in fact, logical occurrence, given the reality of preference falsification (Kuran 1995b). The pachacuti, initially experienced as a force of overwhelming proportions, became in a very short time the reestablishment of continuity after a relatively brief period of earlier reversal. In fact, it may seem more accurate to the people in Huaycopungo today to say that the pachacuti, or period of reversed direction, occurred when they were continuing heavy ritual drinking and experiencing drinking-related harm, despite their long-term commitment to progress and self-determination. Leadership by the viejos chumados was a brief, modern perversion of proper and traditional indigenous leadership.

In addition, the traditional andean perspective on time further supports the unfolding amnesia toward the earlier values. Native andean thought did not imagine one standing in the present, seeing time flow into the future, with the past slipping away behind one's back. On the contrary, people faced the unfolding past with the future unknowable behind. Since, in this perspective, the present does not replace the past in favor of a new future but is ideally the culmination of forces set in motion long before the present and carefully replicated by those closest ancestors people would choose to memorialize, then God's message had vindicated one vision of the past and nullified as corruption what had previously been considered sacred tradition. Valued leaders became drunken old men, and disruptive young political and religious reformers took on the responsibility of perpetuating the ideals of the past.

Not surprisingly, change and continuity have indeed both resulted. The representational weight of certain elements has shifted from acceptable continuity to perverted reversal. Those beliefs and behaviors that previously represented external sources of change came to symbolize[4] and promote indigenous tradition, and vice versa. What once convincingly seemed a tenacious resistance by indigenous people to the dominant society's pressure on them to give up their own traditions and become decultured servants of the hispanicized nation has been transformed into the results of local nonindian domination designed to keep indigenous people from realizing their own traditional march to modernization and progress.

The outside changes they have adapted to and the internal transformations they have created for themselves affect every aspect of living. The next two chapters outline the changes experienced in the economic and political relationship of Huaycopungo to the nation as a whole and the transformations of worldview promoted by activists, primarily religious but also political. Part I attempted to ground us in an understanding of the prevailing native worldview of the 1970s by examining the cultural continuity that was revealed as a shifting shadow cast by the contending clouds of explanatory oppositions current in that period. The focus was on drinking, a symbolic complex central to the construction of indigenous identity, in dialogue both with the spiritual forces and with the dominant society. In contrast, part II sketches the profound transformations of the indigenous way of life in the last quarter of the twentieth century. On the one hand, the revolution in the interpretation of drinking can provide us with a special lens with which to investigate these more comprehensive changes. On the other, this domain of belief and behavior and its metamorphosis deserves an explanation of its own. And part of the explanation comes from the altered assessment of the costs and benefits that events and processes at home and in the wider society brought to this key symbolic complex, leading to a cascade of change in normative choices about beliefs and behaviors. As stated above, Sunstein claims that rational "choice among options is a function not only of a) the intrinsic value of the option—a book, a job, a drink—but also of b) the reputational benefit or cost of the choice and of c) the effects of the choice on one's self conception" (1997, 39).

It will be my contention in the following chapters that all three of these determinants of the choice between different interpretations of drinking, of religious worldview, and of the meaning of indigenous ethnicity experienced change in the decades leading up to the earthquake of 1987. Chapter 7 demonstrates how the evolution of Ecuadorian society in the last quarter of the twentieth century altered the intrinsic costs and benefits of the traditional lifestyle, to which ritualized drinking served as pledge of loyalty. The religious and political movements considered in chapter 8 show how alternatives to the reputational benefits of differing cultures of alcohol use and associated cultural complexes were promoted and strengthened by entrepreneurs both from within and without Huaycopungo's borders. Chapter 9 looks at the intrinsic costs of drinking within the contexts of the altered lifestyle and transforming systems of meaning to more explicitly address the causal explanation of how drinking became a problem when it did.

CHAPTER SEVEN

Runa Gente, Gente Civilizada
Uniting the Contradictions of the Indigenous and the Fully Civilized

The First High School Graduate and the First Potable Water

IN 1982, FIVE YEARS BEFORE THE EARTHQUAKE, a young man named Segundo Aguilar became the first person from Huaycopungo to graduate from high school. He had attended Colegio Fernando Chaves Reyes in Quinchuquí and later went on to complete a doctorate in jurisprudence. Huaycopungo's adults alternated between expressing their fears of losing Segundo and others like him to the outside world and proclaiming themselves thrilled and proud to have Segundo represent their community as an educated man. Isabel and I attended the graduation, photographed the ceremony for the family, and later joined the celebration at his house in Huayopungo proper. That day was a watershed for me personally—in more ways than one, if you will pardon the pun you will recognize below. But the joys and travails of that day help illustrate the conflicts between the old ways of life and the new that were brewing at the time, conflicts that resulted just a few years later in the public acceptance of a generalized radical change. The high school from which Segundo Aguilar graduated was a controversial and much discussed innovation in Otavalo at the time. Although legally established by the federal government, the high school was partially

Fig. 41. Segundo Aguilar graduates
from Colegio Quinchuquí
(PHOTO BY AUTHOR)

funded by USAID and intended to provide both academic and practical learning for the children of indians and poor nonindian campesinos. The first rector was a native Otavaleño who had spent a number of years studying in U.S. universities, coming back to live in Quinchuquí with a North American wife. The school's opening sparked intense competition among Otavalo's many private high schools to admit— indeed, recruit—indigenous students, whom they had actively discouraged before, since the new constituency of elementary-educated indians that resulted from the national government's promotion of education of indigenous children was a potential fee-paying constituency they could not afford to leave to the new competition. During this period, indigenous opinion shifted, gradually at first and then quite rapidly, from fearing public education to sacrificing everything to attain the highest possible level for as many of their children as they could. Segundo's triumph is still used as a model when Huaycopungo's parents talk about their young children's educational future.

The week of Segundo's graduation was notable for another reason. Various public sources of money had been found to bring potable water directly to houses in the town of San Rafael, and pressure had been exerted to extend the service to parts of Huaycopungo as well. Huaycopungo was one of the first indigenous communities in the cantón to become a recipient of this program, although only a small, easily accessible portion of the comuna's sections would benefit, and the materials and engineering of the early stages of this initiative would be found to have been seriously flawed as the years went on. Since comadre Isabel's house lay in Langaburo near the Pan-American Highway, it was going to be hooked up to water. I was doing a research project on colera, or anger sickness, there at the time, and my six-year-old daughter and I were living with my comadre's family. We had purchased the connections and faucets to bring the piped water right inside our one-room house and were eagerly waiting for the date two days hence when the water was scheduled to begin its first flow through the pipes. When we left for Segundo's party, we carefully padlocked the door because no one would be left at home while we were gone. Not only would Isabel's family's belongings be at risk of theft if the house was left unlocked, so would everything I had brought for myself and my daughter for three months of research.

Although I was excited to attend this major event in Huaycopungo, it was not to be a happy occasion for me. As the celebrations in the boda huasi to honor Segundo's graduation progressed, I watched the circling drinks first turn everyone inward to examine their disappointments, grievances with others, sense of general injustice and then cause people to become increasingly violent in word and deed with each other. Mellow conversation, dancing, and warm greetings to the newcomers were all but drowned out by the increasing numbers of angry drunks. With their usual sangfroid, relatives and compadres of the participants separated the individuals who were physically attacking each other and calmed the tempers of those who were screaming nonstop insults, only to see another wildfire of alcohol-fused emotion break out moments later in another part of the crowded courtyard. Often their own patience snapped, and the caretakers had to be separated from the partying crowd for a good cry. Segundo stayed on the edges with his friends—a mix of indians and mestizos from all over the county—and tried to listen to the folk singers who had been asked to play, in a modernizing introduction of urban customs to the indigenous comuna. I remember sitting in a corner of the curridur, avoiding the drinking as much as possible and feeling increasingly depressed, bitter, and angry myself. At that particular boda huasi, for some reason, it seemed that all the symbolic frameworks for interpreting such ritual drinking, featuring self-sacrifice and inebriated communion with the spirits and one's fellows, were nothing but rationalization for simply dysfunctional behavior. Perhaps the only position I could take was that the whole culture, as symbolized by these socioreligious rituals, had become sick. Maybe the fact that I knew fewer individuals at the party and thus had little understanding or empathy for their particular woes fueled the fire of my despair. I asked my comadre if the anger seemed closer to the surface, the drinking faster or more copious, the violence greater than usual, or if it was just me. She wasn't succumbing to the same black mood as I was, and she suggested that I was exaggerating the negative, but she did agree that this boda huasi was suffused with more anger than mellow joy.

As I was fighting despair for Huaycopungo and my research project, a neighbor from our Langaburo house rushed into the party and announced to Isabel and myself that we had to come quickly. Disaster had struck at home. Apparently the potable water we had been so eagerly anticipating had been turned on prematurely and without warning. Our faucet had been left in the on position—not obvious when there was as yet no liquid flow—and waves of muddy water were gushing out from under the door, carrying a few of my daughter's smaller toys with it. All attempts by our neighbors to get in had failed because of the padlock, and the house's mud walls were in danger of collapsing from the pressure. When we returned and unlocked the door, our sleeping mats and mattresses were floating, along with the Barbie dolls, in six inches of water above the dirt floor. The water was swirling around the trunk in which I stored my audiotapes, fieldnotes, and other research paraphernalia. Once we had picked up the toys, determined that only a few audiotapes seemed to have been ruined, and dragged our mattresses out to dry, I admit with some shame that I packed a bag, grabbed my daughter's hand, and headed to the Pan-American Highway to catch the first bus to Quito for a few days of rest and relaxation. As I waited on the edge of the road to flag down a bus, I watched my comadres patiently sweeping the oozing mud out of the house and down the bank. The shadows were beginning to lengthen and I guiltily imagined them working well into the dark to repair the house I had just selfishly fled. With time for reflection, I realized that I needed to do a lot more work to reach a fuller understanding of the role of drinking in Huaycopungo.

The earthquake in 1987 irreparably damaged those water pipes and household connections. They had worked only intermittently, anyway, but it was several years before my compadres had water at home again. When they did reinstall the water, the pipe was placed at a concrete laundry stand in the backyard, not in the house. Before the water was reconnected, the family returned to carting water from the closest spring, Potro Pogyo, when they couldn't get it from Isabel's cousin's house next door.[1] Soon after I arrived for a visit in 1991, my godson Fernando, along with his brother and uncle, both younger than he was, was eager to show me the modernization of Pushic Pogyo. In a community minga, the access path down from the road and the sides of the spring had been covered with concrete, creating steps, places to sit, and sloping surfaces into the water that served as washboards. While it seemed a peculiar innovation to my American sensibilities—paving over a natural spring to which spiritual offerings had so recently been laid, along with prayers—they were quite proud of their modernization. But that same year, most people had to accept that water from Potro Pogyo was good for laundry only. A cholera epidemic took the lives of many elderly people in Huaycopungo within hours after they showed signs of being sick. For the first time since I had been coming to Huaycopungo, public opinion switched from believing that the public health campaigns for clean water were but another form of ethnocide—our spring water may be harmful for white folk but was good enough for our ancestors and is good enough for us—to accepting that the microbial theory of disease might in fact be true and that the springs were polluted. By that time, the mutual dance of offering and accepting such civil rights as public education or public health improvements between the dominant society and the indigenous communities had been continuing at a steady pace for years. The ambiguously desired modernization of the late 1970s had become an integral part of everyday life. In what follows, we examine the changing relations of the indigenous community and Ecuador as whole in the last quarter of the twentieth century.

During the final decades of the century, the members of Huaycopungo and other Otavaleño communities were increasingly claiming publicly to be *runa gente*, a typically Janus-faced symbol of their worth, uniting the Quichua word for a culturally indigenous person, runa, with the Spanish word meaning "people" that petty bourgeois Ecuadorians self-consciously reserved for themselves, frequently coupled with the adjective *civilizada*, or civilized. Otavaleños did not have to cease being runa to be civilized people. Self-determination would allow them to fashion their identity out of whatever streams of meaning to which they had access, no longer employing secrecy and misdirection as the colonial and early national periods had demanded. Their cultural identity and worth could neither be confined nor judged by the dominant society—it was a creative endeavor over which they alone had control and which they could proudly proclaim to the world at large.

Fig. 42. The remodeled spring, *Pushic Pogyo*
(PHOTO BY AUTHOR)

Fig. 43. José Manuel Tituaña and Isabel Criollo's new Red Cross house, 1988. The group of family and friends includes author and ex-husband, P. Sudevan, in center; José Manuel's sister Elena in front row, second from left; his brother José Segundo, front row, far right; Isabel stands to the left of Sudevan
(PHOTO BY UNIDENTIFIED FRIEND WITH AUTHOR'S CAMERA)

Political and Economic Transformations of Local, National, and International Scope

What changes in material conditions underlie the world reversal, the pachacuti in the traditional way of life, of the last few decades? Or, phrased in a rational choice framework, what were the alterations in the intrinsic costs and benefits of traditional socioreligious norms, the norm perturbations, and the activities of norm entrepreneurs that caused most individuals to create a cascade of innovative choices? The three biggest influences, discussed below, are: (1) the country became an oil exporter in the early 1970s; (2) tourism and the export of native handicrafts had been growing exponentially since the 1960s, especially in Otavalo; and (3) public and private education opportunities, and other basic civil rights, were extended to indigenous Ecuadorians. Several other factors, such as migration trends and the expansion of mass media through radio and then television have also had major impacts. One result for Otavaleños was that the peasant lifestyle so basic to Huaycopungo identity until the 1970s became economically impossible to continue. At the same time, new economic opportunities grew and previously closed avenues for income generation were opened. Accompanying the opening of national and international sources of income were profound alterations in the relations between indigenous and nonindigenous Ecuadorians. Interestingly, Meisch also uses images of an earthquake to describe the same period: "an ethnic earthquake that has rearranged the local social strata" and "the seismic upheaval . . . which has brought social and political power that has altered social relationships among indigena and between indigenas and other local groups" (2002, 200), although she is not referring to the 1987 temblor.

OIL AND NATIONAL ECONOMIC GROWTH

In 1967, a consortium of the U.S. oil companies, Texaco and Gulf, launched a costly exploration program in the eastern lowlands of Ecuador, the Oriente. They announced that in Lago Agrio, near the Colombian border, they had found exploitable oil, which had been thought to lie deep below the jungle covering at least since 1937, when the British Shell Oil Company acquired a huge concession for exploration. A combination of fluctuations in world supply and demand, Ecuadorian government policies, and the high costs of drilling and transporting oil from the jungle over the mountains and to the coastal shipping facilities had delayed oil's successful exploitation until the 1960s. By 1972, a pipeline to the northwest coast of Esmeraldas had been built, and Ecuador began to export oil. In the same year, a military junta overthrew the populist elected president, Velasco Ibarra, from his fifth and last term and renegotiated the oil contracts with Texaco and Gulf, ensuring a gradual nationalization of oil. In 1973 Ecuador joined OPEC.

The military government's plan was to invest the significant government oil revenues into the nation's infrastructure and into industrial and social projects (Corkill and Cubitt 1988, 25). Such projects as improved and more extensive highways, hydroelectric plants, and an expanded education system were successfully undertaken. The measures to increase native industrial production produced far less change in the long run. Predictably, this additional revenue also started a period of expanded military expenditure, which ended, in the early 1990s, with Ecuador spending the highest percentage of GNP on the military in all of Latin America, despite its relatively peaceful international relations.

Nonetheless, for about a decade the Ecuadorian economy grew, with a real increase in per capita income. "Formerly one of the poorest countries in South America, Ecuador by 1981 had attained a per capita income of $1,180, roughly equal to that of its neighbors Colombia and Peru" (Schodt 1987, 105). This figure also approximates the median income for Latin America as a whole. A large percentage of the increased money was spent on imports, but the internal markets in both food and manufactured goods also expanded exponentially, even in the previously isolated towns of the country such as Otavalo. The first shiny new stores selling what is known as *electrodomésticos*, or small home appliances and electronics, opened to great fanfare in Otavalo in the late 1970s. Nevertheless, the impact was greatest in the largest cities, which had experienced an explosive growth of the middle class, massive migration from the depressed agriculture regions, and a construction boom.

Quito, the capital and home to most of the government activity, experienced even greater growth than its rival, the larger coastal city of Guayaquil, which was more oriented toward commerce. Quito's growth directly and indirectly affected the lives of people in Otavalo. First of all, Quito's public and private construction boom provided casual labor to large numbers of impoverished Otavalans, who could use this work to supplement their resources in subsistence agriculture. Only a very few were legally employed as full-time workers by construction contractors, with the full complement of legal rights and protections operative in Ecuador. The vast majority of workers were part-time, hired for several days or, at most, a week at a time. On Monday, potential workers would appear before dawn at La Carolina, a public park in prosperous north Quito and wait for contractors to come pick a crew for the week.

The growth of the urban middle class also created an increased demand for food and for domestic and other low-paying services that both mestizos and indigenous people from Otavalo could provide. "Consumer expenditures, corrected for inflationary price increases, doubled between 1972 and 1982" (Schodt 1987, 108). Since Quito was only two hours away by motor vehicle from Otavalo, work there quickly supplanted the longer-term labor on distant coastal plantations, where the heat, mosquitoes, isolation, ethnic harassment, and sky-high prices for every necessity of life often made the costs of this migrant labor greater than its benefits.

Furthermore, the number of public and private vehicles grew rapidly in this period. In the early 1970s privately owned cars were scarce in Ecuador, but the number of cars in Ecuador went from 82,000 in 1970 to 223,000 by 1997 (Schodt 1987, 110). The numbers of buses and microbuses also mushroomed; every few minutes a bus arrived in Otavalo from Quito and another left. Since fuel prices were kept artificially low by the government, bus fares were very cheap. Bus companies made a profit by sheer volume and by speed. The drivers earned precious *sucres* by racing each other up and down the narrow curving highway with terrifying abandon. While many passengers avoided panic by sleeping through the ride, some became enthusiastic supporters of their driver's race—trading notes with others, bragging about who got to or from Quito in the least amount of time on their last trip.

The developing advantages of migration to Quito for Otavalo's mestizos resulted in an indirect benefit for indigenous Otavaleños at home. Otavalo's rural mestizos, who often sought some local prestige through the avoidance of labor, even though they constituted an economically stagnant class, began to migrate permanently to the cities where more opportunities for economic advancement could be found. Rural indigenous parishes had been a resource for poor but enterprising mestizos. There they opened small stores providing goods and services to the locals, who did not manage businesses of their own because they thought that dealing with their fellows through market exchange was immoral. In addition, mestizos had frequently tried to squelch commercial activities by indians and to dominate this type of work. Convenient location and credit were two advantages offered indigenous people for patronizing these establishments, even though prices were often high. A new enterprise would offer respectful treatment, generous credit arrangements, and personal ties of compadrazgo to establish a clientele and even to obtain a plot of land within the indian community, but these advantages would inevitably disappear once an indebted clientele was established. If bills were left unpaid, creditors would get support from mestizo parish authorities to confiscate a plot of land in repayment or to seize the labor of the debtor's relatives for domestic or other service. The opportunity to sell alcohol on credit, either in cantinas or to individuals who wanted it for a boda huasi, was particularly attractive. In San Rafael a couple of families monopolized all the paraphernalia for Corazas, including the costumes, and have used that, along with their *other* exploitative activities, to improve their economic standing considerably (Villavicencio 1973). The economic boom that followed oil exportation lifted a great deal of this local economic exploitation from indigenous communities and decreased the competition for informal sector opportunities locally. The more direct, quick, and secure economic activities in Quito were far more inviting than the marginal benefit gained by squeezing a few sucres here and a few sucres there out of wheedling and whining indians.

Transportation within the province and the cantón also increased throughout the period. Several bus companies began to offer regular service to rural areas, including an indian-owned company. The number of taxis also increased rapidly, with the newer drivers agreeing to take fares to the rural communities in order to stay busy. Private vehicle owners helped pay for their car or truck by carrying passengers for a fee, especially on market days. The lines of families walking to Otavalo from every corner of the cantón on Saturday in the 1960s changed to crowds of people waiting at all outlets to the Pan-American Highway, hoping to catch some kind of inexpensive ride. The growing number of schoolchildren who attended Otavalo's schools used the buses to get there.

Tourism and Commerce

In the early 1970s international tourists often rose before dawn in their Quito hotels, ate a special early breakfast prepared for those going to the feria in Otavalo, and boarded taxis in which they would arrive, dizzy with motion sickness, by midmorning.[2] These gringo tourists were the last wave of buyers, taking home decorative wall hangings, trendy ponchos, and crude wool blankets. By noon, most of the mestizo and indigenous sellers and buyers had packed up their wares and gone home or to a local cantina, while the tourists had driven to see the weavers in Peguche or to marvel at the sparkling crater lake, Cuicocha, high on Mount Cotacachi before returning, tired and sunburned, to Quito. Left were those few unlucky runa whose ponchos or hats had been seized by police, and who were then forced to sweep the littered plaza before getting their property back and continuing home. By the end of the decade, the Saturday textile market lasted until late afternoon and a *feria chica,* small market fair, took place on Wednesday. Hotels were built to cater to foreign tourists as well as to visitors with more moderate budgets. More and more stores on the main streets were converted to the sale of folkloric items to tourists. By the 1990s, every day had become market day in the textile plaza, although Saturday is still the most crowded with sellers and buyers.[3]

Local tourism also increased as a result of the more plentiful public and private transportation. After all, just as the local people could maintain their homes and fields but still take a week off now and then to labor in construction, people in Quito could enjoy the rural charms of Otavalo and get home the same day. The two cities were only two hours apart. While not a suburb, Otavalo was much more closely drawn into the influence of the capital than it had been before the improvement of transportation. Mestizo migrants from Otavalo who had relocated to find better opportunities in the city could still come home to enjoy their native dishes, *comidas típicas,* and visit their grandparents on weekends. Colombian middle-class tourists also began to flock to Ecuador to enjoy the relatively low prices and quaint backwardness they believed they found there. Even today, the number of Colombian tourists in Otavalo equals that of international tourists from North America and Europe. But as Meisch emphasizes (2002), it is important to recognize that even in the early 1970s, outsiders were not simply invading the valley of Otavalo, introducing modernity to the natives glued by poverty and archaic attachment to the land—indigenous Otavaleños were traveling as well, experiencing novel relationships and introducing others to their own traditions. The Pan-American Highway was a two-way street.

Throughout the 1970s, competition between mestizos and indigenous people for direct access to the tourist market was intense. Local mestizos greatly resented the opportunities foreigners gave indigenous people to enter retail marketing, just as they begrudged the other economic achievements of some indian families. For example, the growing migration of Otavaleños into the town of Otavalo, the purchase by a few indigenous families of retail stores for the sale of handicrafts within the town, and the establishment of indigenously owned weaving workshops (Parsons 1945; Chavez 1982)—all were resented. After the Dutch government sponsored a program for the indigenous weavers that resulted in the construction of architecturally designed cement stalls in the Plaza de Ponchos in 1973, frequent legal battles—and sometimes extralegal and violent confrontations—took place between mestizo and indian contestants for places in the market. In the early 1980s the indigenous sellers finally won preferential access to stalls, which are now passed on carefully within families over generations.

Clearly, international tourists found the Otavaleños picturesque as had William Bennett Stevenson in the early 1800s when he said, "I never saw a finer looking people than an assembly of Otavaleños on a Sunday" (quoted in Salomon [1973] 1981, 420). They did not come to photograph the often haughty urban mestizos, so sensitive to slights to their dignity and so dismissive of their indigenous neighbors. Nor did they find the local mestizos visually attractive in their faded, worn, and outmoded versions of the foreign tourists' own clothes or their fusty black suits and hats. "In search of the noble savage" (Meisch 2002, ch. 4 title), tourists found the runa frequently displaying childlike smiles, since they were accustomed to demonstrating humility in order to endear themselves to their social superiors. With their long single braids hanging down their backs, shiny white pants and embroidered blouses, distinguished navy and gray ponchos, and elegant black anacos and fachalinas, they were far more appealing and photogenic. Proud of their few words of French, English, and German, they would try to joke with the tourists, offering relatively low prices and declining to bargain very much.[4] Foreign desire for finding the exotic on the equator gave the indigenous people a kind of monopoly they hadn't had before. They could attract sales by offering a sociable access to themselves.

Here we encounter a different reality from the dark huasi ucu and the sheltered curridures of the introduction and chapter 1, where runa life seems to be self-consciously shut off from the outside world and focused on intimate exchange relations among runa people, runa land, and localized spirits. In the market, indigenous people are plunged into rewarding social and cultural interchanges with tourists from Colombia, the United States, France, and other American and European countries. Because this social interaction is often both pleasurable and profitable, it has become a further source of imaginative reference for interpreting and refashioning their lives.

In the decades under discussion, the social landscape has become further extended. The most inclusive level of the nested series of llacta, places that are characterized internally by an intense mutual responsibility and externally by a combination of rivalry and cooperation between llacta at the same level, is now more levels removed from the smallest. As we saw in chapter 3, the moieties of Janan Shaya and Urai Shaya can be counterposed as opposites in some fundamental way or engage in profitable interchanges. They can be combined to serve as a unit at a higher level of inclusion, and then counterposed with another. So, too, the social worlds we are considering here—indigenous world versus the world of the mestizo, Ecuador versus foreign nations, indians versus gringos—should stand as immiscible opponents on some occasions and on others intermingle for mutual profit. For many people in Huaycopungo in the 1970s, the most inclusive group they recognized did not even include the northern end of the Otavalo valley, including such towns as Peguche and Ilumán, let alone part of a group with other indigenous Ecuadorians or part of the nation as a whole. Today the former sense of inclusion is now universal and the second commonplace.

In addition, they are working out ways to imagine their place in the world as a whole. In their interaction with foreign tourists in Ecuador, or with foreigners they encounter in their home countries when they travel to sell folkloric handicrafts and musical performances, they can choose to think of themselves first as Ecuadorians or first as Otavalo runacuna. With the second choice, they can bypass their stigmatized national identity in pursuit of the advantages that their own exotic appeal and practiced charm can bring. While the interchanges are frequently patronizing, as they involve class distinctions and, often, contrasts between first world citizens and third world subjects, as well as potential racial discrimination, Otavaleños are relatively comfortable with these unequal relationships. More than five hundred years of social interaction with human conquerors and powerful superhuman forces in their environment have taught them ways to develop intimacy with the mighty in order to become recipients of their largesse.

The curiosity of Otavaleños about the world in these years cannot be overemphasized, nor was their curiosity entirely idle. For example, the ethnolinguist Lawrence Carpenter, who served in the Peace Corps in Otavalo in the early 1970s, once found his compadre poring over a book of Escher prints he had found in Carpenter's small personal library (personal communication 1978). Within months, weavings of Escher-inspired juxtaposed frogs and cranes in black and white wool appeared in the Otavalo market and have been a popular design ever since. Even in the late 1970s, when international sales took Otavaleños only to the United States, Mexico, and Spain, I was badgered for tapes of world music. One friend, a Peguche native who was my neighbor in Otavalo, was particularly interested in ragas from India, having first heard them from the missionaries of the Maharishi yogi. I have previously mentioned that José Manuel besieged me with questions about how things worked, including such imponderables for me as airplanes and telephones. Clearly North Americans and other gringos had sources of power undreamed of in Ecuador, and Otavaleños were interested in access to it. Since that time, Otavaleños travel to every country in the globe, usually with only marginally legal papers or completely illegal status, in order to find opportunities to improve their economic and social standing at home. While there are long-standing communities of Otavaleños in such large cities as New York, Chicago, and Madrid, most travel home frequently and state their intentions to return home permanently someday. It is becoming almost a rite of passage for a large number of young men to travel to Europe or elsewhere for one- or two-year stints of casual labor in order to earn money for the construction of a house or to amass the capital to begin a commercial or agricultural project. With those travels, "Many Otavalos . . . have leapt right into the postmodern world, skipping modernity in the process, from serfdom to Amsterdam in one generation" (Meisch 2002, 198). The opportunities for further reimagining and combining identities have become practically infinite.

In chapter 1 we read that José Manuel came from Eugenio Espejo parish, where his landless father had a loom and specialized in long-distance commerce, and his maternal grandparents and mother added meat butchery and sales to their agricultural pursuits. Much to his father-in-law's horror, José Manuel did not have much land inheritance and he was not knowledgeable or skilled in agricultural pursuits. By the prevailing definition of the time, he was a hopeless choice of husband for his oldest daughter. But José Manuel, who had married for love, believed that commerce, especially in textiles, promised a better future than the increasingly inadequate land resources that his mother could give him or that his in-laws would give Isabel and her six siblings. Although José Manuel and Isabel have become increasingly estranged from her family, although they live in Huaycopungo, her home community, they were pioneers in economic strategies that increasingly consumed the labor of men and women in Huaycopungo in years to come.

The unusual community exogamous marriage made by José Manuel and Isabel back in 1973 also presaged a trend for the future. From the 92 percent rate of community endogamy found in the late 1970s, a survey of 294 households conducted by several community members under my supervision in 2000 revealed that of the 228 marriages since 1990, only 156 (68 percent) were endogamous to Huaycopungo. However, 33 (46 percent) of the 72 marriages that were exogamous to Huaycopungo were still endogamous to San Rafael parish, 56 (78 percent) of them were endogamous to the Otavaleño ethnic group, and 54 (75 percent) were endogamous to Otavalo cantón. Only 6 marriages united young people from Huaycopungo with residents outside the province of Imbabura, and 2 of those were identified as being indigenous Otavaleños residing outside the province. A total of 71 (99 percent) marriages united two indigenous Ecuadorians, and in only 1 did a young Otavaleño marry a mestiza from Colombia (the only other foreign marriage was to an Otavaleño residing in Colombia). In the case of indigenous non-Otavaleños, two were from Chimborazo province, which is in the central highlands of Ecuador, and the other nine were Mochos, Quichua speakers from the southern end of Imbabura province and the contiguous northernmost reaches of Pichincha province, neighbors to the east of Huaycopungo.

An expansion of the horizons for inclusion beyond the community of Huaycopungo is illustrated by an only half-humorous remark made to me by a couple of men from Cachiviro, the San Rafael parish community that abuts Huaycopungo on the west side. When I patiently explained that I was accepting proposals for community development projects only from Huaycopungo, because that was where I had done my dissertation research and because I had to draw the line somewhere, they made the claim that the large number of recent intermarriages between Cachiviro and Huaycopungo (particularly the contiguous Langaburo and VillagraPugru sections), made any boundary between them moot. They had effectively become one community (a similar argument was made a year later by two women who had married into a more distant community within the parish). While this underscored for me the conceptual role of marriage as a means to create consanguinity over time and the further role of consanguineal ties in defining territorial integrity, it also provoked me to investigate the contemporary rate of community endogamy. In fact, the number of marriages made by a person in Huaycopungo with someone in Cachiviro (nine) was exceeded only by those marriages with someone from Tocagon (fifteen), the linked Urai Shaya community in the old moiety system.

New economic strategies that made inherited chacras only incidental to making a living completely altered the constraints on exogamous marriages that had operated in the past. As stated in chapter 1, community endogamy restricted rights to land and other community resources to community residents, making the practice of agriculture easier for individual households, given the equal land inheritance of sons and daughters. In the 2000 survey, I attempted to find out if those who identified their primary occupations as agriculture or reed mat manufacture would be more likely to marry endogamously than those who claimed to be involved in some form of commercial activity.[5] Of the seventy-two exogamous marriages identified in the survey, seventy replied to the occupation question. Of those, only ten (14 percent) worked in agriculture and/or esteras. Some fifty (69 percent) identified their occupation as some form of commerce, and the ten who fit in neither category (14 percent) included two in construction, two in *artesanías*, four in paid labor, two who were students, and one carpenter. Since none of the "other" occupations depended on inherited land, some or all of them might be added to the group who would have no incentive besides custom or personal preference for an endogamous marriage. Certainly, in the past, women claimed that given the relative preference for newly married couples to reside with or near the husband's parents, they strongly favored endogamous marriages so that they would not be separated from their parents and other close relatives. Unfortunately, I did not gather information on postmarital residence in the 2000 survey. However, those couples who work in long-distance trade vary their residences frequently, both individually and as a couple, between homes in Huaycopungo and rented quarters in their region of commerce. The likelihood of a strong partnership developing between the prospective spouses and mutually beneficial ties to exchange networks on both sides seem to be more relevant than postmarital residence and land inheritances in making marriage decisions today.

EDUCATION, BILINGUALISM, AND THE MEDIA

Isabel was an educational pioneer in childhood, attending and succeeding in San Rafael's mestizo school and going on to secondary school. This is but one early example of the enormous expansion of educational opportunities that also transformed the Otavaleños' world. The increase in Ecuadorian government revenues from oil during the early 1970s was partially allocated to improving literacy rates and educational opportunities throughout the country, particularly in the underserved rural regions. Small schools offering the first three to six elementary grades sprang up overnight throughout the Otavalo area. With the help of a dedicated mestiza schoolteacher from San Rafael, Yolanda Hidalgo, Huaycopungo's first elementary school opened in 1962. From a situation where rural indigenous children were effectively excluded from formal education, Otavalo embarked on an ambitious program of providing Spanish-language instruction for all children. Opposition to indigenous children attending school had come from both mestizos, some of whom wanted to maintain traditional divisions of labor, and from indigenous parents. Otavaleños living in town in the 1960s were more likely to go to school or to attain higher levels of education (Chavez 1982, 265–66); this had been true even from the 1940s (159–60). More rural parents held out against sending their children to town schools for a number of reasons. Many did not want to lose their childrens' labor help, especially in animal herding and baby minding. Parents also objected to their children being required to dress as mestizos and to speak only in Spanish as well as to the harassment from their classmates and indoctrination by their teachers (159); they feared they would lose their children to the mestizo world. The vast majority of mestizos believed without question that exposure to the civilizing influence of school would automatically convince indigenous students of the outmoded nature of their parents' way of life.

However, the new indigenous community schools were cautiously accepted by indian parents. A community liaison with the school, which people in Huaycopungo colloquially referred to as Padre de Familias, was elected every year along with the cabildo officers in an attempt to give parents more say in the school's development. If children were schooled close to home, fewer hours of their help would be lost while they were in school and fewer expenses incurred for transportation or meals. In addition, throughout the region, the school uniform was modified for indigenous children, with a sweater in the school colors supposed to complete a girl's official attire of anacos and embroidered blouse or a boy's white pants and shirt. Sandals, instead of shoes and socks, were also acceptable for both boys and girls, although some schools specified details of the sandals, like color, type of heel, and length of the laces, to instill the requisite discipline and respect for authority.

In the early 1970s, few indigenous children attended Otavalo's schools, especially secondary schools, and those in school were excluded from school parades for national and regional holidays unless they were dressed as mestizos. How could indians represent the nation? However, by 1978, Otavalo's main streets were enlivened by groups of lovely indigenous schoolgirls, whose white gloves set off their lace-trimmed white blouses ringed with colorful embroidery and white-accented dark anacos. They swung their chumbi-wrapped long ponytails in featured positions of the school processions. Similarly, indigenous boys in white pants, long shiny braid, and school sweater marched together, in a separate group from their mestizo schoolmates. In part, this proud display by Otavalo of its squeaky-clean indigenous youth recognized that Otavaleño runa had become a tourist attraction, bringing new economic activity to native mestizos and indigenous people alike.

In 1977 the revolutionary military government also promoted an ambitious program of adult literacy programs, designed to include previously marginalized people into the lofty national goals of progress. "Let's make of Ecuador one big school" was the slogan announced by General Dobronsky O. in 1977 (Stutzman 1981, 69). According to official publications, the national adult illiteracy rate fell from 25 percent in 1974 to 16.7 percent in 1982 (Corkill and Cubitt 1988, 64), although a national study carried out by the Centro Andino de Acción Popular found that the rate of illiteracy in Otavalo cantón fell only from 76.81 percent in 1974 to 48.32 percent in 1982 (Sánchez Parga 1991, 79). These continuing high rates of illiteracy were due in part to the high degree of monolingualism in Quichua. The ability of native speakers of Quichua to speak Spanish also grew significantly in this period as well. The same study (177) reports on three generations in one indigenous community of Otavalo cantón, Carabuela, estimating that 26.67 percent of the grandparental generation spoke Spanish, while 66.67 percent of their children did, and 72.73 percent of their grandchildren were bilingual. During the late 1970s, it was common to hear indigenous adults tearfully bemoan the fact that they were illiterate or monolingual (Chavez 1981, 265), with such phrases as *Llamashnalla cani; Yanga umata charini; Ñuca umaca chushajllami; Uma ucupi nimata tiyan* {I am just like a sheep; I have a worthless mind; My head is just empty; There is nothing inside my head}, as both Taita Antonio Criollo and Mama Emilia Amaguaña repeatedly told me when they were drunk during the house building and many times since. Many adults in this generation became determined to obtain the benefits of bilingualism for their children. In Otavalo and among migrants to Ibarra or Quito, this period resulted in the loss of Quichua language for the children among some upwardly mobile families. However, in rural parishes, Sánchez Parga (1991, 177) found that the use of Quichua does not decline with the addition of bilingualism in Spanish.

However, the deliberate aims of the expanded schooling in those years were to remake indians in the model of progressive mestizos who spoke Spanish; regularly used chairs, toothpaste, and forks; gave up superstitions; and displayed a recovered dignity (Stutzman 1981, 70–71). It was a form of ethnocide (Crespo Toral 1981; xiii), *blanqueamiento* (whitening), or *mestizaje* (mixing) (Whitten 1981, 15; Stutzman 1981), whereby all Ecuadorians would become more alike, with a mixed ethnic past and modern future. The very presence of indians in Ecuador constituted a drag on its path to progress. The revolutionary government's explicit stance was that indigenous identity had to be eliminated for the good of the nation and all its people; "There is no more Indian problem," stated President Rodriguez Lara in one speech. "We all become white when we accept the goals of national culture" (quoted in Stutzman 1981, 45). The school curriculum was then, and still is to some extent today, rife with lectures to indian children about the depravity of their parents' lifestyle and the need to become civilized by adopting the customs of the mestizo majority. The children's reactions have been variable. When she was in high school in the mid-1990s, Susana once patiently explained to me why one ethnocidal message taught by her high school teachers was literally true; her uncle of about the same age, Ernesto, once proudly told me how he stood up to one of his high school teachers in class and told him why he could not make such racist remarks, much to the thrill of his indigenous schoolmates.

Furthermore, the instruction was entirely in Spanish to monolingual Quichua-speaking children. The local elementary schoolteachers defended the practice to me by saying that the children did not need language instruction, since they learned Spanish quickly through immersion, but I usually exhausted any Spanish conversational gambits with indigenous elementary schoolchildren after a few stereotyped phrases. The children learned very little Spanish in the local elementary school, even though the teachers knew only the most basic Quichua and taught almost exclusively in Spanish. This might account for what Sánchez Parga finds *un dato curioso* (a puzzling fact): namely, that the number of people reporting some schooling in a rural community is greater than the number of people reporting that they can read or write (1991, 176). Any delay in educational progress on the part of indian children was attributed to their stupidity, their culturally impoverished backgrounds, or absenteeism during fiestas more often than to the difficulties of learning in a foreign language.

Nonetheless, by 1982 Huaycopungo had its first high school graduate, Segundo Aguilar, from Colegio Fernando Chaves Reyes in Quinchuquí. Originally led by an indigenous graduate of a North American university and funded by USAID, Colegio Quinchuquí was designed especially for rural indigenous children, although it did not exclude mestizos, and offered a curriculum which was supposed to be relevant to their likely future careers in agriculture and handicraft marketing. The publicity of this venture at the time helped to bring many indigenous children into secondary school, although they soon began to choose other schools over Quinchuquí for a variety of reasons. One explanation was that other, more exclusive schools began to accept more indigenous children. In addition, Quinchuquí had a number of problems, from poor administration to the firing of the rector in a scandal over his alleged role as CIA agent to the relatively poor and declining standards of the school. As even rural indigenous parents began to see the advantages of having the skills to compete with mestizos directly in a growing economy and to diversify their childrens' future away from the failing subsistence agriculture, they wanted to ensure their children's access to the best. In the two decades from, say, 1975 to 1995, rural indigenous parents went from being quite resistant to education, at least beyond basic literacy, to being determined to pay for their children to go as far as they could, at least through most of high school. In fact, most would pay more for private education, since public schools are few in number and generally considered to be of inferior quality. Nonetheless, until the twenty-first century, not many Huaycopungo high school graduates had joined Segundo Aguilar in earning a bachelor's degree.[6]

Over time, the mushrooming numbers of indigenous children in school and a shift in the country from the zealous cultural ethnocide or idealistic mestizaje of the 1970s began to change the cultural and social consequences of that schooling. In the early 1970s in San Rafael, Isabel had to force her way into a school-town celebration from which she and her parents were excluded because they were runa, even though she was a student at the school. Twenty years later, I sat with her and a group of other indigenous and mestizo parents, chatting among themselves with animation and total disregard for ethnicity about their children's progress while waiting for their parent-teacher conferences at elementary school in Otavalo. After the conferences, Fernando and Antonio rushed around with the other children, bringing us treats from the picnic laid out for the parents by the school. Not only were indigenous parents and students fully accepted in the school, the mestizo and indigenous parents acted as social equals in that setting.[7]

In general, the teachers also became more respectful of their indigenous students and careful about criticism, and some indigenous students felt empowered to complain when they were insulted by the curriculum, like Ernesto Amaguaña, the son of Mama Emilia's brother who lived in Pivarinci, whom we mentioned above. What's more, the teachers listened and adjusted their classroom language. While many teachers have been influenced by Marxist ideas about social progress and consequently are concerned to decrease indian poverty and powerlessness, they are as determined as the revolutionary government or Christian missionaries to civilize them away from their supposed atavistic mentality and false consciousness. Still, school taught that all citizens, mestizo or indigenous, had access to legal rights, voting responsibilities, and economic opportunities. Overt harassment by mestizo schoolmates declined, and interethnic friendships were sometimes established. When Isabel's sons Fernando, my godson, and Antonio graduated from a relatively prestigious high school in 2004, kids hugged each other good-bye in apparent disregard for ethnicity; Fernando and Antonio cried in the arms of a mestiza school friend who kept saying how much she would miss them. Both indigenous and mestizo kids received awards for outstanding performance and were equally applauded as they walked onstage to accept them. Indigenous parents carried their fancy digital cameras to the foot of the stage to catch the moment in at least the same numbers as mestizo parents, and perhaps more often. Nonetheless, the indigenous students were still in the minority at the school, despite their numbers in the cantón as a whole.

At the same time, Quichua language and culture were not taught, understood, or considered equal alternatives. Schools taught that the dominant culture is an Ecuadorian version of modern Western progress, although the roots of the national culture and the best roads to that progress were by no means uniformly conceived. However, consensus was achieved about the role of contemporary indigenous culture, which derived from some mix of the primitive past, romantic but obsolete, and the pathological results of five hundred years of extreme poverty and marginalization. The positively valued indigenous roots of the national mestizo culture were visible in a sanitized history, in folk music and dance, in artistic images, and other decorative frosting on the cake of modern progress.

From 1979 until the 1990s, experimental attempts in bilingual education by private organizations began to be promoted, but not funded, by various governments. Then, in the early 1990s, a directorate of bilingual education was established in the Ministry of Education, although the programs remain severely underfunded. In Imbabura, the regional indigenous leaders largely direct bilingual education programs, which have become quite politicized. Here is where my compadre Francisco Otavalo, the son of the Curaga Ila Rafi, found his niche. Nonetheless, sincere efforts continue to be made to fashion a system that will promote the Quichua language and integrate indigenous culture into formal education. Most indigenous parents, however, have more confidence that the well-established educational programs in Spanish offer their children greater hope of advancement in the future than the struggling indigenist schools. Even more significant is the problem of how to translate indigenous knowledge, which has been conveyed through observations in daily living and through ritualized song, dance, and invocation (Abercrombie 1998) into textual form for standardized instruction. It risks becoming a politically correct form of the icing approach to culture mentioned above, giving little guidance to indigenous children in how to live life today, but plenty of artistic images of an idyllic pre-Columbian past. Meaningful bilingual education remains a hope of many but is far from a flourishing reality, except in a few isolated cases.

Although the number of qualified indigenous teachers from Otavalo has grown enormously in the last twenty years, it has been difficult for them to replace the mestizo teachers in the local schools. Since everyone prefers to have a post near home, there is substantial competition for the positions in the valley. In Huaycopungo the same person has directed the school for the last twenty years, and some of the teachers have been there as long. The majority are mestizos from San Pablo.

When my compadre Francisco Otavalo, who now heads the bilingual high school in Tocagon, was assigned his first teaching job in the early 1980s, he was sent deep into the jungle near the Peruvian border to work in a tiny school for the Shuar.[8]

Radio programming in Quichua had an important impact in the 1970s as well. Begun by Protestant missionaries, it expanded to a number of stations from Protestant and Catholic sects through the 1970s and to nonreligious stations in the 1980s. Interspersed throughout the religious programs, the local news and personal messages, and the indigenous folk music hours were messages similar to those given in the schools. Indigenous listeners were exhorted to civilize themselves through use of soap, furniture, eating utensils, shoes, and other essentials of life; to save money and avoid wasteful ceremonial expenditure; to send children to school; to get vaccines; to stop drinking; and to participate in the affairs of the nation. While everyone preferred the music and the news, monolingual Quichua-speaking adults were often as exposed to the messages about the need for their progress from barbarism as were their children.

From the late 1970s, exposure to television became more common as the indigenous communities finally got electricity and the price of televisions fell. By the 1990s, even in Huaycopungo every family tried, not all of them successfully, to own their own television. At first, the main impacts were made by access to presidential campaigns, to World Cup soccer games, and to national news and public health campaigns. In the present, a fuller array of programs is available, and families have developed more diverse watching habits. Movies and TV shows from the United States that feature suspense, violence, and horror are extremely popular. Despite the fact that television is broadcast almost exclusively in Spanish, it has drawn the newly bilingual runa people into the life of the nation, and even the international communities, more than ever before.

Huaycopungo's Response to the Changing Environment

The thirty years leading up to the millennium have been characterized by a major change in indigenous Otavaleños' horizons—at once economic, social, and political.

Fig. 44. Looking from Jurubi toward neighboring Cachiviro, 1979
(PHOTO BY AUTHOR)

Fig. 45. Same scene looking toward Cachiviro, 2000
(PHOTO BY AUTHOR)

Internal population growth severely threatened their peasant adaptation, which emphasized subsistence agriculture and domestic production in order to ensure a degree of social and economic autonomy from the oppressive national society. Because of this productive land shortage, the older generation in Huaycopungo greatly feared losing the majority of their children to the outside world. Without the resources to raise a family within the indigenous community, young adults would be forced to seek unskilled labor as low-status cholos throughout the country, as had their neighbors in the hacienda-owned indigenous communities before the land reform of the 1960s. Cautionary tales were often told of emigrants from the community returning after many years to walk the streets, claiming loudly—and perhaps deliberately—to recognize no places, no people, not even their parents, and these stories regularly reduced listeners to tears. The story told in chapter 1 of Isabel's mother's brother, José Manuel Perugachi, or Chunda Fucu, who had gone to work as a teenager in Santo Domingo de los Colorados, is a case in point. Since he had cut his hair and did not wear the impractical white pants, jute sandals, and wool poncho in the rainforest, people imagined that they had seen him many times in the Santo Domingo markets, where they were selling reed mats, and had not recognized him. When one day he approached one of these mat sellers, the seller from home tricked him into returning by the falsified news of his father's death and his mother's fatal illness. When Chunda Fucu got off the bus in San Rafael, he reportedly did not recognize his sister, Dolores, who was walking into town, nor she him. Not only was this story told and retold, but Chunda Fucu, also called Mocho Jusi Mali, and his children have not one but two nicknames that both refer to this period in his life, although almost thirty years have passed since he returned for good. Like many other parents, Taita Antonio, Chunda Fucu's godfather, prepared his children for that possible fate of having to make a living outside Huaycopungo, equipping Isabel with her advanced education, Cipriano with his railroad job, and Oswaldo with his short hair,[9] so that should their fate take them out of the runa world, they would have an edge on their completely unacculturated, sheeplike (*llamashna*) contemporaries. While Huaycopungo did lose some of its children in migration to Quito, Santo Domingo de los Colorados, the coast, or the Oriente, the numbers were relatively insignificant compared to other indigenous communities throughout the Sierra of that period. Perhaps the heightened speed and anxiety with which potentially escaping individuals were drawn into the web of continuously circling drinks—like Chunda Fucu, who was married off in a drunken haze—was partially responsible for keeping the community a place where people "shared but one heart," however constricted and excruciating that heart had become.

However, instead of this terrible misfortune of raising children for an alien world in which they must look down upon their parents, but still be looked down upon by everyone else, Huaycopungo's parents encountered a dramatically altered national political and economic situation. While the long-term promise of the oil revenues and desired industrial development of Ecuador have by no means borne fruit, and the country is in a serious crisis state today, the hope born of the early oil period altered the rural Sierra forever. Large-scale migration to the cities, with the national urbanization figures going from 28.5 percent urban in 1950 to 41.4 percent in 1974 to 49.2 percent in 1982 and 56.1 percent in 1989 (Sánchez Parga 1991, 5), made Otavalo less of a pressure cooker for ethnic tensions exacerbated by few opportunities to make a living. Poor mestizos, who had been dependent upon exploiting the even poorer indígena in order to survive, sent their children away to the land of opportunity in droves.[10] With less competition from mestizos, Otavaleños could and did insert themselves more forcefully into the market. In Huaycopungo in the 1970s, families increasingly refused to turn their reed mats over to mishu middlemen and organized travel to sell them themselves, braving gangs of teenagers in Guayaquil who would grab them and cut off their braids or slice up their ponchos in recreational ethnic harassment. They refused to patronize mishu-owned cantinas in San Rafael, and most of those eventually closed. An entrepreneur who had spent years living in the Oriente came back and opened a sawmill that marketed to local runa and mishu alike. A few people, mostly evangelist converts (see chapter 8) opened small convenience stores in Huaycopungo, freely competing with local mishus. Huaycopungo's largest mestizo-owned store closed in 1998 after many years of operation, due both to a nasty divorce and declining revenues.

Furthermore, opportunities for part-time construction work in

Quito for young men made long-distance migration unnecessary and kept ties to people and land at home active and alive while supplementing the means of making a living. Not only did money enter the indigenous economy much more than before, indigenous people also became consumers in the national market, spending their money just as the revolutionary government had intended. While there was a great resistance throughout the 1970s to forgoing the limited autonomy provided by a marginal economy of subsistence, the 1980s saw the purchases of watches, blenders, televisions, boom boxes, irons, athletic shoes, jackets for men and sweaters for women, gas stoves, and many other commodities rise exponentially even in the poorest communities. No longer did women say they would not dream of forsaking the *cutuna rumi*, grinding stone, for a new food grinder, justifying their sacrifice with arguments about wasteful, mishulike conspicuous consumption and the ways of their grandmothers being good enough for them, as Mama Dolores and many others did in the early 1970s.

Fig. 46. San Rafael's windswept plaza becomes a civilized park
(PHOTO BY AUTHOR)

These women's sons and daughters all bought themselves and their parents commercial-grade blenders, since the household blenders of the United States could not operate on the high-fiber plant food to which they were subjected.

The expansion of tourism in Otavalo did not affect Huaycopungo in the same way as it did those textile-weaving communities whose crafts were so sought out by foreign visitors. The estera-weaving communities on the lake were slower to benefit directly. Nonetheless, the example of even a minority of indigenous people making fortunes by specializing in commerce made it possible to reimagine their own ethnic specializations. From the late 1980s through the 1990s, the people of Huaycopungo changed their censused occupation from overwhelming *agricultores*, agricultural workers, to *comerciantes*, merchants. The vast majority of families now include long-distance trade in their productive activities, carrying mostly clothing or folkloric items to distant parts of Ecuador, Colombia, Venezuela, and even far western Brazil: mostly to places where stores are unavailable and commercial goods hard to get. By offering a personalized relationship and credit to the isolated populace, they try to create a loyal clientele for further purchases. The competition in this trade is fierce, so as many families as can also send at least one young adult member to sell tourist items and play music in Europe and around the world. The success of a few families has made the class stratification that was noticeable in Peguche, for example, as early as the 1950s, now become visible in Huaycopungo, particularly since the late 1980s. Distinctions in housing are the most obvious sign of class distinction in Huaycopungo, from one-room, windowless, mud-walled or cement block dwellings to two-story, multiroom houses with windows.

Very few people from Huaycopungo have paying jobs, and they do not want to have them. Isabel's daughter, Susana, and oldest son, Ricardo, have turned down offers of good jobs in favor of cooperating with their spouses in a family network of commerce. Just as couples previously joined their plots of land at marriage to form an independent household that nevertheless exchanged labor and produce in an ayllu network, Huaycopungo's families today wish to maintain that independence of action, that stress on marriage as an economic partnership, and that embeddedness in a web of reciprocal relationships, even though they are now engaged in long-distance trade. They would find economists' horror at Ecuador's level of employment in the informal sectors puzzling, as it seems to them a particularly independent form of labor, with small but enticing odds of great personal gain, unlike laboring for a boss. A land of entrepreneurs, however precarious, would seem far healthier to them than one where the vast majority of people are proletariat, just another form of exploitative labor obligation like the huasipungueros and yanaperos of the past.

The increased educational opportunities have further transformed the younger generation. Not only are they fluent in Spanish, they have also largely forsaken the humble indian demeanor of their grandparents. Gone are the daily routines of bowed heads, falsetto voices, and a string of honorifics addressed to most mestizos. In the mid-1990s, the twenty-something and determinedly upwardly mobile son of one of Anga Andu's rivals, Santiago Aguilar (Loco Puente), who used to stand in the path late at night calling Antonio mucusu for not having sponsored Corazas, as he had, was able to buy a truck. Santi Rafi invited me and my comadre Isabel for a Sunday ride around the lake with his family. Spotting a new and luxurious development he hadn't seen before, he drove in, got out of the truck, and proudly strode toward the guard at the entrance. When told, haughtily, that it was a private club, he asked in a confident tone for the membership requirements. I didn't know whether to laugh or cry, knowing that he could never afford to enter, even assuming the absurd—that the urban members, most likely from Quito, would have let him join. But I was nevertheless thrilled that he could behave with such pride and dignity and get away with it. The fact that he did not need me, a prestigious foreigner, to approach the guard and that I could witness his performance probably meant a great deal to him as well. The guard's demeanor was haughty but still extremely respectful. Rafael Aguilar's very proud father, Pata Santi, would have grudgingly humbled himself with raised voice, bent head, and mumbled praises and thanks like the others of his generation. He would have loved to see his son demonstrate such chutzpah so successfully. I do not mean to say that the older man would not have engaged in any organized protest or act of defiance, since he did so quite actively, but in daily face-to-face interaction, he would have obeyed the cultural norms. And rightly so, since even approaching such a high-status development might have provoked violence against an unknown indian twenty years before.

However, in the last few decades and particularly since the start of the new millennium, Otavalo families are increasingly separated by great distances, as they find economic opportunities in the jungles of Venezuela and the parks of Amsterdam. Their young children are now growing up outside of an indigenous community. Their parents vacillate between their desire for their children to know Quichua well and their hope that they will be more fluent in Spanish and avoid the problems they had when they were younger. My godson Ricardo's son Auki Marvin, displaying the modern fashion of combining Inca and English first names, rather than Spanish ones, is known in Lago Agrio, where he lives more than half the year, as Jackie Chan. At four he became a fanatic fan of Jackie Chan movies and had all the moves down.

Runa Gente, Indios Sucios No Longer

The claim of indigenous Otavalans today is that they can be runa and civilized at the same time—*runa gente*, not *indios sucios*, dirty indians. This contrasts markedly with the rhetorical plan of the military government of the 1970s to whiten indigenous people in a cultural sense in order that they become civilized, *gente civilizada*. Runa gente have become part of the national and international economy, although a large percentage of Otavaleños prefer to maintain occupational specializations in which their visible status as indian can serve as a mark of quality. And some mestizos don Otavaleño dress in order to claim indigenous authenticity when marketing to an international clientele. Rather than choose an economic strategy that makes them compete on equal footing with the majority of poor Ecuadorians, they act on the belief that an ethnic niche affords them some advantage. Today's Otavalo runa claim successfully that being indigenous excludes them neither from full citizenship nor from membership in the society of fully human Ecuadorians (Whitten, Whitten, and Chango 1997).

God's pachacuti, as announced by the earthquake, had included a real transformation in the environmental conditions within which Otavaleños made their life choices. In a prevalent scholarly view, the processes that so challenged their lives were controlled by political and economic decisions taken in national assemblies, in transnational board rooms and at the World Bank, or in world system forces beyond the control of any individual or group. Therefore, the Otavalo runa were doubly powerless, an impoverished minority group at the mercy of national and international elites who were themselves constrained by political and economic forces beyond their control. By a similar reasoning, the acculturation visible among the indigenous people of Otavalo in the last two decades resulted inevitably from the globalization of culture, exported largely from the United States. It was not a choice, especially not a choice that preserved a sense of ethnic distinctiveness, but a tidal wave of ethnic homogenization that could only be experienced and eventually absorbed. Personal and group efficacy for such a marginalized group could be encountered only in their own fictionalized accounts of what happened. Their responses to the market changes around them could have only a token effect.

But individuals always have choices within those constraints, and the choices made most commonly by individuals within social groups can have far-reaching effects on their own futures and the larger—and more powerful—frameworks of action within which they are embedded. Changes in the regional, national, and international political economy had altered the intrinsic costs and benefits of the traditional drinking norms, which in turn served as a symbol of and a pledge to uphold a certain way of life. Of particular significance are the decreasing adequacy of the peasant way of life and increasing opportunities for indigenous people in the national and international economies; the norm entrepreneurial projects of the government to increase indigenous access to civil rights as a way to involve them as producers and especially consumers in the domestic economy, to garner their vote, and to improve Ecuador's international standing by removing such obvious signs of the country's anachronistic stage of development and primitive character; and the growth of international tourism and craft export that broadened the horizons of imagination for Otavalo's indigenous people.

This chapter's focus has been primarily the changes in economic conditions that altered the intrinsic costs and benefits of the traditional norms of drinking. However, through the expansion of education, mass media, and even international tourism, people in

Huaycopungo also became familiar with a much larger array of norms, explanatory myths, sources of social value, and relations within hierarchical structures. While traditional norms held sway through the fear of consequences—especially poverty, isolation, and vulnerability to racism—other means of being in the world began to be considered. Some seemed to match evolving ways of making a living and interacting with others in the modernizing Ecuador.

The indigenous Otavaleños found in the idea of pachacuti a reason for greater optimism about their power to direct their own destiny. The earthquake gave credence to beliefs that the changes experienced and initiated in recent years had been mandated beyond this world, at a level superior to the machinations of national governments and international agencies. God intervened in the world in part to guide Otavalo's native people to a new and better path. Such conjectures were popular because they maintained a traditional view that through proper religious behavior, the people could participate in a separate moral economy with both this-worldly and transcendent rewards. Among the former were potent techniques for counteracting the effects of minority status and ethnic discrimination and exploiting ethnic niches. While people were powerless in the face of supernatural forces, a proposition so immediately obvious as to be accepted without reflection, they could, nevertheless, influence the social, economic, and political world around them—or at least their interaction with it. And by continuing their close ties within a community of believers, they could enlist God's help to improve their fate, and God's power was greater than any worldly one. On the other hand, without attention to God's messages, they would continue to be punished in this world. Like the transformations described in this chapter—the greater participation in the market economy, the switch from agriculture to long-distance trade, and the upsurge in educational aspirations— religion, too, was dramatically transformed, as we will see in the following chapter. Paraphrasing Sánchez Parga's definition of pachacuti, a new religious epoch had been installed.

The following chapter examines further challenges to traditional ways of life and worldviews brought by proselytizing missionaries and social activists. The prevailing focus is on religious transformations, rather than on the history of class and ethnic political movements in the region. What begins as uncomfortable challenges to the present balances between contending models of explanation and motivation becomes, with time, an opportunity to refashion native scripts, making the revised versions look like a polishing of the truly autochthonous and some of the old appear to be modern perversions in need of cleansing from the local repertoire. Without the twin wellsprings of self-renewing runa culture—idealized relations with the secular powers of this world and the spiritual ones of sacred space/time—individuals would live, powerless, in a vacuum of meaning. The religious and activist dialogues of the 1970s and 1980s resulted in a renewed social confidence and sense of spiritual strength, especially after the norm perturbation of the earthquake, which appeared to give God's seal of approval for innovation.

CHAPTER EIGHT

Evangelistas, Catequistas, and Activistas

A Challenge to Traditional Andean Christianity

En el mes de Junio de 1974, precisamente en los días que se celebre la fiesta de "Inti Raymi" hoy llamado San Juan, se acercó al hermano Angel Criollo uno de los sujetos que persequía anteriormente y en el sitio de Cali Uma de Río Itambi, luego de una larga conversación éste en tono de broma le dice que "él quería ser evangélico," y así sucedió.

[In the month of June 1974, precisely during those days when the fiesta of Inti Raymi,[1] now called San Juan, was being celebrated, one of the people who had been persecuting Angel Criollo came up to him at the site called Cali Uma of the Itambi River; after a long conversation, he said, in a joking tone, that he "wanted to be an evangelist," and that's what happened. (Aguilar Mendez, Sanchez, and Aguilar Mendez 1997, 3; my translation)]

SO BEGINS THE STORY OF THE FIRST conversion, part of an account prepared, in Spanish, by José Manuel Aguilar Mendez, his brother

Pedro Aguilar Mendez, and Juan Sánchez, leaders of Huaycopungo's evangelical church, Jesus de Nazareth, in June 1997 to present at an evangelical conference. After an introduction, the authors, all norm entrepreneurs whose efforts helped provoke the norm cascade of 1987, outline the antecedent conditions that prepared the people of their community to receive the evangelical message beginning in June 1975.

In 1973, the first evangelical Protestant missionaries came to Huaycopungo. This new challenge to traditional runa culture joined the centuries-old conflicts with the predominantly hispanic Ecuadorian majority to intensify the signaling function of traditional drinking customs. When I began research in Huaycopungo in 1977,[2] each proffered pilchi of asua represented a demand for a loyalty oath to kin and community against the evangelicals, who proclaimed teetotalism to be God's true desire. The new religion's stance on drinking threatened the social and spiritual communion each shared drink was supposed to create. Even today, one of the most popular topics of conversation during San Juan is the number of *evangelistas* who have been seen drunk. However, the meaning of this competition has changed from trying to forestall the evangelist movement to maintaining the proper balance of dualities in a well-functioning community.

The first conversion in the official history involved someone who had delighted in taunting and threatening the missionaries. There should be no doubt that the story above happened, but the details have enormous symbolic significance that foster rich and shifting interpretations. This transforming event occurred during one of the most sacred, and indigenous (as opposed to Catholic) times of the year, and right during the Cali Uma, the least hispanic of the ritual events. Temporary world reversal is a central theme of San Juan, seen in the dances and costumes of the San Juanitos, the relationships with mestizos, and the removal of the celebration from town to the banks of Rio Itambi. Primarily, the inversions acted out in San Juan—of the sun's direction, of runa identity, or runa-mishu relations—are expected to ensure the continuance of the world order, although the possibility of a true and lasting inversion is never fully excluded. What better time to use a joke that ritually engages the still-polarizing alternative of the evangelist message, in order to control the conflict? Angel may have been sincere, but he left the door open to claim later on that he had only been joking, in the traditional San Juan manner. Such an offhand conversion leaves open the possibility of the continuing dominance of traditional Catholicism yet prepares a way for an increase in the interchange with the Protestant alternative.

Angel Criollo, the early convert who later took on the responsibility for evangelizing people in Huaycopungo, was originally from the community and, as an adult, had settled on inherited land there. However, as an orphan, he had been brought up in San Pablo by a mestizo family. He wore his hair short, like mestizos, and was active early in the peasant union movement, Conféderación Campesina, which preceded the indigenist FICI.[3] As a person always on the margins, both indigenous and mestizo, Angel Criollo was in the powerful position of being able to unite two sources of power for the benefit of the people. Of course, as a corollary, the power of his liminal status could also lead to their destruction. Luckily, it would seem, few people today, regardless of their religious preference, would say that destruction was the outcome.

In the late 1970s, Taita Antonio was among those intent on convincing the newly abstemious evangelist sympathizers to accept a drink in the name of the ayllu, compadrazgo, or God, and he and his cronies often succeeded. As discussed in chapter 5, it would hardly be sufficient explanation of this behavior to state that because Antonio was addicted or becoming addicted to alcohol, he strove to increase the consumption of those around him, as alcoholics frequently do, so that his own extraordinarily heavy consumption would appear normal. While that may be true, Taita Antonio's position as a community leader inclined him to exert himself in the time-honored promotion of community unity through the exchange of drinks and the joint experience of intoxication. What he did was not just a personal choice but also the exemplary exercise of his leadership role. While he had been a norm entrepreneur in the issue of education or income supplementation through skilled wage labor, on this issue he was a conservative, publicly advocating a position that may have, in fact, been in accordance with his own private assessment of the situation.

Given the extent to which the members of Huaycopungo desired the continual flow of asua and trago between individuals and groups to resemble the circulatory system of the community as an organic body, the evangelists' prescription of abstinence was radical indeed. In fact, in the minds of many, giving up drinking and ritual sponsorships was the only significant message touted by the missionaries. The new converts believed that they had awakened from the darkness to see, for the first time, that they and their ancestors had willingly submitted to an outside world eager to corrupt and contain their wholesome indigenous work ethic with a perverted religion of exaggerated expenditure and continually available booze. Looking back, it was a leap of considerable faith on the part of the new leaders to believe that a loving and interdependent community could be built anew in the absence of the traditional liquid threads making up the webs of connection. As chapter 10, "Transnational Corazas 2000," demonstrates, twenty-five years later their continuing efforts to reweave the threads of tradition back into the new community fabric, with a Catholic warp and a Protestant weft, have resulted in a surprisingly successful ceremonial event.

The pressure on indigenous people to cure themselves of their drinking pathologies was by no means new. While many mestizos, as individuals and in groups both conservative and Marxist, had long struggled to protect indigenous people from the ravages of too much drinking, the majority of those dealing directly with indigenous people were all too willing to enrich their own purses by selling alcohol to indigenous consumers. That did not stop them from deploring indian drinking; each bottle sold confirmed their views of indian depravity. And this supposed depravity conveniently justified their continued exploitation of indians. Even the government collected taxes on each legal bottle of trago purchased. However, the majority of trago sold came from illegal stills, not from government-licensed distilleries. However, for runa to agree to give up drinking as a result of mestizo pressure would have meant that they surrendered to mestizos' right to make the norms and judge indigenous people by them. Nonetheless, a substantial portion of the indigenous population was willing to consider that drinking was a problem in many of their families, as the mestizos so relentlessly pointed out, without wanting to sell out directly to their oppressors.

The evangelist approach offered several advantages. Abstaining entirely in the hope of God's reward had the appeal of being both simple and coherent. The reward would be a renewed productive partner-ship between God and man that would simultaneously bypass those Catholic sources of religious sanction traditionally dominated by mes-tizos. The fact that some of the early evangelists were also involved in provincewide indigenist movements was another appealing factor, as will be seen in the history below.

Evangelistas

In the 1997 account of the founding of the evangelical church in Huaycopungo, the authors, all norm entrepreneurs whose efforts helped provoke the norm cascade of 1987, outline the antecedent con-ditions that prepared the people of their community to receive the evangelical message, beginning in June 1975.Written ten years after the earthquake, this account shows surprisingly little concern with the problem of alcohol use and abuse, which had been so central to their message before. They mention the omnipresence of mestizo-owned drinking establishments, blaming them for the high level of abusive drinking rather than condemning the indigenous people. This strategy accurately represents the leaders' skill, honed after earlier failures, at picking strategies that would unite rather than divide the community. The alcohol message, however centrally important, had been divisive, while the activist message of struggle against outside oppression united everyone.

The two paramount sources of pressure for change are here described in 1997 as working together in the early 1970s to prepare peo-ple to accept the new religion. First, the community was backward and underdeveloped. Second, its people were engaged in a process of politi-cal consciousness-raising and incipient political activism. Leading peo-ple who are enslaved by paganism or even the Catholic Church out of the dark ages of barbarism into the light of the gospel is a familiar nar-rative in Protestant missionary work. In contrast, the engagement in social and political activism is often thought to be a polar alternative to the formation of an evangelical movement.

> Es triste recordar que las comunidades de la parroquia de San
> Rafael . . . vivíamos en una situación muy dramática, niños

que no terminaban la escuela, familias que se alborotaban por pasar las fiestas del Coraza, Pendón, el Quinche y otras, sin importarle la pobreza, ni la deuda, ni la venta de terrenos. Habían dirigentes que no se preocupaban por el desarrollo de la Comunidad. Mandados y humillados por ciertas personas del pueblo de San Rafael. Cantinas y chicherías por todos los sectores. Grandes problemas de tierras con el Municipio y las haciendas. Comunidades sin estadio, sin luz, casa comunal y agua potable. Es decir teníamos comunidades atrasadas.

En estos tiempos, hallá [sic] por el año de 1972, poco antes de la fundación de la Iglesia existía un problema de tierras de una 10 personas de la zona de San Rafael, justo a las orillas de la laguna de IMBACOCHA, que hoy llaman San Pablo, por cuanto el Municipio de Otavalo, quería tomar unos pedasos de terrenos de la gente pobre, quienes no sabían que hacer con este problema y buscaban a alguién que les ayudara a solucionar a su favor. En esta circunstancia aparecen compañeros asesores como: Doctor Lema, Paulina Lema, Marco Barahona, taita José Otavalo, Isabe Criollo y nuestro recordado hermano Antonio Velásquez. Quienes luego de capacitar nos enseñaron a defendernos de toda explotación, engaño, y miseria por parte de los mestizos.

[It is sad to remember that in the communities of San Rafael parish . . . we used to live in a very dramatic situation, with children who didn't finish school and families that threw themselves into turmoil in order to sponsor the festivals of Coraza, Pendón, El Quinche,[4] and others, without taking into account the resulting poverty, debt, and sale of land. There were leaders who didn't take responsibility for the community's development. [We were][5] ordered about and humiliated by certain individuals in San Rafael. [There were] cantinas and chicherías in every sector. [We had] big problems with the municipal government and the haciendas over land. [We were] communities without a stadium, without electric light, without a community center and potable water. In other words, we were backward communities.

During those times, around the year 1972, a little before the foundation of the church, there existed a land problem with about ten people in the San Rafael area, right on the shores of Lake IMBACOCHA, which today is called San Pablo, because the municipal government of Otavalo wanted to take some properties from the poor people, who didn't know what to do about this problem and who were searching for someone who could help them find a favorable solution. On that occasion appeared comrade advisors such as Dr. Lema, Paulina Lema, Marco Barahona, Taita José Otavalo, Isabel Criollo, and our brother Antonio Velásquez, still with us in memory.[6] After preparing us, they taught us to defend ourselves from all exploitation, deceit, and misery on the part of the mestizos. (Aguilar Mendez, Sanchez, and Aguilar Mendez 1997, 2; my translation)]

The first paragraph takes the perspective we first encountered in the last chapter, so promoted by the military government of that period, that the indigenous communities were uncivilized and backward, needing to be brought into the twentieth century for the good of the country. While the government brought to the nation's attention the exceptional deprivation of Ecuador's indigenous people in a country where the majority of inhabitants were poor, it also took a resoundingly negative view of indigenous culture, especially as it contrasted with the mainstream. As we saw in the previous chapter, the young indigenous adults in the early 1970s who attended school, anyone who could listen to the radio, and all those who conversed with their mestizo neighbors were bombarded with messages about their inadequate way of life. For instance, the absence of clean drinking water in increasingly crowded indigenous communities was clearly a real health problem, and there were others of that nature. But it is less clear that the practice of sitting on the ground, instead of in a chair, or eating the traditional indigenous foods were deleterious in any way other than as symbolic capital in the dominant society. Certainly there is a benefit attached to the earlier peasant lifestyle, wherein fewer natural resources were used, and less nonbiodegradable garbage was generated than in the richer and more urban town of Otavalo, for example. In the next chapter, we will look more closely at our main example, ritualized binge drinking, in which a calculation of costs and benefits is considerably more complex than the absence of potable water or the culturally hegemonic demand that people use furniture.

In keeping with the national and evangelical propaganda, the first paragraph of Huaycopungo's evangelical church history highlights this message of accepting improvement and progress as the responsibility of all citizens. Observers of Protestant missionary work around the world have frequently claimed this to be an essentially politically conservative message that characterizes evangelical work everywhere. If you conform to the social demands of the nation or of the international powers, rather than asserting a cultural autonomy, you might be compensated in this world, and you will surely receive your reward in the next. Learn to wear shoes and the process by which all your earthly problems will be solved has magically begun.

However, this church's history, rather than proclaiming that indigenous backwardness stemmed solely from a lack of religious and social enlightenment in the people, lays some of the blame for the community's underdevelopment squarely on the larger society. Before being ready to receive the word of God as brought by the missionaries, the indigenous people had to be taught "to defend ourselves from all exploitation, deceit, and misery on the part of the mestizos." Whether the message came from the national government or the evangelist missionaries, any call for indigenous people to play by national or international rules in a game for which most mestizos would ensure themselves the only winning roles was unacceptable. When in 1972 President and General Rodriguez Lara entreated indigenous Ecuadorians to join the national culture and encouraged nonindigenous Ecuadorians to accept indigenous people into the mainstream with the words quoted in the previous chapter, "We all become white when we accept the goals of national culture" (Stutzman 1981, 45), he received a mainly negative reaction in indigenous Otavalo. As we have seen in our example of heavy drinking thus far, indigenous people had elaborated a culture of difference that allowed them the freedom to pursue a moral and spiritually blessed life, with the hope of material prosperity, apart from the mestizos. Joining the mainstream would leave the people without a major unifying defense against exploitation, both material and psychological—their cultural difference. On the other hand, if the material conditions of living could be improved and if mestizos could be convinced to extend basic civil rights to their indigenous neighbors, then that part of the proffered deal was intriguing.

The second precondition for acceptance of the evangelical message, as we read in the leaders' prepared history, was political and social activism to improve indigenous access to basic human rights. Even more important to them than giving up their own ignorance and self-destructive behaviors, this message made Protestantism particularly attractive to the young adults of the 1970s. It is significant that the story of political mobilization to protect community land, rather than a set of traditional religious concerns, has a prominent place as a historical precondition of conversion. In fact, in their search for justice concerning the lakeshore properties, the group organized an audience in the Presidential Palace with General Rodriguez Lara himself, and they attribute some of their eventual success in thwarting plans for land development by the military to this visit.

The historical summary above also uses a traditional vocabulary of political resistance. For example, the words *compañeros asesores* (comrade advisors) comes directly from Marxist-inspired political movements. Calling the lake by the Quichua name, Imbacocha, rather than the customary Spanish name, Lago San Pablo, is a self-conscious attempt to reclaim power, in this case the power to name things. The fact that the name is in uppercase forcefully expresses this declaration of political potency, as advocated by CONAIE, the national indigenous political organization that has been so influential since the last decade of the twentieth century. In fact, the account goes on to include the founding of FICI (Federación Indígena y Campesina de Imbabura) in 1974 (called Conféderación Campesina until 1984) as an important precursor of evangelical church organization, although many external critics see the FICI as a hotbed of socialist, Marxist, and anti-American ideologies.

Many people have previously noted the *protest* in Protestantism (see Casagrande 1978 and Muratorio 1981 in Ecuador; Comaroff 1985 and Comaroff and Comaroff 1997 in South Africa), and Stoll (1990) describes similar linkages throughout Latin America in the same period. Nonetheless, the social activism associated here with the evangelical church's history still seems to contradict the conservative message of conformity to Western values and to surprise contemporary North Americans. North American evangelical missionaries of the period in Ecuador were rarely political radicals themselves, although many were unusually flexible in their promulgation of social and economic development and in their passive acceptance of the fact that local people connected their missionary efforts to those of more radical, political groups. Since they were seeking conversion and development in a predominantly Catholic country where the second-class status of indigenous citizens was generally accepted, evangelical missionaries were certainly aware that their work undermined both the traditional Catholic Church and the national power structure. Presumably they did not find that an obstacle, but an especially charged challenge.

Although evangelical Protestants had been active in the Otavalo area for decades, the first missionary came to Huaycopungo from Quito in 1973. At first, the community rallied as it did against all outsiders and threatened violence against the missionaries if they did not cease their efforts. The stories of early persecution are important to the Protestants' view of their relationship to God and to each other today. On the one hand, persecution plagued God's individual loyal followers in the early years of their struggle with the forces of ignorance, as it did Jesus and his disciples, but they were later rewarded for their steadfastness in this time of trouble. On the other hand, Huaycopungo evangelists still believe that God requires communal unity, and persecution continued since the evangelistas lived an immorally individualized life. Their numbers had to grow to the point that it was possible for them to constitute a reciprocally supportive community in God's service. While evangelical Christianity is criticized for its promotion of individualist ideologies in communities with a strong communal tradition, here the evangelists so far have tried to maintain communal responsibility, while freeing families to make risky innovations with the goal of escaping shared but devastating poverty. Until the Huaycopungo converts learned to behave, individually *and* communally, in a way that pleased God, they were subject to his wrath in the form of earthly torture. Individualism is still as suspect to the evangelistas as it is to the traditional Catholics. Evangelists struggle to prove that their generous exchanges with each other exceed those of the more traditional Catholics. Leadership of Huaycopungo's evangelical church has remained constant since its inception, and these individuals never waver from trying to unite people into forms of communal responsibility: both within the ranks of the converted and between evangelists and Catholics.

In the church's historical account, Angel Criollo's conversion marked at least a temporary lessening of persecution and the very slow accumulation of members until, in 1975, they became a church under the pastoral guidance of Antonio Velásquez, the very person mentioned as helping them win the battle for the lakeshore land. Most of the first converts were young men and women in their late teens and early twenties who had learned to read, write, and speak Spanish at the first community school. They had flexed their muscles in the fight for the lakeshore and were willing to confront more traditions if it meant an improved future. The introduction of soccer teams for young men by the activists/evangelists of the time also captivated them. Not only would they get to enjoy the game that was such a national and world obsession, they were also taught to substitute this kind of ritualized combat for the rock throwing between communities that they had engaged in during San Juan. Since the rock battles brought the wrath of mestizo law enforcement agents down on the indigenous communities, caused injuries, and gave indigenous people the reputation for being violent savages in the eyes of the social activists who were intent on guaranteeing their civil rights, they were expendable. Today, soccer tournaments have generally replaced rock fights during San Juan.

Nonetheless, the year following the start of the church was again very difficult, since "no faltaban los insultos, agraciones [sic; agresiones], y maltratos a nuestros hermanos, hubieron además heridos, detenidos y hospitalizados" [there was no shortage of insults, attacks, and mistreatment of our brothers; in addition some were wounded, arrested, and hospitalized (Aguilar Mendez, Sanchez, and Aguilar Mendez 1997, 3; my translation)]. Here one sees that the costs of embracing the Protestant norms fully go well beyond the simply reputational; for some who might have been sympathizers, the threat of violence would act as a powerful deterrent to public support. Even worse, Antonio Velásquez unexpectedly died, leaving the new congregants without a trained pastor. Without his personal inspiration, many people did not want to continue, including Isabel and José Manuel, who had been part of the original activist group influenced by the evangelists. Not only were costs high, the benefits had dramatically decreased with this leader's death. All who speak of him today do so with tears in their eyes, even if they are no longer evangelists, since he was evidently a very charismatic leader in the soft-spoken and self-sacrificing mold the indigenous people so admire.

However, since ninety people were now baptized, those who remained evangelists felt the need for a leader and more formal organization. The first person to become trained at the Bible Institute run by the Christian and Missionary Alliance in the lakeside community of Agato left the church soon afterward. The church dwindled to only eight people. Four dedicated men and women continued house-to-house visiting in their search for converts, and they also began to make more and more contacts with the few converts in the other communities of the parish and the cantón. With the training of two more pastors, the Aguilar Mendez brothers, Damiano Jusi Mali and Damiano Pidru in their Quichua nicknames, the number of interested people again grew. After Pastor Damiano Pidru donated his own land for the construction of their first chapel, the group joyously celebrated their first evangelist wedding. Fifty converts and one hundred curious observers came to enjoy the event. Subsequently the group split up again and the few remaining "evangelical brothers and sisters" (Aguilar Mendez, Sanchez, and Aguilar Mendez 1997, 3) had to begin the process of recruiting followers over again. At the very least, one can see that the threshold for embracing some modified form of socioreligious norms, as promoted by the evangelists, or sticking to traditional Catholic practice was rather fragile. The costs of public support for removing drinking from its central religious place, especially in the form of claiming Protestantism, far outweighed the benefits. Nonetheless, interest in the benefits seems relatively high, causing the numbers of followers the faithful converts managed to attract to shift repeatedly back and forth.

While today's evangelist leaders combine a story of persecution by the infidels, a failure of faith, and a tendency to factionalism to explain the repeated depletion of their church members, those who were never involved in the evangelist movement or those who no longer are have a different version to tell. First of all, they cite the pressures by ayllu and neighbors to continue to participate in the rituals that bound them into a moral community, ones that evangelists were unable to share at the time because of the stricture on drinking alcohol. Personal networks would shrink as the evangelistas within them refused drinks and thus the mutual obligation to exchange labor and food that shared drinking implied. It was almost as people had feared earlier from labor migration—they would lose their children, even if, in this case, they were still physically present. Their children would wander like disembodied spirits through the chaquiñancuna of Huaycopungo, refusing to recognize their drinking parents anymore. Furthermore, in the nonconverts' eyes, evangelists immorally hoarded their own production, rather than let it flow naturally into the reciprocal exchanges that characterized kin and community. Would they not all be punished if the supernatural forces of the universe did not receive their expected ritual attention at many times throughout the year? In their accounts, the multiple factional splits of the fledgling evangelista community arose when the followers caught on to the many instances of immoral selfishness displayed by the most active proselytizers and church leaders. Hoarding, personal aggrandizement, and theft were believed to be the inevitable results of their beliefs in not drinking, not sponsoring festivals, and seeking nuclear family improvement. True to small town life, nasty accusations and bitter rumors were far more common than proof.

In the 1980s the small group of Huaycopungo evangelists joined with other local congregations to found the Asociación de Indígenas Evangélicos de Imbabura, AIEI, an organization sponsored by the Gospel Missionary Union with many counterparts around the world. In the 1997 history, the authors speak of this decade as one of growth and relative peace, although a few years ago, the memories of these years were painful indeed. As their organizational skills and their connections with regional and international evangelical organizations grew, they became eligible for international sources of aid. What Stoll (1990; 268) called the "new wave in missionary work: social responsibility" had come to Huaycopungo, which he spells Guaicopungo (297). The timing of Huaycopungo's evangelical missions is critical. An era of unprecedented cooperation among international evangelical organizations in their Latin American operations and a shift to relief and development over the previous emphasis on moral instruction and child sponsoring coincided with government calls for development and Marxist-inspired peasant and indigenist federations' promotion of active protest. A number of Quito lawyers had begun to specialize in taking civil rights cases. Three very different ideological sources had aligned at this point to support an improvement in indigenous standard of living—the activists, the government, and the evangelical church. Although there were voices for similar change in the Catholic Church, they were of less significance at that time in Otavalo. Their contribution to this discourse, which followed soon after, will be discussed below.

Two advantages that the missionaries had over the secular alternatives were the assurance that God approved their efforts and an orientation toward North America and away from the traditional sources of mestizo authority, whether religious, Marxist, or of the governing elite. Even though the presence of North Americans in the missionary work was relatively rare, the local people and especially the missionaries saw a somewhat hazy connection between North American prosperity, locally visible in the increasing number of North American tourists, and Protestant means of religious worship. After the Spanish conquest, many native people had eventually come to believe that they could multiply the means of attracting spiritual and material prosperity to themselves by combining three sources of supernatural power: that they had inherited from their ancestors, that they had been taught by the Incas, and that they had been forced to accept by the Spanish. Similarly, some people in Huaycopungo felt that the addition of evangelical Protestantism promised another increase in supernatural power. By pleasing the Protestant God, they might share in the prosperity he had bestowed upon his people in North America. No evangelical missionary would argue with the connection made between a moral life and increased prosperity, either, since pulling oneself up by one's bootstraps was part of God's wishes for all good Christians. Nor would the international evangelical community, so dominated by North Americans, deny that the humble North American believers represented a good example to their South American brothers in Christ.

The Huaycopungo church's first successful grant of international aid came from Compassion International. One of the more conservative organizations, Compassion International had been accused of attracting "rice bowl Christians" by sponsoring children only if they were offered Bible teaching (Stoll 1990, 268). The provision of food and Bible instruction became an integral part of the Huaycopungo church's programs for children. Funding by Compassion International continues to this day. The church programs have since expanded to include after-school recreation; tutoring and homework supervision; instruction in crafts, typing, computer, and sports summer camps; and numerous other programs, open to all children in three local communities, even if they regularly attend mass or catechism. Since most people's religious life is flexible, with tentative loyalties and a mixed practice, it is much more accurate to refer to individuals' participation in certain religious activities than to label them evangelists or Catholics. Nonetheless, at the beginning of the program from Compassion International, the provision of aid to the children of evangelists who were receiving Bible instruction provoked great envy and anger in Huaycopungo. It was a clear sign to the unconverted that the evangelistas were selfishly hoarding resources meant for the community, just as had been expected.

Far more damaging was the involvement of World Vision, in part because it claimed to aid the development of all Christians without trying to convert Catholics to evangelical Protestantism. In fact, however, true to its evangelical roots, World Vision channeled all its funds through local evangelical organizations. Particularly resented locally were loans to Huaycopungo's evangelical leaders, such as Damiano Jusi Mali, so they could open stores and sell to their compatriots. The evangelist organizations most likely thought they were helping indigenous people become free of commercial exploitation from their mestizo neighbors, a problem local people often discussed among themselves. However, nothing the church leaders could have done, other than openly stealing from all their neighbors, could have so violated community norms. What else besides the taboo on selling to each other could so unite a poor community, and what other proscription would so clearly ensure that community resources would keep everyone alive, rather than contribute to class differentiation and exploitation? The strength of the outrage was probably fueled by envy. Only the first person to violate the taboo on selling to his fellows would benefit financially. The cost of obeying local norms had mushroomed at the moment someone else dared to break them. Others claimed that the money World Vision donated for the reconstruction of the chapel was being siphoned off into individuals' pockets. Despite such opportunities, the evangelical leaders have not outstripped most of their neighbors in wealth over the years, although they probably generated their share of the lost funds experienced by World Vision in Imbabura through "administrative ignorance, culturally approved sharing of resources with kin, and theft" (Stoll 1990, 290). From that time on, they have become scrupulous about keeping clear and open accounts and with sharing development funds to all those in the community who wished to participate.

During this period, World Vision's easily available funds for development did even more to destabilize regional evangelical politics than it did to destabilize Huaycopungo. Ecuadorian nationalists complain that World Vision wanted "freedom to interfere in local affairs, no government opposition to its projects, and indigenous people who accepted its evangelistic message without question" (Goffin 1994, 90). The ecumenical Protestant agency Brethren and United Foundation complained to Stoll (1990, 297) that World Vision had destroyed forty years of their patient work in the region. And the Evangelical Indian Association broke apart in 1984, when some of the churches, although not Huaycopungo's, left the Christian and Missionary Alliance. Still, when the international organizations throw up their hands at the extreme factionalism among indigenous evangelicals, it is worth remembering Sánchez Parga's caveat that structural unity implies differentiation in andean societies (1989). As we have seen in our analysis of moieties and religious sects, the community is formed not only through webs of reciprocity and mutual responsibility but also through real combat, symbolic competition, and bitter rivalry between divisions arranged in ever-more inclusive levels. Church hierarchy as interpreted by indigenous followers would never mirror the visions held by the foreign missionaries.

Some of the more conservative Protestant denominations were uneasy about the potential of their programs to stir up revolutionary fervor among their indigenous converts. Nonetheless, their message of self-directed socioeconomic improvement, their freedom from the provincial and national governments, the organizational and leadership training they gave rural indigenous people, and their failure to make clear to the local people the distinctions between Marxist and evangelical ideologies all contributed to the mixing of radical political and religious efforts.

Nonetheless, as in other arenas, Huaycopungo's leaders seem to prefer to remain on the fringes of regional and national organizations, using them for whatever advantages can be obtained but withdrawing whenever their own autonomy is threatened. Despite the rhetoric of political activism in the official history, the leaders of Huaycopungo's evangelical church are not committed radicals. They accommodate to whomever can help them serve their community and its neighbors. In fact, Mormons, Seventh-Day Adventists, and the Baha'i were also active in the Otavalo area, and most people in Huaycopungo made little distinction between them; they were all "evangelistas." In their spirit of experimentation and search for knowledge, Isabel and José Manuel have been short-term members or at least visitors to all these sects at one time or another. And they are not unusual.

In a certain respect, the story told above is one about the conversion of a number of Otavaleños from Huaycopungo to evangelical Christianity, as supported by huge international organizations based in the United States. In that way, it resembles many other such stories. But at the same time, the story is somewhat unusual in the extent to which the people in Huaycopungo have been relatively free from dogmatic or oppressive supervision by outside authorities. They have been allowed to pick and choose from a variety of alternatives in an attempt to remodel a way of life that had become economically unsustainable and remained politically impotent. Furthermore, they have been free to construct their religious life in a way that continues to reflect the power of paradoxes. They continue nourishing opposing forces that can in turn enliven and enrich the world where humans live. We will return to the subject of the new religious order after the earthquake following a review of some additional history of the ideological changes in Huaycopungo. The paradoxes engendered by the mix and opposition of traditional Catholicism and evangelical Protantism in Huaycopungo cannot be understood without examining the changes in the Catholic Church that, in many ways, mirrored the Protestant innovations.

Fig. 47. Inside the evangelical church
Jesus de Nazareth, 1992
(PHOTO BY AUTHOR)

Catequistas

In the wave of changes beginning with Vatican II and continuing through the development of liberation theology, some segments of the Catholic Church have also challenged traditional religion throughout Latin America. Aware of the institutional church's role in sustaining, even benefiting from, inequalities of wealth and power, a new wave of Catholic theorists and practitioners strove to reform their practice with the poor. God's kingdom is not to be confined solely to heaven, since the goal of all good Christians working together is to create it right here on earth. Rather than being passive tribute payers to the church, native peoples were encouraged to read the Bible and other church teachings and learn more about true Catholic teachings and worship.

In addition to the democratization of religious knowledge, poor communities were taught to unite spiritually and participate actively in personal and community improvement in order to overcome social, economic, and spiritual domination by the wealthy and powerful. While Ecuador has not been a leader in revolutionary Catholicism, it did have a well-known Catholic proponent of social justice in Bishop Proaño, from another highland province with a large indigenous population, Chimborazo, far to the south of Otavalo. Chimborazo was also the area of earliest evangelical missionary activity in Ecuador, and the history of the clashes between Catholic activists and Protestant evangelists there is quite interesting (Casagrande 1978; Muratorio 1980, 1981; Stoll 1990). Most of the church hierarchy, clergy, and lay Catholic leaders in Imbabura province who sympathized with the new social consciousness, including the current bishop, would have considered Bishop Proaño their spiritual leader.

Although the influence of liberation theology in Otavalo was less overall than that of evangelist missionaries and came to Huaycopungo at a later date, it was important in providing a parallel alternative to conversion to Protestantism. The creative discourse promoted by this new opposition helped shape the resultant religious and normative balance that so transformed Huaycopungo in the last few years. The liberal policies of the local bishop were undoubtedly factors as well, although particular priests' impacts were extremely varied.[7]

One of the innovations promoted by the new Catholic priests, nuns, and lay leaders was the training of lay catechists, *catequistas*. Catequistas were encouraged to study the Bible, a practice the parishioners had traditionally been discouraged from attempting. After the appropriate training, they became religious mediators and sometimes religious leaders for their own people. The extension of schooling in Spanish made this possible within indigenous communities. But increased literacy in Spanish also presented an opportunity for those Catholic leaders who wished to bring official Christianity to the majority of indigenous people who did not understand the languages of the church. Catequistas could be translators of the official teachings to the priests' indigenous flocks, thus undermining local religious traditions. Previously, most priests had considered their indigenous charges to be like children, incapable of understanding orthodox Catholicism, and so tolerated in their immature perversions of the true faith. Still, the training of catequistas also allowed the parishioners to have a more active role in their religion or, in the case of indigenous communities, a more informed dialogue between their own Catholic practice and the teachings of the priests and nuns. This devolution of religious power to local communities mirrors the teachings of some Protestant missionaries and is also consistent with political trends in Ecuador that give indigenous people the means to fashion and communicate their own identity within the national discourse, rather than be marginal to it. However, the tension between devolving power to the local people and using native intermediaries to help bring people into the fold of the new dogma promulgated by the liberated clergy should not be ignored.

As we saw in chapter 3, Huaycopungo runacuna valued priests as intermediaries with God and considered them essential for such religious procedures as masses and prayers on special occasions, like funerals or ritual sponsorships. However, they did not consider themselves under the authority of the parish priest whose dictates they were obliged to obey. Although priests could deny burial in consecrated ground or baptism to those they believed had fallen away from the church's teachings, it was always relatively easy to bypass the controlling local cleric and pay a priest in San Pablo or Otavalo or even Ibarra to carry out the sacraments for a price. Especially from the 1980s onward, whether priests were attracted to the social messages of liberation theology or trained under more conservative conditions caused vast differences in individual priests in the parishes of Otavalo cantón. That and the involvement of lay catechists made closer relationships with a priest more appealing, and thus the shopping for priests became somewhat more intense.

Catholic Church innovations in Ecuador also responded to the growing success of Protestant denominations in various urban and rural contexts (Casagrande 1978). While this was by no means the only influence, the enthusiastic response to the evangelists' democratizing practices, the greater participation in worship by the congregation through singing and testifying, the use of the Quichua language, and the creation of a community of "brothers and sisters" were all models that Catholic innovators who desired to increase and motivate their flocks had reason to copy.

In many ways, the people of Huaycopungo believed that the catequistas and evangelistas were parallel alternatives, not because they were both Christian denominations, since that was not generally recognized, but because of their similar messages of social activism and economic and moral improvement. Radio Catolica's programming in Quichua sometimes competes successfully with the extremely popular Radio Baha'i in Otavalo and certainly outdoes the much older evangelical HCJB, the Voice of the Andes. Pamphlets given out on market days by Protestants and Catholics explaining God's love for individual and family self-improvement are sometimes almost indistinguishable.

Many of the younger generation even began to accept the idea that the way they were drinking had to be changed. People in Huaycopungo now say that catequistas, like evangelistas, do not drink. But for catequistas not drinking means not getting publicly drunk, which is consonant with the nearly synonymous use of the Quichua words *ufyanajun* (they are drinking together) and *machanajun* (they are getting drunk). Since they are not getting drunk, they are not drinking. For evangelistas not drinking means not taking a single drink. In contrast, catequistas attempt to limit their drinking and avoid the days'-long binges that used to be so common.

The story of the one-time curaga, Ila Jusi Otavalo, introduced in chapter 5, illustrates some of these similarities. As a local leader, he is one of the original activist leaders mentioned in the evangelist church history discussed above. However, unlike the leaders in the previous section, he has remained a loyal Catholic, although he has carefully investigated the Protestant alternative. As long as I have known him, Ila Jusi has cultivated relationships with as many priests as he can—in San Pablo, San Rafael, Otavalo, and Ibarra. Through them he has been in touch with all the changing social currents in the Catholic Church that have promised indigenous people a stronger voice in their homeland. In the 1980s Ila Jusi was trained as a lay religious leader by a bishop in Ibarra and became one of Huaycopungo's first catequistas. Ila Jusi got a Bible of his own, which he once excitedly showed me, telling how he had compared it carefully to the evangelist Bible and other copies of the Bible he had been able to examine. Despite his only three years of elementary school education, he has struggled like many others of his generation to read and develop an intellectual relationship to the written word.

In a taped interview in 1990, Ila Jusi told me that until 1989, *Yapa ufyadur carcani* (I was an excessive drinker). It was part of the traditional exercise of his leadership role in the community. But he found it increasingly got in the way of his living the life he valued. *Ñuca partimanda, juyaj juyajta causarcani. Shinaca sintirircani yapa ña ufyajuni, yuyayta charircani* (From my point of view I was living lovingly, but nevertheless I felt that I was now drinking too much, I had that thought).

In his account, what made him stop drinking was not being able to go to church on Sunday, even when his sisters and his daughter came to get him, because he was too drunk or too hungover. His wife had warned him that he was killing himself with his drinking and begged him to change. As community leader, Ila Jusi traveled often to Ibarra, the provincial capital, where he came across a pamphlet, which told him: *Canpaj vida ñami cambiarigrin, canga shimi taita diusta mañana cangui. Jipamanca imashta alichirishpa causangui, taita diusta ña mañanami cambaj vida cambiarijun* (Your life is about to change; you must ask for God's word. Afterward, if you improve your way of life and pray to God, then your life will be transformed [my translation]). In Ila Jusi's account, which makes the event seem very much like an evangelical conversion, two weeks later he gave testimony in church and vowed to God to stop drinking: "Both of my sisters together, one on either side" (*Ishcandin pani ladu ladu*), "they led me as if I were drunk" (*igualmanda machashcashna aparca*). "Me and both of my sisters cried, my wife cried, and even my mother cried" (*Nucaca, ishcandin pani huacarca, ñuca warmi huacarca, ñuca mamitapash huacarca*). *Machashcashna*—as if drunk—has more than one reference. On the one hand, drunks are often led by their women relatives, especially wives, to care for them and get them home safely. The visual image would have suggested a drunk man being led by his "designated caretakers." At the same time, a person who is drunk no longer is exercising rational self-control. As described by Carpenter (1992), he inhabits only his interior and uncontrollable self. This is the self that can be united freely with sacred and perpetual space/time, making drunkenness a spiritual act in traditional religion. This seems to be the same self, without the ambiguous power of alcohol, that Ila Jusi brought to his conversion experience.

Even so, the pressure continues to this day to get him to drink again. His nephew begged during his house building, saying, "I, too, pledged my soul to God, but I still drink." They accused him of becoming an evangelist. Once he came to blows over it and finally took the cup of trago in his hands and held it a long time, "praying to god in his heart" (*taita diusta shungullapi mañashpa*); finally he returned the cup.

After he became stronger in his faith, Ila Jusi organized a catequista group in the poor neighboring community of Caluqui, whose inhabitants are the Mochos or Puendos, descendants of former huasipungueros, who speak Quichua but rarely intermarry with Otavaleños. In 1990 he claimed there were thirty followers and the group was growing all the time. He was also helpful in establishing a new Catholic chapel, run by foreign missionaries, in Huaycopungo Chiquito.

While highlighting the similarities, Taita Ila Jusi's religious experiences also capture some of the differences between the catequistas and evangelistas. Just as an *evangelista* refers both to someone who dedicates him- or herself to acquainting people with God's word and to anyone who belongs to an evangelical church, the term *catequista* is often used to refer to a particular orientation to Catholicism in addition to its use for a particular role in the religion. Although Ila Jusi has been very active, with some success, in trying to attract funds for a Huaycopungo church that would free the worshippers from dependence on the usually mestizo-dominated congregations of San Rafael, Gonzalez Suarez, or Otavalo, he has served as assistant in many far-flung churches, especially when indigenous masses are celebrated. The centralizing of a community of worshippers into a congregation and into a church building or compound as a focus for religious worship has not taken place with the Catholics to the same extent it has for the Protestants. While some groups of Catholics may feel a special relationship to a local congregation, they also make use of whatever resources they find available in a wider area. In this case, the strategies of Catholics seem far more individualized or focused on the nuclear family than those of the Protestants, who energetically gather people together on many different occasions, and for whom the transfer of worship from outside to inside has been more complete. However, before judging the Catholic form of worship as unduly atomized, it is worth remembering the andean practice of constituting unity through continual motion between families, between communities, and between sites of dense sacred meaning, creating invisible webs of connection as individuals and families crisscross the pathways through the animated landscape. The seeming chaos of the movement, like the cacophony of competing San Juanito flutes, comes together to unite earth, sky, people, animals, and plants into a regenerative energy. So when Catholics choose to attend mass in Gonzalez Suarez one Sunday, a baptism in Otavalo the following month, and mass at the San Rafael chapel on the eve of San Juan, they are continuing the tradition of activating ties, and schisms, at ever greater levels of inclusion through movement. The catequista practice of traveling through the landscape for worship continues, in an attenuated form, to unite the geographic sources of power through reciprocal exchange much more than is the case in the evangelista confinement in their impressive church. This is not to say that the evangelistas do not travel to visit a variety of other congregations, but they focus more of their worship inside their own sacred building.

What is missing for the catequistas is the opportunity to freely construct an indigenous church community and practice, as to some extent the evangelistas feel they are doing. Catechists remain subordinate to the Catholic Church hierarchy to a much greater extent than do the pastors of the evangelical churches. Nonetheless, a group of catequistas raised funds to build a Catholic chapel on the border between Langaburo, a section of Huaycopungo, and Cachiviro, Huaycopungo's neighboring community. There the group held meetings and worship services, short of the mass, expressly without the interference of any Catholic clergy. The local priest was sometimes invited to officiate in their chapel but was not considered to have any direct authority over it.

Just as the freedom of the indigenous Catholics is constrained by the institution of the Catholic Church, the independence of the evangelistas may be something of an illusion, since they remain embedded in particular evangelical dialogue about the religious life that goes on at an international level. At some time in the future, interference from outside evangelical authorities may increase, causing them to relinquish their sense of control over the reordering of their future. San Rafael Catholic parish's hiring of a priest who is himself indigenous, although from another part of Ecuador, has gone a long way toward promoting the view, supported by some clergy, that the popular Catholic Church can accommodate the needs of indigenous people for culturally distinct worship. Such additions as Sunday mass conducted at least partially in Quichua, indian singing groups within the church service, and the congregation's singing and giving verbal responses have been influenced by international Catholic Church innovations and by the success of Protestant practices. Although that priest speaks Quichua and is a sincere promoter of indigenous people, he is nonetheless under the strictures of the very hierarchical Catholic Church, which does not always support its more flexible and socially sensitive members.[8]

Evangelistas and *Catequistas*—The New *Shayacuna*

Andean people frequently employ kinship metaphors to characterize relationships of things in general, highlighting the particular combinations of similarity and difference, hierarchy and equality, trust

Fig. 48. The Catholic chapel
Langaburo-Cachiviro, 1991
(PHOTO BY AUTHOR)

and suspicion, and mutual responsibility desirable among parents and children, siblings or in-laws. Using those to analyze the relationship of the evangelistas and catequistas to each other, some people in Huaycopungo spoke as if the religion of their grandparents had spawned two siblings—evangelistas and catequistas, in that order. Catequistas followed evangelistas, with all that implies about a prevailing equality between the sects, qualified by the evangelistas' leadership role, as found in the relationship of older to younger sibling. The facts that the catequista chapel between Langaburo and Cachiviro was built after the evangelista church, that the Protestant church is larger and more luxurious than the Catholic chapel, and that the international funds garnered by the catequistas remained behind those raised by the evangelistas are all concrete examples that support this mildly hierarchical relationship. Others who would promote the catequista religious option over the evangelista alternative see the relationship differently. For them, the traditional Catholic option confronted the Protestant one not as a sibling or as a parent to its child, but as an unrelated opponent and potential affine. But as the sparks flew, they ended up mating and thus combined the two religious perspectives. Runacuna could continue to approach a God both distant, as emphasized in the Protestant alternative, and immanent in the environment, as traditional Catholic practice represented, with the multiple forms of the localized virgin(s), saints, and mountains. At the same time, they could embrace the new prescriptions to become more rational and moral, as defined by international Western standards, in order to please Achil Taita, the most powerful and distant god. In this formulation, catequistas are the legitimate offspring of this battle and union.

Evangelistas, catequistas, and traditional Catholics all have relatively easy social relationships now as individuals and families, unlike in the late 1970s, when many people called the new converts traitors. Community members of all religious affiliations coexist relatively peacefully, and parents, children, siblings, and spouses may separately declare themselves old-time Catholics, catequistas, or evangelistas. Furthermore, individuals and families frequently share more than one affiliation or change it back and forth. In the summer of 2004, when my family accompanied me to Huaycopungo for the first time as a group, each of us three sisters was asked to become godmother to a different child in the extended family of Isabel and José Manuel. We were short of time, so they made a plan to hold the ceremonies at the Catholic church in Gonzalez Suarez, even though one of the couples were faithful members of the evangelical church in Cachiviro. It was only after the pastor of the evangelist church disagreed—not on religious grounds, but because he wanted to host me in his church to repay me for some financial help in the past and keep the reciprocal gifts coming in the future—that we agreed to hold one child's baptism in Cachiviro immediately after the ceremony in Gonzalez Suarez. All members of the extended family enthusiastically attended both ceremonies, and we all adjourned to Isabel and José Manuel's house for a celebration afterward.

Catequistas and evangelistas intermarry, although it is common for one to join the other in church either at the time of marriage or at some later date. For example, one mixed couple decided to be married as catequistas when the evangelista pastor prescribed a year of premarital church counseling, whereas the priest was ready to marry them after only six weeks. In fact, since so many people speak of marriages as crossing religious borders when they do not actually know the details, it seems to me almost as if the model of a marriage today is one where the prospective spouses favor different religious options. It is not a prescription for real marriages, although not proscribed either, but an appropriate symbol of the marriage relationship. Since marriages between ayllus represent the union of opposites, then the religious contrast complements the expected kinship contest in theory and in practice.

Somewhat like the ritualized relationships between moieties during the pre-earthquake era that were examined in chapter 3, the social interactions between evangelistas and catequistas combine cooperation and conflict, both in controlled and stereotypical actions and in engagement with real issues of the day. I have seen several recent examples of the cooperation. When José Manuel Aguilar, the president of the evangelista church, thanked an international donor during Sunday service in 1992, he also announced the parallel donation to the catequista chapel, saying that such balanced donations represented true love for the community, as Jesus advocates. When

I visited him very briefly in the summer of 1998, Damiano Jusi Mali led me to the roof terrace of his church to show me a Catholic church being erected with the help of Belgian missionaries, on land he had generously donated.[9] In another example, an enthusiastic member of an expanding evangelista church in an adjacent community glowingly described how in the recent building effort of his church, believers and nonbelievers alike cooperated in the provision of labor and food. Even his own elderly father, who has stated categorically that he will never convert to Protestantism, donated labor and supplies. Finally, in 1995, a group of secular and religious leaders of the community, parish, cantón, and province agreed to open the San Rafael Catholic church graveyard to all Christians. The initiative had been promoted for many years by Huaycopungo's evangelical church president, Damiano Jusi Mali. Since fear of not being buried in consecrated ground motivated many not to join the evangelists, this would presumably remove a significant barrier to the growth of his church. Nonetheless, at the same time, it promoted community unity in an ecumenical spirit.

During San Juan, the two religious sects now symbolize the ritual contrast and complement more meaningfully then do the moieties, since festival sponsorship has been significantly reduced. While evangelistas used to be prohibited from dancing as San Juanitos during the summer solstice celebrations, there are now both evangelista and catequista dancers, although they rarely combine in one group. Whether groups of dancers gather at Cali Uma for informal competition or line up in front of a panel of judges seated on a platform hung with loudspeakers, today's opposition of evangelistas and catequistas partially substitutes for the rivalry of dancing groups from Janan Shaya and Urai Shaya of yesterday. The evangelist church schedules several events based on sports competitions, music group competitions, and big church celebrations to compete with the mass singing, dancing, and house-to-house visiting of San Juan that is expected to be lubricated with shared alcoholic drinks. During San Juan, individuals are always identified as evangelista or catequista and their behavior judged accordingly, even when their practice has been eclectic indeed. This is one time of the year when you should be one or the other. As mentioned above, one of the most amusing pastimes of those who are thus considered old-time Catholics or catequistas is to entice their teetotaling neighbors into drinking or other related behavior. This competition between the sects over drinking also replaces more traditional intermoiety competition.

In recent years, some individuals and families have continued to sponsor the Gallos Pasai festival during San Juan. A few have used that festive period to sponsor Corazas, which represents a major change in the ritual calendar. The change is convenient, since so many people return from long-distance sales or otherwise rearrange their schedules to come home to dance and visit during San Juan. Unlike agriculturalists, the newer entrepreneurs do not have natural stopping times during Holy Week, San Juan, August, and October that they can use for festival participation. Nor do the new Corazas rely as heavily on the mestizo dressers in San Rafael who so enriched themselves in this trade in early years. The evangelistas come out enthusiastically to constitute the audience and express very little negative opinion about the practices. In fact, they discuss how the ritual could be resuscitated, highlighting those aspects that represent their culture in a positive way, in accordance to the indigenist rhetoric so common in Ecuador today, while eschewing the alcohol consumption and excessive spending that characterized the fiestas in the past. Protestants do engage enthusiastically in dramatic portrayals of past customs, including Corazas, in folkloric venues for church and secular tourist consumption, along with their Catholic neighbors.

The logic of the Janan and Urai Shayacuna, where two fields of social relations are mapped onto opposing and complementary sides visualized as up and down, spatially or hierarchically, is in evidence here. The social reproduction of the community as a living whole is ritually enacted now most clearly during San Juan/Inti Raymi, whereas in the past several fiestas during a seven-month ritual season carried this responsibility. And rather than Janan and Urai Shaya, as geographic designations, carrying the weight of this social symbolization, the two forms of Christian religiosity today serve much the same purpose. Sánchez Parga suggests (1989, 58) that this system of differentiation is fundamentally a way of organizing social relations that is also used to socially structure space. He goes on to argue that historically the verticality of the symbolism gained potency from the strategic importance of controlling and managing land at different altitudes.

Since the role of land use in making a living has been so reduced in the last few decades in San Rafael, this spatial differentiation, illustrated by the juxtaposition of Tocagon's suitability for potato cultivation with Huaycopungo's more abundant corn production, is no longer the most potent way to express life's key issues, both social and spiritual. In contrast, differing ways to manage money, to exercise social or self-control, to engage God as immanent in a multitude of localized deities or as a transcendent power, or to centralize or decentralize the worship of sacred power can serve the same purpose as the most salient concerns of social organization. In addition, along the lines set down earlier for this general social theory, these complementary and oppositional units can engage in transpositions, both horizontally and vertically; can interchange essence; and should continue to engage in social relations, which means reciprocal exchanges of goods and services. Metaphors of siblingship and sexual encounters continue to be employed, along with other relationships of consanguineal and affinal kinship, to characterize the range of relations between them.

Both evangelistas and catequistas see themselves as active change agents in the community, and neither sect restricts its members from joining any of the regional political organizations. In fact, Huaycopungo is known as a particularly dangerous part of the Pan-American Highway to get through during a national strike, as young men, regardless of religious affiliation, actively and enthusiastically attack passing cars to disrupt the nation's business. Since 1985, Huaycopungo has been the lead community in an organization of five local indigenous communities (Asociación de Trabajadores Autónomos "Huaycopungo") founded to make a land claim on three hundred adjoining hectares owned by a cooperative of nonindian absentee owners who leave it mainly uncultivated. After years of entering into litigation and negotiation, particularly with IERAC (Instituto Ecuatoriano de Reforma Agraria y Colonización), having decisions alternately support and deny them their claim, the Asociación members decided to occupy the disputed territory in 1990. During that year, some of their mestizo opponents hired mercenaries to try to scare them back into the confines of Huaycopungo. In several escalating raids, the occupiers' huts were burned, their crops destroyed, and their animals killed. On one day armed men chased them right up to Huaycopungo's operating day care center, and finally two leaders were secretly ambushed and murdered. The group continued, with much hardship, until they received the right to purchase about one-third of the disputed land, and they are now receiving agricultural extension aid to best utilize this resource. Intensive strawberry cultivation has recently yielded enough profits to begin to pay back the debts on the property. The Asociación, whose membership includes traditional Catholics, evangelistas, and catequistas, has been active in the *levantimiento indígena* (national indigenous uprising) that began in May 1990. The levantimiento's lead national organization, CONAIE (Confederación de Nacionalidades Indígenas del Ecuador), has joined religious voices for change, and religious affiliation does not influence to what extent CONAIE's efforts have been judged as worthwhile or suspected as another form of domination.

Conversion to the Secular Religion of Progress

After the earthquake, a new religious epoch began. No longer was the dominant social and religious alternative the traditional one, with shared drinking and the celebration of costly fiestas with intermoiety competition the center of cultural reproduction. Instead, the weight of community opinion shifted to favor the previously insurgent messages from the Catholic and Protestant churches about self-improvement and political resistance. And the Catholic/Protestant split represented the new bipartite form of community. Runacuna were now to pursue fuller citizenship in the secular realm, new opportunities in the economic sphere, a moderation in the expenditure of money, alcohol, and time in festive activities in honor of the spirits. What would result would be renewed social and material prosperity resulting from God's replenished pleasure with his runa people's behavior toward each other and toward his manifestations in the universe.

With the provision of possible new norms, whose reduced costs and increased benefits were touted by norm entrepreneurs, and new norm clusters, in which those with fragile thresholds between public and private beliefs might find fellows to join, the stage was set for a potential norm cascade. But as emphasized by Kuran (1991), any small change in the array of thresholds might have prevented a cascade from occurring and resulted in a new equilibrium very close to, if not identical with, the first. In the next chapter, I want to present a change in the intrinsic value of taking those drinks which, along with the larger socioeconomic transformations of Ecuador, the religious movements for change so productive of revised models of indigenous peoples' place in the sacred and secular worlds, and God's message of the earthquake, together can explain the factors leading to the norm cascade of 1987.

CHAPTER NINE

Yapa Ufyadur Carcanchic
We Drank Too Much

Huaycopungo Relabels
Its Heavy Drinkers as Alcoholics

FOR MY BIRTHDAY IN MAY OF 1999, Isabel called me from the new phone in the *casa comunal* (community building),[1] which had once housed Huaycopungo's first day care center, a campaign promise kept by a successful presidential candidate, later killed in a mysterious plane crash. Finally reaching the head of a line of runacuna trying to reach their distant relatives around the world, she clutched the phone handed to her by the operator, trying to ignore the smell of toddler urine that never seems to fade from the rough concrete floor. The young mothers recruited to run that first day care center had never had to use diapers before or clean children's waste from a concrete floor, accustomed as they were to holding the children over the dirt floor and then sweeping up the wet dirt and disposing of it outside. They carried buckets and buckets of water to wash the floor of the casa comunal every week, but they were eventually defeated and had to require diapers for their charges, the popular disposable ones that are now piling up in Ecuador's growing landfills at the bottom of ravines.

I received the call sitting in my warm kitchen sipping coffee and was forced to make the enormous imaginative leap between our two lifestyles instantaneously. After receiving my birthday wishes, I asked about her mother-in-law, Mama Emilia. Several months before, Mama Emilia had arrived at Isabel and José Manuel's home, trying to hide her black eye with her bruised arm, once again seeking refuge from her abusive, alcoholic husband, Sebastian. This time she surprised everyone by filing for divorce. Mama Emilia's own problems with alcohol were of long standing, and José Manuel and Isabel had used her previous stays with them to try to reduce and control her drinking. Others of her children had also taken their turns, with short-term satisfaction and long-term frustration. So I asked whether Mama Emilia was still sober and whether she was still living with them or if she had returned to Sebastian. Isabel complained that an angry Sebastian, at least sixty years old, had been sneaking up behind the house at night and, in his cups, whistling for his estranged wife to come back to him, and that Mama Emilia often sat at the window listening for his whistle. I understood this to be a metaphorical expression of her take on the subject and a justification of her own feelings and actions rather than a literal description of events. Isabel lamented that she hadn't been able to stand either his hanging around like a thwarted teenager or Mama Emilia's drinking and causing fights at home, so she had sent her mother-in-law on to another son's house in Mama Emilia's hometown. Isabel sounded guilty and frustrated, so I tried to console her by saying that her mother-in-law is an alcoholic and not entirely responsible for her behavior. "Yes," she said, and I paraphrase here, "we *do* know she is an alcoholic. A couple of weeks ago, we wouldn't let her drink for several days and she got quite sick. So José Manuel took her to a boda huasi and begged her to have just one drink to see if it would help. Then we would take her home. After that drink, she felt better, so we know that she is really an alcoholic who can't quit drinking," Isabel was referring to the presence of withdrawal symptoms, which signal physiological addiction. Mama Emilia then escaped from their care and wasn't seen for several days as she continued her binge. A few days after the phone conversation, I happened to get a letter from yet a third son of Mama Emilia, who lives near Quito, in which he complained that he needed counsel but could not get it from his mother: *Mi madre ya no comprende lo que es vivir, ella es como un vejetal que crece por orden de la naturaleza* (My mother no longer understands what it is to live; she is like a plant that grows at the command of nature). "She's like my father now," Isabel told me on the phone in Spanish. "She doesn't know how to reason anymore."

This focus on the physiological effects on the person is significant for a number of reasons. On the one hand, it further illustrates the inroads that information and education from the wider world have made on the general knowledge of people in Huaycopungo. Although people have long recognized that some individuals drink too much, too often and wreak more than their share of harm on themselves and others, the acceptance of the terms *alcoholism* and *withdrawal* was new. Like the recognition of polluted spring water and its effects on whites, mestizos, and indians alike, this new understanding demonstrates that indigena no longer must resist information if it is promoted by outsiders. More important, it calls attention to the fact that despite the world of meaning constructed by people in any culture or subculture in which the experience and significance of alcohol use is set, there are general bodily effects in both the short and long terms with which any community of users must attune their beliefs. This chapter connects these material factors of alcohol use and abuse with the more symbolic context in which they are embedded in order to further extend our understanding of the transformations of both.

These few comments about one person who has struggled through a painful life but has also consistently abused alcohol and thus made the conditions of her life worse illustrate the ravages that alcohol dependence can create for the family and community of the affected person. Little by little, they lose a vital person who is, in fact, still alive. While a few personal stories of alcoholism do not demonstrate a high rate of alcohol abuse and addiction in a community, especially if the examples are confined to one extended family, such tales of suffering occurred in many families in Huaycopungo in the late 1970s and early 1980s. To these must be added the many boda huasicuna where the celebrants didn't feel cushishsha, alishsha anymore but became engaged in bitter brawls, the numerous drinkers who fell prey to accidents or stolen property, the many women who tried to conceal the black eyes inflicted by their drunken husbands, the children who hid at a relative's house to escape a drunken father, the neglect of work or family members, and the verbal and sexual abuse of women by their drunken husbands and other inebriated men. What do these stories have to do with the fact that between the 1970s and the year 2000, with a turning point in 1987, people in Huaycopungo switched so quickly from a defense of ceremonial binge drinking to a conviction that the community members drank too much?

In the last two chapters, we examined the change in general socioeconomic conditions that mandated a change in the way indigenous Otavalans made a living and related to the outside world, and the religious norm entrepreneurs who offered new sacred scripts for living and tried to reduce the reputational benefits of supporting the traditional norms. In this chapter we turn to an alteration in the intrinsic costs and benefits of drinking as presumably calculated by a large percentage of Huaycopungo's population, who, before the earthquake, were nonetheless constrained by their desires for continuing group unity and personal reputation in their home community from putting these calculations into practice.

It is not enough to say that the people of Huaycopungo underwent a transformation in their interpretation of the meaning of drinking because the way of life it symbolized became untenable or because religious and secular missionaries educated them about alternatives and exhorted them to change their system of meanings. Traditional alcohol use might have been maintained as a symbol of indigenous culture and pride, even though the culture had changed in many ways to include market participation and bilingualism in Spanish, for example, and pride was diverted into new arenas, such as a high school diploma or success in international trade. Other symbols, such as traditional Otavalan dress and pride in the Quichua language, were maintained. But ritual drinking was not. For that reason, it was not solely becoming educated in the ways of civilized people or Jesus' disciples that provoked the change; there was an increase in suffering brought about by local alcohol consumption. This new message was accepted and the symbols of group loyalty and ethnic distinctiveness were modified, in part, because alcohol use had increasingly affected them negatively in a direct and bodily fashion. In this way, the norm cascade represented here more closely parallels the cases in the literature of smoking, genital mutilation, and foot binding than the political or ethnic revolutions in the former Soviet bloc nations, the Balkans, or South Asia. The information received by the individuals who had to choose whether or not to participate in such practices is not merely transmitted verbally from others, it is experienced directly. In the case of drinking ceremonially, in contrast to foot binding and genital mutilation, the effects are felt first and foremost on the bodies of those who are most in charge of upholding community norms—adult male leaders. Secondarily, as in secondhand smoking, there are often direct physical effects on the women and children closest to them—through physical abuse and neglect. I suggest that the negative physical effects increased—not only that these costs were no longer outweighed by the benefits but that they increased absolutely—almost guaranteeing an altered cost-benefit analysis for most individuals.

Although the costs and benefits of alcohol use and abuse in this chapter will be treated in a very materialist fashion, with attention to measurable symptoms or behavioral facts, these can be understood only in the context of the particular world of symbolic interpretation in which they are embedded. Given the more hermeneutic slant of part I, following the caveats issued in chapter 1 about blithely interpreting alcohol-related behavior in Huaycopungo with models derived from the United States, we are now in a stronger position to analyze the effects of this psychoactive drug on the population of Huaycopungo. It is only by analyzing the interactions between the symbolic and material worlds in which people live that we can fully understand human behavior, especially in our attempts to integrate models of individual decision making, where symbolic meaning is made and acted upon, with more systemic analyses of social structures and adaptive processes.

Alcohol Abuse and Addiction

Before we proceed to address these issues, however, what is meant by alcoholism and other alcohol-related problems or pathologies needs to be defined. I assume that alcohol use frequently, but by no means universally, results in a certain set of negatively evaluated human experiences and behaviors—physical, psychological, and social—through a number of complex pathways. I assume that these symptoms, if you will, are generally recognized socially as problems all over the world, although there may no particular label for them or no general acceptance that alcohol use is the cause. That is, scientific effort could result in a culture-free description of alcohol-related syndromes, as it can more readily for measles or even diabetes, even though a culture-free understanding would be incomplete in any given environment. Alcohol has the potential of affecting individuals and groups in a negative fashion everywhere, although some of the specifics of how they are affected or how the effects are conceptualized are culturally relative.

Let us start with the commonly delineated syndrome of alcoholism, alcohol addiction, or alcohol dependence, which I will treat as synonyms.[2] First, I assume, although the evidence is as yet by no means definitive, that genes predispose some individuals to both physiological and psychological addiction to the substance of alcohol and to physical and psychophysiological harm resulting from heavy alcohol use, whether that use is continual or intermittent. While a genetic basis could mean that certain populations around the world have a greater frequency of one alcohol-related pathology or another, the preponderance of evidence has shown no such link (May 1994). The theory, common in both North and South America, among native and nonnative people alike, of a special Native American susceptibility to addiction and alcohol-related harm is the result of racist stereotyping. Rates of addiction, death, and other alcohol-related harm are extremely variable in indigenous populations of the Americas, in some cases lower than in corresponding nonnative populations. The overall high rate of alcohol-induced problems in Native Americans of the United States and Canada can be explained by such factors as risky environments, lack of access to medical care, risky drinking and postdrinking behaviors, and poor measurement strategies, among others (May 1994). Nonetheless, in both the general population and some segments of the scholarly community, the prevailing myths die hard.

We are forced to assume, in the absence of evidence to the contrary, that genetic factors do not influence the culture of alcohol use in Otavalo, although it could explain individual susceptibility to alcoholism or the relative frequency of addiction in particular families. But such genetic detail is beyond the scope of this study. My perspective is that we will slowly come to understand more and more about the biology of what we now call alcoholism, which may be a loosely connected group of drug-body interactions. Nonetheless, social and cultural factors will always be necessary to fully understand the particular manifestations of the human biological reactions to heavy alcohol use. What is particularly indigenous here is the culture in which the alcohol use is embedded, not the biological dimensions of human-alcohol interaction.

Physiological addiction, indicated by the presence of withdrawal symptoms when the drug use is stopped, is one important part of what I mean by alcoholism, as suggested by Isabel's discussion of her mother-in-law's addiction. With heavy use over time, the brain becomes dependent upon receiving alcohol and will show signs of neuropathology, such as uncontrolled trembling, visual and auditory hallucinations, and seizures when the alcohol use ceases. However, the amount of time necessary to become addicted varies greatly among individuals and between groups of people, distinguished by such factors as age and gender. In addition, the extent and type of withdrawal symptoms varies so greatly in those diagnosed as alcoholics as to make this evidence insufficient in a description of the disease.[3] For that reason, a less biological description of alcoholism has come to be accepted.

A useful working definition would be that a person who continues to use alcohol heavily, despite repeated and serious problems attributed to alcohol in a number of important areas of life, as generally agreed among that person's peers, could be said to be an alcoholic. This definition mandates an attention to local beliefs about what are important areas of life, how alcohol is likely to affect a person, and whether or not those effects constitute a problem. As MacAndrew and Edgerton say, somewhat tongue in cheek, "Since societies, like individuals, get the sorts of drunken comportment that they allow, they deserve what they get" (1969, 173). But for a person to be considered an alcoholic, the comportment must consistently violate cultural expectations. For example, if people expect alcohol to result in a loss of control over emotions, and then sometimes drink so that they can, say, engage in a crying or screaming jag without censure, then such emotional excess would not necessarily be a sign of problems with alcohol among those people. Contrarily, emotional outbursts might be a sign of an alcohol-related problem in another society in which alcohol is acceptably used only to enhance mild-mannered sociability or communion with the spirits.

Similarly, one has to take into account whether the behaviors frequently displayed by drunks, such as being more outgoing or being more withdrawn, are valued or accepted, or whether they are states most people try to avoid. Thus, a problem suggesting alcoholism in one society may be repeatedly entering into a state of extreme sociability that violates norms of privacy and propriety, while that same behavior would be nonproblematic in another, where an increase in sociability is seen as one of alcohol's beneficial effects. Some negative consequences of heavy drinking, such as an increase in accidents and an escalation of violence among people who are supposed to treat each other nonviolently, are prevalent around the world and would likely contribute to a universal depiction of alcoholism.[4] One would simply have to accommodate their specific cultural manifestations, such as what kind of accident is more common or whether the favorite victim of violence is a wife, a neighbor, or one's brother-in-law. Furthermore, MacAndrew and Edgerton's review of the literature in *Drunken Comportment* (1969) present examples of what they call "a series of infinite gradations in the degree of 'disinhibition' that is manifested in drunken comportment"(17). Whatever the universal, general, or particular consequences of heavy drinking may be worldwide, they may or may not rise to the level of generally recognized problems.

Despite the specific social and cultural guides for how alcohol-related pathologies manifest themselves, it is my contention that the effects on the brain of high levels of alcohol are highly comparable worldwide, and so are the multiple pathways to addiction. Individuals may be genetically predisposed to feel certain pleasures, such as an alcohol-induced high, more intensely, or certain pains, such as a hangover, less distinctly. We all have particular itches to scratch and irritations or anxieties to overcome. In some bodies, alcohol can more easily provide that pleasure or relieve that itch, irritation, or anxiety (Leutwyler and Hall 1997) or fail to cause much pain as the drug wears off. Thus, consumption may continue or escalate over time, enough for accumulated changes, both physical and psychological, to occur.

Given the distribution of these biological susceptibilities in a given population, it is necessary to find out the common and acceptable patterns of drinking in that population. If drinking heavily is an option, that is, when a certain group of people with whom a person might wish to associate uses alcohol heavily, then some people will avail themselves of that option to drink a lot. Another subset of that same group of drinkers will continue to consume alcohol heavily until their physiology has been altered and they have clearly become addicted to alcohol. Of course, where heavy drinking is never a socially acceptable alternative in any available subculture, there will be few alcoholics. A complex combination of social, cultural, and biological factors, then, are necessary to create the patterns that we may label as alcoholism, and the patterns themselves may vary widely. Despite the fact that alcoholism may be overdiagnosed in some social contexts and under-diagnosed in others, I believe it is a reasonable gloss for a complex of physiological and behavioral changes in people worldwide.[5]

Heavy drinking increases the risk of other alcohol-related problems or pathologies besides alcoholism. Both alcoholics and heavy drinkers who are not dependent on alcohol may be responsible for increasing their own suffering and the suffering of others. While it is too simplistic to say that high levels of alcohol use alone cause violence or a neglect of responsibilities, for example, it *is* accurate to say that heavy drinking does generally increase the risk of these and other problems worldwide. In addition, in a culture where men, but not women, are expected to drink, and drink heavily, the bodies of women and their babies are protected from the ravages of the drug, but they then suffer disproportionately as innocent victims of any behavior that gets out of control. I say innocent victims, because drinking men frequently verbally and physically abuse one another, but do so reciprocally and so they are less likely to see themselves or be seen by others as innocent victims. This special position of women and their children is significant worldwide in movements to reduce or eliminate alcohol consumption, including this case in Otavalo, as will be seen below. All alcohol consumption does not increase these kinds of social problems significantly, but heavy drinking in certain conditions does do so. As explained above, the particular negative behaviors that increase in frequency and the positively desired experiences that become less common can vary to a degree in different cultures.

The Effect of an Increase
in Consumption in Huaycopungo

What follows, then, is an explication of the reasons for a measurable increase in community suffering due to alcohol. The first potential causative factor I want to consider is the possibility that the quantity of alcohol consumed had actually increased in recent decades. I cannot verify that this took place. Were I to examine legal records of alcohol purchase, should such things be available, they would not contain the myriad sales of moonshine trago or the asua brewed in indigenous homes. Descriptions of past indigenous drinking by nonindians were and are notoriously unreliable because the belief that indigenous drinking is pathological had become so ingrained in commonsense perceptions that an unbiased study was extremely unlikely. Self-reports by indigenous people today are also colored by the ideological positions they have chosen to take, so that direct questioning on the subject would not be useful. Nonetheless, I will give some indirect evidence to suggest that this may have been the case.

Although anthropologists have generally criticized the position that alcoholism and alcohol-related problems vary directly with the quantity of consumption, what Heath calls the "distribution of consumption model" (1987), it will be demonstrated that it does apply to the case in Huaycopungo. An increase in consumption need not lead to more problems if it occurs because, for example, a particular population that did not drink, or drank very little, in the past begins drinking moderately and in a well-socialized fashion. In his brash critique of America's demonizing of alcohol, Barr points out as an example that the U.S. Department of Health and Human Services in 1990 declared its intention to reduce alcohol-related pathology by reducing the overall consumption of alcohol in the United States by 21 percent (1999, 222–23). The policy betrayed no hint of recognition that the desired decrease could have zero affect on alcohol-related pathology if it occurred solely among moderate drinkers who exhibited few if any problems. In the case of Huaycopungo, however, given the drinking norms already in place, the consumption by already heavy drinkers increased, and younger drinkers got access to high quantities of alcohol.

I suspect that there were multiple periods in the past, from the conquest to the present, when major changes occurred in the types of alcohol available, occasions to drink, places to drink, or simple quantity of booze in Otavalo and throughout hispanic America. For example, Taylor (1979) describes four major changes from the conquest through the eighteenth century for colonial Mexican natives, most of which seem to have affected Otavalo as well. They are an increase in general consumption, particularly by the common people; the introduction of aguardiente and other new forms of drink; an intensification of drinking on Sundays and feast days; and a greater commercialization of liquor production, distribution, and consumption (69) in the new urban centers created by the Spanish to which indigenous people were either forcibly removed or successfully attracted. These and other alterations in the culture of drinking led to an increase in alcohol-related problems in colonial Mexico, as they presumably did in colonial Otavalo. In contrast, poor harvests, a scarcity of money, renewed religious control by the orthodox Catholic Church, or increased government controls on drinking are all factors that could have decreased drinking among indigenous Otavalans at times during the last half millennium. Some version of the account given here for Huaycopungo must have happened in other places, especially those undergoing urbanization at an earlier time, and is likely still taking place in other locations in Ecuador.

Several recent factors led to an increase in alcohol quantity consumed in Huaycopungo. As people became increasingly active in the money economy, they increased their consumption of distilled sugarcane brandy, trago, either by itself or as a supplement to asua or *guarapo* (fermented sugarcane). Since trago is distilled, potentially reaching a maximum alcohol content of 40–50 percent, compared to the maximum alcohol content from fermentation of only 12 percent for asua, a small increase in the amount of trago consumed would have exposed the drinkers to a greater quantity of alcohol. As the total percentage of alcohol in drinks increased when the celebrants added and partially substituted trago for asua, so did the number of drinks, because increased monetary resources resulted in binges becoming extended to days or even weeks, as life-cycle ceremonies and calendrical religious festivals were lengthened. Either quantity of absolute alcohol in drinks or length of drinking occasion alone could have increased quantity consumed and resulting problems.

Secondly, trago existed in almost unlimited quantities for those with the money to buy it or the guts to charge it, whereas asua most often had to be brewed at home from grains they had to grow themselves, bargain for, or buy. The several days necessary for the grains to ferment to the proper stage also helped limit the quantity of asua consumed and, even more, the amount of alcohol in the asua. While maximally fermented asua was preferred for its strong kick, after the supply of it was finished, celebrants at a boda huasi often had to be satisfied with asua that had not yet reached that stage. When women were required to drink, they always preferred the lighter, mishci asua, but men were more likely to be disappointed with the lighter brew.

Although the commercialization of asua production began in the colonial period, until recent decades most people in Huaycopungo were constrained by the lack of time, money, and public transportation from drinking at public cantinas except rarely. Since cantinas serving asua and other forms of alcohol were more of an urban phenomenon than a rural one, it is true that visits to Otavalo and other urban centers were often scenes of inebriated violence, accidents, and victimization.

Public health campaigns carried out throughout the twentieth century to stamp out unlicensed asua production, especially home production by indigenous people, futher eroded asua consumption. As late as the 1970s, an inspector was appointed in San Rafael to collect taxes from those who had registered their homes as cantinas and to smash the pottery jars of asua discovered at unregistered houses. In such an impoverished mestizo town as San Rafael, a main way of making a living was exploiting the local indigenous population. Predictably, then, the laws were interpreted as an opportunity for mestizos to control the commercial production and sale of alcohol. Failing that, they could always gain income by illegally licensing any indigenous household that would pay them enough for a license or by accepting bribes to overlook homebrew in an unlicensed home. San Juan was a particularly lucrative time for the San Rafael inspector, who was forced to appoint deputies to deal with the work. It was an extremely tense period for those in Huaycopungo who wished to offer their neighbors a pilchi of mishci asua along with a rosca of hard homemade bread in celebration of the summer solstice. Some women were particularly anxious to continue their responsibility to provide asua, perhaps as much to stop or at least slow the purchase of trago by their husbands as to fulfill their traditional responsibilities, demonstrate their excellence at their work, and contribute to the prestige of their household. As the quantity of corn decreased relative to the population and the price for corn increased on the market, the temptation to substitute cheaper, and more potent, trago for homemade corn beer grew. That way, corn could be reserved for food or sold on the market in order to purchase other necessities. Over time, as money resources became more common and prices for agricultural commodities increased,[6] the extremely low price of trago, especially the bootlegged variety, made it more and more attractive as a substitute for homemade asua. It was cheaper to buy trago than to make asua at home, reversing the cost differential cited by Hassaurek for the mid-1800s ([1868] 1967, 104).

Binge Drinking as a Risk Factor for Alcohol-Related Harm

As stated above, an increase in quantity is not always a sufficient condition for an increase in alcohol-related problems in a given population. What in the nature of drinking in Huaycopungo before, during, and after an increase in total quantity consumed led to an increase in alcohol-related problems? Any examination of the interaction of risk factors for alcohol abuse and addiction over time, and of the practices that protected people in Huaycopungo from them, must begin with the practice of binge drinking. By binge drinking is meant a pattern of abstaining ordinarily from alcohol consumption but drinking heavily to the point of inebriation on intermittent occasions. Taken alone, drinking intermittently does not increase risks for problems, but drinking to the point of getting drunk whenever one imbibes probably does have a generally negative effect. Even though binge drinkers in Otavalo are expected to learn how to drink properly over a number of binge experiences, someone who is drunk is more likely to suffer an accident or lose property accidentally than someone who has consumed moderately. Both accidents and property loss affect the whole family, not just the drinker. In Huaycopungo, however, people expected that heavy drinking would most often result in a highly valued state, such as the ability to engage in public celebration to the gods for hours on end, and that those who abstained were denied necessary social and spiritual resources. The increase in accidents or lost property or occasional fights was considered well worth it, given the benefits gained by periodic drunkenness.

Nevertheless, a significant increase in the amount of alcohol available can increase the risk of many additional alcohol-related problems in the context of a binge-drinking pattern, regardless of the types of behaviors expected while drunk. This happens when the quantity of alcohol consumed increases to the point of making the bingeing occasions more frequent, multiplying the numbers of persons allowed to reach intoxication on any one occasion, or increasing the extent and duration of inebriation of any segment of society. Note that the important factor is inebriation, not simple consumption. Some practitioners in the Alcohol and Other Drug Abuse community in the United States consider binge drinkers alcoholics even if they drink as infrequently as once a year, as long as they consistently violate their own expectations of acceptable behavior and cause significant problems for themselves and others when drunk. However, this pattern of drinking is less likely to result in long-term physiological addiction, as defined by the presence of withdrawal symptoms. Still, some individuals may be particularly inclined by their neurophysiological responses to continue drinking once started or particularly likely to engage in unacceptable behavior when drunk, and their problem, while perhaps not accurately termed addiction, can be considered a pathology of both biological and social dimensions. Among binge drinkers who become alcohol addicted in the classical sense of physical dependence are those, like Taita Antonio and Mama Emilia's husband, Sebastian, who daily searched out events at which to binge, including special visits to compadres or distant relatives who, like them, frequented local cantinas. Their families repeatedly suffered violence, lost property, community feuds, and reduced resources at their hands. Mama Emilia is a binge drinker, but her drinking bouts may go on for months and then be separated by months. Both José Manuel and his two younger brothers have experienced problems with binge drinking of a few days. Their infrequent binges were usually damaging to their economic situation, physical health, social relations, and senses of well-being and self-respect. Of course, since alcohol addiction is progressive, there is the risk that this could be a precursor to the same pattern exhibited by their mother. Their sister almost never touches alcohol.

A cultural pattern that favors binge drinking over other forms can still incorporate restrictions of the total quantity consumed, whether these be limits on the quantity consumed, the duration of the binge, or the behaviors exhibited. However, in Huaycopungo drinkers did not expect to limit their consumption themselves. It was limited by the quantity available only. In the traditional view, the intervention of God in the provision of alcoholic resources was the limiting factor, as mediated by the success of those sponsoring the drinking event in the previous year. The symptoms of drunkenness were not restrained but exaggerated in an attempt to demonstrate and attract supernatural blessing on people, to "facilitate the flow of vitality among different categories of living beings" (Allen 1988, 173), and to prime the pump of reciprocity at the heart of andean life (93). In the context of an increase in total quantity available, this absence of self-control, indeed this value on drinking to excess, which is an ever-multiplying amount in the absence of outside limitations, also increases the risk of problems. A sacred emphasis on excess (*yapa*) is particular adaptive in an environment of extreme scarcity, but not one where the scarcity is more relative than absolute.

Another negative effect of valuing excess in social spiritual offerings to ensure what Allen (1988) describes as the vitality of the circulatory system of the total environment is that it leads to a competitive one-upping of each other in the reciprocal offer of drinks, as described in chapter 2. With multiple motives, from the maximization of individual household prestige and future assistance to mobilizing spiritual forces on behalf of one's own household and community, individuals try to give as much as they can possibly afford to others during a boda huasi, on the paths during San Juan, or in their sponsorship of the fiesta of Corazas. When alcohol resources are cheap and in an endless supply, as long as money or credit holds out, and with the ubiquity of aggressive marketers, then such competitive drinking practices can be carried to a dangerous level. While individuals try to maximize their gift in the context of managing their resources, the competitive nature leads them to exceed their budgeted amount on almost every occasion. To do otherwise would be stingy.

Perhaps more important, an increase in the overall quantity of alcohol available can override some of the protections built into the traditional system of binge drinking. The practice of distributing drinks preferentially to important male leaders, to those who are older and politically or economically more successful, can reduce the number of people who can become significantly drunk in a context of scarce resources, whether in the form of grains or money. In addition, contrary to the usual pattern of surrendering enthusiastically to slurring words, weaving walks, and general incapacity for anything serious, those men who are drinking in the fulfillment of their leadership roles attempt to maintain their ability to reason, to speak wisely and gently, and to lead communal action as long as possible while they continue to accept drink after drink. It is not so much that they try to hide their growing symptoms of ataxia, but that they attempt to be efficacious in their leadership roles despite a growing and physically noticeable intoxication. It is precisely this ability to undertake such a heavy responsibility to the community, expose themselves maximally to the intervention of supernatural forces and keep being effective that earns them the respect of others. While these men, like others, may fall prey to accidents, to theft, to outbursts of violence while drunk, and to a general ill temper when hungover, they are much more likely to try to control their own behavior, more likely to have others watch over them, and less likely to allow their leadership to cause harm to themselves and others. If they did, they would not have been leaders in the first place or would not remain leaders for long. Mama Juana, the Huaycopungo cantina owner and healer, and the curaga Ila Rafi are two examples of the older generation of such leaders.

Three sectors of any population probably cause the most social and physical problems when they become frequently drunk. They are children, child-rearing women, and young men, although the kinds of problems each causes is different. Since children still do not drink in Otavalo, there is no reason to linger on the specific problems they face.[7] Suffice it to say that addiction and physiological harm may develop more quickly in the very young, and that self-destructive or antisocial behavior may be harder to control in those who have, as yet, such incomplete preparation and such little stake in adult society. For women of child-bearing age, the biological risk of harm to unborn children and the risk of abuse and neglect of living children are particularly great. Women's work in Otavalo focuses on a continuous presence and care of others in terms of food preparation, personal supervision, laundry, and protection of the house. In contrast, men's work is harder physically but more intermittent, and they are more frequently away from the house. Without minimizing men's ability to abuse and neglect children, their periodic removal to drinking parties and drunkenness alone is by no means as detrimental to children as the periodic absence of their drinking mothers, especially since the roles of men vis-à-vis drinking wives do not parallel those of women to their imbibing men. Not only would husbands be less likely to serve as designated caretakers to their wives, they would also most likely be drinking in the same boda huasi as their wives, leaving the children alone or with relatives. No less important, from the local point of view, is the sexual vulnerability of drinking women. They are vulnerable to their own fleeting desires as well as the unwanted attentions of drinking men. Since women's unfaithfulness may result in pregnancy or the disruptive desire to leave the father of their existing children, endangering those childrens' care, it is considered more serious than men's infidelity. This is not to deny that women may feel jealous and start fights over their husbands' infidelity. Older women, in contrast, no longer have young children, often have work assistants at home, and are less likely to be so sexually vulnerable, so their occasional drinking has fewer negative effects on themselves and others.

Finally, we come to the problem of young men. This is the problem that Huaycopungo has been most concerned with in the last few years, as young men's access to alcohol has increased. It is a common finding that teenaged and young adult populations tend to have much higher rates of alcohol-related harm than do children, the middle aged, or the elderly (May 1994, 125). Similarly, female alcohol use rates and rates of alcohol-related problems are lower than those for men. One of the reasons may be a greater tendency of young men to take risks, whether that involves risky drinking practices per se or engaging in other dangerous behaviors while drinking. In addition, it seems that there are several aspects of young men's lives generally, which are heightened in certain societies at a given time, that make them more vulnerable to the negative effects of the emotional and behavioral disinhibition that is associated with drinking.[8] For example, during the first two decades of young adulthood, men are so affected by their desire for sex, their competition with each other, and the need, especially in monogamous societies, to monopolize the sexuality of their chosen women that drinking can greatly increase social conflict with their peers and their spouses. In general, younger men are not yet so constrained in their behavior by the social webs of responsibility to superiors, peers, and subordinates that they have spun for themselves as are men in the middle of their life. Their reputations in the eyes of other men and women are yet to be earned, and their reputation is a combination of their ability to work and their success in competitive endeavors.

In short, the particular form of binge drinking to inebriation, with self-control of quantity being neither expected nor commendable, that was common in Otavalo predisposed those who were likely to drink often to more and more alcohol-related problems in the context of an increase in overall quantity of alcohol. The competitive nature of sharing drinks, the potential inclusion of ever younger men into the pool of heavy drinkers, and the continuing expansion of the acceptable occasions to binge, as alcohol became cheaper and more readily available, also contributed to higher rates of alcoholism, violence, injuries, and neglect of responsibilities. Whereas the evangelista solution to alcohol-related problems is abstinence, the catequista position stressed the elimination of binge drinking controlled only by the quantity available. While the former will certainly address the problem, the latter does seem focused on one of the most significant sources of the suffering.

Other Risk Factors in the Context of an Increased Quantity

While binge drinking is by far the greatest risk factor for increased alcohol-related problems in the context of more potent, cheaper, and more prevalent alcohol, a number of other changes in the lives of the people of Huaycopungo probably overrode protective factors in their traditional culture of drinking or contributed to greater risk. Among these changes are the switch from a peasant lifestyle to one more urban and dependent on the national economy, shifts in their religious lives, and an increasing openness to local mestizo, and even transnational, cultural interchanges.

PEASANTS TO ENTREPRENEURS

Despite the traditional pattern of binge drinking to intoxication, several aspects of the mixed peasant lifestyle that once generally characterized Huaycopungo (but which has been slowly disappearing) served to protect people from a high level of alcohol-related problems. Among the factors that have reduced protections against problems are those discussed above under the rubric of the increase in the quantity consumed, such as an increase in the money indigenous people controlled, a cultural restriction on the disposal of money, the national promotion of trago production and limits on the home production of asua, the decrease in trago price and increase in asua price, and the decrease in relative social and spatial distance between rural and urban milieus for all indigenous people.

Another feature of peasant life that reduces the effects of heavy alcohol use on any one occasion is the necessity for continual agricultural labor, which burns calories quite quickly. As work in subsistence agriculture became less able to support the population and haciendas became converted to tourist hotels, men, in particular, had to shift their work responsibilities elsewhere, which in turn further decreased the supplies of homegrown food. This shift had two effects on how alcohol affected the population. While men continued to work very hard and those who worked in construction probably worked as hard physically as agriculturalists, those who became long-distance traders and who relied heavily on public transportation were probably burning fewer calories and burning them more slowly. This is evidenced in more people becoming overweight in recent years. The rapid burning of calories resulting from heavy manual labor allows bodies to process higher amounts of alcohol more quickly, reducing the cumulative effect and the duration of a drunken state. It also reduces any hangover effects. However, if people who work less continue to drink as much as they did before, they will become drunker and stay drunk longer than they did before.

Secondly, as homegrown food resources were reduced, people

tended to serve less and less ceremonial food at a boda huasi. This change in food supply occurred at a time when the only proper food to be offered was food grown by the family or received in exchange from other families on the community's land or on the plots of their far-flung relatives or friends across the country. The celebrations of plenty were supposed to consist of a demonstration of that plenty. It was considered shameful to serve purchased food, but homegrown food was increasingly scarce, especially in quantities necessary to host a public ceremonial. The dried corn that was their agricultural staple could no longer be expected to feed the family through the year, let alone be ground up to make the festive corn gruel soup, api. Because of a growth in population relative to land, an increase in agricultural costs, and an extremely low valuation of agricultural products in the market, indigenous subsistence agriculture was failing as a way to make a living. During the late 1970s, people told me that a boda huasi was always characterized by *boda*, special food treats, but I often attended a boda huasi in which no food was offered at all. It was if the local people willfully failed to recognize the reality of the reduction in food; it was polite to ignore that people could not grow enough corn for a good api and plate of muti. Men contented themselves with getting drunk and forgetting about food, while women tried to stay away.

Today, a boda huasi is always characterized by a large quantity of food to share, although the majority of it is now purchased for the occasion. That it is purchased is a major innovation, one that took the transformative effects of the last few years and the supernatural approval of the earthquake to ratify. There are no set mealtimes, but it is a point of honor to serve each guest as soon as he or she appears. It is competitive in the same way that alcohol offerings were competitive and the food flows from kitchen to guests incessantly. Alcohol taken with food is processed more slowly, reducing the speed at which it affects the brain. While food may increase the time that alcohol's effects are present, it reduces the overall effect. Of course, for those who accept many drinks in succession and do so for hours or days at a time, it hardly matters that they eat. But for those lower in the hierarchy for the circling drinks, whether or not they eat may have an effect on how drunk they get. A change in food supply on drinking occasions can change the numbers of people who get drunk.

In the past, when all young men expected to become agriculturalists, they frequently had to wait until their parents died or began to divest themselves of productive property in order to attain full adult status in the community. Only with a sufficient land inheritance could they establish their own independent household that would become a full participating unit of society. All of this had direct effects on the level of alcohol abuse and addiction. Younger adult men were somewhat protected from alcohol-related antisocial behavior by their need to continue to please their parents in order to attain the only resources that could make them full members of society. Furthermore, when the quantity of alcohol and money were limited, they could only infrequently achieve this altered state. In the transition period we examined in part I, young men's fathers were agriculturalists, but the young men themselves knew that the land resources would not be sufficient to support them, their siblings, and their families and were thereby freed somewhat from the burden of obeying and humoring their parents. If they were not entirely relieved of moral responsibility toward their parents, they would at least suffer fewer economic consequences if they fell short of the older generation's demanding standards. In addition, they were faced with the stress of trying to find another long-term source of support in the mestizo world, which might encourage them to look more favorably upon mestizo norms of drinking, just as they tried out other aspects of mestizo culture.

In summary, then, a peasant lifestyle provides such protective factors as self-sufficiency, poverty, hard physical labor, and the control by elders of both productive resources and the festive consumption of surplus in the form of food and drink.

THE REDUCTION OF SPIRITUAL POWER IN EVERYDAY *RUNA* LIFE

Festive drinking, especially when it is done for spiritual reasons, has sometimes been associated cross-culturally with a lower level of alcohol-related problems (Bales 1946; Snyder 1958). Presumably, there are several possible reasons for this association, some of which apply to this case and some of which do not. While adherence to a ritual calendar can restrict the frequency of consumption, in the andean case a number of factors counteract that form of protection. According to Taylor (1979, 59) the number of feast days celebrated by Native

Americans increased with the imposition of the Catholic ritual calendar. However, this was in an attempt to forestall the consumption of alcohol during communal labor activities, which had traditionally required celebrating the sacred webs of reciprocity that tied people together in community and united them with the spiritual powers in the animated landscape and beyond. As a symbol of access to supernatural power, sometimes monopolized by the political and religious elite during both pre- and post-Columbian eras, and as a source both of enjoyment and of the formation of social bonds, there was always reason to multiply the occasions for drinking in this culture.

Religious reasons for drinking have sometimes ensured social control over the quantity, speed, and duration of consumption cross-culturally (Snyder 1958) and have thus been associated with a lower level of alcohol-related problems. Although the religious responsibility to consume alcohol to the point of advanced intoxication in as many significant social/spiritual occasions as quantity would allow certainly worked the other way, increasing consumption, certain spiritual traditions could limit alcohol abuse. In the rural Otavalo case, one would have to cite the association of drinking with the combination of secular and spiritual wealth, power, and authority. This meant that those who had the most to lose if their drinking got out of hand monopolized the alcohol resources, thereby reducing the consumption by those who might never reach the levels of achievement desired if they spent their energies and their economic resources on binge drinking. In the precolonial period, this sometimes meant that the nobility attempted to maintain a monopoly on the production and distribution of alcohol to support their position, making the common people grateful for whatever consumption they were allowed to enjoy.

Most important, Otavaleños were motivated by a fear of spiritual power in their ritual drinking that has been diminishing over the years. Since the presence of alcohol invited the presence of supernatural forces, both good and bad, and since inebriated individuals were particularly susceptible to the whims of the spirits, people were careful to be in a spiritually strong and healthy state before submitting to that supernatural danger. In Otavalan psychological theory, people are born with a certain spiritual constitution, which may make some people susceptible to spiritual harm and others relatively resistant to it. Experiences and practice during life can alter that basic constitution, especially those experiences that cause a temporary soul loss and debilitate people in ways we would call physical, psychological, and spiritual. On the other hand, individuals with a particularly strong spiritual constitution may choose to become healers or even shaman, since shaman must be able to repeatedly and deliberately interact with the supernatural realm without personal harm. In addition, their special strength must help them influence the spiritual powers to undertake the healing (or harm) of others. When a potential patient visits a powerful supernatural healer, yachaj, literally "possessor of knowledge," the first thing that is measured is the spiritual constitution of the person to be healed and that of any accompanying relatives. One reason for excluding foreigners from witnessing healing rites, as I was told when the healer reluctantly let me stay for a spiritual cleaning with a guinea pig early in my research, is that their strength is notoriously hard to measure. They may be so weak they may attract the harm that will be released in the cleaning and succumb to it. Or they may be so strong as to somehow misdirect the dangerous forces and harm the other participants. A healer's wife in Quito was once puzzled when trying to measure my spiritual force by thrusting a candle inside my shirt and rubbing it up and down my chest and back. On the one hand, some indices suggested a powerful spiritual constitution to her; others indicated a complete absence of strength. She wasn't sure what to recommend to her husband about his coming interaction with me.

When the sun set, spiritual forces that the daylight hours kept at bay had free rein in the land of the people of cunan pacha, the everyday time and space of living people, and could easily harm those who walked out freely. In urban areas, public lighting may have made nighttime drinking seem safer. Especially common were the annoying evil spirits called cucu who tried to lure people to harm or even death, sometimes by crying like a baby in distress. They were sometimes said to be the unhappy souls of those colicky babies who died before being baptized.[9] A relatively invulnerable spiritual constitution was recommended when one wished to make late-night forays, as binge drinking often required. A person with such a spiritual strength was also expected to remain calm and wise under the influence of alcohol. An emotionally volatile person was in greater supernatural danger.

In addition, someone who lacked a designated caretaker was expected to avoid drinking heavily by day or night, since that person would then lack protection from natural and supernatural disasters. Since people came to a boda huasi to accept an obligation for future support to the host, they might be expected to make sure that their emotions and social goals were on the right track before embarking on drinking to become drunk, lest they either promise more than they could afford or get angry and alienate their desired supporters. The social costs to living people from obstreperous drinking could be exacerbated when a quarrelling community attracted God's intervention and punishment. Finally, the social costs could extend even further, beyond the relationships of runacuna with each other and with God and other spirits to include interethnic relations. Drunken violence that escalated quarrels and drove individuals and families apart would help neighboring mestizos exploit the fractured indigenous community.

In some parts of the world, the customary and religious consumption of one form of alcohol over another, usually a fermented beverage, like wine, instead of one that is distilled, is associated with low rates of alcohol abuse and addiction. Among orthodox Jews, for instance (Bales 1946; Snyder 1958), daily and ritualized consumption of sweet wine coexists with a very low level of problem drinking. The pattern of considering a fermented beverage a food as well as a sacrament, but not as a recreational substance, is also less likely to be associated with a high rate of alcohol-related problems. The Mediterranean pattern of using wine in small doses as a weekly sacrament and as a daily food is a case in point. If asua had remained the only acceptable form of alcohol, as both food and spiritual medium, or if the Spaniards in the Andes had early been able to produce good and cheap wine in the New World, perhaps something of that pattern might have persisted in the Andes. However, distilled sugarcane alcohol rapidly joined corn beer as an adequate way to get drunk with and for the spirits. The use of asua as food persisted in some areas of the greater amazon rainforest but diminished in the Andes. The association of a spiritual state with advanced inebriation perhaps encouraged this acceptance of trago; the desire for a more moderately altered state would have prevented its quick adoption. Once trago became available in almost limitless quantities at a very low price to the rural people, alcohol-related problems were bound to increase, despite the supernatural meaning and sanctions associated with alcohol use.

RUNA-MESTIZO CULTURAL INTERCHANGE

Chapter 4, "*Cantina* and *Boda Huasi*," laid the groundwork for examining how the "pidgin" culture of drinking shared by runacuna and mestizos in San Rafael and beyond could exacerbate indigenous drinking problems in Huaycopungo. Let us concentrate first on what it means to drink and try to unravel the mixed hispanic and native andean cultural influences of the past from the more recent effects of the modern Ecuadorian indian, mestizo, and "pidgin" cultures of drinking on the beliefs and behaviors of today's Otavaleños. Above we have reviewed some of the ways in which, in andean conceptions, an alcohol-induced altered state of consciousness unites the social realm of living humans with the social, and we would say spiritual, world of the eternal spirits immanent in the surrounding landscape and more distant natural environments and transcendent in the inaccessible realms deep within the earth, the sea, and the sky. To drink is to act on the world, creating, ratifying, and enacting threads of interdependence that weave the world of today and of forever into a harmonious tapestry of contrasts and complementarities. This notion of the religious meaning and effect of drunkenness is quite foreign to orthodox Christianity and marginal at best to its many local manifestations in Europe and Euro-America, where the notion of contracts and social bonds being made through offered and shared drinking took place between people and between people and God only in the context of moderation. Drunkenness, although sometimes tolerated, was believed to lead to evil temptation rather than to increase the sanctity of human life.

The origins of the notion of drinking to escape and unburden oneself from negative feelings, which is so common in indigenous and mestizo Ecuadorian culture today, is harder to trace. This pattern is associated cross-culturally with an increase in alcohol-related problems. Estrella and Estrella (1982, 153) suggest that this was an additional pattern adopted by the Ecuadorian indians as a response to the brutal Spanish conquest and colonization. It certainly has a place both in earlier times in Europe and in today's Euro-American culture.

"I need a drink" is a Euro-American cliché in any stressful situation, even among those who have no intention of actually imbibing alcohol. Otavaleños frequently use the Spanish term *desahogarse*, which means "to seek relief through venting one's feelings," to justify their own or others' drinking. It is difficult to speculate with any confidence how long this has been part of their world of drinking. Certainly, it has been part of Spanish, hispanic Ecuadorian, and North American writing on Andean indians (Estrella et al. 1982) for a long time. However, that may represent the outsiders' interpretations of indigenous drinking rather than an accurate expression of the natives' motives for drinking. For instance, Abercrombie's ethnographic and ethnohistorical study of a community in Bolivia finds that "In K'ulta the road one travels through drink is not that of amnesia but of its opposite, memory" (1998, 346). Through the songs and prayers that accompany and are enhanced by ritual drinking, the spiritually adept tries to retravel the road from the eternal past to the present, recapitulating and strengthening the social and spiritual order. Abercrombie continues: "That drinking alcoholic beverages should serve as a mnemonic technique is surely at odds with the commonplace in so-called Western culture that one drinks in order to forget."

It does seem to me that the younger people today who have had greater education in the mestizo culture and Spanish language make this argument more often than the older generation. Nonetheless, these younger people suggest that the older people drink for this reason, even though the older men themselves are more likely to claim that they are doing it for legitimate social and religious reasons. Both mestizos and indigenous people claim that the venting of feelings while drinking heavily is potentially helpful, if not positively health enhancing. However, as suggested in chapter 4, mestizos are more likely to expect the unburdening to lead to mildly antisocial behavior, which may tempt drinkers further into evil, whereas some runacuna believe that drinking heavily can be emotionally cleansing and spiritually uplifting. It is the antisocial aspect of drinking in the mestizo worldview that has most altered the indigenous world of drinking, as will be explored further below.

The feelings that are most commonly vented in Huaycopungo during bouts of drinking are laments of the inadequacy of love and material resources to meet one's desperate needs and the ease with which either can be diverted or stolen from one's grasp. I must emphasize that while we in the United States think of love and material gain to be both morally incompatible and separable in practice, Otavaleños consider them to be the emotional and practical sides of the same phenomenon. People demonstrate their feelings of love, both familial and romantic, through material aid to each other, and they feel the pangs of unrequited love when resources, not endearments or caresses, are clearly withheld. To carry the argument one step further, to be able to offer someone alcohol, to be the potential giver of love and esteem in pursuit of moral and material support, is to be in the superior position, however momentarily. But, paradoxically, the giver of alcohol is very vulnerable since the offer may be refused, leading to a tremendous public humiliation and loss. There is a parallel here to the time in North American culture when only a man could propose sex, while a woman had to wait for the proposition. Although men were thought to have the upper hand in sexual encounters, a man might feel more insecure than a woman, because a refusal by the less powerful woman could unman him. The emotional and material needs for interdependent ties of love and material aid in the family, the neighborhood, the community, and to the world beyond are so great and so often and easily thwarted that these issues form a running commentary to peoples' everyday lives. People are particularly likely to erupt into despair or anger during the festive times of heavy drinking.

Another influence from hispanic culture might have had a different effect on drinking behavior, calling into question a source of alcohol-related violence attributable to indigenous cultural rules. It is a famous stereotype in Ecuador, with probably as much mix of truth and exaggeration as in any stereotype, that native women expect to be beaten by their drunken husbands and will go so far as to defend their husbands' right to do so if someone steps in to protect them. Clearly, Otavaleño women have said as much, to me as well as many others. However, one must think carefully about what that means. Has the rate of violence against women, especially wives, always been the same? We don't know. A study I did about child rearing in previous generations on the Stockbridge-Munsee indian reservation in Wisconsin might suggest another way of looking at the matter. In this study, designed to aid parenting classes, we interviewed elders—men and women—about their experiences as children and as parents. They all claimed that discipline was very strict in their childhood. Their parents and grandparents had the right to inflict stiff and sometimes violent punishments on children, and today's elders said they had been physically afraid of misbehaving. However, none of the elders could give any examples of having been violently punished, except in the church-run boarding schools. They gave examples of the many difficult activities they performed without question, beyond what parents can today enforce, and they spoke meaningfully of their fear, but they themselves seemed to have been rarely punished. It seems possible, if not provable, that although a threat of parental violence existed, its actual occurrence was at least as rare as it is today. Could this have been the situation in the Andes at some time in the past? A relationship that balanced conflict and cooperation could be expected to yield justified violent retaliation by husbands against their wives' misbehavior, as well as by women against men. Alcohol intoxication could further be expected to increase the perception of wrong by spouses, disproportionately on the part of men because they drank so much more often, and also magnify the vehemence of their reactions against these imagined spousal infractions. But at times of restricted alcohol availability, the rate of alcohol-related violence against women could have been small enough not to challenge the assumed right to violent punishment. This would change in those periods when alcohol consumption increased significantly, especially among men not in positions of community leadership. During the 1970s, women certainly complained frequently of men's violence while drunk, and casual observation seemed to confirm a high rate of domestic violence. Could there have been a period (or periods) when it was common for women to justify a high rate of spousal violence, which represented a temporary, and conservative, response to changing events, like their short-lived acceptance of foodless boda huasicuna, despite the name that refers to special foods, as drinking in homes began to increase? I do not know the answer to this question, but given other misunderstandings of indigenous culture, especially as regards drinking, it seems as likely a hypothesis as the more commonly accepted theory that drinking-related violence against women among indigenous people was always at a level higher than among their nonindian neighbors due to their lack of a civilized culture.

Furthermore, this defense of husbands in the face of mestizo outsiders also reminds me of women's tight-lipped silence and pretence that they did not understand the Spanish language when mestiza cantina owners tried to engage them in conversation about their inebriated husbands. Loyalty to husbands—indeed, to their whole ethnic group—certainly precluded any complaint to a mestizo or a white outsider, however sympathetic she seemed to be. A related interpretation has always been that wives apparently agreed with their husbands that keeping the violence at home was a safer way of exorcising the immense frustration with social injustice that welled up uncontrollably when drunk—much safer than attacking the mestizos who so regularly exploited them. While protecting abusive husbands is called *enabling* in the AODA literature of North America today and considered dysfunctional for the individual and family, a more complex analysis is required when the other alternative is risking retaliation by the ethnoracial majority.

While domestic violence committed under the influence of alcohol is common among hispanic Ecuadorians, their belief that it is morally abhorrent and directly connected to alcohol abuse, rather than an inevitable and justifiable source of suffering in this imperfect world, is significantly different from what was common among indigenous Ecuadorians. This perspective has contributed to a major change in current indigenous worldview. In hispanic culture, domestic violence while drunk has often been connected to challenges to masculinity, part of which entails controlling one's domestic females to a much greater degree than among the New World's peoples. Coupled with that is the belief that women are weaker than men and thus, like children, should be spared masculine violence. This second part of the equation makes the violence immoral, but the first makes it fairly common. These beliefs, then, added to the worldview of older runacuna through drinking in mestizo cantinas and younger runacuna during the many years in hispanic-dominated schools, become a double-edged sword for native women. They are a source of righteous outrage against domestic violence, but come at the price of viewing women as the weaker sex and of advocating male protection and dominance in the home.

In fact, the whole hispanic cultural complex of gender behavior and its trajectory over time probably increases the potential for ceremonial binge drinking to lead to problems, especially among younger adult males. As we discussed in chapter 4, "*Cantina* and *Boda Huasi*," in hispanic culture it is considered inevitable, if not positively desirable, for young men to be mildly antisocial, competitive with each other, predatory toward women, and insecure about their status, all of which feelings and behaviors are maximally displayed during recreational drinking. Over time, these behaviors are supposed to disappear with the assumption of mature responsibilities, as does frequent drinking outside the home. For young indigenous men, who only recently have acquired access to unlimited supplies of booze, the melding of these goals and interpretations of male drinking, so familiar to them now, with those that have long encouraged competitive drinking to maximum inebriation for social and spiritual prestige, the stage is set for an increase in behaviors expressing strong negative emotions and interpersonal violence relative to those of respectful and mellow communion with one's fellows and the spirits. This contributed to the increasing dissatisfaction with the traditional drinking culture among women. It also contributed to the general frustration of older drinkers, who no longer could coax their sons and sons-in-law to accompany them, remain relatively sober, and care for them during ceremonial binges. If the younger men became inebriated, they might need more care from others than their older, more experienced relatives.

A Real Increase in Alcohol-Related Suffering, Not Just a Reevaluation of Its Significance

This discussion of how the changing social and economic environment resulted in an increase in alcohol quantity, the exacerbation of risk factors in the traditional culture of drinking, and the overriding of protection factors has been designed to demonstrate that the incidence and prevalence of alcohol-related problems rose in Huaycopungo in the past several decades. It was not just a case that Ila Rafi Taita was relabeled a "viejo chumado," an epithet that fit Anga Andu Taita a bit more. Nor was it only that Mama Juana, the Huaycopungo cantina owner, more likely to be lumped with the dysfunctionally drinking elders like Mama Emilia. People like Anga Andu and Mama Emilia were actually more likely to become alcoholic than in the past. In other words, fewer prosperous and ambitious individuals were like Mama Juana and Ila Rafi Taita, and more people were like Anga Andu and Mama Emilia than had been the case long ago, although alcoholics still constituted a tiny minority of the community's members.

An increase in real suffering does not always result in major changes in the beliefs and behaviors of individuals and communities. As in the case of foot binding in China or female genital mutilation in the Sudan, people can come to believe that the alternatives to the painful practices of today are clearly worse. But in Huaycopungo, many other aspects of their way of life had changed. They were becoming educated, bilingual, voters with real political power and access to national and international markets. Simultaneously, secular and religious authorities and social activists were competing to reinterpret indigenous life in the modern world. It is my contention that the traditional adaptation encouraged a dialogic relationship to cultural differences, making their culture both dynamic and relatively healthy. All of these factors allowed people to do what is rare, make an about-face in their alcohol behavior.

But the burden of this book is to show that the analysis of the culture of alcohol in Huaycopungo and its changes cannot be treated as a hermetic isolate; it inescapably engages the most basic moral and spiritual foundations of local religious conceptions, which in turn serve as the template for their ethnic identity, as a minority in their native land, subordinated to the descendants of their conquerors. How they treat alcohol illuminates the most sacred postulates of who they are. The following chapter will return to the religious life by examining one contemporary example of the continuing effort to retain the most positive aspects of traditional life while accommodating to the realities of the present by defining themselves, and their relationship to spiritual powers, in a dialogic relationship with polarized alternatives.

In the year 2000, the Protestant head of the cabildo promoted one of the most successful Coraza fiestas that had occurred in Huaycopungo in two decades, although his own written history of the evangelist church three years previously had singled out the traditional Corazas fiesta as a reason for the local Protestant revolt from the Catholic Church.

CHAPTER TEN

Transnational Corazas 2000

The Corazas Fiesta Is Resuscitated

IN JULY OF 2000, my comadre Isabel tracked me down by phone to where I was vacationing in New Hampshire. Thrilled to have found me, she was breathless and giddy and I knew something was up, but the formal conversational gambits had to be completed first. When we finished asking after everyone's health and well-being, she revealed that there was a secret she had to share with me. She said that I would never guess what she had to tell me. For my visit to Ecuador a few weeks hence, the comuna president, José Manuel Aguilar (Damiano Jusi Mali), had planned a major Corazas fiesta to celebrate the completion of the potable water project. With the help of my family's charitable foundation, the system had been renovated and extended to almost everyone in the community. That Damiano Taita was organizing Corazas by itself was shocking news, since Corazas had not been fully staged for sixteen years, although I had seen some mini Corazas during recent San Juan festivities. Furthermore, how could he, a major leader of the evangelist church, sponsor a traditionally Catholic religious fiesta, partially in honor of San Luis? And why was it going to be on August 6, when the traditional date was the 19th? As Isabel hemmed and hawed, I realized there was more to tell. When she finished telling me, we were both wordless and flustered. Damiano Taita had appointed the president of the Potable Water Commission to be Coraza, and he planned to surprise Isabel and myself by giving us the honor and responsibility of serving as the *Corazapac Huarmicuna*, or female cosponsors: literally his "wives" (in this unusual case, there would be two). Word had leaked to her and she thought I should be forewarned. My scheduled visit to Otavalo that year had determined the early date; they couldn't wait until the 19th if I was going to be back in the United States by then. Furthermore, Isabel's second son, Alberto, had agreed to act as the Loa, the junior companion of the Coraza, who, similarly costumed, recites the long invocations at different points during the ceremony. After our conversation, I called my close friend Tracy Honn, a book artist, who was coming to Ecuador with me for the very first time, officially to give workshops in women's cooperatives associated with the Maquipucuna Foundation but also to visit Huaycopungo, about which she had heard so much from me for the last seventeen years. She was excited about witnessing such a major cultural event and assured me it would not inconvenience her in the least. A further surprise awaited us, however, on the day of the ceremony; when comadre Isabel and I presented ourselves to be outfitted for the Corazas procession, the women organizers decided on the spot to gather together a third costume for Tracy and give the Coraza a third—and very tall, red-headed—wife, who spoke very little Spanish and no Quichua at all.

Appointing the main participants was a significant innovation, since in the past, an ambitious family would volunteer to be *prioste* (sponsor of a ritual event) in order to increase the family's prestige, forestall criticism that they selfishly hoarded their wealth, and attain full elder status for the heads of the family. How comadre Isabel and I happened to be chosen as Corazapac Huarmicuna deserves some explanation. Isabel was chosen partly on her own merits. She is considered by some to be an inspiration to younger people because of her past activities in defense of community land, as we saw in chapter 7. In addition, she still tirelessly receives people seeking advice in her home day or night, sometimes to the irritation of her own family. The other reason for her being chosen is that she and I have worked together all these years and she has helped channel my contributions for the benefit of all, rather than hoarding it for her own benefit, as gossips and people from the shifting factions whisper that she does. As discussed in the preface, over the years I had donated a part of my salary to community development projects in Huaycopungo as proposals were made to me in person or submitted to me in writing. In addition, I enlisted assistance from my parents' charitable foundation, usually to valuable projects of a larger scale; the potable water project had been the largest of those.

In 1999 evangelist church president Damiano José Manuel was elected community council president as well, with the express hope that he would direct the fund-raising ability he had demonstrated developing outreach programs as church leader to the community needs identified by the council. The largest project for which the community council sought funding was the overhaul of the potable water system. At that time the system served only about two-thirds of the community and suffered breakdowns over half the time. An impressive proposal, complete with engineering diagrams for the repair, extension, and improvement of the system, was drawn up and taken to a large number of potential donors. The system had been designed by a French water engineer who had stayed two years beyond her holiday, so taken was she with the place, the people, and their need for her expertise. As usual, the community members would donate labor and the food to pay the labor—an ancient tradition common throughout Ecuador—the municipality would put up the cost of the engineering, and the materials would be purchased by the outside source of funds. The reply received from potential donors, mostly international governments, was that, while the project was worthy and the proposal excellent, the funding priority had to be those communities with no potable water system. Since Huaycopungo had a partial, if poorly working, system, the project was a low priority. The Butler Foundation decided to fund the project.

While Huaycopungo's leaders knew that nothing seemed to galvanize community interest and involvement like a good source of water, even they were surprised by the community response to the news of funding for the potable water, something they had come to appreciate especially after the waterborne cholera epidemic in the early 1990s. Now, in the midst of a national economic and political crisis that threatened to tear the whole country apart at the seams, the people in Huaycopungo received the promise of abundant clean water, a gift of life. When the materials were ready and the day scheduled for the minga, or communal labor party, dawned, the turnout astonished the leaders. Elders, children, and able-bodied adults all assembled, with picks and shovels or their bare hands to help lay the pipes. Isabel said that two weeks had been scheduled to lay the lines from the regional reservoir to the new community tanks, but she expected it would take longer. It was finished in three days. José Manuel Aguilar said that he spent the whole day assigning jobs to people, and, at the end of the day, there were still people waiting to be put to work. A family's minga obligation is fulfilled if one member of the family is present and working. If no one appears, then the family pays a fine. For this minga, whole families showed up to get the job done as soon as possible. People who worked in traveling sales internationally came home to labor in this minga.

This level of excitement and enthusiastic commitment in Huaycopungo and throughout the parish carried over to the Corazas celebration preparations as well. The generation now entering adulthood was fascinated, since none of them remembered the traditional celebrations of twenty years ago. Many of the retired elder generation were likewise thrilled, but with the possibility of passing on their remembered knowledge to the generation of today. The active elders of today, who had criticized and attempted to hijack the festival twenty years ago, were in charge of the preparations. All families were expected to contribute food, money, and labor in proportions suitable to their resources. Foods and drink specially suited for fiestas had to be prepared in advance. *Yamor*, the asua made from sprouted corn, which takes longer and requires more care to make than the version fermented with brown sugar, was prepared by a large group of volunteers. Barrels and barrels of ordinary asua were also prepared for the date. Everyone soaked sacks of white maize in limed water to remove the hulls, making mounds of muti. For the first time in years, I ate *champus*, a special fermented and slightly sweet corn gruel, which was once among the few sweet dishes that people ever ate, and which they greatly relished during fiestas.

Fig. 49. *Corazas* 2000: the sponsors—
from left to right Isabel Criollo Perugachi,
Juan Mendes, the author, Tracy Honn

(PHOTO BY LUIS RICARDO TITUAÑA)

Fig. 50. *Corazas* 2000: a procession around the stadium

(PHOTO BY AUTHOR)

Transnational Corazas 2000   347

Corazas Once Seemed a Thing of the Past

When I began my research in Huaycopungo during the late 1970s, the most costly and elaborate fiesta sponsorship, Corazas, was a bone of contention for many different groups in the region, especially those advocating for modernizing progress among Otavaleños. Those Catholics and Protestants who promoted religious change found Corazas outmoded, too embarrassing a mix of paganism and colonial-era Catholicism. The sponsorship's extreme cost, determined by a competition to outdo one's rival Corazas in expenditure, was abhorred by those who thought people in Huaycopungo should invest their surpluses for economic rather than spiritual ends. People with many points of view believed that the local parish mestizos were tricking indigenous people into spending their resources for spiritual reward, so that they could get rich from the sale and rental of the paraphernalia and supplies that they alone controlled. Finally, the central themes of the Corazas fiesta were highly political, addressing a traditional balance of power within and among the indigenous comunas of the parish, as well as the negotiated balance of power between San Rafael's runa and mishu. The Coraza's impersonating an exalted figure of power, along with the other indigenous performers and audience of the five comunas, rehearsed a reversal of the local hierarchy, using a Catholic religious idiom to raise indigenous power and authority above that of their supposed betters. Although the reversal was temporary, it proclaimed the mestizos to be in a position of first among equals, rather than conceding the inherently and significantly superior status that these lowly mestizos of San Rafael liked to claim for themselves. And, like San Juan/Inti Raymi, it was a warning of local indigenous power and the potential cost of treading too heavily on their toes.

Yet at the same time that social and religious activists tried to convince the local people of the error in their traditional ways, folklorists and cultural preservationists wished to record what they believed was the tradition's imminent and regrettable demise. The Instituto Otavaleño de Antropología, under Plutarco Cisneros, was particularly noted for these attempts and still displays a wonderful scale model of a Corazas procession from San Rafael in the 1970s. Of course, individual observers could hold both views at the same time, sometimes working to preserve in the local museum what they decried in political rallies. The force of modern Westerners' desire to preserve in purity the practices and beliefs of people who once lived in societies more isolated and less complex than their own seems to defy explanation, conflicting with their central ideologies of progress and development. However, these two stances seem more compatible if you see the passion for preservation as a means to triumphantly display our full control over ways of life that once competed with our own, cultures that have thus been relegated to the ranks of evolutionary failures. Once they appropriate these "outmoded" cultures for their amusement, elites in the world system can undertake to domesticate the living descendants of those cultures as well, better preparing them to serve their own economic and political goals.

In the late 1970s, local leaders in Huaycopungo usually reacted to both sorts of outside pressure by generally rejecting the presence, observation, interventions, and suggestions of outsiders. Then it was considered mildly dangerous for an outsider to attend Corazas in San Rafael unless you were invited—and even if you were invited. Drunken indigenous revelers could be expected to verbally assault the visitor, while threatening physical violence, and to seize any cameras and tape recorders they found. Alternatively, some natives tried to charge extortionist prices, by local standards, for each photograph an observer wanted to take. In Otavalo, San Rafael had the reputation of being fiercely closed, shunning outsiders and clinging desperately to an ancient way of life. I remember late one morning when Chunda Fucu arrived at the house of Antonio Criollo, who was both his brother-in-law and his godfather, to hilariously recount his morning's adventures playing the dangerous indian, hurling insults in Quichua and a few rocks at suspicious Ecuadorian outsiders of official mien found straying within Huaycopungo's borders, with who knows what nefarious purpose in mind. People in Otavalo, both indigenous and nonindigenous, told me that the folk in Huaycopungo were backward and dangerous for throwing rocks or refusing to allow photos; within Huaycopungo it was considered both useful defensive maneuvering and funny playacting. Knowing that these Huaycopungo natives were the same people who had cannily defeated the proposal for a military base on their community's lakeshore just a few years earlier should have given pause to a too-quick acceptance of the prevailing stereotype of monolingual and isolated rural traditionalists. Their resistance to outside interference and potential theft of their resources, whether material or spiritual, was not quite so archaic and unthinking as it seemed.

During my fieldwork in 1978, a Coraza sponsor from Huaycopungo invited me to take photos during the fiesta so that I could later present him with a photographic record of his triumph. Since I was busy with other research and my new friends and assistants were loath to plunge me into the reciprocal drinking at a boda huasi, I did not accompany the Coraza at his house but attended only the most public parts of the fiesta. Nonetheless, local friends, including, on one occasion, the tipsy Coraza himself, who was luckily passing on horseback at the right moment, had to frequently defend my right to take photos against those who were pushing me out of the way, haranguing me in Quichua, demanding money, and reaching for my camera. I kept my tape recorder carefully concealed but activated, and today people are thrilled to hear the songs I recorded.[1] That year I witnessed a full Corazas season, in which three married couples in the parish, including one from Huaycopungo, served as ritual sponsors on three occasions between April and October. And in 1979, I saw the *fiesta chica*, or small festival, that begins the season's Corazas sponsorship around Easter, just before I left Otavalo to return to graduate school.

Although, during my dissertation research between 1977 and 1979, the criticisms of Corazas were common currency among the young adults who had been exposed to some education, to missionaries, and to political activists, they spent countless hours discussing what they might do to preserve the best of the festival while making it less burdensome and exploitative. Many of the young men in these groups were on the community's first soccer team, and some were, or had once been, evangelistas, since the first evangelical missionary had initiated soccer competitions in Huaycopungo. These conversations revolved around how to make Corazas a more purely runa festival, more on the lines of San Juan. On visits home to the United States, I was given the job of searching for a good source for the dyed ostrich plumes and sequins. If they could supply their own vestments instead of renting them, they reasoned, they could stop the unscrupulous exploitation on the part of the few local mestizo families who had control of the necessary paraphernalia. We felt daring when we contemplated defying the formidable dowager Sra. Cristina, who always demanded imperiously that the runacuna cede the first seats in the San Rafael bus to her, frequently cowing even the local rebels. As head of her family, she was in charge of the largest store of Coraza paraphernalia, which had been rented to the San Rafael runacuna for generations. Therefore, I remained skeptical of the claim that Corazas was a thing of the past.

Less than a decade later, two published books—Ares Quejía's ethnography of the fiesta based on fieldwork in 1976 (1988), and Naranjo's more recently researched Imbabura volume of a series on Ecuadorian popular culture (1988)—reported that the numbers of competing Corazas had been diminishing over the years. Naranjo suggested that the traditional fiesta had come to an end with the celebration in 1984.

In the early 1990s, a few individuals sponsored attenuated versions of the Corazas, especially as a folkloric accompaniment to the San Juan festivities during the summer solstice. Since the Gallos Pasai sponsorship is associated with San Juan, there was a good traditional reason to add another fiesta sponsorship at that time. In June of 1993, during San Juan, I witnessed an ambitious father and young son from Tocagon don the traditional Corazas vestments, which they had rented from the San Rafael mestizo owners. What struck me as surprising as I watched the procession during my short visit that year was that the fiesta attracted sympathizers of both religious approaches. Evangelicals gathered excitedly on the sides of the processional path alongside traditional Catholics and catequistas, even though the celebration still honored the patron saint of San Rafael, with the participation of the parish priest. Nonetheless, most people in Huaycopungo saw it as a local cultural resource and occasion for pride. Of course, the usual snickering wagers on how many watching evangelistas would succumb and take a drink ensued among those who were not followers of that church. Although Naranjo's prediction sounded plausible to me, so did the possibility that those young leaders who had argued so passionately for a less exploitative festival in the future would find a way.

Traditions and Innovations

However, when first contemplating the celebrating of Corazas with appointed sponsors to inaugurate the new potable water system, rather than the parish saint's day, it seemed very strange to me, far removed from the calendrical festival I had known over twenty years ago. These were striking innovations that underlined the general transformations of Huaycopungo over the years. Nonetheless, as many people as could obtained copies of Berta Ares Quejía's now out-of-print book entitled *Los Corazas: Ritual Andino de Otavalo* (1988), based on fieldwork in San Rafael in 1976, to make sure they got it right. Unsuccessful efforts were made to use the Web to locate her in Spain, so that they could request her permission for a reprinting.[2]

Despite these real changes, the more I compared the old and the new in my mind, the more faithful to traditional themes seemed the interweavings of innovations and faithful reenactments in this year's Corazas fiesta. Past symbolism was not gone but diverted into other channels of emphasis. The focus on water itself is a case in point. In the years of my field research, the mingas for the cleaning and repair of the water supply for people, animals, and plants, which were focused most heavily on the several springs and the river Itambi, had become rare. Similarly, the associated propitiatory rituals at water sources in order to ensure that they promoted human life rather than threatened it—through floods, droughts, dangerous water spirits, and the like— had diminished significantly. But as we saw in chapter 3, water from the skies, water in the earth, and the rains and mountain springs that mediate between the heavenly and earthly halves of the cosmos are all central to the geospiritual bases of andean religious theory. While explicit religious ritual had diminished, the overwhelming importance of water in the cosmic relations of humans and their environment was not entirely forgotten. That this event, the provision of abundant clean water to everyone, should be the impetus for a major community ritual of thanks was not as novel as it first appeared. In some ways it revived a tradition that had seemed to be lost in the 1970s.

Another major innovation was the centralization of authority in the hands of the community's secular officials. Community leaders chose the Coraza and his several wives, set the date, engaged music

Fig. 51. *Corazas* 2000: the crowd around the dais
(PHOTO BY AUTHOR)

groups, printed a schedule for the day (in Spanish), and constructed a dais for official speeches and awards in the afternoon program. Perhaps it should not have been a surprise given the concerns of the young adults during the late 1970s. They had discussed at length how to modernize the celebrations and take them into community hands. Concerns at that time included how the festival could maintain its local purpose of serving the community while avoiding the impoverishment of successful individuals, who now commanded a far greater portion of their resources in easily alienated money than in productive land, and preventing the further enriching of San Rafael's mestizos. No longer was the priest, or even San Rafael's secular authorities or the few families in control of Coraza paraphernalia or even the mestizo cantinas significant players in Huaycopungo's year 2000 Corazas fiesta, as they had always been in the past. There *had* been a kind of centralized authority before, but it was outside of the indigenous community. While Huaycopungo's runa tried to ignore and marginalize these mestizo actors when they could, the local mestizos had still directed many aspects of the ritual. The native character and organic feel of the fiesta was a partial fiction that the local inhabitants tried hard to present as the most significant truth.

In the past, every day's performance began in the house of the sponsor and slowly worked its way to distant corners and central religious spaces, both indigenous and mestizo, of the parish. It ended again in the boda huasi of each prioste. This individual family–and huasi-centered pattern contributed to this sense of local and family control over the shape of each year's fiesta. In 2000, instead, the performance began and ended in the casa comunal, literally "communal house" in Spanish, but in practice a community center, under the direction of a few community leaders. Neither the Spanish word *casa* nor the uses to which the casa communal is put suggests a parallel with a *huasi* to local residents. This move supported both a greater centralization and an increased formalization.

One more general change in society that this innovation reflects is the new place *within* national society, rather than marginal to it, that indigenous communities have taken in the last decades. Now, runa have national political efficacy, in a new de jure capacity as well as the de facto sense of the past. Huaycopungo is more like a mestizo town than it was before, especially since the legal registering of Huaycopungo's land in the national system, which began as a desperate measure to protect indigenous land resources against mestizo encroachment in the early 1970s. The assigning of tasks for Corazas by a centralized committee reflects these other centralizing and formalizing forces, as discussed particularly in chapter 6.

Probing a little further, one can speculate that this innovation may also have represented an attempt to rescue an endangered moral principle. At a time when each family has become more independent of others, more focused on its own economic performance and more protective of its economic resources, community identity was ritually presented less as the organic by-product of individual houses caught in a web of reciprocity and more as an formal entity in and of itself. The ritual emphasis shifted to the production of a more inclusive and civic identity, as threats to the natural reproduction of both communal interests and a functional geosocial unity through everyday family activities grew in strength and number. In 2000, each house contributed food, labor, and money both to the water project and to the preparations for the fiesta, but neither the individual huasicuna nor the heads of households were the focus of ritual to the same extent they were in the past. Each house became generic and undifferentiated, while Huaycopungo as a whole community, represented publicly by its elected leaders rather than its male heads of household, took on a higher profile than in the past, when its symbolic concreteness appeared only as the result of its competitions with other communities, like its paired shaya, Tocagon. In fact, there was more discussion of the rivalries and differing contributions of the community's sections than those of different families. It was necessary for the contributions to have been symbolically, if not factually, equal from Langaburo, Villagran Pugru, and Huaycopungo. Theoretically, we might say that the production of an apparently concrete social structure, to the eyes of the outside observer, through the interaction of material conditions and unexamined *habitus* as described by Bourdieu (1997) for traditional societies gave way to the *imagined communities* analyzed by Anderson (1991), where community leaders self-consciously create a "national" identity, in this case a community identity, for presentation to the people included as well as to the outside world.

At a time when economic realities made "the community of one heart" seem harder to attain through the daily interactions of the constituent households, whose members no longer worked regularly on community land, the staging of this festival in the name of that ethos took on a special importance and poignancy. As my godson Ricardo Tituaña said to me in February 2005 (my paraphrase): "Otavaleños used to compete for pride and prestige through Corazas, now they do it by buying and displaying the latest in technology." From the point of view of Huaycopungo's members, the new innovation was a resounding success, with a minimum of modern technology, such as microphones, loudspeakers, and our own videographers from CONAIE. "Everyone," in their words, even people from Huaycopungo who live or work in far-flung places, returned to play a part in the reenactment of sacred community. I heard visitors from other communities grumble about Huaycopungo's reputation in the national media for providing drug couriers and gunrunners to the cartels and rebels in Colombia.

No doubt expressing some intercommunity rivalry, they claimed to be "afraid" of those dangerous fellow runa. They also gossiped about the supposedly menacing split between Catholics and Protestants in Huaycopungo, but the local inhabitants' talk was overwhelmingly about the inspiring collaboration of every family to make this year's Corazas work.

From a Catholic Church-sponsored event in honor of the parish's patron saint to a community fiesta under the direction of the evangelist church's president and most enduring leader, albeit in his role as community council president, is a giant leap. Since an effort was made to be as faithful to rituals of the past as possible, this made for some awkward moments in the actual festival. There was some discussion about whether the main procession should go to the Catholic church in San Rafael at all. In the past, the eve of the saint's day was celebrated by a mass in church in which all the Corazas appeared in their regalia with their attendants. The Loa traditionally recited his full invocation there, hands lifted in front of him, from a place next to the statue of San Luis. This part of the celebration, called *cultu punlla*, "Catholic cult day," was eliminated this year. The *pasai punlla*, or "sponsorship completion day," constituted most of this year's festival. During the procession, which is the central part of the pasai punlla, it was decided to parade to the church steps after all, as tradition dictated, before going on to conduct the novel celebrations at the water tank, which included a ceremonial ribbon cutting. The main assistants arranged themselves on the church steps facing the plaza, with some difficulty since there were fifty or so people already crowded onto the steps to see the festivities. The Coraza and Loa, still on horseback, faced the church and the Loa gave his first invocation. It was beautifully presented, although some of us realized he had forgotten a large chunk of the verses in the middle.

Just before the Loa began the recitation, the parish priest emerged from the church, somewhat at loss what to do. He was greeted warmly and politely and the principals shook his hand. With the crowd pressing all around us, his face and mine were only inches apart. He expressed his disappointment that he had not been included in the fiesta and that the bishop in Ibarra had also not been consulted, since the bishop was a long-standing supporter of progress in Huaycopungo. When the invocation was done, in which the church, the local priest, and the bishop are saluted, people respectfully bade their leave and the procession continued. Perhaps the priest was then asked to come to the ceremony at the stadium later, because he took his seat on the dais in the afternoon and presented the crowd with a message of support from the bishop.

During the rest of that day and in the days following, people argued about what the proper role of San Luis and the church as a whole should have been. Many traditionalists felt that it was wrong to so remove the ceremony from its older religious roots. Others recognized that it was more inclusive of all Huaycopungo's citizens, especially its evangelistas, that it be done in this less Catholic way. But if it was always celebrated in church with the priest's participation, and if they are trying to preserve their traditional customs, countered the first group, shouldn't they continue to celebrate the patron saint?

Another unspoken motive for marginalizing the church may have been the long-standing desire to make sure that the indian fiestas, and religion in general, be under runa control, and not directed by anyone in the dominant society. Given the significance of the ritual split between the Catholics and the Protestants, I was surprised that there were so few public recognitions of this division during the festivities, although they may well have been more salient during the preparations, when I was absent. Instead, community unity was proclaimed. To do so, the ritual had less Christian focus, despite the references in the Loa's memorized address.

Most evangelicals in Huaycopungo are pretty tolerant of the music and dancing of the traditional fiestas, although the national and international denominations with which they are loosely affiliated prohibit dancing. José Manuel Aguilar did agree to dance with me on the evening after Corazas, although he looked miserably uncomfortable the whole time, and later told friends that when one foot moved he wasn't sure what to do with the other one and felt paralyzed. His friend, another long-term evangelical loyalist, thought the story was exceptionally funny and kept repeating it, although he agreed it is humiliating to dance when you don't know how. He was pleased, however, that the church president and I had shared a dance. It was an honor we owed each other. But earlier in the day, when I was off resting, my compadres Isabel and José Manuel and a group of family and friends had asked Damiano José Manuel to dance in a group with them. Since Isabel had also been honored as Corazapac Huarmi, it would have been an appropriate gesture of mutual honor for them to dance together. However, as reported to me, his wife made a scene, dragging him away by his poncho, while he protested vainly that he wasn't going to do anything wrong. There was no suggestion made by anyone who witnessed the event of sexual jealousy; it was a question of whether or not evangelicals could dance. There still are some evangelicals, including Taita Damiano's wife, for whom church orthodoxy is more important than the preservation of indigenous culture.

However, in the group was my compadre José Manuel Tituaña, who had been drinking heavily. Such drinking is still considered a relatively serious offense in the evangelical church. The connection of drinking and dancing is what most often worries evangelistas. On the previous day, there had been some question about whether José Manuel Aguilar had joined in a toast, but a photograph subsequently proved that he had taken no cup of wine into his hands.[3] Even so, people who normally side with the evangelicals are often reported drinking and returning safely to the fold. For all but a few, it is a forgivable offense.

Nonetheless, the music and dancing had changed significantly. As explained in chapter 4, in the past, women could only dance and sing when drunk and their dance movements when sober approximated the movements of someone who is intoxicated. Dancing and drinking were synonymous with each other, the presence of one implying the other. This year we Corazapac Huarmicuna did not weave significantly in our processional dancing and there was little complaint. Group dancing in the evening also demonstrated more self-conscious control of movement while dancing than drunken ataxia. Coastal and urban Ecuadorians claim that Otavaleños are repressed and prudish because they move their bodies as one piece, rather than allow their hips to sway independently from their shoulders or use their arms and hands to further complicate the movement. In general, the dancers were able to maintain that desired illusion of dignified flowing movement.

Berta Ares Quejía spends some pages of her monograph (1988) examining the songs sung by the wives of the Coraza and his attendants when they are under the influence. Two that she includes and translates are opposites of one another. The first song recounts, without expressed irony, the wife's unflagging devotion to her husband's desire to undergo the sponsorship and complete his transition to elder status. The second song expresses the experience of a woman soldiering on in support of her husband, while simultaneously bemoaning her suffering in search of her husband's chimerical goal to achieve recognition while he squanders family resources. Both of these are typical of andean women's music, which is often considered a personal critique and commentary on public behavior that they are licensed to express especially when they are drinking (Harrison 1989). No one suggested we sing one of these songs or even called our attention to them. Possibly the twin themes of presenting a modern community that is a source of progress and one that is relatively free of the alcoholic miasma of the past won the day.

The absence of women's singing and other changes in our performances are also consistent with more general changes in women's roles. Women today can exercise public leadership more openly than before, and thus may be less inclined to use the oblique criticizing they were known for in the past. Both the appointment of women to named roles in order to honor their community leadership and the speeches and plaques presented on the dais represent a major transformation toward a greater, and more formal, public role for women. This parallels the feminist challenges to traditional female roles in Ecuadorian national society as a whole. For example, the officer of the immigration police who examined my papers this year at the airport was a woman, which astonished an elder Ecuadorian man returning for a visit from Chicago after a number of years. When he expressed his surprise to her, she proudly announced that she was the first of her kind.

On the other hand, with increasing accommodation to the dominant society, there has been an increase in the belief that men rule over women and that they have the license to intimidate them. Women were once equal partners, and sometimes the dominant partners, at home, although undifferentiated females in public venues. Despite this depersonalization in public, women's *collective* power was still felt, and individual women could exercise their will by making seemingly personal but very cutting critiques of men's affairs as if they were gossiping loudly among themselves during public events, especially when they were required to drink. Both of these forms of women's power, formally in the home and informally in public arenas, have diminished. Now they are less different, but basically unequal, although more conscious of gaining status than losing it. This may be partially explained by the fact that the dominant hispanic Ecuadorians have long believed emphatically that indigenous women were in a more oppressed position than hispanic women, although outside observers have most often seen it to be the other way around. Before, women were overwhelmingly different but most often equal.

A man describing our role during the Corazas festival in 2000 said we were there just to serve our men. On the other hand, a useful counter to that statement is my comadre Asciencia Criollo Perugachi's high school thesis in which she claims the Coraza and his wife preside as king and queen, not king and wifely servant (1995–96). This is also supported by the honor given comadre Isabel and myself. When Damiano Taita appointed the sponsors, and individual households no longer volunteered for the job, both male and female roles were considered important to bestow on worthy persons. Corazapac Huarmi was not simply the wife of the Coraza, but a female position parallel to the position of Coraza, one that could be held by women completely unrelated to the man appointed to serve as Coraza.

Finally, Urai Shaya and Janan Shaya, the traditional moiety division, were significantly absent from almost all of this year's festival, although it had once been central to it. The only reference to them came in the Loa's invocations, memorized from accounts written in the past. At one point during the festivities, our Loa, Alberto, asked us to explain what the shayas were all about. On the one hand, this celebration was not parishwide as it had been in the past, when several Corazas from the many San Rafael communities competed with each other for the most lavish display. Since it took place only in Huaycopungo, and not in Tocagon, Urai Shaya Huaycopungo's Janan counterpart, the issue was moot anyway. Even so, representatives of UNCISA, Union de Comunidades Indígenas de San Rafael (Union of San Rafael's Indigenous Communities) appeared for the formal ceremonies on the dais and gave both a presentation and plaques to those responsible for the potable water project. The parishwide references were made in mestizo idiom more than in traditional andean terms. In fact, without the ritual enactments of the moiety interrelationships in the last decade or so, the shayacuna have lost their significance. More salient now is the Catholic/evangelical split in Huaycopungo, as suggested in chapter 8, which has partially replaced the function of the upper and lower sides to produce generative competition and collaboration. Similarly, Huaycopungo has grown so much that the rivalries between Langaburo, Villagran Pugru, and Huaycopungo proper also serve a similar role.

The Burden

Service as prioste[4] is expected to burden and challenge the personal resources of those impersonating the highest secular and sacred realms of power. Not only is this heavy responsibility the price someone must pay for these moments of glory in the lavish display of wealth and power, it also symbolically represents the desirable outcome of hierarchical relations. Wealth and power should serve not the individual but the group. Should that message fail to reach an ambitious individual, the ceremony may also serve to significantly reduce his wealth and subject his pretensions to public humiliation.

The procession that is the central event of the fiesta is one manifestation, both literal and symbolic, of this heavy load. This year the day dawned completely clear and the equatorial sun beat relentlessly down upon us, decked out in more clothing than normal, as we paraded up from the lowest point of the community to the highest over a period of several hours in the middle of the day and then danced slowly back down again. The darker-skinned natives ended the day with sunburned faces and necks just as did the light-skinned American visitors. As is common in the dry summer months, the dust was at least an inch thick on some parts of the paths, which left us all with red-rimmed eyes, hoarse voices, and nagging coughs when the procession finished. Somewhere along the way, a friend pointed, laughing, at my face and then handed me a tissue to wipe the big dirt smudges from my nose and forehead. The constant repetition of the same movements, especially on the dancing return down to the stadium, as we huarmicuna whirled in our places, first dipping and then coming out of the dip to raise our paper bouquets in salute toward the mounted Coraza and

Loa, all while avoiding the crowds pressing in on us, our personal care-takers one step behind us and the looming horses, was exhausting and hypnotizing in equal measure. We arrived back at the stadium after about five hours of processing, with ritual stops along the way at the church, the water tank, and key corners. Despite a continual source of water and the occasional soft drink or beer, we were hot, hungry, light-headed and dizzy from the sun, and exhausted. I kept thinking that if I whirled too energetically one more time, I would keel over. My native comadre was only marginally less depleted than I was. The following day, my friend Tracy suffered from sunstroke.

While seated on the dais, we listened to unending speeches and received a number of plaques and tributes ourselves. The local notables from outside Huaycopungo used this opportunity to wordily promote their own political agendas in Spanish. Meanwhile, women representa-tives of family after family approached us, the Corazapac Huarmicuna, with baskets of cucavi, cooked snack foods. Before I realized that we were figureheads receiving largesse to redistribute, I snatched a couple of cooked beans and toasted corn, to the indulgent giggle of spectators, who are used to seeing the ethnologist as a child. All baskets were directed to my comadre Isabel, whose feet, she later told me, hurt ter-ribly each time she stood to receive an offering and hand it to our *cuin-tayuccuna* (assistants) seated on the ground in front of the dais. I did not think to intervene, but even if I had, my offer might not have been accepted, since my efforts to participate at that level have often been turned away in the past. Indeed, I do not know everyone's name and kinship position by heart, nor have I developed the ability to remember clearly who gave what and when, which is so important in the compu-tations of social networks, so I remain pitifully inept in any case.

After lunch, they staged the limai, the part of the fiesta during which the Coraza is chased on horseback by his assistants, who attempt to injure him by throwing candies in his face. Isabel's son Alberto, the Loa, was proud of his success in inflicting two wounds. The limai was followed by a concert given by a local well-known folkloric group. Couples dancing, another relatively recent innovation from the mes-tizo world, attracted people to the stadium until almost dawn.

While we, the foreign participants, escaped for a rest in the after-noon and retired early from dancing in the evening, since I had been very sick the day before, the Coraza had to continue throughout the fiesta. Because there was still money left the next day, the committee decided to continue the celebrations, and the Coraza, Loa, and Yumbo were redressed and made to appear publicly, without the full procession, again. Since Tracy was in bed with sunstroke, Isabel and I returned to other responsibilities on what was to be my last day in Otavalo that year.

While our liquor consumption was tiny during the whole day, by choice and prearrangement, the Coraza and his assistants consumed steadily. Pedro Mendez, the Coraza, is not a regular drinker, but he did get drunk on more than one occasion, as did the Yumbos and their wives. Nonetheless, moderate drinking, not general and advanced drunkenness, characterized the celebrations. Alberto, only eighteen, claimed to have gotten a bit tipsy a couple of times, but never really drunk. Of course, there were unfortunate incidents among those who have a problem with drinking. Once again, for example, compadre José Manuel lost his hat. His mother, however, surprisingly remained sober.

In the past, the burdens of the sponsorship had more of an actual leveling effect, although the symbolism of cutting the Coraza down to size at the same time that he is raised to exalted heights continues today. When prosperous and ambitious men or couples used to choose to sponsor Corazas themselves, every attempt was made to goad them to compete in spending their resources to the point of incurring significant debt. While the mestizos desired to have the indians in debt to them, as a source of income, fellow runa were interested in seeing that everyone remained equally poor. The sponsors would significantly increase their symbolic capital in the community, but their economic capital would be depleted, sometimes even permanently eliminated. This year, the sponsors did not spend their own resources on the food, costumes, strings of coins, fireworks, alcohol, horses, and musicians. Nor were the sponsors responsible for mobilizing the largest possible personal support network. The community leaders enlisted aid from among all the community's members, rather than just from their own personal support networks, even though the latter undoubtedly volunteered the greatest help. No longer did the Coraza's family's role include overseeing the many aides they had appointed for the various named positions of keeper of the alcohol, the horses, the costumes, the food, the persons of the priostes, the coins, and so on. The fiesta organizers did that, too.

Nonetheless, despite the absence of personal expenditure in the sponsorship of the new version of the Corazas festival, the participants were chosen by the community to honor them for spending their time and other personal resources on service to the community rather than increasing the resources of their own family before the ritual event. The festival recognized past expenditure and voluntary leveling, instead of requiring it in the present.

In addition, however, the hierarchical position of the sponsors and their assistants is *symbolically* leveled during the fiesta, at the same time that it is elevated, through the forced drinking, the deliberate wounding of the symbol of grandeur during the limai, and the enthusiastic pressure to exhaust the honored sponsors in the long procession and continuous dancing. The same community that views with awe the magnificent costumes, strings of ancient coins, decorated horses, and fireworks that represent the exalted elevation of the sponsors is also licensed to push these impersonators of grandeur to ever greater personal resource depletion, even to the point of humiliating exhaustion. Everyone enthusiastically recounts each time the Coraza was hurt, the Coraza fell down drunk, the Coraza fell asleep at his duties, or the Coraza displayed a burst of temper.

Depersonalization

In addition to the symbolic burdening, the ritual serves to depersonalize the individual sponsors, a result of the ritual that became much clearer to me as a participant than it had been when I was only an observer. While we were chosen for our personal achievements, our honor during the main procession consisted of our impersonating a figurehead of great power, without the experience of actually possessing that power. Rather than singling out my personal characteristics or achievements, the traditional part of the ritual depersonalized me as one of three Corazapac Huarmicuna.

One part of the depersonalization experienced was the traditional public role of women. Where men can be distinguished as individual heads of families in public events, women are usually lumped together as generic representations of their gender. In keeping with this distinction, we were given no instruction about our role beforehand but were guided step-by-step by others along the way. The Capitan de Corazas and Loa were given more guidelines and rehearsal than we were, but their roles were also more complex. Nonetheless, the Coraza and Loa were more depersonalized by their costume than were the women. For example, their white-painted faces made it difficult to recognize them except when up close. And when the uma was in place, you could not see their faces at all. They, too, became generic representations of exalted power.

As Corazapac Huarmicuna, we were simply told to show up at a particular time and place, the stadium at 8:30 a.m. We were instructed to appear in native dress but told that we would be given new outfits once we arrived. Once there, we were hustled off into a room of the casa comunal and instructed to undress quickly. Our cuintayuccuna, keepers of our person, then dressed the three of us carefully in entirely new outfits. Attention to the details of the folds of our anacos and angle of the fachalinas was greater than I had ever experienced before. We were given a new maroon rebozo, a color then representing special honor, to wear folded on our shoulders, and I also wore the sash I had been given the day before in honor of my contributions to the evangelical church. Throughout the first couple of hours of the procession, my cuintayuk continued readjusting details of my rebozo, fachalina, sash, and anacos as we walked to ensure perfection in my appearance. We were handed elaborate carved candles in one hand, the paper flower-topped staffs that belonged to the Coraza and Loa for our other hand; the Corazas' hats were put on our heads, and we were ready to be presented to the crowd. After joining the Coraza, Loa, and Yumbos in the stadium, we all began dancing in a circle, which periodically switched direction, to the sounds of the runa musicians. Then we were ready for the procession, our husband and his assistants following us on horseback, as the mestizo town band from San Rafael began to play. Little girls we passed reached out their hands to touch the hem of my anaco. The glory of the moment was impressed upon this youngest generation.

During the procession, our cuintayuccuna whispered in our ear when to start, what to do, and periodically handed us bottles of water to prevent dehydration. Customarily we would have been offered asua, but in recognition of the delicacy of gringos, bottled water had been prearranged. When the Corazas' horses got too close, we were told—or prodded, due to my friend's lack of either Spanish or Quichua and the difficulty we sometimes had hearing or paying attention in the noisy crowd—to move faster, and when our pace got too swift, we were told to slow down or hauled back by the fachalina. After a great deal of discussion about when to walk and when to dance, it was decided that we would parade up the hill, and on the return from San Rafael's church and the new water tank, we should dance back to the stadium. On that return procession, we were given periodic guidance in how to dance properly by our cuintayuccuna as well. At one point, Tracy's cuintayuc, tipsy and frustrated by poor Tracy's inability to understand speech, grabbed her by her clothes and physically swung her into more desirable whirls. Luckily my comadre and I remembered some of the steps from observations in the past. Still, because all my movements were guided by someone else, and my only responsibility was to keep doing what I was told, I felt more like a doll than a person.

This depersonalizing effect is undoubtedly greater now that the prioste and his entourage are no longer strictly speaking the sponsors but figureheads chosen by the sponsor, which is the community. However, the entirely new part of the ceremony, which took place on the dais after the procession, partially counteracted that depersonalization. All of the main participants, including the organizers, were singled out for awards, while perhaps one thousand people watched from the ground. Everyone on the dais had a chance to address the crowd in front of the microphone. At the same time, a new room in the local elementary school was celebrated and the school's principal honored as well. Although most of the speeches were given in Quichua, including the moderation by the female indigenous broadcasters of a local radio station, the format would have been much more familiar as a public ceremony to honor public service in the mestizo community than what had gone before. The growing individualization of Huaycopungo's culture that results from its increasing similarity to the nonindian culture of Otavalo was represented in the ceremony but partially counteracted as well in the more traditional parts.

Taming Hierarchy

The central theme of Corazas today, just as in the past, was taming hierarchy, which the symbolic burdening and depersonalizing discussed above served to promote. While individuals were singled out because of their special achievements, they were then made to impersonate an idealized, even exaggerated, figure of authority in an exhausting ritual for the viewing pleasure of the community and their guests. The symbolic capital we gained—prestige for laboring in benefit of the community—was recognized as having preceded the ritual in the modern version, rather than being the result of the ritual sponsorship itself, as it had been before.

In response to this change, the motive to mock or challenge the Coraza beyond his capacities was therefore reduced, since his participation was not a personal bid for greater status in the community but a recognition of services rendered, given by community leaders in the name of all. In general, all of us were treated with great dignity and courtesy. People were clearly thrilled with the whole process. Particularly touching were the elderly community members who would accompany us for a while, periodically shouting things like *Viva nucanchic runa causai* (Long live our indigenous way of life), and coaching us or congratulating us on how we were fulfilling our role. The now elderly ritual clowns had a blast, weaving in and out of the group, making lewd jokes, insulting adults, harassing children, and getting drunk.

Pedro Mendez, the head of the potable water project chosen to play the Capitan de Corazas, was the ideal sort of leader in the local tradition. He was dignified, soft-spoken, and somewhat hesitant to seek the limelight. Alberto Tituaña, the Loa, at eighteen was young enough to play an inconspicuous role, although once he is an adult, he will not be known first for his mild-mannered humility. Like his father, he is gregarious, humorous, and strong-willed. Both made it clear that they resisted this honor and responsibility, although I know that Alberto was in fact thrilled to be so singled out, as his maternal uncle had been once long ago.

One result of the ritual that astonished me was that almost everyone I had ever spent time with in the past twenty-three years came to greet me or at least saluted me from afar. Especially noteworthy was the behavior of a number of people who had recently ignored me, or even refused to talk to me, because of feuds with others with whom I was associated. Everywhere I went, people tried to catch my eye, claiming a relationship and recognizing my honor and their own gratitude by their glance. My depersonalized dancing self nonetheless saw in the faces I passed a review of my history in Huaycopungo, almost like watching one of my own slide shows. But they were all smiling directly at me.

An example of one of the major transformations from distant to friendly includes the wife of one of the Yumbos. In 1978, my comadre and I helped rescue a teenaged girl, who had once lived as a foster daughter in my comadre's parents' house, from an abusive forced labor situation with a local mestizo store owner. Her parents were too poor to support her and had placed her in service with the mestizos once she was old enough. What prompted the rescue was her employers hiding a ring and accusing her of theft in order to cease paying her or buying her clothes. As in previous cases, the criminal complaint brought by her employers was supported in San Rafael's court. Later, because of a complex series of family disputes and factional feuds, the same young woman claimed we had hurt, rather than helped, her at that time. For this year's Corazas, as we processed and danced through the community together, she repeatedly made sure I still remembered the details of how I had helped her when she was young, laying claim to our long-standing and intimate relationship. As she consumed more and more alcohol, her comments became increasingly repetitive.

Another example involved the parents of one of my godchildren, Francisco Otavalo, the educated son of one of the curagas and community leaders and comadre Isabel's younger sister Asciencia, an educated leader in her own right. However, Asciencia also played a large part in perpetuating the feud within her sibling set, and neither had spoken to me in years. When I was still being dressed as Corazapac Huarmi in the casa comunal, compadre Francisco begged for a moment to approach me and presented me with two gifts from Asciencia—a coral bead necklace with an elaborate religious medal and a copy of her thesis on the traditional culture of Huaycopungo for a high school equivalent degree in the local bilingual institute (Criollo Perugachi 1995–96). He begged my forgiveness and stated his intention of resuming our relationship.

Later in the day, a young girl approached me during the procession, holding tight to her younger sister and grabbing my arm as I danced past. "Allow me to present you to your goddaughter," she said. I realized I was talking to Francisco and Asciencia's older daughter and tried to greet young Rocio, who buried her head in her sister's clothes. We huarmicuna danced on, and the moment was gone. These are but two of the poignant examples of the reconnections explicitly made because of the fiesta.

There are at least two, seemingly conflicting, motivations for this setting aside of old slights and factional feuds during Corazas. The first is self-serving. Once a person is publicly recognized as a resource for aid in a number of forms, it is not in one's best interest to snub that potential largesse. In fact, it is a good idea to publicly claim any social connection one has.

On the other hand, the whole focus of Corazas as a religious ritual is to celebrate the elevation of some individuals but in the process mold that elevated status into a moral form that benefits the majority. Through ritual, people are ratifying a social order in which sources of extraordinary resource richness, whether human or spiritual, can be cajoled, feted, and honored to the point that they share their wealth and other bounty with others less fortunate. This reciprocity not only gives the cosmos a sacred order, binding humans to powers greater than themselves, it also creates a community. Elevating people to such exalted status creates the moral obligation for them to continue to remain enmeshed in the webs of reciprocity, to which they can contribute so much more than the ordinary. Leadership and even periodic expressions of extreme hierarchical divisions between people can be made to bind people together into mutual obligation as effectively as they can be united by symmetrical reciprocity. Francisco and Asciencia, an ambitious couple, would aspire to rise to the top of that system rather than remain outside it. Finally, the extent to which the leaders of the whole are exalted is a measure of the wealth and power of the group as well.

Almost certainly the sense of unity and resource bounty experienced by individuals in the community, in which I was included for the extent of the ritual, would be ephemeral. Nonetheless, the public acceptance and commitment to those norms means that such community unity is believed to be real and attainable. Also real is the idea that individuals of unusual material and immaterial resources can be a resource for the whole. Certainly Huaycopungo has individuals who pursue personal and family wealth by cheating their family and neighbors, hoarding their excess, and avoiding reciprocal responsibilities. All economically successful individuals and aspiring leaders are suspected of exploiting others in that way, although fewer do so. People who have been successful leaders for a number of years often do conform to the expectation of being soft-spoken, self-sacrificing, and humble. They successfully mobilize the labor of others and, under their direction, generally desired outcomes are realized, like the provision of abundant potable water. Leaders regularly tell stories of their suffering in the service of others and of the unfair suspicion directed at their labors by their fellows. But they also support the traditional morality that a good person ceaselessly helps others in the name of community. The Corazacuna—prioste, Loa, Yumbos, and huarmicuna—act out that self-sacrificing suffering under public scrutiny during the ritual. They are publicly honored and recommitted, along with the participating community, to a moral order in which the power of the mighty has a sacred base, and as such serves the interests of the weaker majority.

Again, this ritual must have seemed particularly necessary to some of the organizers now that Huaycopungo is divided by economic class. Could local class distinctions, and even international divisions of wealth, be transformed into resources for the whole? Could Huaycopungo continue to be characterized as a field of continual reciprocity and mutual aid despite the fact that everyone was no longer equally poor? Quoting Appadurai, Colloredo-Mansfeld states that "'generations easily divide as ideas about property, propriety, and collective obligation whither [sic] under the siege of distance and time' (Appadurai 1990; 18). Migration and the expanding economy erode the commonalities of Otavalo's social world" (1999, 27). Could the efforts of Huaycopungo's leaders forestall this "irreversible fragmentation," as Colloredo-Mansfeld terms it? How potent for the symbolic message of Corazas must have been the participation of a foreigner, who, despite her higher social status and superior economic resources, and despite lacking a birthright in the runa culture of Otavalo, nevertheless publicly accepted the moral order proclaimed in the ritual and provided an uplifting example for those who were born in Huaycopungo. The answers to the questions posed here, however, remain for the future to answer. Still, in 2000 an ideological recommitment to the goal was made.

Transnational Corazas

In conclusion, the seizing of the reins of control of Huaycopungo by the indigenous secular authorities from the local mestizos has been counterbalanced by an opening of the desired field of relations well beyond the community. When Huaycopungo's relations with the outside were almost uniformly exploitative, the leaders sought to seal it off ideologically, if not actually, from the outside world. The desired fiction was that it was an autonomous world unto itself. Now that the balance of power over indigenous issues has shifted into indian hands, not only in Huaycopungo but in Otavalo and perhaps even Ecuador as a whole, Huaycopungo has become ideologically part of the world. Not only do its citizens travel to every corner of the globe selling handicrafts, andean music, and their own charm, and not only do they make efforts to attract foreign tourists to them at home, they define their own relevance and identity with a much more transnational reference. Natives of Huaycopungo can live in Amsterdam and, contrarily, native North Americans like myself can be treated as genuine parts of the community. This bid to use generous gifts of love, exoticism, and service to compel return largesse in the form of economic aid and a boost to their own symbolic capital may be a short-lived strategy. The heady thrill of a soaring symbolic capital will fade as it becomes less novel, and unless a boost to economic capital follows, another strategy is likely to be devised. Still, taking the risk of committing the andean version of orientalism, I confess to being amazed at how successfully these Otavalans can take on the world and make it conform, at least in their own eyes, to long-standing andean goals and values.

Que Viva Runa Causai
Long Live Indigenous Culture

The Postcolonial Derivation
of Seemingly Ancient Andean Culture

WITHOUT SOME SENSE of continuity and the confidence in local expertise that results from that sense, people can become overwhelmed and directionless, especially in a period of rapid change. Cultural traditions, the guidelines for living that are passed on with transformations over the generations, can provide that sense of purpose and faith for one's self and community. At the same time as they provide ballast to keep the society afloat and on course, cultural fields must change to adapt to both minor oscillations and more permanent alterations in the environment as broadly conceived. In the Andes, as in many other places, it is impossible to separate the physical from the cultural environment; the mountains are personages as well as places. The pace of that change worldwide has presumably quickened in the last century as the last outposts of isolation from the expanding centers of political and economic complexity have succumbed to inclusion, and ethnically defined peasantries around the world have become incorporated into the global economy. The need for cultural continuity takes on a particular poignancy among the descendants of conquered peoples who, for whatever complex of reasons, have been neither completely

Fig. 52. Long live Huaycopungo
(PHOTO BY JACQUELINE PURCELL CALLISTER)

displaced nor completely assimilated in their native lands, but who have remained ethnically distinct.

When we attempt to understand people who have self-consciously maintained traditional continuity as minorities within an encompassing and dominant society, we can focus either on the continuity or on the change, on the authenticity or falsity of either tradition or innovation. With the exception of some sectors of academia, the most common perspective has been to see cultural persistence as doomed, ceding to incorporation in one uniform transnational culture; this is taken for a truism without need for explanation in many self-congratulatory sectors of the United States. Nonetheless, even the United States continues to have indigenous people who, while vastly different from their ancestors of one hundred or two hundred years ago, are still recognizably different from the majority in the United States in aspects of their cultural identity and still demonstrate thematic continuity with their cultural past. This cultural persistence can manifest itself in surprising ways and linger far beyond what would be predicted by the inevitable assimilation model. In addition, "traditions" can be found to have shallow roots, even if they seem to link to the distant past. If not strictly speaking "invented" in the sense of inauthentic (Hobsbawm and Ranger 1983), they can be shown to be a half-conscious attempt to connect to the past as imagined. In some respects, Otavaleños may be more "andean" than they were a century ago. Lastly, we must examine the fuzzy border between reenactment and authentic performance. I remain convinced that, however much a mix of the two, the 2000 Corazas displayed a rich and sincere symbolism that went beyond a dramatic portrayal of something that had been authentic ritual in the past. However invented or reimagined, ritual by its nature penetrates and projects the consciousness of the participants. Cultural continuities in the face of substantial change deserve more recognition and explication.

Nonetheless, it is not the persistence or continuity per se that this book has taken some pains to demonstrate, but the form and process of combination, innovation, redirection, and change of emphasis that result in the balance, or potential imbalance, of persistence and change that characterizes this case from highland Ecuador. The explanation for cultural continuity lies partially in the creative transformations that are made to adjust the traditional and make it contemporary and vice versa. Although Huaycopungo and other communities of Otavaleños have undoubtedly experienced peaks and valleys in their adaptive success and sense of pride and accomplishment as a people given their social and physical environment, the overall trajectory of history from the present vantage point seems to suggest considerable efficacy and buoyant ethnic pride under challenging circumstances. Certainly, the size of this indigenous population in the region is both a reason for this success and a measure of it.

This balancing act has entailed performing mini-pachacuticuna, using the Quechua term loosely, on a regular basis. Such symbolic reversals could ensure continuity while simultaneously making 180 degree shifts in ways of making a living, interacting with local authorities, and relating to the dominant Catholic Church and its rivals, among other adaptive strategies. A number of cultural themes and practices that loom large in depictions of the precolonial and early colonial periods in the Andes still hold true in Huaycopungo today, despite five hundred years of immersion in a hispanic American world. In fact, in many cases, these cultural patterns have seeped into the hispanic American world as well. Among those that have persisted among the indigenous Americans are the following patterns, which we have examined in the previous chapters. Precolonial andeans drank asua as part of religious ritual, in a religion that was not a separate domain of its own but integrated thoroughly into political, economic, and domestic life. Secondly, ancient andean religion was particularly characterized by the union of what we would call secular political concerns with sacred matters and the enactment of these themes and principles in public rituals (as was Christianity in the colonial period and beyond). Lastly, paradoxes and other dualistic forms were useful in social organization, philosophical thought, and ritual to anchor the sacred to the physical and social environments through movement that united space and time. As we have seen, these patterns are still alive in Huaycopungo.

But rather than representing the faithful transmission of pure native culture over five hundred years despite the odds, alcohol use, politicoreligious ritual, foundational polarities, and an emphasis on creating order through motion between places and states shifted considerably over time, becoming part of a new Ecuadorian interculture, even a global interculture (Meisch 2002). In the introduction we examined how ritual alcohol use probably gained greater symbolic stature in native culture after the conquest and the imposition of Christianity than it had held before. Ritual drinking could be continued under the pressure of Catholic evangelization, whereas other native religious practices could not, because the hispanic cultural models of drinking provided an excuse for the practice that protected it from accusations of religious heresy. It was not considered religious behavior at all. However, this continuance of ritual drinking under the pressure of cultural domination entailed an increasing combination of two ethics of drinking—one that was believed to ensure spiritual health and fortune for native people and another that severely threatened their wellbeing in both senses. Shared drinking served Huaycopungo's natives as a positive symbol of their resistance and spiritual validation, but was for nonindians a devastating sign of indian degradation. This parallels the distinction between clean mestizos and dirty indians so important to mestizo racial views, as analyzed by Colloredo-Mansfeld (1999, chapter 2). When agriculture was a viable way to make a living, being "dirty" could be embraced by indigenous people to mean a positive and morally superior choice to plunge one's hands and feet into one's own patch of earth, but when making a living entailed travel and marketing in more urban environments, it seemed closer to the stigmatizing of their whole bodies meant by mestizos. The view that alcohol use was an embarrassing weakness was by no means unknown or without influence within the indigenous community as well. Complex combinations and juxtapositions of these two ways of judging the morality and social benefits of drinking characterize what it meant to drink in Huaycopungo, and other andean communities, in the recent past.

The salience of the dynamic interrelationships of polarities and the fecundity of paradoxes can be subjected to similar analysis. Did this premise persist, and perhaps even take on added significance, in the local worldview into the modern period? Or might these purposed cultural survivals from the precolonial era be some form of "invented tradition" (Hobsbawm and Ranger 1983)? The historical record and the wide distribution of certain dual forms and their interactions throughout the Andes ensure their authenticity as traditions in the present. In addition, a principle this ubiquitous and persistent must still convey significant benefits to those andeans who claim to be indigenous in their home regions. Indeed, with the prevalence of international travel, trade, and television in the contemporary indigenous world today, there may be a potential for global advantages as well. When searching for factors in the interaction of the indigenous and dominant societies that could explain the seeming persistence, and perhaps even intensification, of the principle of dynamic polarities, one immediately encounters the centrality of dualism in the colonial and postcolonial enterprises of the conquerors, their descendants, and their apologists. Elites in both colonial and national governments typically use such concepts as race and ethnicity to define and confine native peoples to a low position in the status hierarchy and ensure their own monopoly on societal privilege and power. We, the progressive and civilized, are contrasted to the others, defined by complex intersections of race, ethnicity, and class, who are backward, brutish, or inferior. Boundary making is a constant preoccupation, however contentious the terms of definition and enforcement may be. Images of dirty, drunken indians versus clean and civilized mestizos represent the polarizing tendencies of Western hierarchies of value at least as much as some andean philosophical dualism.

Nor is this Euro-American dual model and concern with boundaries entirely static, since hispanic migrants to the Americas have been preoccupied with the proper status of intermixtures as well. Mestizo is a significant category in the status hierarchy all over Latin America. However, in some important respects, its symbolic boundaries with other, purer categories have been more often essentialized than fluid in Ecuador. At certain times and in certain places individuals have been able to cross into higher categories, and the acceptable symbolic behaviors within a status may be somewhat flexible, but to be mestizo is to be not-indian.[1] As Townsend demonstrates for Guayaquil on Ecuador's coast in the early nineteenth century, since there was little hope of social mobility in what she calls the "middling ranks," effort for social prestige was placed in distinguishing themselves from the indigenous masses (2000, 153). This pattern continued well into the modern period, especially in those regions of the Andean highlands where there continued to be significant numbers of indigenous masses from which to distinguish oneself. Individuals may be able to move from one status to another, but they can't be two things at once. Even more important, the hierarchical relationship of categories cannot be flexible and context sensitive. While mestizos and indians can share some aspects of character and history, these social and cultural interchanges do not equally empower both groups. Indians are overwhelmingly indigenous and inferior because of it; mestizos are only touched by the stigmatized characteristics of indians and at best only in a romanticized past.[2]

Still, the rhetoric of Ecuadorian nationhood today claims that national identity springs from a certain relationship of oppositions and mixing that can be employed in a chameleonic way (Klor de Alva 1995, 263). To be a true Ecuadorian, as in many Latin American countries, is to represent the historical mix of colonists from Europe with descendants of the conquered native populations of the coast and the mountains and, to a lesser extent, African slaves. For nonindian Ecuadorians this mestizaje, or process of mixing, was combined with an ethic of progress that always led to an overwhelming commitment to the Spanish language, Catholic Christianity, and modern development. Unlike a

Euro-American heritage, an indigenous ancestry cannot serve as both a link and a springboard to a contemporary center of political and economic power; all Native American empires were destroyed over five hundred years ago and have not risen from the ashes. Again, the difference between the indigenous and mestizo perspectives is one of emphasis. Here, this national formulation proposed a single trajectory, with one thing becoming another, with the indigenous providing the base but becoming progressively obsolete with the developmental advances. Of course CONAIE and other successful indigenous political contenders for national authority are currently challenging this model.

Despite the centrality of the Westernizing model for Ecuadorian mestizos, the promotion of the mestizo character of the nation can be used pragmatically in different ways. For instance, it can indicate an Ecuadorian connection to and sympathy with the indigenous perspective, resulting from the past genealogical connection, which is missing among pure white Europeans or North Americans. In turn, this connection has resulted in alternate advantages and disadvantages for real living indigenous people. An extension of civil rights to indigenous people and a willingness to appreciate differences in culture is one alternative. Contrarily, subverting indigenous political power by claiming the right, by mixture, to represent the interests of this segment of society and flaunting the more colorful aspects of indigenous tradition in order to garner the cachet awarded the indigenous by the national or international elite for themselves (Crain 1998) have both been results of this claim to a mixed heritage. Both of these tendencies have influenced the indigenist political movements of the recent past in Ecuador, which have nonetheless achieved previously inconceivable levels of national efficacy. The envy of whatever advantage indigenous people may claim—the moral legitimacy given Amazonian natives by the Western left or the economic success in marketing folklore internationally achieved by Otavaleños—is powerful right through the upper middle class (Meisch 2002) even as it is utterly baffling to them, brought up as they were in the idiom of hygienic racism (Colloredo-Mansfeld 1999. 85).

Andean people of the past, faced with this preoccupation with dualisms among their colonial and postcolonial masters, must have at least partially recognized the similarity to their own dualistic formulations and the even greater difference in the Western models' lack of dynamic character. In this context, their own traditions became imbued with a renewed and transformed meaningfulness. While the conquerors sought to limit their own acquisition of native habits and beliefs, many native people actively tried to maximize their control over sources of power both indigenous and European in origin. While the conquering elite remained pure and thus more powerful in their own eyes, they could be construed as incomplete in the minds of the conquered masses, like a man or woman without a mate, an upper moiety without its lower counterpart making a productive whole, an indigenous community without both Taita Inti and Taita Dios. If the indigenous people could furthermore imagine contemporary socio-cultural hierarchies as shallow and reversible, at least in theory, they could experience themselves as possessed of double power of a sacred kind, rather than condemned by their inferior culture to a supposedly natural powerlessness. And they could act it out in the Corazas fiesta or during San Juan/Inti Raymi. Since the colonial, and postcolonial, condition is to be immersed in supposed binaries of inside/outside, oppressor/oppressed, civilized/primitive that must be both suffered and resisted (Klor de Alva 1995), then a two-sided perception of the world made doubly perfect sense. It offered a cultural escape from the realities of domination and impoverishment in their own lands. The impoverished people who manage to believe in their own sources of power are more likely to maximize the available practical opportunities to enhance their position by finding loopholes in the system or by orchestrating strategic resistance than are those who succumb to imposed powerlessness. Again, it is the addition of their status as conquered *masses*, rather than tiny minority in the statistical sense, that fosters and reinforces this symbolic source of power.

Cultural mixing among indigenous Otavalans has been demonstrably greater than among Ecuadorian mestizos, despite the latter's name and definition. While modern socially conscious mestizos in Ecuador often eschew guinea pig and home-brewed corn beer as too indigenous,[3] and thus stigmatizing, in favor of chicken and aguardiente or bottled beer, native Otavalans require the serving of both guinea pig and chicken, both chicha and aguardiente when they celebrate publicly. The clothing that people in Huaycopungo wear daily to proudly proclaim their separate ethnicity combines elements of Incan, colonial Spanish, and more modern Western provenance. While indians mix cultural elements and do not consider themselves mestizos because of it, mestizos try to be as Western as they can, while proclaiming their past genealogical mix with indians. For example, well-meaning mestizo parents lectured me repeatedly against allowing my six-year-old daughter to wear the indigenous jewelry she loved so much because of its stigmatizing effects. This separate strategy for cultural mixing can be seen as another opportunity, or sociocultural niche, that people who claim a persistent indigenous identity and social adaptation have found to exploit. It has developed within a hegemonic series of narratives that falsely essentialize binary distinctions in order to maintain social dominance and political control.

Just as the ability to mentally accept and behaviorally enact two cultures of drinking, preserving the best of the past while giving the dominant society what they wanted, led to the persistence and transformation of ritual alcohol consumption, the conceptual emphasis on binary oppositions in their transformations helped outwit the religious literalists among the conquerors intent on converting indigenous people to some form of Catholic orthodoxy in order to better control them, or the nationalist forces committed to modernizing the nation by eliminating stigmatizing remnants of the indigenous past. The Janus-faced reality made plausible by andean ways of thinking was a perfect adaptation to a social system bent on eliminating cultural heterogeneity as part of nation building while simultaneously dependent on keeping the descendants of the conquered people an economically and politically dependent class easily identified by observable cultural difference.

One way the local elite adapted to postcolonial regional stagnation was to allow the descendants of the conquered people to remain on the land to which they had sacred and historical ties, leaving them enough freedom to enable them to feed themselves while sufficiently restricting their self-determination so that their labor could be mobilized in the service of the majority at any time. This pattern had a historical precedent in colonial times, when there were too few Spanish immigrants to successfully run the country, and indigenous communities were administered through their local headman and middlemen of a variety of ethnic backgrounds. Full acculturation to the majority by indigenous people in such conditions was neither probable nor desired. Acculturation generally removed individuals and families from the indigenous category altogether, making them impoverished mestizos or, somewhat more likely, a category of mestizo wannabes called cholos. This strategy was therefore rarely chosen in those areas where indigenous identity gave individuals rights to productive resources, whether in free communities or on haciendas. In contrast, it was the reluctantly pursued option of those who, for one reason or another, could inherit no land (Crespi 1975). An opposite determination to wholly resist hispanic cultural imperialism would have been possible, and then only partially, solely for those who fled to establish a life of extreme geographic isolation in areas with harsh environmental conditions. Nonetheless, armed uprisings did occur and probably contributed to a mitigation of oppression, if not its overthrow (Moreno Yanez 1978). The resulting partial economic self-sufficiency and independence of the peasants had an unfortunate side effect for the architects of hispanic hegemony; it gave the native people space for reinforcing cultural autonomy as well.

The andean tolerance, even a preference, for paradoxes—equally powerful, but opposing, explanations or sources of power—gave their particular adaptation to colonial and postcolonial processes a unique character. Rather than being restricted simply to choices that pleased, or did not merit the censure of, the dominant society, there were a number of choices the indigenous people could employ to demonstrate satisfactorily to the outside that they were leaving behind their primitive native ways and simultaneously to strengthen a renovated religion and worldview with deeply native roots—right under the noses of the national agents of control.

In fact, religion likely took on a new importance as a particularly potent source of legitimization and justification of a way of life when that way of life became threatened by outside control. Religion is not just a refuge from political and economic realities but also an expression of the nature of power in the universe. This power takes on a particularly political character in the intersection of cultures among peoples of vastly unequal power. After all, the Inca ruling elite had used overarching religious forms very effectively to bind culturally distinct peoples of the Andes, with their own shrines, deities, and ancestors, under the cultural umbrella of the empire and thus to sustain political dominance. The Spanish had contrarily tried to eliminate native religion and replace it with a sacred justification of their own power and hegemony, only to accept, grudgingly and in a piecemeal fashion, a similar melding of two traditions, with their own religious tradition overwhelmingly supporting the structure of imperial and later national power. But local people could turn the process on its head, with religious forms helping an embattled minority maintain some cultural self-determination in the context of encapsulation and domination. In the absence of demonstrable political or economic power of their own, their control over sacred sources of efficacy could not be so easily disproved or dislodged. The spiritual domain provided a real source of psychological power for seizing every small opportunity that presented itself for gaining an advantage.

Many peoples around the world have experienced the problems of forced acculturation in the wake of colonialism and its aftermath, and the most successful have made compromises that satisfy the oppressors while preserving some separate sources of cultural self-definition and judgment, especially through religion (for example, Comaroff 1985; Comaroff and Comaroff 1991, 1997). However, the forms of and justifications for the resulting syncretisms and juxtapositions of earlier and imposed or borrowed beliefs or behaviors are not all the same. Some may consider themselves fully acculturated, while continuing to practice forms with a long precolonial history, or contrarily find the hybrid state to be the most meaningful, even the default position (Amselle 1998). What is deeply andean about the patterns I am investigating is the emphasis on polarities persisting while engaging in multiple permutations over time, leading to Isbell's often repeated description of andean culture as "a kaleidoscope of mirrored images" (1978, 11).

Staying within the framework of postcolonial categories and dualisms but moving away from issues of cultural mixing in Latin America, we might also consider the generalization made over half a century ago about the status of African Americans in the United States by W. E. B. DuBois ([1903] 1969). As he noted so insightfully many years ago, suffering an inescapable subaltern status, whether for reasons of race, ethnicity, class, or gender, creates a "double consciousness," a two-sided and contradictory consciousness of self and culture. What DuBois was particularly interested in naming, and then working to eliminate, was the part of African American consciousness or identity that accepted the judgment of the dominant society that African American persons and culture were inferior and backward. This kind of inferiority complex arises when people grow up enmeshed in social relations and webs of signification that degrade their person and exploit their lives—such as viejos chumados or indios sucios, old drunks or dirty indians.

Like others in similar conditions, indigenous people in Ecuador frequently experience this reluctant and partial acceptance of the inferiority attributed to them by their oppressors. However, the ability to see—or rather the culturally inspired inability to ignore—the imposition of inferiority by ethnic others as necessarily calling up its opposite, a sense of great self-propelled ethnic pride, is the strength offered by the opposed nature of reality among such andean societies. If we go back to Carpenter's (1992) proposal that the andean self has two sides, one that can be influenced from outside and the other that wells up unbidden from inside, we find again a formulation of possibly ancient derivation that served remarkably well as a defense against the sort of double consciousness that DuBois was so angry to report. Otavalans do, in fact, suffer the conflict of a negative and outside-imposed view of themselves and a contrasting and inwardly generated positive sense of identity. However, the cultural schema that explains these perceptions and feelings as a source of spiritual strength and generative power would certainly have an intense appeal for individual actors in this system. Furthermore, the availability of this explanatory model would have different consequences than the one that African Americans seem to be burdened with, which challenges them to seek and attain the positive and eliminate the negative.

In fact, more modern formulations of the subaltern condition, especially in "postcolonial" contexts, highlight the opposite aspect of the double consciousness described so early by DuBois. For example, Klor de Alva speaks of the emergence of a "contestatory/oppositional consciousness . . . which fosters processes aimed at revising the norms and practices of antecedent or still vital forms of domination" (1995, 245). The dominated usually know their oppressors more thoroughly than the latter know them, so that they can better oppose or subvert the hegemonic control over political processes or systems of meaning. The power of those above one in the social hierarchy must be truly appreciated in order to be able to find the available, and ever-changing, niches for self-expression and a limited autonomy of action. Until recent decades, the contestatory/oppositional consciousness was more likely to be expressed in ritual, such as during San Juan or Corazas, as a counterfoil to an opposite demonstration of the divine right of contemporary hierarchical forms. Exalted leadership was alternatively symbolized as of a sacred nature and productive of the best of all possible worlds and lampooned as the delusions of grandeur of those who failed to see their own human failings or misguided cultural myths. This relationship to hierarchy applied both within the indigenous community, to relatively powerful local individuals and families, and outside, to the mestizo and white elite, whether local, regional, or national. The power derived from the ritual overthrowing of authority was more likely to mobilize people to find weak points in the walls that confined them than to directly assail those walls. Since the levantimiento indígena begun in 1990, overt political opposition has taken precedence over more ritualized and symbolic forms of resistance, likely continuing a pattern of alternation with a long history.

Finally, the introduction of new contrasts and conflicts has been spurred on by the expanding global system. Otavalo, through the tourist industry, the international export of native handicrafts, and the explosion of long-distance travel for sales and performance, has been immersed in international systems of meaning for several decades. The segment of the modern international markets in which Otavaleños work exposes them most often to quite complimentary versions of their own identity. Rather than directly facing the exploitation of the undereducated and impoverished minorities that is the reality of North America and Europe, for example, they experience the attraction felt by relatively prosperous and adventurous Westerners to the exotic "Other," especially in the form of ruthlessly clean, carefully dressed, and respectful andean natives. Foreign anthropologists, middle-class tourists, and travelers seeking spiritual or drug-enhanced enlightenment all serve as mirrors to native Otavalans, holding up to them an image of an exploited but pure, attractive, and spiritual version of mankind that they have paid money to come see. What a difference from the more common local mestizo image of their indians as dirty, drunken, uneducated louts! Still, Ecuadorians from outside the highlands are likely to consider the native Otavalans the most civilized of the degraded and pitiful indigenous Ecuadorian lot.

In these new polarities, pitting Ecuador against the United States or European nations and the troubled national economy against a global market in which they can sell their ethnic wares, the Otavalan natives have again found entrances into sources of power through the manipulation of contraries. They can accept the management of money, modern conveniences, and the status of international travel as forms of capital, both social and material, for the improvement of their lives, while doing so strictly in the idiom and for the purpose of enhancing their identity as indigenous people, as they define it. And they can recognize the compliment, and potential economic competition, offered by the mestizo Otavalans who now grow their hair long and don ponchos in order to board a plane to Europe, Japan, South Africa, or the United States, where they will play folkloric andean music and sell handicrafts to the foreign middle classes hungry for the ethnically exotic.

It is true that many cultural traditions, such as the moiety system, have become decreasingly meaningful to the people of Huaycopungo in recent years with these social and economic transformations. However, now the distinction between Protestants and Catholics has absorbed some of the same functions. Groups of Protestants and Catholics are sometimes united in cooperative enterprises, sometimes counterposed in bitter conflict: nearly equal, but generally ranked, with Protestants the older siblings of modern Catholics. They engage in oscillations of relationships over time, assuming special importance in the ritual season, now mostly confined to the week following the summer solstice and dedicated to both San Juan and the Sun. So, too, do foreign communities of Otavalans in Madrid or Chicago still sometimes behave as if their outposts were both replicas and parts of home. Lund Skar (1994) noted this pattern for contemporary Peruvian Quechua colonists from the highlands to the jungle and the city, Colloredo-Mansfeld (1999) described "transnational archipelagos" for the Otavaleños who make their homes abroad, and many researchers have detailed the same pattern for the Incan outposts in the multiethnic Andes of the precolonial period. While the intensity of reciprocal relations and density of social networks created at home have waned somewhat, Otavalans attempt to create intense, if not socially dense, relationships to substitute all over the world. If travel is necessary for economic survival and success, then far-flung compadres and in-laws will substitute nicely for those at home who used to share agricultural labor during labor-intensive seasons in the past. As Colloredo-Mansfeld notes, "Relationships, not formal contracts, structure much of Otavalo's million-dollar transnational industry" (150).

What the Future May Hold

Despite the renewed life that modern conditions can give to ancient forms, both symbolic and behavioral, the cultural complex that gives people the most meaningful choices today is not at an end point but in a transitional period between yesterday and tomorrow. Let me further explicate my perspectives for this analysis of continuity and change in Huaycopungo by considering what I think the future might bring. This is attempted with all the humbleness a respectable social scientist can muster, since individuals and events not anticipated could greatly skew the likelihood of any particular outcome. And by the time this is published, it will be recent history rather than a contemporary portrait, in any case. Let us take in turn the fate of ritual drinking and problem drinking in Huaycopungo, of the balanced opposition of Protestants and Catholics, of the unorthodox and "indigenous" forms of religious expression in both forms of Christianity, of dual forms in dynamic interaction as a principle of social organization and more general systems of thinking among indigenous Otavalans, and, finally, of the self-projection of indigenous ethnicity among Otavaleño Ecuadorians who are eagerly becoming part of the global village.

Huaycopungo cannot go back to the drinking norms of the past, where control over the quantity consumed lay in the sacralized environment, not the individual. Self-control of consumption, whether it will be through moderation or abstinence, is now inescapably part of what it means to consume alcoholic beverages in this community, as it is among most Otavaleños and Ecuadorians in general. In some respects this is a general process associated with greater urbanization and integration of peripheral areas into a modern nation (Segal 1987) worldwide. Moderation can be defined as an attempt to exercise self-control over the amount, speed, or duration of consumption. Catholics in Huaycopungo generally believe that escalating binge drinking was the problem. Drinking on a few ritual occasions to a point short of maximum intoxication for a duration of only one or two days would be an acceptable model of moderate drinking. They also support supplying less potent forms of alcohol during these occasions, nonalcoholic beverages to supplement or substitute for alcohol, and abundant food to go along with alcohol to reduce the effects of binge drinking. Faithful evangelists support total abstinence. Since a combination of these two practices is supported around the world today as means to avoid alcohol-related problems, both are likely to remain as options in Huaycopungo as well.

However, this change in orientation did not eliminate problems with alcohol altogether. For some, their plight has most likely worsened. Some alcoholics of the previous period continue to suffer from this addiction. No longer can they be seen as basically upstanding persons who suffer one of the inescapable risks of human existence in the pursuit of generally treasured social and spiritual states. Now they are personal failures, individuals who cannot seem to uphold the moral values of their own community. Chunda Fucu is one of those unlucky individuals. He and others like him have become doubly afflicted by alcohol. Furthermore, there is greater stigma attached today to the minority of families whose troubles are exacerbated by a heavy drinker in their household.

Nor can the new values entirely overcome the more modern expectation from the outside world that alcohol abuse is part of the rebellion of adolescents and young adults. As they become more assimilated to their nonindian schoolmates, many younger male Otavaleños will become tempted to try alcohol and other drugs to be hip and daring. Perhaps young men will become more susceptible to alcohol addiction than they were before, while the risk for developing dependence will be reduced among older men and women. If addiction is developed at a younger age, problems of drained family resources, domestic violence, and child neglect may increase in both frequency and duration. This seems to be a greater problem in other communities of the cantón so far, particularly the town of Otavalo, with the more traditional family relationships and cultural continuity serving to discourage adolescent males from following this path in Huaycopungo.

On a positive note, women today have a greater expectation that they can form the productive partnerships with their husbands lauded in the ideal form of traditional families, which the Protestants have made part of their reformist platforms. It is with a visible relief that women report and promulgate the new views about drinking. For Catholics, a few binges are manageable, even pleasurable, if kept relatively short-lived, but the vast majority of money coming into the family will now be used for education, food, clothing, and small household appliances—in that order—and if finances permit, a car and a modern house. For Protestants, the hope is that alcohol will not take one dime away from these family expenses, although more money can be spent on decking the church building out in splendor.[4] The financial investment in spiritual benefit has not ceased altogether.

What is important about this case is not that a group was able to eliminate alcohol-related problems, but that they could enter a period of greater suffering due to binge drinking and rather than being overcome by such dysfunction, turn the community around and take steps that would reduce new cases of addiction and opportunities for abuse. Frequently, minority communities that experience increased alcohol-related problems are reported as having succumbed to an inevitable and nearly irreversible process of social and cultural devastation, whether blame is placed on the minority cultural heritage or the effects of social and economic marginalization by the dominant society. Clearly, some communities in Otavalo are not as lucky as Huaycopungo in mitigating the problems so quickly and effectively. Norm cascades are not predictable (Kuran 1995a); small changes in the choice thresholds of a few individuals in different communities could prevent a cascade altogether, despite a situation similar in most respects to that in Huaycopungo. So can an earlier or more thorough growth of class distinctions, resulting in the poorer drinking more than the more prosperous, as happened in some of the more northern communities of the cantón.

However, another reason for the poor prognosis reported for minority communities could be that the expectations for enduring problems constitute a self-fulfilling prophecy much like the expectation of inevitable cultural extinction in the face of global expansion. Whether they are condemning or sympathetic, observers from dominant societies may see what they expect to see. And when the minorities are not so large or protected by alternative sources of ethnic pride, their ability to triumph over adversity may be overcome by the prevailing prophecy.

The division of Huaycopungo into evangelistic and Catholic halves, with which individuals can align themselves rather freely, is probably an enduring adaptation. Some possible challenges to that pattern could come from increasing reincorporation into the regional, national, and international institutions of either denomination. The local bishop is very liberal, having told José Manuel Aguilar, for instance, and much to the latter's surprise, that Catholicism and Protestantism are sister forms of Christianity. Like others in Huaycopungo, Damiano Taita grew up believing that only Catholics were Christians. However, in the fall of 2000, Pope John Paul II announced that the bishop's view was an error and that the Holy Roman Church was the prior and truer form of Christianity. Should this renewed conservatism become a crusade of the church under this pope's successor, liberal clerics in the Ecuadorian Catholic Church could be marginalized and pressure put on native Catholics in Huaycopungo to leave the church or toe a conservative line. Cardinals are increasingly being selected from Latin America, not only to represent the proportion of the world's Catholics in that part of the world but presumably to reinvigorate them with commitment to the contemporary church's conservative positions. Similarly, a renewed and successful movement on the part of the international evangelical organizations to reincorporate the diffuse Latin American flocks into the fold could marginalize José Manuel Aguilar and others like him in favor of those who would fight for the primacy of the Protestant Church, conservative Christian orthodoxy, and the exclusion of non-Protestants or unfaithful Protestants from the church family. For the time being, the independence of the local religious sects seems secure and related to the general sense among Otavalans that they are seizing power over their persons, their communities, and their territory that they lost over five hundred years ago.

Similarly, the balance of religious traditions from orthodox Christianity and indigenous Christianity and older forms of religion will continue for some time to come. The example in the last chapter is a case in point. And since 2000, San Rafael has witnessed self-conscious public rituals led by yachaccuna that purportedly reproduce pre-Columbian practice faithfully, without the admixture of Christianity, although the participants are all *also* Christians. The efficacy of ritual performances in a number of domains, from fixing sacred values and goals in the local people to attracting international tourism and engaging in symbolic national political action, make them invaluable in the present. The lack of detailed indigenous knowledge in the young adult generation, whose members have spent too much of their life in a monolingual and monocultural school system that still preaches vestiges of the progressive rhetoric designed in the 1970s to homogenize Ecuadorian citizens, makes the continuity of a rich local tradition vulnerable. Counteracting that, however, is the keen interest of young adults, international visitors, national indigenous organizations, progressive national elites, and activist organizations within and beyond the country's borders for researching and resuscitating native traditions. Such pressure will ensure a great effort is made to revive seemingly dead traditions and reactivate ones, like Corazas, that seemed on the verge of extinction a short while ago. In an interesting trend, the communities of San Rafael are trying to claim a monopoly on the performance of Corazas, claiming, inaccurately, that it was solely a tradition, and now a touristic product, of their region, making the Peguche Corazas bogus. Beyond that, there is enough overlap in local rural culture across the indigenous boundary to help keep certain traditions alive and to amplify the enduring ways of thinking that will always survive the pressure of the national and international hegemonies.

The fate of the dynamic interrelationship of polarities as a preferred format for thinking and social organization is more difficult to explore. Up until the present, this conceptual tradition has been so deeply ingrained in Otavalan life, bodily memories, and thought that it flourished without any conscious attention. Since it included the more familiar form of treating oppositions preferred in Western thought— where boundaries were primary, conflict the norm between opposing groups, categories, or concepts, and hierarchies fixed—the contrast between the two ways of thinking could go unnoticed most of the time. Indians and nonindians could certainly agree on the fixed, conflictual, and hierarchical aspects of the relationship of oppositions, while the former could add to that other sorts of relations and transformations at will and without any discomfort. But it is precisely this overlap that makes a slow and painless slide away from the andean dual world into the contemporary Western one, much as must have happened over centuries in Europe after the Middle Ages, a possible outcome. A similar example already discussed in chapter 4 is cantina drinking, which did slide imperceptibly over time from a slightly more commercial form of a boda huasi, whose goals were the reinforcing of social and spiritual values, into a capitalistic form of exploitation and mildly antisocial recreation. Another is the area of gender relations, which have become more basically patriarchal at the same time as public rights for women have expanded. Traditions that are cut so deeply that they are traversed without conscious effort, but which nonetheless share a portion of track with outside traditions of an overwhelmingly opposed destination, can lead to a similarly unconscious shifting of direction toward the alien cultural destination.

The most insidious force against the continuation of such forms of knowing comes from the school system that Otavalans have embraced so enthusiastically in the last few years. Just the sheer volume of time that young Otavalans spend in the company and direction of agents of the dominant society, with few exceptions, and the corresponding lack of time they spend with elders or on traditional tasks whose customary forms so often underscored these more general themes, gives nonindigenous ways of thinking priority. Despite heroic and well-meaning attempts to have bilingual education counteract this cultural shift, several factors work against its overall success. First, since it is a relatively new form of education, it suffers from a lower reputation than the more established schools. Second, the rectors and teachers and curriculum developers, like my compadres Francisco Otavalo and Asciencia Criollo, themselves got their positions after a thorough passage through the modernizing school system. Finally, traditional kind of knowledge is implicit rather than explicit and was transmitted in the past through reiterated examples and embodied memory practices (Abercrombie 1998; Wogan 2004) rather than through teaching. Just as it is hard to find out how children in the United States with ardent feminists for parents learn stereotyped gender roles so well and so early, it is hard to counteract the early influence of mestizo thinking and inculcate indigenous alternatives in the school model.

Similarly, the activist movements that have so galvanized the indigenous civil rights movement in Ecuador over the last three quarters of a century come from the same tradition of progress toward a more rational future. Since contemporary indigenous culture so clearly arose in conjunction with domination and oppression, it must be thrown off like other shackles in order for the people to be free. Even though some of these movements are explicitly indigenist, some of them have moved into a more essentialized notion of what it means to be indigenous and away from the focus on bipolar self-direction toward univalent self-assertion.

Nonetheless, one must assume that certain habits of action and expression will continue to carry forward this preference for the dynamic interrelationships of polarities, even as they become weaker in their force. One finds loud echoes of older Native American ideas in the modernized tribes of the United States today, even though the young often have trouble integrating them into their world. Since popular culture in the Andean region of Ecuador has partially expanded to include indigenous songs and music forms, for instance, to some degree stimulated by tourism and the international interest in "world music," local hip-hop can easily promote more indigenous ways of perceiving and processing reality. Lastly, the desire to keep fiestas alive in some capacity must provide opportunities to rehearse older forms of social and spiritual orders to the younger generations. Anywhere indigenous adults occupy roles of creative authority will be found the possibility that they will develop social and symbolic forms that convey that traditionally paradoxical sense of meaningfulness.

Like both Colloredo-Mansfeld and Meisch, I worry about the effect that developing class differences will have on the future of traditional Otavaleño values. The former even suggests that the new "real" indigenous Otavalan will be the wealthy: "As the market unevenly elevates the amount of cash circulating within society, the basic means of social participation, from rituals to architecture to outfits, becomes more expensive" (1999, 222) although he recognizes that in Ariasucu in the 1990s "being a good *runa*, a good indigenous man or woman, means continuing to farm and to invest in and to honor obligations of mutual assistance with family, neighbors and compadres" (220). The process began later in Huaycopungo, and the particular leaders of the last few decades have been truly gifted in rekindling the communitarian values in the altered economy. I wonder about the next generation, more subject to the propaganda of the mestizo school system, but also increasingly exposed to self-conscious indigenous revival. Ultimately, Colloredo-Mansfeld, Meisch, and I all seem to remain in awe of the abilities of the native people in Otavalo to persist and change in equal measure and remain linked to the past and efficacious in the global present. "My basic argument is that Otavalos are coping with globalization by relying on a combination of traditional values and practices and modern technology to preserve as well as market their ethnic identity, including others' (mis)perceptions of them as Incas or noble savages" (Meisch 2002, 10).

The Difference between
Preservation and Self-Determination

Especially for my students and others with the same influences on their thinking, I want to argue from my experience with the literature on Latin America and with the people of Huaycopungo that a lot of time is wasted in the United States concentrating on cultural preservation as the best and only hope for ethnic minorities who suffer from ethnic/racial stigmatization in the social hierarchy. The greatest tragedy is not that they were exposed to a stronger foreign group that forced them to change, since that is presumably the condition of most of humankind at one time or another in history. The worst devastation to a conquered people occurs when the victors have the desire and the capacity to remove all self-determination from those they now dominate and then to blame the victim when social problems ensue within the subjugated group. Cultural mixing is one of the great creative strengths of being human, right along with cultural innovation. Having one group of people's mix of cultural continuity, innovation, and borrowing be almost entirely determined by another group deprives the former of social agency and therefore threatens the mental health of many of its individuals. All peoples are constrained by others in their social arrangements and cultural themes, even superpowers. When that constraint becomes a straitjacket, simultaneously restricting initiative and serving as a stigmatizing sign of inferiority, people's initiative in finding alternate sources of validation, pushing back the walls of confinement, or turning their attention into making their little patch of space a garden of delight becomes critical.

All North Americans have become partially African American in culture, partially Jewish, partially hispanic, although no one has attempted to force them in that direction and they remain relatively unaware of the fact. Some scholars even claim that Native American political ideas influenced the founding fathers of the United States, especially as regards the implementation of a federalist system. Depending on where we live, our cultural makeup is more or less affected by any sufficiently large minority group with whom we share our towns and neighborhoods, whether we realize it or not. The point is not to preserve perfect minority—or majority—identity and heritage, whatever that could possibly be given the variations within any labeled group, nor even to have individuals replicate faithfully the lives of their own grandparents. The point is that to the extent that individuals and families wish to make a group identity part of their own, these groups should be free to interpret their past and fashion their future in their own creative way, as do those groups who occupy the more powerful positions during any particular period. This is not to say that we can escape the legacies of unequal power, since that is also a fact of life, but I would suggest we lament more the attempts to keep individuals from wearing running shoes on the grounds that it would violate their "indian" heritage than we weep for the sandals they no longer wear or their bare feet. If the Incas had invented that combination of rubber and canvas shoewear, with light-emitting diodes on the side, we would be favorably impressed. We should lament a group's lack of power to fashion its own identity through tradition, innovation, borrowing, and mixing more than any specific elements of the past that have become forgotten. Otavalans, as have many other ethnic minorities that resulted from colonial and postcolonial processes, have been creative and agile enough to keep their eye on the validating past while leaping into the future and landing on their feet.

Appendix One
Issues of Ethics and Objectivity

In 2000, journalist Patrick Tierney published *Darkness in El Dorado: How Scientists and Journalists Devastated the Amazon*, a book that accused journalists and scientists of cultural imperialism of the worst kind in the northern Amazon. The book caused an uproar in the anthropological community, made front-page headlines in many U.S. newspapers, and led to upheavals in Amazon regions. His sensationalist claims were a mix of detailed and careful research and reporting; the uncritical acceptance of personally, professionally, and politically motivated exaggerations of questionable practices; and sloppy science regarding vaccinations and the spread of disease. Tierney's accusations were unfortunately sometimes facile, such as accusing someone of an unacceptable practice by the standards of 2000, when the practice was considered acceptable in 1960, when it was performed, or grossly exaggerated, such as claiming that Yanomamo warfare was the result of Napoleon Chagnon's research interests, or just plain wrong, such as the charges that Chagnon and James Neel spread measles and refused vaccinations to people they knew to be at risk or gave vaccinations they knew to be dangerous. Some of the results of these accusations were tragic in the short run. For example, some native groups began to refuse all vaccinations for fear of poisoning. However, the intense soul-searching it prompted in the anthropological community was one of the best results of the book's publication. According to Jane Hill, chair of the El Dorado Task Force established by the American Association of Anthropology: "The most critical thing we learned is that these people [Yanomami Indians] are really in terrible danger. . . . This is a critical situation that threatens their very existence." One incidence of ethical violation by anthropologist Chagnon was substantiated by the committee: that he bypassed official channels when he was denied a permit for research from Venezuelan authorities and enlisted wealthy, and purportedly corrupt, associates of the Venezuelan president to continue this work, without taking any standard precautions to protect his research subjects. Furthermore, although this did not rise to the standard of an ethical violation, it was agreed by the committee that Chagnon did not work hard enough to prevent his oversimplification of Yanomamo culture from being used by others in ways that stigmatized them and supported the abuse of their human rights.

The scandal that erupted in the anthropological community as a result of Tierney's book prompts me to try to reach an even deeper level of transparency with regard to the research that produced this book. Particularly, I would like to address the potential of my actions over the years to cause, fail to prevent, or perpetuate harm to Huaycopungo and its people, and secondly, to the possible effects of my involvement on the research results. In some respects, this is a chimerical attempt, since it would be precisely what I cannot recognize myself, rather than what I have pondered deeply and am able to articulate, that could be the source of problems for the people and this written account.

Regarding the ethics of anthropological research first, let me use as a guide the charge given the American Anthropological Association Committee on Ethics in response to Tierney's book. The committee was asked to consider the following:

1. their [anthropological researchers'] responsibility to provide assistance when study subjects experience health emergencies
2. the level and kind of remuneration to subject populations and individuals that is both appropriate and fair
3. the impact of material assistance provided to subject populations

4. the potentially negative impact of factual data about a study population on such population
5. what constitutes valid and appropriate informed consent in anthropological studies. (AAA, e-mail to members, December 14, 2000)

Taking these concerns in order, I will make a few observations about my own experiences. Like many anthropologists working in rural areas at the time of my dissertation research, I brought along copies of *Donde no hay doctor: Una guía para los campesinos que viven lejos de los centros médicos* (Werner 1980) and the *Merck Manual of Diagnosis and Therapy* (Berkow 1977). The first, which was published in English as *Where There Is No Doctor*, is a user-friendly guide to basic medical practice for nonspecialists, and the second is written for people in the medical field but is also useful for dealing with patients who have no easily accessible Western medical care. But San Rafael had a clinic, staffed every two years by another young doctor doing his or her compulsory rural residency. And Otavalo had a hospital. One way I maintained reciprocal exchanges with local people was through informal health aid, such as providing transportation to medical centers, dispensing a layperson's advice on illnesses, and advocating with doctors. The latter was probably the most significantly beneficial. I left my health books with women who were training to be health promoters when I left. During two health crises, the 1987 earthquake and the 1991 cholera epidemic, I was not in Ecuador, although I do remember some shoveling to clean out the school in response to a damaging mudslide in 1978. In general, this concern did not apply during my research.

The second charge to the AAA Committee on Ethics is to consider "the level and kind of remuneration to subject populations and individuals that is both appropriate and fair." This has been a delicately negotiated terrain that has shifted over the years, as my potential to pay and their need and expectation for greater monetary remuneration have both increased. In the late 1970s and early 1980s, I made gifts of Polaroid snapshots of the family to any household that consented to an interview. To my research assistants, I gave occasional gifts and later paid slightly over the local minimum wage for hours spent going house to house for formal interviews. When my research is more informal and unsuited for hourly compensation, I have relied on gifts and favors. Because Isabel Criollo has frequently been my research assistant since 1978, I have made it a point to aid my two godchildren generously while providing gifts to her, her husband, and her other four children. With such relationships, I have attempted to reduce the potential for my becoming simply a foreign benefactor and maximize my participation in local webs of reciprocity at a level appropriate to my greater source of funds. To some extent, this is a fiction in which we both collaborate.

Furthermore, I decided to reimburse the community for allowing my study of them with a portion, roughly 10 percent, of any salary I received based on the Ph.D. I was able to earn with their help. I solicited and received proposals for community projects and, using my own experiences in grant writing, I guided community leaders toward practices in soliciting and administering grants that could also help them with future national and international funding. In addition, completely independently, my parents had established a charitable foundation whose main interest was in natural resource conservation and whose largest project was in Ecuador. During the late 1980s, the Butler Foundation began making a number of small grants to Huaycopungo's community projects in response to requests too large for me to consider. The largest project with the greatest impact was contributing to a major expansion and overhaul of the community's inadequate potable water system in 2000.

It is hard, probably impossible, for me to fully assess the impact of this material assistance on Huaycopungo. Could it have harmed individuals or the community as a whole? Since community envy and infighting over resource allocation is inevitable and ceaseless, I am accustomed to accusations that I have favored some over others or that certain people have taken advantage of me and left their fellows empty-handed. Since I live so far away, I can usually ignore such complaints, taking comfort in the arguments of the responsible individuals who defend my actions and in the fairness and transparency of the actions of those who assist me.[1] My closest associates have personally suffered, however, but then that is the price of leadership at all times. The value of my contributions to Huaycopungo seems to me and to others to outweigh my implication in some of the infighting or the personal pain of my closest associates, who have never asked to be relieved of their role. Overall, the small sums of money involved, the careful procedures followed for choosing which projects to fund, and ensuring that the funds are spent in the proposed manner have made significant long-term harm relatively unlikely.

In fact, I believe that the benefit to the community has been significant, far outweighing any harm. Furthermore, my decision to repay the community through financial contributions seems ethically defensible as a means to reduce the significant differential of both symbolic and financial power that gives me greater access to them as research subjects than the reverse. The arrogance of academia in my country, the superior resources available to American researchers, and my own relative good fortune in recent years have made it possible for me to attempt to interpret them for publication. They could not do the same for my community, should they so desire. I cannot merely revel in their quaint customs and ecologically friendly technology without recognizing that they suffer many of the disadvantages of poverty anywhere, including poor health, food shortages, and discrimination. I cannot solve these problems, but I would argue that it is ethically better to provide some kind of help than none at all. According to their own ideals, we have continued to engage in exchanges from which we both benefit. Let me quote a recent letter (dated December 30, 2000) from José Manuel Aguilar:[2]

> En los próximos años, queremos presentar *proyectos productivos*, que generen fuentes de trabajo, para que la inversion sea dirigído para el progreso de toda la gente que habitamos en Huaycopungo. Tenemos en la mente realizar proyectos de Salud, agricultura, artesanías, capacitación o educación, becas y intercambio de estudios técnicos y científicos con otros países. Con estas obras la gente indígena seguirá progresando y mejorando su calidad de vida y contribuir a la solución de la crisis del Ecuador. Para lo cual rogamos que no nos abandone nuestra area de trabajo, es decir a la comunidad de Huaycopungo, por cuanto con sus proyectos estamos seguros que saldremos adelante toda la comunidad.

> [In the coming years, we wish to present *productive projects* that generate job opportunities, so that the investment will

be directed toward the progress of all the people who live in Huaycopungo. We plan to accomplish projects in health, agriculture, crafts, training or education, scholarships, and exchange programs in technical and scientific studies with other countries. With these efforts, the indigenous people will continue to progress and improve their quality of life and to contribute to the solution of the crisis in Ecuador. For this reason, we beg that you not abandon our area of work, that is to say, the community of Huaycopungo, because with your projects we are confident that we, the whole community, will come out ahead. (my translation)]

The fourth concern of the ethics committee was "the potentially negative impact of factual data about a study population on such population." This book examines the use and abuse of alcohol and the extent to which heavy ceremonial drinking led, given particular circumstances, to addiction and other problems in an indigenous community. It is conceivable, although unlikely, that this book might foster a reputation for being "The Drunk People," comparable to Chagnon's epithet "The Fierce People" for the Yanomami. In Venezuela and Brazil, this reputation for fierceness was used opportunistically—by politicians, miners, and others whose interests were inimical to the Yanomami—to justify inflicting all sorts of human rights abuses on these previously isolated people. However, the study of the ritual use of alcohol among the indigenous peoples of both the Andes and of Mesoamerica has a history that begins in print from the colonial period. More importantly, in Ecuador, the indigenous reputation for being a bunch of hopeless drunks has been used opportunistically for centuries to oppress the native people. I can only hope that my account, which lays bare this history of cultural conflict, prejudice, and discrimination, causes no further harm.

Finally, let me consider informed consent. At no time during my stays in Huaycopungo have I been confident that the majority of people have a good grasp of what I am doing there as a professional anthropologist. Only in recent years has formal education made more than a handful of people sufficiently sophisticated about my goals. Still, most people are more likely to accept me simply as a person rather than form a judgment based on the merits of my professional role and credentials—as long as I avoid doing anything of which they disapprove, they allow me to continue taking notes or asking questions. The increasingly informal nature of my visits has obviated the need for strictly formal requests for consent as well. In practice, a careful explanation of what I am doing to everyone who asks or whom I interview and a consultation with a variety of local leaders about my goals and plans have constituted seeking informed consent. When my visits were for longer periods of time and included more formal research agendas, I also sought permission from the appropriate Ecuadorian authorities for the acceptance of foreign researchers within their borders. Additional consultations with community leaders and other individuals named in the book have accompanied the preparation of this manuscript, although I have not made the manuscript available to be read in its entirety by anyone in Huaycopungo.

Turning to the second set of concerns articulated by Tierney in his critique of Napoleon Chagnon and others but outside the scope of the AAA Ethics Committee, let me share some of my thoughts about how my long-term involvement may have influenced the account you read. Despite its multitude of weaknesses, Tierney's *Darkness in El Dorado* echoes many other, more reputable sources on the subject in suggesting that despite Napoleon Chagnon's claims to have obtained unbiased data in his study of the Yanomami, his social relations and interests indubitably influenced individuals and events he recorded and witnessed. Since humans are such social creatures, a researcher who actually achieves a position on the local social radar, particularly if he or she is perceived as representing a source of power that the local people cannot access directly without the researcher, will influence local events.[3] In the context of social relations where the subjects want what the researcher is perceived to control, an ethnographer's research and personal interests, such as Chagnon's on male competition and violence, may have an effect on what the researcher actually sees and records.

One of the main themes of this book is how the culture of an ethnic group and its social boundaries are created and maintained in joint production between groups across those boundaries. I am but a bit player in that process. Certainly my presence over the years has barely registered on the consciousness of the majority of Huaycopungo's inhabitants and, until recently, while many people may vaguely recognize me during my short visits, they forget who I am most of the year and have to be reminded when they see me again. I was an important part of the childhood of a few individuals and thereby became an indelible part of their world. Many more children have become adults without our ever having meaningful contact. They don't know who I am and I don't know them. Nevertheless, the symbolic meanings associated with my relatively high status in Ecuador and my being a native of the United States are extremely provocative for considerations of ethnic identity and the nature of ethnic boundaries.

In fact, several individuals tell me repeatedly that I am a major force in their personal lives. While some percentage of such statements is flattery, there may be something to what they say. Two individuals in particular, Isabel Criollo Perugachi and José Manuel Aguilar Mendes, are leaders in their community—the latter perhaps the most important of the last ten years. It is entirely possible, but not certain, that their perceptions of my values and beliefs color their decisions about how to relate to individuals or plan activities for groups. What follows are examples of how I may have influenced individuals' judgment in Huaycopungo, some of which were intentional, some unwitting, and others even against my will.

An example of my most deliberate intervention might be my strong insistence on complete transparency in requesting grants. The problem is not so much that someone may want to hide information from potential grantors but that conventions of how much to reveal and how much to gloss over in order to be polite, to please, and to convince are different in anglo and hispanic America. Since a group of early Protestant converts had suffered greatly from not doing so in the past (see chapter 8), and since such transparency upholds the highest community ideals although it violates more pragmatic community practice, my views were not the only ones that influenced behavior, although I was verbally given a lot of credit.

In a less intentional example, my apparent approval of traditional values of leadership, an approval so lacking in the local nonindian society (if idealized by educated nonindians living distant from concentrations of indian people), has motivated the individual leaders I referred to in their work, although I had no intention of influencing them. They feel empowered to continue the soft-spoken, self-sacrificing, and group-cohesive roles that brought prestige in their pasts rather than adopt a more assertive, even aggressive, leadership style, which would be more generally valued in the dominant society. Leaders have repeatedly told me—and I am now beginning to accept its truth—that my moral support for their efforts has been extraordinarily beneficial: my single most important contribution.

Lastly, my behavior may have helped justify a change of which I do not entirely approve. In my early fieldwork, I struggled to emotionally accept the view, then popular among young educated Americans, that the material poverty of people in Huaycopungo—living in a one-room, dirt-floored house without electricity, running water, or even furniture—was more ecologically sustainable than our way of life and potentially as healthy. After all, weren't Boy Scouts and Girl Scouts made virtuous and healthy by going camping with only a sleeping bag and mess kit (in those days before fully equipped campers)? I wanted to convey the notion to the people of Huaycopungo that they were not inferior because of this aspect of their lifestyle. Material poverty, with the exception of poor food and health care, could be seen as evaluatively neutral or even, perhaps, morally superior to the accumulation of material wealth. They themselves, using Christian ideals, often claimed the same thing, denouncing their greedy nonindian neighbors.

However, at the same time, I took my closest collaborators, particularly Isabel Criollo, with me to elite restaurants and other public places in the capital and elsewhere, where indians would not have been allowed entry without my presence. It was difficult for both of us sometimes, and we both wavered occasionally in our stubborn defiance, but my impression was that it was as gratifying for comadre Isabel as it was for me. She was already engaged in indigenous activism before I ever met her, having even spent time in jail for her activities. We practiced looking aloof and comfortable chatting with each other while the patrons stared at us with a mixture of surprise, curiosity, amusement, and disgust. By doing this, I wanted to convey the message that in my view the indigenous Otavalans had equal rights to any kind of lifestyle, just as I had been taught as an upwardly mobile middle-class white person from the East Coast of the United States.[4] Far from being detached, then, I actively fought for my egalitarian values in their defense. But now that they have incorporated innovations like birthday parties (complete with paper plates, cups, and napkins; commercial cakes; and streamers); have begun to accumulate nonbiodegradable garbage; and have purchased blenders, refrigerators, bicycles, boom boxes, televisions, and sometimes even cars, they expect my wholehearted approval. Perhaps my view that they had the right to anything they could afford was added to the other justifications people used to so thoroughly change their lifestyle, even though I would have preferred that they see more clearly the dangers in materialistic consumerism and adopt a more ecologically friendly compromise.

I am still open to charges that I have bought my results, that people tell me what I want to hear and stage what I would like to see in order to please me and keep the funds coming their way. Of course what I have seen and been told has sometimes responded to my perceived desires, despite my efforts, irritating to them sometimes, to remain noncommittal about important local issues. Still, it is not possible for everything reported here, or even the majority of my description and analysis, to be a joint production for our mutual benefit. First of all, despite the importance of interacting positively with powerful outsiders in order to improve their view of themselves and their image in the larger society, my impact—personal and financial—has not been that great. The weight of the daily life of a community with a few thousand people in a complex society with a far-reaching national media—print, radio, and television—overwhelms my contribution, as do their history and their goals for the future. As we are well aware in the wake of postmodern challenges to simple empiricism, it is not possible for me to achieve an account unmediated by my interests, my ideologies, my biases, my interactions with the subjects of the study. We can only hope that the balance is reasonable and the most striking potential sources of biases transparent. However beneficial, my material assistance has only reinforced directions and accomplishments that would have occurred without my presence.

Appendix Two

The Sounds and Writing Conventions of Ecuadorian Quichua

This is a simplified version for speakers of English, so that they will be able to read the words in the text relatively accurately. Among further refinements necessary for a more authentic pronunciation of Otavalan Quichua, particularly significant would be rules of aspiration.

The Sounds of Quichua

a	=	as in *father*
ay	=	as in *high*
b	=	as in *book*
c	=	as in *cook*
ch	=	as in *church*
d	=	as in *dog*
e	=	as in *Katy*—not as long or diphthongized as in one-syllable English words such as *bay* or *made*; not a Quichua vowel; used sometimes in Spanish words; often substituted by *i*
f	=	as in *fun*
g	=	as in *good*

gu	=	as in *quick* (with more aspiration than *way*); from Spanish; used only for proper names with this conventional spelling
hu	=	as in *quick* (with more aspiration than *way*)
i	=	as in *accordion*
j	=	between the sound in **head** and *Ba**ch***
ju	=	as in *quick* (with more aspiration than *way*)
ɪ	=	as in **l**ook
ɪɪ	=	as in *measure*
m	=	as in **m**easure
n	=	as in **n**ot
ñ	=	as in the kid's taunt **ny**a, **ny**a, **ny**a**ny**a, **ny**a, **ny**a
o	=	as in **o**at; not a Quichua vowel; used sometimes in Spanish words; often substituted by *u*
p	=	as in **p**at
qu	=	as in **c**at
r	=	pronounced either as an initial "r" with the tongue in retroflex position against the alveolar ridge (flapped as in Spanish; no English equivalent) or the same flapped "r" preceded by the sound in *measure*
s	=	*as in* **s**un
sh	=	as in **sh**oe
t	=	as in **t**alk
ts	=	as in *Bo**ts**wana*
u	=	as in **d**o
v	=	as in **v**et or **b**et or in between
y	=	as in **y**et
z	=	as in **z**oo

In multisyllabic words, the stress consistently falls on the penultimate syllable. That rule continues to hold when words are modified by grammatical infixes.

The Conventions of Writing Quichua

The orthographic conventions of writing Quechua (or Ecuadorian Quichua) have by no means become generally accepted, although there are a number of relatively politicized efforts to accomplish this unification. Ecuadorian Quichua is a variant of Quechua that lacks the phones /e/, which is an allophone of the phoneme [e,i], and /o/, which is an allophone of the phoneme [o,u] in other dialects of the language. In general, Ecuadorian Quichua is more phonologically assimilated to Spanish than some other variants of Quechua. An example would be the elimination of separate phonemic status to some aspirated and nonaspirated consonants.

My own exposure to written Quichua has been quite variable. Some formats are closer to international linguistic conventions and others are more assimilated to Spanish orthographic conventions. The Universidad Católica in Quito has been in the forefront of an effort to promote an orthographic system, called *Quichua Unificada*, that will facilitate the reading of Quichua by people who speak the range of dialects found from north to south in Ecuador.

To add to the difficulty of choosing a way to write Quichua, the phonology has been changing somewhat in recent decades and has become more assimilated to Spanish. More Spanish words are acceptable in general Quichua speech, and pronunciation of Quichua words has changed. So decisions must be made whether to write a word in a form that more closely replicates its older pronunciation or whether to approximate the most common speech of today. Most particularly, as Quichua speakers become bilingual in Spanish, they have begun to use the phones /o/ and /e/, which they did not use in the past. In the 1970s, a common male given name was universally pronounced /Jusi/ in Huaycopungo; today it is pronounced /José/. Words and names derived from Spanish, or sometimes Quichua words that merely seem similar to Spanish words, are first to experience the substitution of /e/ for /i/ or /o/ for /u/, often in a pattern of hypercorrection. In other words, some /e/'s are substituted for some /i/'s when /i/ is in fact correct. For example, they may call a *misa* (Catholic mass) a *mesa* (table). The spelling of the name Huaycopungo has changed over time, but that is the most common variant used today, including the letter *o*, which represents a sound not previously used in local Quichua. The name is still often pronounced more like *Huaycupungu*.

I prefer the conventions that most approximate the Spanish because (1) most native Quichua speakers learn to read first in Spanish and

I have seen native speakers who read Spanish well unable to read the "unified" Quichua promoted by the Universidad Católica; and (2) because Spanish has a long history in the Andes. I do not see the advantage of teaching people who are—most optimistically—going to be literate in two native languages to learn two different orthographic conventions. Of course, there are precedents in other parts of the world—even multiple orthographic conventions for one language, such as Japanese. Nonetheless, it would seem to slow the advancement and acceptance of bilingualism in Quichua, which is a threatened if not imminently endangered language in Ecuador, to teach those generations newly literate in Spanish another set of orthographic conventions (or linguistics) before they can read their native language. Further, it is very hard to accommodate proper names of Quichua origin or Quichua words commonly used in Spanish that have a conventional spelling— like the capital Quito or the nearby city of Guayllabamba. It seems a bit overly restrictive to insist that they are written differently when one is using them in a Quichua-language context rather than a Spanish-language context.

Every system that I have seen includes advantages as well as characteristics that I find distinctly annoying. I also have a high tolerance for mixing multiple orthographic conventions; I frequently fail to notice inconsistency when I am reading, and I have been known to use two or more forms in the same sentence myself. However, I know that my using mixed conventions in this book would be a disaster for the reader, so I recognize my responsibility to pick one consistent form.

I have studied with Dr. Carmen Chuquín, former instructor of Ecuadorian Quichua at the University of Wisconsin–Madison, off and on for a number of years. She promotes an orthographic form different both from the "Unified Quichua" and from the hispanicized conventions. She takes a much stronger stand than I would advocate on preserving older phonological conventions and eschewing the addition of Spanish or Quichuaized Spanish words in the lexicon. However, since I do not feel either qualified or entitled, as a native English-speaking professor of anthropology—not a native speaker, an Ecuadorian, or a linguist—to take a public stand in the political struggles being waged over this unifying effort, and in honor of Dr. Chuquín's efforts to maintain and promote the Quichua language at the Universities of Illinois and Wisconsin, I have decided to choose the orthographic convention she uses for this book, with some minor modifications. Rather than use the letter *w* for the /w/ sound, I generally use the hispanic convention of *hu*. And rather than using the letter *k* for the sound in *cat*, I will most often use *c* when that is the more long-standing convention and, more rarely, *qu* when that spelling has a long history in Ecuador.

Notes

Preface

1. *Mestizo* and *mestiza* are the masculine and feminine nouns (or adjectives) referring to people of presumed *mixed* Spanish and indigenous genealogical heritage. More practically, it means those who may have indigenous ancestry but who embrace the hispanic-Ecuadorian culture and Western ideologies of civilization and progress today. It literally means "mixed," but in the period under discussion here, however mixed the cultural fields may have been in actual fact, the prevailing goal of nonindigenous Ecuadorians (and some indigenous Ecuadorians) was to escape the stigmatizing indigenous past, wipe out any indigenous elements they could identify, and clearly demonstrate their modernist outlook.

2. A cantón is an administrative unit of territory similar to a county.

3. *Mama* and *Taita*, Mother and Father respectively in Quichua, are honorifics like Mr. and Mrs. then in use for most adults. *Tia* and *Tio*, Aunt and Uncle respectively in Spanish, were used for young adults only. In other parts of Otavalo at the time, Tia and Tio were much more general, Mama and Taita being used only for elders. This pattern has spread to San Rafael in the intervening years.

4. Although Berta Ares Quejía has never returned to Ecuador, for a number of years she kept in contact with the family. At some point the connection lapsed and for some years people have made unsuccessful attempts to locate her, including through the Internet. In 2004, I successfully found her on the Web and, I hope, helped bring them back in touch. I say I hope because both parties keep telling me how their phone calls and e-mail messages are never answered.

5. Transnational identity usually refers to native people who maintain ethnic identity and even community in the developed countries. However, I think it can sometimes be applied to natives of developed countries

who have a lifetime of involvement in native communities in the developing world, especially when it is the latter who are determined to have the prestigious foreigner play that role.

6. The other godchildren include a girl, now a young woman, from a neighboring community, unrelated to Isabel and José Manuel; Isabel's sister's daughter; José Manuel's sister's son; and José Manuel's maternal uncle's son.

7. The words *hispanic* and *indian* will not be capitalized in this book in order to draw attention to their use as a conventional—but very inexact and sometimes inaccurate—generalization. The hispanic people we are talking about are not literally from the hispanic peninsula but from Ecuador, and the indian people are not from India at all. When *andean* is used to call attention to a culture area, rather than as a geographic designation, it also will appear without capitalization. All these generalizations mask a great deal of social and cultural variation among the peoples so labeled.

8. Since 1987 I have also served on the board of directors of the Fundación Maquipucuna, a nonprofit organization dedicated to the conservation of Ecuador's biodiversity and the sustainable use of natural resources

9. Throughout Latin America, the relationship between godparents and the parents of the godchildren is as important—and sometimes more important—than that between godparents and godchildren. They are called co-parents and one always uses the title compadre for a man or comadre for a woman in both reference and address. Furthermore, all the relatives of the ritually established co-parents (excluding the actual godchildren) are co-parents with each other as well. To use the term is to make a claim for certain kinds of respectful behavior and mutual aid.

10. The indigenous pronunciation is *culira*.

11. In the interest of full disclosure, my father was a very successful businessman before his retirement and in 1987 began sharing his acquired wealth with his daughters. Before that I was rich in Otavalo's terms only.

12. Quite reasonably, many Ecuadorians from the majority culture see Americans as being dupes of the politically savvy indigenous people, who struggle to convince the naïve foreigners of their superior innocence.

Acknowledgments

1. Adults are most commonly known in their own community by nicknames, which are frequently passed on to their children. There is a greater likelihood for men to acquire nicknames in their lifetime (as also stated for the Salasaca area of Ecuador [Wogan 2004, 54]), but both men and women inherit nicknames from their parents, most often their father. The nicknames of illustrious individuals persist long after their death.

2. When I was preparing my dissertation proposal, Casagrande gave me some advice, which I confess I ignored. He suggested that I look at nonverbal communication in the broadest sense as a way to investigate the ethnic boundary in Ecuador. How do mestizos and indigenous strangers recognize each other as such? In Otavalo, where the indigenous people so proudly proclaim their ethnic identity in clothing and hairstyle, these more subtle distinctions were less relevant.

Introduction

1. The dual nature of the relationship between the hispanic and the indian exists most clearly at the level of ideology or folk social analysis, while the relationships of people with a variety of connections to one genealogical history or cultural exposure or the other are far more complex than this statement about "two social groups" implies.

2. It is a source of resentment for many Ecuadorians that white people like me from the United States can benefit from racism in our own country and then come to Ecuador and criticize so vociferously the racism there. I share their frustration because they do the same to us, but I recognize that in the social hierarchy of the world system, we North Americans can see ourselves as superior from our exalted "first world" perch while we look down on their "third world" backwardness. Thus is our criticism that much more galling. To that I can say only that I recognize my extraordinary privilege and assert that all the European-derived and American-molded blends of tolerance and intolerance can be found in both countries, each with its own particular flavor and permutations of ingredients.

3. Although *blancucuna* or "whites" was a labeled category, this formulation plays a less significant role in the period under discussion, in part because the indigenous people rejected the claims of the majority of nonindians in Otavalo to racial purity and extreme social superiority. It is also a measure by some Otavalo's mestizos to deny special blanco status to some in their midst. Meisch discusses it as a category, like cholo, which has dropped out of use or been combined, as in blancos-mestizos, in recent years (2002, 203). I think it is also because the traditional blancos—high-class Ecuadorians by anyone's standards—have not lived in Otavalo for decades or more, having forsaken it for the city.

4. Coca leaves became the source of cocaine during the latter part of the nineteenth century, when Europeans isolated that alkaloid from the leaves. When they chewed the leaves, as was their practice, Andean natives received only a very small quantity of the psychoactive alkaloid that gives cocaine its power, and that was mixed with small amounts of other alkaloids present in the leaf. The main effects were a mild relief from tiredness, cold, and hunger, which some say was like a combination of caffeine and nicotine. Its addictive potential was more similar to caffeine than to nicotine.

5. Nonetheless, in some areas of the Andes, home-brewed corn beer became a standard drink of the mestizos. In other areas, mestizos shunned it, considering corn beer solely an indian drink.

6. Since beginning this book, my own life has been painfully rearranged because of alcoholism. While I can't say that personal experience has motivated or facilitated the writing, I hope that it has further deepened my understanding.

7. Unlike in North America, sex is almost exclusively symbolized as a battle. My runa friends laughed with paternalistic indulgence at our customs of giving flowers and writing love letters to further a romance. For native men, flirting involved stealing an article of a woman's clothes or managing to sneak a pinch of her nipple against her will, and for women devising clever verbal insults that displayed personal knowledge of the individual man.

8. Literally it means "We were drinkers of too much."
9. Pronounced *sentro*, as in Spanish.
10. Meisch explains that this style was copied from the folkloric group Charijayac, formed in Barcelona by transnational Otavalans in the late 1980s (2002, 146).
11. While Ecuador had no legal slavery from the nineteenth century, it was customary to consider the indigenous people who resided on large land-holdings to belong to the land. As late as 1972, I saw an only slightly worn sign saying, *Se vende esta propiedad con sus indios* (This property is for sale, with its indians).
12. The five names represent a conservative and now somewhat outdated geopolitical division of the parish.
13. Huaycopungo Chiquito was later recognized as a separate community that in fact belonged to Gonzalez Suarez parish, not San Rafael. It begins on the other side of the *huaycu* that gives Huaycopungo its name.

Chapter One

1. The suffix *-yuc* is possessive, but in this case is better translated as having a wife or husband be attached or belong to you than as you possessing a wife or husband, since "possession" has such strong connotations of private property in contemporary English.
2. The fact that, when referring to their parental status in general, men are more often said to be churiyuc (possessing a son) and women huahuayuc (possessing a child, no gender specified) deserves some discussion. The other formulations, such as a man being huahuayuc, are equally correct but somewhat less commonly used. Men are by no means considered childless when they have only daughters. But conventionally in Quichua the gender of a group is often specified by the person in the group that the speaker is most closely associated with or whose participation in a group is singled out. A group of people with a mix of genders is referred to as "the women" when your sister is the head of the group or the only person you know personally in the group is a woman. Similarly, it is often appropriate to talk of men's children as their "churicuna" even though they may have boys and girls. This does not really imply a gender preference, only a gender parallelism that is considered particularly salient. Why in this case it is not as common to talk of women's children as their *ushicuna* (daughters) is somewhat puzzling. However, the word *huahua* (child) connotes a young child in a dependent state. My guess is that people emphasize the more symbiotic relationship between women and children over the sex-distinguished parent-child relationship of two individuals. Ten-year-olds take mild offense when they are referred to as *huahua* and not as *cuitsa* (girl child on the verge of or in the unfinished process of puberty) or *huambra* (boy child on the verge of or in the unfinished process of puberty). Still, there is nothing wrong with using *huahua* with a possessive (my, her, their) to refer to an adult when what is communicated is the parent-child relationship. What does *not* seem to be the case is that men prefer to have sons rather than daughters. Both men and women lament when they have only daughters or only sons. Not to have both is considered the unfortunate case.

3. During the writing, in the spring of 2000, Antonio died suddenly of cardiac arrest while carrying out his daily activities. A few days before his death, perhaps with some inkling of what was to come, Antonio approached Isabel to tell her, all rumors aside, that he had not already divided his land assets among his other children but had kept her portion intact as was her due as his eldest child. By asserting that he had safeguarded her inheritance portion throughout the years, he clearly stated that her place in his heart had never wavered.

4. Frequent drinking to intoxication by women was quickly deemed a problem in Huaycopungo, since before menopause women drank infrequently.

5. Susto is a folk illness throughout Latin American with a variety of symptoms (see Rubel 1964; Rubel, O'Nell, and Collado-Ardon [1984] 1991).

6. Rappoport's comments refer to kinship affiliation, specifically agnation, for the rules to exclude when necessary, but this is not meant to imply that the kinship meaning of ayllu is in any way prior in the Andes as a whole, although my own direct experience in Otavalo would lean me in that direction for that region.

7. Ayllu is best described with the term "field of social relations" instead of group or category of people, because the former term refers to the actual people in interaction, not a group of people fixed by lineage or territorial affiliation. The members of an andean group defined by kinship or territory may share a responsibility to behave in a reciprocal way, but the individual members may or may not do so (Sánchez Parga 1989, 39–44). Given this disposition to engage in reciprocal exchange and the differing contexts in which reciprocity is practiced, it can *seem* that people are actively exchanging in this aid *because* they are members of an ayllu, by right of membership according to the operant definition, be it territorial or consanguineal (Bourdieu 1997). In other words, an entity like an ayllu, with its own prescriptive practices, can seem to determine people's relations while it is really an outcome of those relations. Furthermore, in order to preserve the processual generation of differing outcomes in social practice over time and, conversely, to avoid having to explain away the people treated as group members who are seemingly not eligible for membership, I am concentrating on the fields of social relations rather than on social groups. Andeanists have argued a great deal over what ayllu really means, and perhaps we would benefit by considering the act of enmeshed reciprocal obligation as definitive of an ayllu. We would then treat the two types of putative categorical reasons for membership—consanguineal kinship or, alternatively, coresidence in a specific place—as the most common *reasons* for an ayllu developing, rather than as constituting the definitional elements.

8. From *Alabado sea Dios* (Praise be to God). Hassaurek ([1868] 1967, 71) suggested also, based on his stay in Ecuador during the 1860s, that it developed from *Alabado sea el santísimo sacramento* (Blessed be the most holy sacrament). These linguistic origins are no longer in use or recognized, and the single word is used as a polite way to hail and greet someone from a distance, especially when requesting entrance into their space, whether it be a field, storage area, or a house.

9. As Carsten and Hugh-Jones (1995, 3) put it, "In Andean countries, implicit rules concerning the approach of visitors—whether they remain at the gate or enter yard, patio, porch or house—reflect social distance from household members."

10. Cancian (1992) calls attention to the problem of descriptive emphasis; does it matter more that a larger minority of Zinacantecos are well off or that the majority are still resolutely poor? Both have serious consequences. I suggest that the presence of Otavaleños who have not only been economically successful but who have had that weatlh and its social concomitants recognized in mainstream Ecuador, even if they are the minority, opens new horizons for everyone. The stories that more humble Otavaleños feel justified in telling about themselves or dreaming for their children's futures affect what they are subsequently able to accomplish.

11. The younger generation was almost unanimous at the time in asking me to teach them about effective birth control. They thought my having but one child, at the time by choice, was admirable. Government programs provided IUD's in family planning clinics with varying results. Isabel herself was one of the women who developed serious infections with their use. All other forms of birth control at that time had even greater deficiencies for local use.

Chapter Two

1. When I returned to graduate school in Rochester, New York, I unconsciously used these greetings with acquaintances met on the quad. It provoked a mixture of consternation and affront, as I appeared to be prying.

2. Margarita became my comadre when I baptized her daughter in 2004. She is married to Isabel's younger brother Oswaldo.

3. Evangelical Protestantism was part of the mix in the 1970s but was still considered the disloyal challenge of a few. See chapter eight for fuller discussion of the interplay of the two forms of Christianity.

4. It is very difficult to separate imposed Incan beliefs and practices from native ones (Salomon [1973] 1981), and the persistence among contemporary Otavaleños of such Incan practices as the Quichua language and Inca-style clothing for women suggests an active process of syncretism that continued long after the imposition of Spanish rule. One theory is that the Sarance/Otavalo native elite imitated their Incan conquerors in an attempt to acquire the privileges that the Spanish were granting to the Incan elite. The assertion that the last Inca emperor, Atahualpa, was born in Otavalo and/or of an Otavalan mother (he was born in his mother's homeland, which is now Ecuador) was another part of that effort. In any case, the association of chicha with combined political and religious power persists.

5. Skar (1982) speaks of sharing drinks as a "part of Indian hospitality," but the kind of social-spiritual obligations given and received through visiting are too serious and formal for the word "hospitality" to suffice.

6. Montes del Castillo (1989), in a study of compadrazgo in another Ecuadorian indigenous community, stresses the uses of these means to consolidate power over others. My position is that there is always a tension between the interests of reining in individual or family power and the interests of individuals or families to increase their power. Each moment in any society must be examined carefully to ascertain what sort of balance pertains at the time. Both a tendency to level community members' wealth and power and a trend toward the sustained dominance of some individuals or families can predominate in any society, but this balance can easily shift again as circumstances change.

7. This is a clear example of the self-referential aspect of ritual as discussed by Rappoport (1999), whereby the participant has a binary decision to make—to participate or not participate. To participate indicates public acceptance of the canon proposed in the ritual itself.
8. The main grammatical form denoting this combination of intimacy and respect, that so contradicts our own linking of respect with social distance, is the verbal infix -pa-. See a further discussion of this grammatical form in chapter four.
9. While godparents are usually a married pair, and my husband at the time was made godfather in absentia during his namesake, Ricardo's, baptism, the lead godparent in a baptism is often the woman, who holds the baby. *Guaguacuna*, especially *llullu guaguacuna*, who are still nursing, are the special province of women. According to local church practice, for confirmation, the lead godparent of the pair has to be the same sex as the child. This led to a humorous incident when Ricardo's paternal great-uncle chose the author to be godparent to his second son at his confirmation (he was already baptized). We dressed Ramiro as a girl and gave his name as Romelia to the church authorities in order to complete the ceremony. Again, my now ex-husband was not present to make things easier. In the marriage ceremony, the godparent pair is more important than either of the two alone, as they serve both bride and groom equally.
10. At the time of publication, José Manuel had finally managed to take advantage of the changing norms of drinking to maintain his friendships while moderating his drinking by shortening its duration to a couple of hours in any ceremonial event.

Chapter Three

1. The province of Imbabura also takes its name from this dominant mountain. Taita is generally used to address or refer to social superiors, somewhat like *Mr.* in English. More generally, Taita can be used to denote a male ancestor or any social superior, whether living in this world or in eternal space/time. When used in this way, the term implies a social responsibility on the part of the person or personified agent so addressed for the physical welfare of those using the honorific, and, correspondingly, for the speaker's obligation to enhance the prestige, pleasure, and other symbolic capital of the title's recipient.
2. At the time, however alternative and critical my educated perspective, I was ever the North American of my generation. I arrogantly assumed he thought I knew everything, since I came from powerful North America, and I laughingly protested that I was just an ordinary person with but ordinary knowledge of the world. Now I understand that he had been exposed to all kinds of novel information and knowledge in my presence, the limits of which he had no a priori way of divining. Only by trial and error, by blindly asking all sorts of questions, could he get a sense of what I knew and what I didn't. My questions of them could hardly have been less naïve. We seemed equally childish to one another, but my role as professional interpreter of them made my ignorance potentially more dangerous.

3. As Otavalans became more in touch with panandean movements and sources of symbolism, Indi has taken on a greater role in the religious symbolism of Huaycopungo.

4. Auca was the name given by Euro-Americans to a particular rainforest ethnic group in Ecuador, now called the Haorani (see Kane 1996).

5. Nor did I ever make the special efforts needed to study Otavalan shamanism, a somewhat secretive art.

6. Pachakutik is the name of a major political party in Ecuador today, staffed largely by indigenous leaders and emphasizing indigenous issues.

7. Levi-Strauss (1963, 139) discussed the contrast between dual structural models featuring two sides and those featuring a center and periphery. He claimed that the former was more likely to be an egalitarian form, and the latter one would emphasize hierarchy. The two-sided form here references a shallow intraethnic hierarchy and the center-periphery form a very pronounced and ethnically divided hierarchy.

8. Vichai, like janan, signifies above, and here the direction indicated is toward Cerro Cusín, a hill that flanks the high pass at Cajas. Mt. Mojanda is the other flank of the pass and is the orienting point for the janan distinction. All southward travel must go through that high pass. Ladu comes from Spanish *lado*, meaning side, and may have been chosen because it is a synonym for the Quichua word and thereby avoids the ambiguity present in the native language, which distinguishes the different spatial references from context only. The urai distinction in the next line is oriented toward Mt. Cotacachi. In the earlier janan/urai pair, urai referenced Mount Imbabura. Northward travel follows the valley between Cotacachi and Imbabura. Travel toward Colombia, which those of European heritage would call northward, is *uraiman*, signifying downward. Travel to Quito, which we would term southward, is called *vichaiman*, or upward through Cajas pass.

9. In the year 2000, I had told some people in Cachiviro who were seeking my financial help that my collaborative efforts were directed toward Huaycopungo because that is where I had done my Ph.D. research. On the spot several people made the argument that Huaycopungo and Cachiviro are now intermarrying to such a high degree (and they quickly pointed out a number of marriages of people I knew well) that they had become like one community. Therefore, I should extend my aid to Cachiviro. See chapter seven for the recent reductions in the rate of community endogamy.

10. Ares Quejía (1988) searched for derivations of this term, which is only used in this context, and found one reference: in a dictionary of Ecuadorian Quichua y Moreno Mora (1955), which defined *lima* as a scar or tattoo.

11. To be historically precise, the Yumbos lived in the cloud forests to the west and were either in very close interrelationships to the people of Otavalo prior to the conquest or in fact were of the same language family and greater ethnic group. One meaning of the word, then, is to specify a named ethnic group in a specific geographic region. However, since the word in Quichua was also used as to designate the kind of person who lives in a cloud forest or rainforest, it is applied to the Amazonian lowlands as well. It carries the connotation of people closer to the primordial state in all its linked savagery and spiritual power in opposition to the structural order, religious sophistication, and current time placement of the andean runa.

12. A good description of early colonial sacred/secular pageants directed at consolidating the conquest over the natives' minds as well as persons is described in Gutierrez 1991 for New Mexico. Additionally, Dean (1999) describes how the Catholic ritual of Corpus Christi glorified both secular and sacred triumphant conquest over opponents in the Iberian peninsula during the Counter-Reformation and later was transformed with conquered Inca participants in colonial Cuzco, Peru. In the latter case, the indigenous subjects simultaneously acted out a glorification of their own subjugation as directed by authorities and used available opportunities to pervert the colonial intent by performing and interpreting their own political and sacred messages during this most important Catholic feast day.

13. The word most often used, *bailana*, is a Quichuaized form of the Spanish verb *bailar*. The Quichua infinitive for dance is *tushuna*. While the adoption of the hispanicized word may be arbitrary, there is often some reason of interethnic adjustment or hispanicization of native practice in any use of Spanish words when there is a good Quichua word available. I would like to offer the wild guess that this phrase to describe San Juan—to dance—is the mutually acceptable explanation of the holiday. Indigenous people adopted it first when speaking to their hispanic neighbors because it satisfied the latter's prejudices. It stripped the fiesta of its complex and very non-Catholic symbolism and made it secular and entirely understandable as entertainment. Who isn't attracted to an opportunity to dance one's heart out, while, of course, having a drink?

Chapter Four

1. This part of the New World has been very little influenced by the other, and later, European conceptions of the wilderness as the true habitation of God, with the cities representing humans' corrupt nature.

2. This perspective on indigenous prestige hierarchies, first put forward for Central America, has been very controversial. A dissenting view for Ecuador is represented by Montes del Castillo (1989), who claims that the prestige hierarchies enshrined personal wealth rather than leveling it. Similarly, Colloredo-Mansfeld claims that he never met someone in Otavalo who believed in the idea of limited good or "that one family's material success—if gained through hard work—threatened the livelihood of the community" (1999, 93). Huaycopungo in the 1970s was considerably more devoted to subsistence ideologies than Ariasucu in the 1990s, and my view is that the people in Huaycopungo struggled in the last decades to balance the two poles so that they would reap the benefits that the successful can share with everyone without succumbing to a class split. Colloredo-Mansfeld's own insightful discussion of the "discursive force" (114) of the native's use of the adjective *yanga* would lend support to this idea of a more nuanced and variable set of indigenous ideologies of individual, family, and community, dependent on how the particular political and economic environment affects racism and ethnic discrimination and their own participation in the wider economy. Native people frequently refer to what is theirs as *yanga cosas*

(things), *yanga kawsay* (way of life), and *yanga shimi* (language), with *yanga* variously meaning "everyday," "simple," "humble," "worthless," "useless," and sometimes even "indigenous" in a particular reflection of nonindian negative stereotypes. When indigenous people are more rigidly confined, they can make a virture for themselves out of the vice of nonindigenous others. This is where I think so many critics of these older notions, such as "limited good" or the "culture of poverty," went too far. If culture is in fact discursive, then such notions can enter the discourse and affect behavior, even though they are by no means fixed or determinative in any simple way and will wax and wane in importance over time.

3. The most fastidious would express horror at eating guinea pig as well.

4. Here you might want to remember that this is being written by a middle-class woman who has not done research in the cantina.

5. With some regret, I acknowledge that I never made close friendships in San Rafael. When I started my research in 1977, the situation seemed to require a choice between the mestizos in San Rafael or the indigenous people in the comunas, although it was the first schoolteacher to Huaycopungo's children who introduced me to my indigenous research assistant. The former was godmother to the oldest child of the latter. Too many people in San Rafael tried to convince me the indigenous people were dangerous and depraved, or they tried to justify themselves and their own superior civilization too relentlessly. While I have had many friendly conversations with the schoolteachers in Huaycopungo, most of whom are from San Pablo across the lake, we too share very few perspectives. My view of San Rafael is therefore necessarily incomplete and one-sided.

6. So did the indigenous parents with their own toddlers. Mestizos and indians competed with each other to tell my daughter how dangerous the others were. Thankfully she didn't understand.

7. The Spanish-language swear words that indigenous drunks commonly utter in a slurred but emphatic fashion in ordinary conversation, like *chucha* and *carajo*, can stand metonymically for a drunken person.

8. Unfortunately, now that he is grown, it is apparent that no such facility was transmitted.

Chapter Five

1. A reed, like bamboo, which grows in the *páramo*, high-altitude grasslands, and which is used to weave baskets and hats.

2. I presume he means Calpaquí, since I know of no Calpanquí.

3. Ecuarunari was the forerunner of CONAIE, the all-indian political organization active today. Its founding led to the establishment of the Conféderación Campesina in Otavalo in 1974, which later led to the provincial indigenous organization of today: Inrujta-FICI.

4. In many ways this set of laws paralleled the Indian Reorganization Act passed in 1934 in the United States, which similarly established elected tribal councils that would cooperate with the Bureau of Indian Affairs and replace traditional leaders.

5. Anthropologists have written a lot about chiefs and nobles in Polynesia, where native people believe that a special source of power in the world, called *mana*, can reside in people as well as objects. Noble lineages, and especially chiefs, are full of mana, which thus justifies their position. Theoretically, one only needs to know how closely related someone is to a past chief to judge whether he or she had sufficient mana to make a good chief in the future. Nonetheless (Sahlins 1963), the presence of superior mana is also judged by achievement, so that superior achievement can lead to chiefly power even with a merely distant tie to a chiefly family.
6. In recent years, a conception of panindian identity uniting these neighboring communities has developed.

Chapter Six

1. Barbara Bode gives a moving account of the destruction of a Peruvian town by earthquake and its subsequent renewal in *No Bells to Toll: Destruction and Creation in the Andes (1989)*.
2. There is clearly a lot of overlap in the material being investigated by Picker and Sunstein. However, Picker is concentrating on the change in people's behavior due to information about the consequences available to them; Sunstein is taking a more radical leap into social psychology and sociology in using the concept of "norms," generally accepted guidelines for behavior, which may mediate between individuals' information and individuals' behavior. He claims: "For the individual agent, rationality is a function of social norms" (1997, 54). Both norms and information are relevant in these examples.
3. As a legal scholar, Sunstein is particularly interested in specifying what public policies have successfully promoted norm cascades that are generally considered positive, like antismoking campaigns, and asking in what conditions government agencies should intervene in public norms. An example he cites concerns the differential rates of change in adolescent smoking among African Americans and white Americans. In 1965, 38.4 percent of white teenagers smoked; the rate dropped to 27.8 percent in 1987 and 22.9 percent in 1993, persisting at a similar level to the end of the millennium. Among African American teenagers, the rate began at the slightly lower rate of 37.1 percent in 1965, dropping to 20.4 percent in 1987 and to 4.4 percent in 1993. One of the reasons suggested for the difference is the successful management of feelings of public pride and shame in a campaign in inner-city neighborhoods that said, "They used to make us pick it. Now they want us to smoke it," displaying the image of "a skeleton resembling the Marlboro man lighting a cigarette for a black child" (Sunstein 1997, 33).
4. To **predominantly** symbolize one or the other, since each proposition embodies its antithesis as well.

Chapter Seven

Much of the material in this chapter is prefigured in Meisch's 2002 book *Andean Entrepreneurs: Otavalo Merchants and Musicians in the Global Arena*, which appeared after this was originally written. However, as that book concentrates on the indigenous communities to the north of

Otavalo, particularly Peguche, the material here will serve as a comparison and contrast between Peguche, which "has a reputation for being on the cutting edge of social change" (157), and San Rafael, south of Otavalo and previously known as a more traditional community.

1. They had the funds to repair and replace the damaged equipment at a time when Isabel and José Manuel did not.

2. Otavalo's hotels of the time generally did not meet international standards. An expensive exception was the Hostería Cusín in San Pablo, which had been established by the absentee owners in the old manor buildings of the same hacienda where Huaycopungo runa continued to labor in exchange for the rights to harvest totora.

3. The definitive study of the growth of tourism in Otavalo during this period is Meisch 2002.

4. Since bargaining on prices is common in Ecuador, and since Otavaleños are adept at lowering the asked price when they are the buyers, even in the Otavalo textile market, I am inclined to believe that the insistence that the prices were fair and relatively fixed was an adaptation to the preferences of the majority of North American and northern European tourists of the time. Some bargaining is necessary for the buyer to save face, but the prices do not alter dramatically, as they might in other venues, even in Otavalo.

5. The question (in Quichua ¿Imapitaj trabajapangui?) was "In what do you work?" Responses are fairly standardized, since the national ID card requires an occupation to be listed. The most common responses were comercio/negocio, agricultura, esteras (reed mats), and artesanía (handicrafts). Only three people listed skilled labor—two bricklayers and one carpenter. The responses were often mixed. If agriculture was mentioned or commerce mentioned, I placed the responses in that category. Those who mentioned esteras alone were placed in the agriculture/esteras category, since that is considered a very traditional occupation and does not necessarily require ties outside the community. Nonetheless, while some estera manufacture depends on the inheritance of plots of land where totora reeds grow, a great deal of totora is acquired through other arrangements, like the cooperative that has rights to totora harvested from Cusín. Those who mentioned commerce and esteras were placed in the commerce category. Those who listed student and commerce were listed as commerce; those who said student and esteras were listed as agriculture/esteras. While the nine students may be more likely to meet mates outside of Huaycopungo or to take up occupations that differ from agriculture or esteras in the future, the more conservative strategy of listing them with their current way of making a living seemed preferable. Similarly, those who listed another job or artesanías with esteras were grouped with agriculture/esteras.

6. In January 2004, I visited Segundo Aguilar, J.D., to consult on a legal matter. He was a thorough professional in his own law office in downtown Otavalo. His advice was very helpful.

7. Meisch (2002) talks about segregation of mestizos and indigenous children, harassment by mestizo peers, and racist put-downs by mestizo parents toward indigenous parents and their children in 1993. Without a doubt, these things still occur but have become increasingly rare as the ethnic climate in the schools has continued to improve in the years since.

8. In 2004, I brought my compadre Francisco an old photograph of Ila Rafi, his father, that he had requested. In it, Francisco was a high school student. He appears barefoot and somewhat scruffy, because the picture had been taken during a minga to construct his older sister's house. For many people in Huaycopungo it was a thrilling revelation and reminder of the past to see the illustrious don Francisco barefoot. He began to use it in his speeches to demonstrate his humble origins and similarity to them, despite his higher education.

9. Oswaldo and I experienced the story of Chunda Fucu in reverse. When I returned to Huaycopungo in 1987 after five years, I encountered a strapping adolescent with a thick braid washing at a water pump in the street. I did not recognize him. Oswaldo had to prod me many times before I realized who he was. It was the hair for me too.

10. The difference for rural mestizo parents was that they were seeking family upward mobility within their own society. While success on the part of their children would likely result in some disdain for their rural parents, it could be counterbalanced with gratitude for the sacrifices that led to the family's socioeconomic rise, in tune with the national ideals. This rural mixed past is the official legacy of all Ecuadorians, but being indian was not, and would have to be denied in the recent past for social advancement (see Butler [Rivero] 1981).

Chapter Eight

1. This is a term popular in Huaycopungo only since 1992 and the indian uprising when CONAIE took up the Incan term for the celebration in its struggle to make San Juan a rallying point for indigenous protest.

2. I came to Otavalo prepared to accept drinks publicly in order both to proclaim my interest in reciprocal social relations and to deny that I was an evangelist missionary. As mentioned in the introduction, some conspicuous episodes of drunkenness did indeed cement my relationships with many individuals in Huaycopungo, including Taita Antonio. For many years, I carefully dissociated myself from the group of loyal evangelists. While my own religious background did not prohibit drinking, it was nevertheless Protestant, not Catholic. Nor was I an active participant in any religion. Despite my early care to distance myself from the most loyal evangelists, they have seen me as a natural ally, since I come from a country they associate with progress and with international evangelism. After the earthquake, I became much closer to some of the evangelist leaders while maintaining relationships with continuing Catholics.

3. Peasant movements, being Marxist, stick to the line that economic class differences are far more basic than ethnic differences and the only hope for the powerless is to eschew ethnicity and unite as a proletarian class. The major weakness of this approach for indigenous peoples is that mestizos tend to remain in control of the movement, thus perpetuating the ethnic domination from which the indigenous people wish to escape. The 1970s saw the beginnings in Ecuador of ethnic organizing, sometimes in cooperation with and sometimes in opposition to Marxist formulations of social change promotion.

4. El Quinche refers to a pilgrimage to La Virgen del Quinche in El Quinche, Pichincha province. In Imbabura the pilgrimage is traditionally undertaken on October 22. During the colonial period, a virgin reportedly appeared to a local peasant farmer in Oyacachi and was later taken to a church in nearby El Quinche. It is an important religious pilgrimage site for many people in the country as a whole, since it speaks to the early creolization of the Catholic religion, presaging the development of the Ecuadorian nation.

5. The words in square brackets were added by me, as is necessary in both Spanish and English for a grammatical and fully interpretable sentence. Although this was written in Spanish, it is influenced by Quichua grammar, which would not require a verb or explicit subject to be both correct and clear. A validator suffix -*mi* on one of the words in the noun phrase would suffice to form a grammatical sentence.

6. The people mentioned here are Dr. Lema, the U.S.-educated founder of Colegio Quinchuquí, who was then very active in indigenous political movements but was later accused of having been a CIA infiltrator; Paulina Lema; Marco Barahona; Taita José Otavalo, a native and curaga of Huaycopungo; Isabel Criollo, the educated native who is my comadre and research assistant; and Antonio Velásquez, a native of Imbabura who, unbeknownst to the people of Huaycopungo at that time, was actually an evangelical pastor. He died very young and is remembered as the bringer of the evangelical message to Huaycopungo, first through political protest and only second through God's word.

7. I write this at a time, in 2000, when Pope John Paul has just declared Catholicism to be the original Christian faith: the mother, not the sister, of the other denominations. I wonder how this will impact Ibarra's bishop and other more liberal Catholic leaders.

8. In 2000, this priest was chosen to continue his religious study in Rome. Perhaps he will more closely toe the conservative church line when he returns.

9. In fact, he sold the land for a fair market price. But since the agreement to sell land to someone else (unless in exchange for a more desired plot) is undertaken only in the direst emergency, the word *donation* seems to capture the spirit of the transaction much better than *sale*. The money would never make up for the loss of land, which is forever, while money is always used up.

Chapter Nine

1. One of her sons has since bought her a cell phone.

2. There are certainly useful efforts in the literature to distinguish between two or more of these terms, but for the purpose of this more general discussion, I will treat them as synonyms.

3. It can certainly be used to challenge any particular diagnosis of addiction as well, but we are here concerned with definitions, not diagnoses. The fact that definitive diagnosis is difficult does not by itself refute the existence of alcohol addiction.

4. This is the case even though not all intoxicated individuals are likely to become violent toward others or even themselves. While some individuals are likely to become more quiet and withdrawn, there is no questioning the fact that a large percentage of heavy drinkers increase their violent behavior.

5. I have avoided using the term *disease* in this discussion in order to sidestep the reams and reams of controversy over its use. I believe the term does buy us some things we might want, such as a relief from an overemphasis on individual responsibility for addiction or its absence, health insurance coverage of alcohol treatment, and an acceptance that the biology of alcoholism deserves more attention. But it also brings with it some factors that are less favorable for our understanding and, more importantly, for our achievement of desired goals. These include a tendency to search for simplistic explanations (one gene) or simplistic cures (one drug) or simplistic social policies (declaring addicts disabled and supporting them financially for life) to deal with the problem.

6. This increase was felt locally, caused more by competition with urban populations for scarce native commodities than by price raises that kept up with general inflation. Agricultural production in the whole country fell in this period, with the exception of some products produced for export, because prices for most agricultural commodities remained low. It was cheaper to import food than to grow much of it commercially in Ecuador (Schodt 1987).

7. As in any population, it is completely possible that in households where both parents have serious drinking problems, children drink and develop a dependency or act out when drinking as well. But this remains a rare and totally unacceptable social problem in everyone's eyes, not a sad fact of life that is sometimes accepted.

8. The reduction of emotional inhibition is a symptom of drinking that is facilitated, but not determined, by neurophysiology. In this case, it is both expected and emphasized by the local people. See below. In the social context where disinhibition is not thought to be an important result of drinking, it may not be so clearly exhibited by those who are drunk.

9. My first godson, Ricardo, was a colicky baby and, at the advice of his grandparents who could not sleep with his crying, we baptized him relatively early to stop his crying and prevent his dying and becoming a tortured and torturing cucu.

Chapter Ten

1. That this taping without permission from anyone in charge was unethical was clear to me at the time. However, I let my friends' encouragement convince me to proceed. Looking back, the use to which the tapes have been put makes the ethical violation seem relatively insignificant, and community leaders are happy I did so. Nonetheless, it is not professional to take such steps, regardless of my motives and eventual use of the data. Researchers must respect the natives' rights to their own cultural patrimony by following the decisions made by group representatives rather than relying on the opinions of selected natives who are favorable to them as persons.

2. I finally found her in 2004.
3. "Oh," joked my comadre Elena Tituaña, a faithful and traditional Catholic who lives in Quinchuquí, "I could have told you that. If he had sipped his wine, there would have been at least an earthquake," thereby making fun of his supposed religious beliefs about what God would do to drinkers.
4. Loosely speaking, all named roles are *priostazgos*, including the Coraza, Loa, Yumbos, and Huarmicuna. Strictly speaking, the Coraza and his wife are the priostes. This is that familiar part/whole distinction so important to Quechua theorizing. On the one hand, the Coraza is the leader and the only really important figure. The other figures are his lowly assistants. From the other point of view, the Coraza is the primary figurehead of a whole made up of all components. Each of the components can serve as representative of the whole, or as a double for the Coraza, even though overwhelmingly it is the Coraza who stands in that place of first among equals.

Conclusion

1. This is far more the case in North America, excluding Mexico, than in the countries to the south as a whole. There are degrees along a continuum of essentializing ethnic categories and treating identity as creative matter of groups (indigenous Ecuadorians) or individuals (much of Brazil).
2. While I think this is generally accurate over time in Ecuador, I do not believe that such a perspective is either monolithic or inevitable. The value of the indigenous in the country as a whole, or in some part of the country, could shift to make the lower and middle classes of mestizos proudly display a wide array of elements from their supposed mixed heritage and contemporary culture, rather than the selective aspects claimed today. In fact, something of a shift in this direction may be seen in the example of those contemporary Otavalan mestizos who masquerade as Quichua speakers outside their country. However, it is impossible to tell to what degree it will affect the national status hierarchy in the future.
3. And in other Andean countries, guinea pig and chicha are acceptable, while something else—coca leaves and roasted caterpillars, for example—are the stigmatized symbols of primitive indian life.
4. In an amusing inversion of the stereotypes of my childhood, it is the evangelist churches that are shiny, decorative, and opulent by local standards while the new community Catholic chapels are simple and humble representing the traditional *yanga causai*, "simple and fruitless lifestyle," of Otavaleños, so well analyzed by Colloredo-Mansfeld (1999, chapter three).

Appendix One

1. José Manuel Aguilar, the evangelical leader who has borne so much personal criticism over the years and whose projects have been frequently funded by international organizations as well as myself, has recently been elected community council president, honoring his service to the community, his successful leadership, and his transparency in the use of all donated funds.

2. José Manuel Aguilar was the lead signer of the letter, along with Pedro Aguilar and Juan Sánchez, but it was most likely drafted by several people, including younger people with a greater command of formal Spanish than any of these leaders, now middle-aged, can command.

3. And it seems somewhat disingenuous of Chagnon to claim such personal distancing, since he consistently and consciously used both his financial and personality resources in order to get the people's reluctant cooperation with his research, with a clear view of the effects of his actions on local individuals and groups.

4. While this view can be said to characterize the U.S. middle class as a whole and is not specific to the East Coast, my years in Wisconsin have shown me that the right and responsibility of the middle class to claim elite privileges is not so strong in all areas of the country. Many Wisconsinites seem to be more likely to disclaim the value of elite privileges in a similar attempt to proclaim their equal worth.

Quichua-English Glossary

Notes: the suffix *-cuna* indicates plural; it can be added to any noun below. The suffix *-yuc* indicates possessive; tt can be added to any noun below.

Achi-Huahua	Godchild
Achi-Mama	Godmother (*Achi* is probably a shortened form of *Achil*, meaning "shining" and serving as an epithet for the supreme being; therefore it is a literal translation of God Mother)
Achi-Taita	Godfather
Achil Taita	God, literally "shining father," probably an ancient epithet for the Sun as God (and may once have been *Achij Taita*, Father Light); despite the similarity, the terms *Achi-Taita* and *Achil Taita* should not be considered synonymous, but something like "Godfather" and "Father God"
Aclla	Maiden (sometimes referred to as a virgin) dedicated to a life of spiritual service
Aclla-huasi	Residential/religious complex where the *aclla* resided for life
Alabadu	Word used to hail and greet distant people you wish to approach; from *Alabado sea Dios* (Spanish): Praise be to God
Ali	Good, right (adj.); well (adv.)
Alishsha	Really well, great, superlatively pleasant (*-sha* is a mellow superlative and is sometimes doubled, as here, *-shsha*, for further emphasis)
Alpa	Land, earth

Amaru	Primordial snake deity
Anaco(u)	Woman's wrap skirt; two are typically worn—a rectangular piece of cloth of white or cream for the lower layer, and one either black or in a shade of dark blue for an upper layer
Api	Ground maize soup
Asua	Home-brewed beer, usually from corn (see *chicha*)
Auca	Savage; once used by Spanish speakers to refer to the Amazonian group who call themselves Haorani
Ayahuasca	Hallucinogenic plant (literally "soul vine" in Quichua), any of several species of the genus *banisteriopsis*
Aya Uma	A mask representing a spirit, meant to be scary and worn during a Cali Uma by dancers
Ayllu	Relative, family, cognatic kindred, localized relatives
Bailana	Quichuaized form the Spanish verb *bailar*, to dance; *bailangapac* means "in order to dance"
Blancu	Quichuaized version of the Spanish *blanco*, used to refer to light-skinned and high-status people in Ecuador of supposedly undiluted European ancestry, whereas the majority of the population are considered *mestizos*
Boda(a)	Festive food, always including a soup and boiled hull corn. The word's meaning may be derived from the Spanish word *boda*, meaning wedding. Weddings are included in the list of celebrations for which *buda* is served
Boda huasi	Open house in which household heads are sponsoring a ritual event and thus hosting ritualized eating and drinking
Cabildu	Community council, from Spanish *cabildo*
Cali Uma	A ceremonial dance event with costumed dancers, uniting several groups
Camlla	Toasted corn
Canlla	Outside
Caru	Far, distant
Caru ayllu	Distant kin
Catequistas	Literally "lay catechists," parishioners trained by progressive Catholic clergy to assist in various church functions; used to refer to all those individuals involved with the progressive movements in the Catholic Church. For *runacuna* this means those who are moving away from the traditional mix of Catholicism and native andean religion
Caticcuna	Those who follow
Catic huahua	Second child or next youngest child
Causai	The state of being alive, or way of life (nominalized form of *causana*—to live)
Cazarana	To marry; Quichuaized form the Spanish verb *casar*
Chacra	Demarcated agricultural field owned by an individual or set of siblings

Champus	Sweet soup made of maize traditionally served only for the most festive occasions
Chaquiñan	Footpath
Chaupi	Half
Chuchuca	Maize first cooked and then dried for future use
Chugllu	Sweet corn (*choclo* in hispanicized form)
Chumbi	Woven belt—used to fasten *anacos*, to wrap women's long hair, to hold up old-fashioned men's pants, to bind young babies' legs, etc.
Chunta	From Spanish *chonta*, a palm tree or palm wood
Churi	Son
Churros	Tiny land snails. Used for the ringlets worn by the Coraza or anything in the curled shape of a snail shell
Cocha	Lake
Colera	Folk illness comprised of a variety of symptoms that can prove fatal; it is caused by too rapid a rise of anger or anger sustained too long
Comuna	Word for indigenous communities that became common after the 1937 *Ley de Comunas,* which provided national recognition of their political status and established self-governing procedures. While other words, such as *parcialidad*, were favored by Otavalo *mestizos*, Huaycopungo *runacuna* most often used *comuna*, perhaps because of it meant a positive recognition of supposedly indigenous traditions at the national level
Comunal	Communal; jointly owned by the *comuna*
Corazapac	Belonging to the *Coraza*
Corazas	Name of a major sponsored calendrical festival. The sponsor is called *Curazas, Capitan de Corazas,* or just *Coraza*
Cucavi	Lightweight cooked foods, such as toasted corn kernels mixed with boiled beans, which can be carried and eaten as a snack or while traveling
Cucu	Dangerous spirit out at night; cries like a baby to attract the unwary
Cuichic	Rainbow; a spiritual manifestation that is dangerous to humans
Cuicocha	Local crater lake
Cuintayuc	*Coraza*'s assistant; a "keeper of accounts"
Cultu	Central religious ritual; reserved in the Catholic Church for mass
Cunan	Now
Cunan pacha	The here and now, as distinguished from eternal space/time
Curaga	Semihereditary leader of the landed community who has guardianship over the land resources
Curridur	Roofed patio on the front or back of a house where guests are received
Cusa	Husband
Cushi	Happy, pleased

Cushishsha	Extremely happy, blissful (happy and mellow, not happy and excited)
Cutuna rumi	Grinding (*cutuna*) stone (*rumi*), used mainly for maize
Cuy	Guinea pig; used for food and for curing rituals
Cuy asado	Roast guinea pig; this combines the Quichua word for the animal with the Spanish word for the cooking method
Fachalina	Woman's rectangular shoulder wrap that reaches just below the waist and forms a sort of two-piece outer-wear with the dark *anaco*, as in a suit. One is completely dressed with the blouse, *anaco*, and *fachalina*, but informally and incompletely dressed with just the *anaco* and blouse
Fishta	Quichua form of *fiesta*, or religious festival
Fucuna	To blow. It refers equally to blowing in a literal and material sense and to ritual blowing by a spiritual healer
Gallos Pasai	Festival sponsorship, involving the offering of chickens and guinea pigs, traditionally associated with San Juan at the end of June
Gringu	Quichua form of *gringo*, referring to foreigners, especially North Americans
Gringu shimi	Foreign language—especially, but not exclusively, English
Huaca	Found objects or features of the landscape imbued with spiritual power; today most often used to refer to pottery and other archeological artifacts dug up while plowing
Huaccha	Orphan; impoverished person
Huahua	Young child
Hualca	Indigenous woman's necklace, made of gold-colored and many-faceted glass beads, coral beads, or coral-colored glass beads
Huambra	Boy in his teens
Huangudo(a)	Otavaleño, indigenous person with a long braid; considered disrespectful by indigenous people. *Huangu* is a Quichua word meaning "bundle of thin things"; only the ending—*udo*—is Spanish. It means "having the characteristic of"
Huanlla	Special food treat
Huarmi	Woman or wife
Huasi	House, building
Huasichiy	House building
Huasipungo	Arrangement similar to serfdom. The labor arrangement in which the resident laborers received a small plot to cultivate on their own time, which they could pass on to one of their children. In exchange, all family members were variously responsible for work in the fields and in the house. If the land were sold, the laborers would be sold with it

Huasipunguero	Person in a *huasipungo* labor situation; frequently shortened to *huasipungo*, making the word for the arrangement and the person in the arrangement the same
Huasi ucu	Inside room(s) of an indigenous house
Huaycu	Deep ravine caused by water erosion, usually a seasonal stream
Imbaburapac	Belonging to Imbabura
Inti (Indi)	Sun
Jachun	Daughter-in-law; treated as an unpaid servant who will nevertheless be treasured, especially by her mother-in-law, if she can work ceaselessly and well without complaint. Treated with either sympathy or disdain, the daughter-in-law is not a butt of jokes as is a son-in-law. It is a term of reference; the term of address is *Panicu*, the diminutive of the word for the sister of a male. Everyone in her affinal family, including in-married spouses, addresses her by the term
Janan Pacha	The heavens, the eternal time/space of the heavens (as opposed to *Pacha Mama*, which centers on the earth)
Janan Shaya	Upper Side; moiety that is first among equals
Jari	Male; used for humans and animals alike. When expressed as *Jari-huarmi* it means a married couple or the gendered dyad that is a constituent principle of the universe
Jayaj	Bitter, strong
Jipa	After, behind, younger
Jurubi	Named elevated corner to the northwest of Huaycopungo at the border with Cachiviro. From Jurubi, a good portion of the community can be seen
Ladu	Quichuaized form of Spanish *lado*, meaning "side"; corresponds to *shaya* in Quichua
Limai	Part of *Coraza* festival in which the assistants attempt to wound the *Coraza* himself; wound
Llacta	Homeland, applied in a nested series, starting from community section and extending through nation
Llactapura	Among people from the same homeland (as adverb) or people from the same homeland acting together, with "homeland" applied in a nested series. See *llacta*.
Llama	Sheep
Llamashna	Sheeplike
Llamashnalla	Simply (*lla*) like (*shna*) a sheep (an insult when applied to humans)
Llamingo	The animal called llama in English
Llapingachos	Hispanicized word referring to sauteed potato patties stuffed with cheese and green onions
Llullu	Unripe, newly born, infant, tender (*llullicu* is the diminutive)
Loa	The *Coraza*'s second in command
Machana	To get drunk

Machanajun	To mutually get each other drunk (the morpheme -*naju* adds a reciprocal dimension to the action of a verb)
Machapashun(chik)	Let's you and I (or we, more than two) get drunk
Mama	Mother; as an honorific it means a woman with a full complement of adult statuses
Mana	No, not
Mana ali	Bad, wrong, badly
Mana vali	Worthless, of no value
Masha	Son-in-law; can be pushed around and made fun of by his affines. It is a term of both reference and address
Minga	Communal labor party
Mingachihuai	Request for permission to enter another's territory, literally "Give me orders or permission"
Misa	Altar made for displaying offerings in traditional worship; possibly from Spanish *mesa*, meaning table
Mishci	Sweet, delicious; also comparatively mild when applied to *asua*
Mishu	*Mestizo*; used by indigenous people for those who are not indians and who are not of the highest economic, political, or religious rank. The richest, most politically powerful, and the religious elite are termed *blancus*, strictly speaking "whites"
Mishu jinticuna	*Mestizos*; a more polite reference since the Spanish mass noun *gente*, from which *jinti* is derived, means civilized or decent people
Mishu shimi	Spanish language
Mocho	Man without a braid; man or woman (*mocha*) whose hair or clothes suggest an allegiance to the *mestizo* majority; in the latter sense, often used for the indigenous neighbors of Otavaleños to the south
Muchicu	Man's felt hat
Mucusu	Literally "snot-nosed," from Spanish *mocoso*; figuratively an unsuccessful adult, a failure
Muti	Hull corn, called *mote* in Spanish, hominy
Ñanda mañachi	Greeting given on a footpath when passing someone else's territory; means literally "Lend the path"
Oca	Small native root vegetable
Pachacuti	World reversal. It can signify a transformation of cosmic proportions, ending life as we know it, or a revolutionary change of more limited dimensions. It represents both devastating destruction and the beginning of a new era
Pacha Mama	World Mother, the supernatural and personified world of space/time
Pasai punlla	Day of the *Corazas* sponsorship involving the most important ritual
Pascana	To open; *pascai* is a nominalization—the act of opening
Pendoneros	Name for a sponsored fiesta whose defining features are staffs topped by red flags, carried by the sponsors and their aides

Pilchi	Gourd bowl
Pogyo	Natural spring (Potro Pogyo is one of the named springs in Huaycopungo)
Pondo(u)	Large ceramic jar with pointed bottom; it is stored by placing the end into a small hole in the earthen floor
Puendos	Local nickname for the neighboring *runa* who are not Otavaleños
(Puenducuna)	and who live on the southern edge of Imbabura province and northern Pichincha province; *puendos* are literally the pleated skirts made of yards and yards of fabric worn by the women
Pungu(o)	Door
Quilla	Moon, month
Raymi	Ritual festival
Rosca	Bagel-shaped bread roll. See entry in Spanish glossary
Ruana	Poncho, for men
Runa	Indigenous person
Runacuna	Plural form of *runa*
Runa shimi	Quichua
Sacha	Forest; *Sacha Runa* are indigenous people of the lowland forests and forested slopes of the Andes to the east and west of the highlands
Sara	Maize
Shamupay	Request to come toward the speaker, "Please come toward me," *(Shamupaychic)* often used as we would say "Please come in." The two forms here represent (1) the request addressed to a single person; and (2) the request addressed to more than one person
Shaya	Side; especially a partition in a bipartite or quadripartite division
Shimi	Mouth, speech, language
Shuk	One
Shungu	Heart
Sumac	Superlative of good, great
Taita	Father, honorific for adult male, honorific for male spirits
Tanta	Bread
Tincui	Violent clashing of two opposing forces, natural or social
Tiyaripai	Polite verbal command/request to sit, "Please sit down"
Totora	Marsh reeds from which mats and fire fans are woven
Tragu	Quichuaized form of the Spanish *trago*, meaning sugarcane brandy
Tushuna	To dance
Uchu	Hot pepper, usually cayenne; also sauce made from ground hot peppers, salt, and green onion
Ucu	Inside
Ufyanajun	They are drinking together by serving each other (the morpheme *-naju* adds a reciprocal dimension to the verb)

Ufyapashun(chic)	Let's you and I (all of us) drink together
Ufyay	To drink. *Ufyadur* adds the Spanish suffix *-dor(a)* to make it a person who engages in the activity of the verb, in this case a drinker
Uma	Head (headdress of a costume)
Urai	Spatial direction with first meaning being "down." Used to refer to the mountain slopes toward the Amazon and also north to Colombia
Urai Shaya	Lower Side; moiety that is second among equals
Vichai	Direction, usually meaning "up" or south toward Quito
Yachac	Someone who "knows," especially esoteric knowledge; used as the term for shaman
Yalipay	Polite command to keep going—"Please go ahead" or "Please pass"—when literal forward movement is meant
Yamor	*Asua* made from sprouted corn—the most labor-intensive form and therefore the most highly valued; also refers to Otavalo's main town festival, held at the start of September
Yanapero	Person in a particular labor contract who owes labor to a landowner in return for some rights of usufruct on the owner's land, such as rights to harvest reeds, glean fields, cut firewood, gather medicinal plants, pasture cattle, or similar activities. Traditionally the landowner had coercive power over the *yanapero* but not vice versa; it was not an exchange between equal parties
Yanga	Worthless, useless, humble, fruitless
Yanga Shimi	Quichua; Worthless Language
Yapa	Too much, extra
Yumbo	Natives from the forested slopes or lowlands
Zambu	Large green squash

Spanish-English Glossary

Activistas	Activists, individuals involved in any organized movement for change
Agricultor	Farmer
Aguardiente	Distilled alcoholic beverage from sugarcane. See *trago*
Ají	Sauce from ground hot peppers, salt, green onions, parsley, and cilantro
Artesanía(s)	Handicraft(s)
Artesano(a)	Craftsperson
Asado	Grilled or roasted
Blancos	Whites, once honorifically applied to elite *mestizos*, now in disuse except for a few native Ecuadorians and sometimes for white foreigners
Blanqueamiento	Process of becoming whiter, literally in skin color or, more likely, in cultural orientation
Cabildo	Community council; mandated for indigenous communities in the *Ley de Comunas* of 1937
Campesino(a)	Peasant
Cantina	Storefront bar
Cantón	Administrative unit, similar to a county
Carajo	Swear word, similar to "hell" in English
Castillo	Castle; also used for the roof-shaped frame on which offerings are strung in religious festivals
Católico(a)	Catholic
Centro	Pleated skirt made of yards and yards of material worn by the *runacuna* of southern Imbabura and northern Pichincha provinces

435

Chica	Small; also used as slang for a young woman
Chicha	Home-brewed beer, usually from corn. See *asua*
Cholo	Ecuadorian word for low-status people whose ethnic identity is socially ambiguous although their self-identity is hispanic rather than indigenous. Sometimes used to refer to individuals with known indigenous ancestry living as *mestizos*
Chucha	Swear word, literally referring to female genitalia
Civilizado(a)	Civilized. See *gente* below for a definition of *gente civilizada*
Comadre, Compadre	Co-mother and co-father; term used by godparent for the parents of the godchild and vice versa
Comerciante	Merchant
Comida típica	Regional folk cuisine
Compadrazgo	System of fictive kinship establishing godparents, godchildren, and co-parents
Comunidad(es)	Community(s)
Dios	Christian God
Electrodomésticos	Small home appliances and electronic devices
Enganchadores	Labor contractors; literally "people who hook one"
Estera	Reed mat woven from *totora* reeds
Evangelistas	Either Protestant missionaries or those who are involved in Protestant worship or a Protestant church
Familia	Family
Feria	Market fair
Fiesta	Religious festival
Gente	People, particularly "decent people"; *gente civilizada* is a very common expression in Ecuador referring to those who have an Ecuadorian-hispanic orientation and aspire to middle-class norms or above. It specifically excludes indigenous people and the very poor
Gringo(a)	Foreigner, especially, but not exclusively, a white or North American foreigner
Guarapo	Fermented sugarcane juice
Hacendado(a)	Owner of a *hacienda*
Hacienda	Landed estate
Hostería	Inn
Imbabura	Northern Sierra province in which Otavalo cantón is found
Indígena	Indigenous person; considered a polite form
Indio	Indian; considered a derogatory term for indigenous person
Indios sucios	Dirty indians; common derogatory expression in Ecuadorian Spanish
Lechero	Tree with a milky white sap
Lengua	Tongue; also a language
Levantimiento	Uprising
Loma	Hill
Longo	Demeaning term for indigenous person
Madrina	Godmother

Mediano	Formal offering of cooked food to thank someone for a service. Typically it includes at least one, ofen more, boiled chicken and roasted guinea pig, boiled potatoes, and sweet corn, all heaped to overflowing in a basin
Melloco	Root vegetable native to the Andes
Mestizaje	Process of becoming more *mestizo* and less white or indigenous; from the majority point of view, especially in the 1970s, this would be a significant improvement of Ecuadorian society, since it would eliminate the indigenous
Mestizo(a)	Literally a person of mixed ancestry; in Ecuador that ancestry can be either social, genealogical, or a mixture of both; for some Ecuadorians only the mestizos, formed in the encounter of white Spaniards and the native people, are the true Ecuadorians
Misa	Catholic mass
Mocoso	Literally snot-nosed; figuratively an unsuccessful adult, a failure
Mote	Hulled corn, hominy
Natural	Indigenous person; once considered a polite euphemism, the term has come to be viewed as disrespectful in the last few decades
Oriente	Eastern lowlands in Ecuador; literally "the east"
Otavaleño	While literally referring to a person from Otavalo cantón, as in Otavalan, it is restricted to indigenous people with roots in Otavalo cantón who wear distinctive Otavaleño dress and hairstyle. *Mestizos* from Otavalo are not called *Otavaleño*, except in jest. They are *de Otavalo*, from Otavalo, or *Imbabureño*, referring to the province
Padre de Familias	Indigenous community liaison with the community school who represents the interests of the indigenous parents to the mostly *mestizo* teachers, who are from other towns and even regions of the country
Padrino	Godfather; *padrinos* means godparents (inclusive gender)
Pagar	To pay
Panela	A brown sugar cake with a relatively high degree of molasses. Very popular for traditional sweet dishes in Ecuador and Colombia
Páramo	High-altitude grasslands
Parcialidad	Word used since colonial times for indigenous communities. While it is a very common word in mestizo speech and Ecuadorian social science, I do not use it because it is not used by the people in Huaycopungo.
Pascua	Easter
Peón	Unskilled laborer
Plaza	Open square in a town. Can be used for a market surrounded by important public buildings
Político	Political (adj.); a person involved in politics (n.)

Prioste	Sponsor of a ritual event
Provincia	Administrative unit, a province
Rebozo	Large, rectangular shawl, often brightly colored, that indigenous women wear when away from home to protect them from the evening chill or to serve as a carrying cloth when needed
Rosca	Donut- or bagel-shaped and barely leavened bread made earthen ovens; among indigenous people a special treat during San Juan
Sierra	Geographic region distinguished by mountain ranges
Sucre	Ecuadorian unit of currency, recently replaced by the dollar
Susto	Literally "fright," sometimes used to refer to illnesses caused by fright, with or without temporary soul loss
Tapia	Packed mud walls
Teniente	Lieutenant; *teniente político* is the civil head of a parish, under the authority of the municipal mayor
Trago	Distilled alcoholic beverage from sugarcane. See *aguardiente.*
Tu	You (singular and informal)
Usted	You (singular and formal)
Vecino(s)	Neighbor(s)
Viejo chumado	Old drunk, drunken bum
Vos	Old-fashioned term for you (singular and intimate)
Yamor	Otavalo's main town festival, held at the start of September
Yanapa	Labor contract in which land-owning peasants owe periodic labor to a neighboring landowner, who then allows them limited rights to harvest from his land certain resources that he himself is not exploiting
Yanapero	Person in a particular labor contract who owes labor to a landowner in return for some rights of usufruct on the owner's land, such as rights to harvest reeds, glean fields, cut firewood, gather medicinal plants, pasture cattle, or similar activities. Traditionally the landowner had coercive power over the *yanapero* but not vice versa; it was not an exchange between equal parties
Yuca	Manioc root

References Cited

Abercrombie, Thomas. 1998. *Pathways of Memory and Power: Ethnography and History among an Andean People.* Madison: University of Wisconsin Press.

Aguilar Mendez, José M., Juan Sánchez, and Pedro Aguilar Mendez. 1997. "Historia de la vida de la iglesia evangélica 'Jesus de Nazaret' de la comunidad de Huayco Pungo." Unpublished manuscript, July 6.

Alexie, Sherman. 1993. *The Lone Ranger and Tonto Fistfight in Heaven.* New York: Harper Collins.

——— 1998. *Smoke Signals.* Miramax Films.

Allen, Catherine. 1988. *The Hold Life Has: Coca and Cultural Identity in an Andean Community.* Washington, D.C.: Smithsonian Institution Press.

Amselle, Jean-Loup. 1998. *Mestizo Logics: Anthropology of Identity in Africa and Elsewhere.* Trans. Claudia Royal. Stanford, Calif.: Stanford University Press.

Anderson, Benedict. 1991. *Imagined Communities.* London: Verso.

Appadurai, Arjun. 1990. "Disjuncture and Difference in the Global Cultural Economy." *Public Culture* 2 (2): 1–24.

Ares Quejía, Berta. 1988. *Los Corazas: Ritual andino de Otavalo.* Quito: Instituto Otavaleño de Antropología y Ediciones Abya Yala.

Ayala Mora, Enrique, and Rodrigo Villegas Domínguez. 1988. *Historia de la Provincia de Imbabura.* Monographs of Imbabura, vol. 1. Ibarra: Centro de Ediciones Culturales de Imbabura.

Bales, R. F. 1946. "Cultural Differences in Rates of Alcoholism." *Quarterly Journal of Studies on Alcohol* 6: 480–99.

Barlett, Peggy. 1980. "Reciprocity and the San Juan Fiesta." *Journal of Anthropological Research* 36 (Spring): 116–30.

Barr, Andrew. 1999. *Drink: A Social History of America*. New York: Carroll & Graf.

Bateson, Gregory. 1972. "Culture Contact and Schismogenesis." In *Steps to an Ecology of Mind*, 61–152. New York: Ballantine.

Berkow, Robert, ed. 1977. *The Merck Manual of Diagnosis and Therapy*. 13th ed. Rahway, N.J.: Merck, Sharp, & Dohme.

Bhabha, Homi. 1994. *The Location of Culture*. London: Routledge.

Bode, Barbara. 1989. *No Bells To Toll: Destruction and Creation in the Andes*. New York: Scribner.

Bonifaz, Emilio. 1975. *Los indígenas de altura del Ecuador*. Quito: Varela 190.

Bourdieu, Pierre. 1997. *Outline of a Theory of Practice*. Cambridge: Cambridge University Press.

Buitrón, Aníbal. n.d. *Taita Imbabura: Vida indígena en los Andes*. Quito: Misión Andina.

Butler (Rivero), Barbara. 1981. "Indian Identity and Identity Change in One Ecuadorian Andean Community." Ph.D. diss., University of Rochester.

Cancian, Frank. 1992. *The Decline of Community in Zinacantan*. Stanford, Calif.: Stanford University Press.

Carpenter, Lawrence K. 1992. "Inside/Outside, Which Side Counts? Duality-of-Self and Bipartization in Quechua." In *Andean Cosmologies through Time: Persistence and Emergence*, ed. R. V. H. Dover, K. E. Seibold, and J. H. McDowell, 115–36. Bloomington: Indiana University Press.

Carsten, Janet, and Stephen Hugh-Jones, eds. 1995. *About the House: Leví-Strauss and Beyond*. Cambridge: Cambridge University Press.

Casagrande, Joseph. 1978. "Religious Conversion and Social Change in an Indian Community of Highland Ecuador." In *Amerikanistiche Studien*, ed. Roswith Hartmann and Udo Oberem, 105–11. St. Agustin, West Germany: Haus Volker and Kulturem, Anthropos-Institut.

Chavez, Leo Ralph. 1982. "Commercial Weaving and the Entrepreneurial Ethic: Otavalo Indian Views of Self and the World." Ph.D. diss., Stanford University.

Collier, John Jr., and Aníbal Buitrón. 1971. *The Awakening Valley*. Quito: Instituto Otavaleño de Antropología.

Colloredo-Mansfeld, Rudi. 1999. *The Native Leisure Class: Consumption and Cultural Creativity in the Andes*. Chicago: University of Chicago Press.

Comaroff, Jean. 1985. *Body of Power, Spirit of Resistance*. Chicago: University of Chicago Press.

Comaroff, John L., and Jean Comaroff. 1991. *Of Revelation and Revolution*, vol. 1: *Christianity and Colonialism in South Africa*. Chicago: University of Chicago Press.

——— 1997. *Of Revelation and Revolution*, vol. 2: *The Dialectics of Modernity on a South African Frontier*. Chicago: University of Chicago Press.

CONAIE. 1989. *Las nacionalidades indígenas en el Ecuador: Nuestro proceso organizativo*. Quito: Ediciones Tincui-Abya Yala.

Corkill, David, and David Cubitt. 1988. *Ecuador: Fragile Democracy*. London: Latin American Bureau.

Crain, Mary. 1998. "Performances of San Juan in the Ecuadorian Andes."
In *Recasting Ritual: Performance, Media, Identity*, ed. Felicia Hughes-
Freeland and Mary M. Crain, 135–60. London: Routledge.

Crespi, Muriel. 1968. "The Patrons and Peons of Pesillo: A Traditional
Hacienda System in Highland Ecuador." Ph.D. diss., University of
Illinois. Ann Arbor, Mich.: University Microfilms.

——— 1975. "When Indios Become Cholos." In *The New Ethnicity*,
ed. John W. Bennett, 148–66. St. Paul: West.

Crespo Toral, Hernán. 1981. Foreword to *Cultural Transformations and
Ethnicity in Modern Ecuador*, ed. Norman E. Whitten Jr., ix–xiv.
Urbana: University of Illinois Press.

Criollo Perugachi, Asciencia. 1995–96. "Estudio socio-cultural de la
comunidad de Huaycopungo." Instituto Pedagogico Intercultural
Bilingue "Quillerac," Extension Imbabura.

Crosby, Alfred. 1972. *The Columbian Exchange: Biological and Cultural
Consequences of 1492.* Westport, Conn.: Greenwood.

Dean, Carolyn. 1999. *Inka Bodies and the Body of Christ: Corpus Christi
in Colonial Cuzco, Peru.* Durham, N.C.: Duke University Press.

DuBois, W. E. B. [1903] 1969. *The Souls of Black Folk.* Greenwich: Fawcett.

Eber, Christine. 1995. *Women and Alcohol in a Highland Maya Town: Water
of Hope, Water of Sorrow.* Austin: University of Texas Press.

Espinosa Soriano, Waldemar. 1988a. *Los Cayambes y Carangues: Siglos
XV–XVI: El testimonio de la etnohistoria.* Vol. 1. Collección Curiñan.
Quito: Instituto Otavaleño de Antropología.

——— 1988b. *Etnohistoria ecuatoriana: Estudios y documentos.* Quito:
Ediciones Abya-Yala.

Estrella, Eduardo, Ramiro Cazar, Edilma Benitez, and Oscar Carranco, eds.
1982. *Estudios de salud mental.* Quito: Unidad de Psiquiatria Social.

Estrella, Eduardo, and Ramiro Estrella. 1982. "Evolución historica de los
patrones de consumo de alcohol en el Ecuador." In *Estudios de salud
mental*, 136–75. Quito: Unidad de Psiquiatria Social.

Foucault, Michel. 1983. "Afterword: The Subject and Power." In *Michel
Foucault: Beyond Structuralism and Hermeneutics*, 2nd ed., ed.
Hubert L. Dreyfus and Paul Rabinow, 208–28. Chicago: University
of Chicago Press.

Geertz, Clifford. [1966] 1973. "Religion as a Cultural System." In *The
Interpretation of Cultures: Selected Essays*, 87–125. New York:
Basic Books.

Goffin, Alvin M. 1994. *The Rise of Protestant Evangelism in Ecuador: 1895–
1990.* Gainesville: University Press of Florida.

Gramsci, Antonio. 1971. *Selections from the Prison Notebooks.* New York:
International.

Griffiths, Nicholas. 1996. *The Cross and the Serpent: Religious Repression
and Resurgence in Colonial Peru.* Norman: University of Oklahoma
Press.

Gutierrez, Ramon A. 1991. *When Jesus Came, the Corn Mothers Went Away:
Marriage, Sexuality, and Power in New Mexico, 1500–1846.* Stanford,
Calif.: Stanford University Press.

Harrison, Regina. 1989. *Signs, Songs, and Memory in the Andes: Translating
Quechua Language and Culture.* Austin: University
of Texas Press.

Hassaurek, Friedrich. [1868] 1967. *Four Years among the Ecuadorians.* Carbondale: Southern Illinois University Press.

Heath, Dwight. 1987. "A Decade of Development in the Anthropology Study of Alcohol Use." In *Constructive Drinking: Perspectives on Drink from Anthropology,* ed. Mary Douglas, 16–69. Cambridge: Cambridge University Press.

Hobsbawm, Eric, and Terence Ranger, eds. 1983. *The Invention of Tradition.* New York: Cambridge University Press.

Isbell, Billie Jean. 1978. *To Defend Ourselves: Ecology and Ritual in an Andean Village.* Austin: University of Texas Press.

Kane, Joe. 1996. *Savages.* New York: Random House, Vintage.

Klor de Alva, J. Jorge. 1995. "The Postcolonization of the (Latin) American Experience: A Reconsideration of 'Colonialism,' 'Postcolonialism,' and 'Mestizaje.'" In *After Colonialism: Imperial Histories and Postcolonial Displacements,* ed. Gyan Prakash, 241–78. Princeton, N.J.: Princeton University Press.

Kuran, Timur. 1991. "Now Out of Never: The Element of Surprise in the East European Revolution." *World Politics* 44 (October): 7–48.

——— 1995a. "On the Inevitability of Future Revolutionary Surprises." *American Journal of Sociology* 100 (May): 1528–51.

——— 1995b. *Private Truths, Public Lies: The Social Consequences of Preference Falsification.* Cambridge, Mass.: Harvard University Press.

——— 1998. "Ethnic Norms and Their Transformation through Reputational Cascades." *Journal of Legal Studies* 27 (June): 623.

Lebret, Iveline. 1981. *La vida en Otavalo en el siglo XVIII.* Coleccíon Pendoneros. Quito: Instituto Otavaleño de Antropología.

Leutwyler, Kristin, and Alan Hall. 1997. "Closing in on Addiction." *Scientific American,* November 24.

Levi-Strauss, Claude. 1963. "Do Dual Organizations Exist?" In *Structural Anthropology,* trans. C. Jacobsen and B. G. Schoepf, 132–63. New York: Basic.

Lucas, Phil, and Janet Tanaka. 1986. *The Honor of All: The Alkali Lake Indian Band, Williams Lake, British Columbia.* Videotaped film, Phil Lucas Productions. Sponsored by Chief Dan George Memorial Foundation, 4 Winds Development Project, and National Native AODA Program of Medical Services Branch, Health and Welfare Canada.

Lund Skar, Sara. 1994. *Lives Together, Worlds Apart: Quechua Colonization in Jungle and City.* Oslo: Scandinavian University Press.

MacAndrew, Craig, and Robert B. Edgerton. 1969. *Drunken Comportment: A Social Explanation.* Chicago: Aldine.

MacCormack, Sabine. 1991. *Religion in the Andes: Vision and Imagination in Early Colonial Peru.* Princeton, N.J.: Princeton University Press.

Mackie, Gerry. 1996. "Ending Foot-Binding and Infibulation: A Conventional Account." *American Sociological Review* 999: 1015.

Marshall, Mac. 1979. *Weekend Warriors: Alcohol in a Micronesian Culture.* Explorations in World Ethnology Series, ed. Robert B. Edgerton and L. L. Langness. Palo Alto, Calif.: Mayfield.

Marshall, Mac, and Leslie B. Marshall. 1990. *Silent Voices Speak: Women and Prohibition in Truk.* Belmont, Calif.: Wadsworth.

May, Philip A. 1994. "The Epidemiology of Alcohol Abuse among American Indians: The Mythical and Real Properties." *American Indian Culture and Research Journal* 18 (2): 121–43.

Meisch, Lynn A. 2002. *Andean Entrepreneurs: Otavalo Merchants and Musicians in the Global Arena.* Austin: University of Texas Press.

Montes del Castillo, Ángel. 1989. *Simbolismo y poder: Un estudio antropológico sobre compadrazgo y priostazgo en una comunidad andina.* Barcelona: Anthropos.

Morales, Edmundo. 1995. *The Guinea Pig: Healing, Food, and Ritual in the Andes.* Tucson: University of Arizona Press.

Moreno Yanez, Segundo E. 1978. *Sublevaciones indigenas desde comienzos del siglo XVIII hasta finales de la colonia.* Quito: Universidad Católica.

Muratorio, Blanca. 1980. "Protestantism and Capitalism Revisited in the Rural Highlands of Ecuador." *Journal of Peasant Studies* 8:37–61.

——— 1981. "Protestantism, Ethnicity, and Class in Chimborazo." In *Cultural Transformations and Ethnicity in Modern Ecuador,* ed. Norman E. Whitten Jr., 506–34. Urbana: University of Illinois Press.

Murra, John. 1973. "Rite and Crop in the Inca State." In *Peoples and Cultures of Native South America,* ed. Daniel R. Gross, 377–89. Garden City, N.Y.: Doubleday/ Natural History Press.

Naranjo, Marcelo. 1988. *La cultura popular en el Ecuador, Tomo V., Imbabura.* Cuenca: CIDAP.

Ohnuki-Tierney, Emiko. 1990. "The Monkey as Self in Japanese Culture." In *Culture through Time: Anthropological Approaches,* 128–53. Stanford, Calif.: Stanford University Press.

Ortner, Sherry. 1990. "Patterns of History: Cultural Schemas in the Foundings of Sherpa Religious Institutions." In *Culture through Time: Anthropological Approaches,* 57–93. Stanford, Calif.: Stanford University Press.

Otavalo Andrango, José. 1990. Interview by author. Tape recording. June 19.

Parsons, Elsie Clews. 1945. *Peguche, Canton of Otavalo, Province of Imbabura, Ecuador: A Study of Andean Indians.* Chicago: University of Chicago Press.

Picker, Randal C. 1997. "Simple Games in a Complex World: A Generative Approach to the Adoption of Norms." *University of Chicago Law Review* 64 (Fall): 1225–88.

Posner, Eric. 1998. "Symbols, Signals, and Social Norms in Politics and the Law." *Journal of Legal Studies* 27:765.

Rappaport, Joanne. 2004. *Cumbe Reborn: An Andean Ethnography of History.* Chicago: University of Chicago Press.

Rappoport, Roy A. 1999. *Ritual and Religion in the Making of Humanity.* Cambridge: Cambridge University Press.

Rodriguez Sandoval, L. 1945. "Drinking Motivations among the Indians of the Ecuadorian Sierra." *Primitive Man* 18: 39–46.

Rubel, Arthur. 1964. "The Epidemiology of a Folk Illness: Susto in Hispanic America." *Ethnology* 3: 268–83.

Rubel, Arthur, C. W. O'Nell, and R. Collado-Ardon. [1984] 1991. *Susto: A Folk Illness.* Los Angeles: University of California Press.

Rubio Orbe, Gonzalo. 1956. *Punyaro*. Quito: Casa de la Cultural Ecuatoriana.
Rueda, Marco V. 1981. *La fiesta religiosa campesina*. Quito: Universidad Católica.
Sahlins, Marshall. 1963. "Poor Man, Rich Man, Big-Man, Chief: Political Types in Melanesia and Polynesia." *Comparative Studies in Society and History* 5:285–303. Cambridge: Cambridge University Press.
Salomon, Frank. [1973] 1981. "Weavers of Otavalo." In *Cultural Transformations and Ethnicity in Modern Ecuador*, ed. Norman E. Whitten Jr., 420–49. Urbana: University of Illinois Press.
——— 1986. *Native Lords of Quito in the Age of the Inca: Political Economy of North Andean Chiefdoms*. Cambridge: Cambridge University Press.
Salomon, Frank, and George L. Urioste. 1991. *The Huarochirí Manuscript*. Austin: University of Texas Press.
Sánchez Parga, José. 1988. "Del temblor de tierra (*pachakuyuy*) a la construccion de la casa." In *Respuesta andina al sismo: Cayambe 87*, ed. Eric Dudley et al., 155–91. Quito: Centro Andino de Acción Popular.
——— 1989. *Faccionalismo, organización y proyecto étnico en los Andes*. Quito: Centro Andino de Acción Popular.
——— 1991. *Educación y bilingüismo en la Sierra Ecuatoriana*. Quito: Centro Andino de Acción Popular.
Schodt, David W. 1987. *Ecuador: An Andean Enigma*. Boulder, Colo.: Westview.
Segal, Boris M. 1987. *Russian Drinking: Use and Abuse of Alcohol in Pre-revolutionary Russia*. New Brunswick, N.J.: Rutgers Center of Alcohol Studies.
Shkilnyk, Anastasia M. 1985. *A Poison Stronger Than Love: The Destruction of an Ojibwa Community*. New Haven, Conn.: Yale University Press.
Skar, Harald. 1982. *The Warm Valley People: Duality and Land Reform among the Quechua Indians of Highland Peru*. Oslo: Universitetsforlaget.
Snyder, Charles R. 1958. *Alcohol and the Jews: A Cultural Study of Drinking and Sobriety*. Glencoe, Ill.: Free Press; New Haven, Conn.: Yale Center of Alcohol Studies.
Somer, Murat. 2001. "Cascades of Ethnic Polarization: Lessons from Yugoslavia." *Annals of the American Academy of Political and Social Science* 573 (January): 2–83.
Stoll, David. 1990. *Is Latin America Turning Protestant? The Politics of Evangelical Growth*. Berkeley: University of California Press.
Stutzman, Ronald. 1981. "*El mestizaje*: An All-Inclusive Ideology of Exclusion." In *Cultural Transformations and Ethnicity in Modern Ecuador*, ed. Norman E. Whitten Jr., 45–94. Urbana: University of Illinois Press.
Sunstein, Cass. 1997. "Social Norms and Social Roles." In *Free Markets and Social Justice*, 32–69. New York: Oxford University Press.
Taussig, Michael. 1980. *The Devil and Commodity Fetishism*. Chapel Hill: University of North Carolina Press.
Taylor, William B. 1979. *Drinking, Homicide, and Rebelliion in Colonial Mexican Villages*. Stanford, Calif.: Stanford University Press.
Tierney, Patrick. 2000. *Darkness in El Dorado: How Scientists and Journalists Devasted the Amazon*. New York: W.W. Norton.

Townsend, Camilla. 2000. *Tales of Two Cities: Race and Economic Culture in Early Republican North and South America*. Austin: University of Texas Press.

Urton, Gary. 1992. "Communalism and Differentiation in an Andean Community." In *Andean Cosmologies through Time: Persistence and Emergence*, ed. R. V. H. Dover, K. E. Seibold, and J. H. McDowell, 229–66. Bloomington: Indiana University Press.

Villavicencio R., Gladys. 1973. *Relaciones interétnicas en Otavalo: ¿Una nacionalidad india en formación?* Mexico City: Ediciones Especiales 65.

Vreeland, James M. Jr. 1999. "The Revival of Colored Cotton." *Scientific American* 280 (4): 112.

Wachtel, Nathan. 1977. *The Vision of the Vanquished: The Spanish Conquest of Peru through Indian Eyes, 1530–1570*. Trans. Ben Reynolds and Sian Reynolds. Hassocks, U.K., Harvester.

Weismantel, Mary. 1988. *Food, Gender, and Poverty in the Ecuadorian Andes*. Philadelphia: University of Pennsylvania Press.

Werner, David. 1980. *Donde no hay doctor: Una guía para los campesinos que viven lejos de los centros médicos*. Palo Alto, Calif.: Hesperion Foundation.

Whitten, Norman E. Jr. 1976. *Sacha Runa: Ethnicity and Adaptation of Ecuadorian Jungle Quichua*. Urbana: University of Illinois Press.

——— 1981. Introduction to *Cultural Transformations and Ethnicity in Modern Ecuador*, ed. Norman E. Whitten Jr., 1–41. Urbana: University of Illinois Press.

Whitten, Norman E. Jr., Dorothea Whitten, and Alfonso Chango. 1997. "Return of the Yumbo: The Indigenous Caminata from Amazonia to Andean Quito." *American Ethnologist* 24 (2): 355–91.

Wogan, Peter. 2004. *Magical Writing in Salasaca: Literacy and Power in Highland Ecuador*. Boulder, Colo.: Westview.

Wolf, Eric. 1955. "Types of Latin American Peasantry: A Preliminary Discussion." *American Anthropologist* 57: 452–71.

——— 1957. "Closed Corporate Peasant Communities in Mesoamerica and Central Java." *Southwestern Journal of Anthropology* 13 (1): 1–18.

Index

446

andean cast, 123; and forced evangelization, 20; and good and evil, 51

Chunda Fucu, 45, **47**, 47–48, 70, 76–77; and alcoholism, 387; and binge drinking, 78

circle dances, 19, 142

Cisneros, Plutarco, 348

clothing, 200

colonial Mexico, increase in alcohol-related problems in, 322

comuna, 34, 55, 57, 64

communalism, 57

communitas, 109

community identity, 355

compadrazco, 71, 255

compadres, 70, 71, 100

Compassion International, 293–94

competition, 177, 307; for tourists, 201, 257

Conféderación Campesina, 206, 223, 224, 282

Conféderación de Nacionalidades Indígenas del Ecuador (CONAIE), 288, 310, 355, 378

contra dances, 17, 19, 85

Cooperative Preñadilla, 209, 212, 220

Coraza fiestas, 123, **132**, 143, 145, 154, 255, 308, 342, 346, 348, 379, 390; of 2000, **353**; and Capitan de Corazas, 132, 150, 151, 152, 365, 367; and hierarchy and humility, 149–56; and setting aside old slights and factional feuds, 369; and taming hierarchy, 367; transnational, 371

Coraza paraphernalia, 351, 353

Corazapac Huarmi, **155**

Corazapac Huarmicuna, 344, 358, 360, 364, 365

Corazas (characters in drama), 134, **153**; costume of, 151

corn, 90, 331

corn beer. *See* chicha

Corpus Christi celebration, 224

cosmological axioms, 87, 123

cosmovision, 87

Criollo, Angel, 280, 282, 289

Criollo Criollo, Antonio, 43–44, 45, 46, 69, 71, 72, 74–76, 191, 194, 211, 212–20, **213**, 225, 264, 271, 282, 341–42, 349; and alcohol-related absenteeism, 217; and alchoholism, 78, 219–20; and binge drinking, 325; death of, 75; and reputation for drinking too much, 216

Criollo Perugachi, Asciencia, 360, 368, 391

Criollo Perugachi, Isabel, vii, ix, xiv–xv,

xxvii, 40, **42**, 65–79, 110–13, 194, 204, 211, 220, 223, 245–49, 266, 271, 290, 296, 306, 312–14, 343, 344, **347**, 358, 360, 402, 403; death threats made against, 73; estrangement from her family, 260; new Red Cross house of, **251**; as research assistant, 398; served prison sentence for cattle theft, 229

Criollo, Rafael, 193, 194, 207, 208–12

cuichic, 127

cultural continuity, 374

cultural identity, 173

cultural imperialism, 395

cultural mixing, 379–80, 392

cultural myths, xi–xii, 114

cultural schemas, 87, 123

curagas, 62, 194, 203–7, 212, 220, 223

curers, 108

Damiano José Manuel. *See* Aguilar, José Manuel

Damiano Pidru. *See* Aguilar, Pedro

dancing, 137, **155**, 158, 160, **185**, 308, 361, 362, 365, 366, 368; and altered sense of time, 139; as central symbol of San Juan/Inti Raymi fiesta, 157; and circle dances, 19, 142, 365; and competition, 160–61; and connection to drinking, 358; and contra dances, 17, 19, 85; evangelistas and, 307, 357-58; house to house, 159, 163; as synonymous with drinking, 358; and women giving appearance of being drunk, 184

demons, 126

depersonalization, 364–66

designated caretakers, 109, 335

differentiation, 57

dominant metaphors, 87, 123

drinking rituals, 88

drinking to intoxication, 22, 107, 190, 191, 330; as form of rebellion for young men, 190; Otavalan vs. hispanic Ecuadorian attitude concerning, 191; as pleasure and burden of social life, 11; as problematic behavior, 231; and promotion of community, 282; sacredness of, 12, 14; and support of social order, 191; surrendering to drunkenness as a morally enjoined duty, 176; as symbolic act of sharing, 11; as threat to civic order, 5; by women, 440n4

Drunken Comportment (MacAndrew and Edgerton), 319

dualism, 16, 17, 51, 376

Dubois, W. E. B., 382–83

Tituaña, Ricardo, 355
Tocagon: compared to Huaycopungo, 143, 219
totora reeds, ix, 65, 143, 164, 188, 195, 208, 214; harvesting of, **66**
tourism, 198, 201, 202, 215, 251, 255–58, 264, 277, 293, 308, 384, 390; and Colombian middle-class tourists, 256; expansion in Otavalo, 274; and North American tourists, 293; and Otavaleño runa as tourist attraction, 264
trade, 34–35, 187–88, 198, 262; long-distance, 275
trago, 14, 84, 89–94, 100, 106, 178, 212; alcohol content compared to asua, 92, 322; and men, 93; money and, 94; purchased rather than home-brewed, 323; as substitute for asua, 324

ucu, 170
uma, 151, 365
Unión de Comunidades Indígenas de San Rafael (UNCISA), 360
Urai Ladu, 143
Urai Shaya, 141, 143, 144, 258, 307, 308, 360

vaccinations, 395
Velasco Ibarra, José María, 252
Velásquez, Antonio, 290
Vichai Ladu, 143, 144
viejo chumados, 212, 224, 243
violence, 148, 149, 161, 216, 309–10; in cantinas, 176; domestic, 29, 232, 319, 325, 335, 338–40, 387; threat of, 290
Virgin Mamacuna, 121, 125
Virgin Mary, 121, 124; author likened to, 217–18; Pacha Mama as manifestation of, 125

Virgin of El Quinche, 125
Virgin of Las Lajas, 125
virgins, and brewing of asua, 93
vulnerability, 177

wanlla, 160
water, 345–46, 351
weaving, 68, 82, 215; commercialization of, 201
wine, 5, 6, 169, 335
Wogan, Peter, xviii
women: and alcohol consumption, 12, 45–46, 440n4; and asua, 93, 96, 324; and cantinas, 181, 184; and chacras, 62; of child-bearing age, 328; drinking and sexual vulnerability, 328; and drinking obligations, 97; endogamous marriage favored by, 262; indigenous vs. hispanic, 360; and limited opportunities prior to menopause, 61; and maize harvesting, 93; and music, 359; and new views about drinking, 387; opinions of, viii; and pressure for sex, 108; and rape, 108, 182; role of, 60, 359; and serving food, 61; and unwanted pregnancies, 185; as victims of intoxicated men, 320; views on alcohol, 240–42; violence against, 338–40
world reversal, 123; and sharing of drinks, 281; and world renewal, 163
World Vision, 294–95

yachac, 129, 130
yachaccuna, 128, 129
Yumbos, 146, **147**, 152, **153**, 363, 365, 368, 370

zuro, 195